War Injuries

Jaroslav Krasny

War Injuries

Historical and Legal Perspectives on Unnecessary Suffering

palgrave
macmillan

Jaroslav Krasny
RECNA
Nagasaki University
Nagasaki, Japan

ISBN 978-3-032-00736-0 ISBN 978-3-032-00737-7 (eBook)
https://doi.org/10.1007/978-3-032-00737-7

This Palgrave Macmillan imprint is published by the registered company Springer Nature Switzerland AG.
The registered company address is: Gewerbestrasse 11, 6330 Cham, Switzerland

To the loving memory of my father, Jaroslav Krasny (1958–2021). To my always cheerful daughter Reina, son Seiji, and my remarkably understanding and patient wife, Yuka.

Preface

The interpretation and application of fundamental principles of the law of armed conflict, particularly the norm prohibiting superfluous injury or unnecessary suffering stemming from the principle of humanity, has long been a subject of both legal and ethical debates. Legal scholars engage in discussions on how to define unnecessary suffering and, most importantly, how this principle can be applied in real life to means and methods of warfare. Based on my doctoral dissertation from September 2022, this book is the culmination of years of research to uncover the historical, legal, and health-related dimensions of one of the most fundamental principles of the law of armed conflict, the prohibition of superfluous injury or unnecessary suffering. The book aims not only to trace the development of the norm from its first codification in the nineteenth century to the present but also to explore its relevance and application in the context of modern warfare, particularly regarding the use of nuclear weapons and other contemporary weapons and weapon systems. Therefore, the book centers around examining the legal nature of controversial weapons and how they reconcile with the prohibition of unnecessary suffering under weapons law, a subfield of the law of armed conflict. The impetus for this work stems from a deeply rooted concern about the humanitarian consequences of armed conflict. As someone who has studied and witnessed the impacts of war, I have come to believe that the principle of unnecessary suffering is not merely a legal idea but a vital safeguard against the worst excesses of human violence. However, as this book demonstrates, the interpretation and application of the principle have been anything but static. The interpretation and application of the prohibition of unnecessary suffering needs to evolve in response to changes in military technology, shifts in international norms, and advances in our understanding of the long-term health effects of certain weapons.

This work is, at its core, an interdisciplinary exploration. It draws from international law, history, public health, and case law to carefully analyze how the prohibition of superfluous injury and unnecessary suffering has been understood and applied over time. It challenges the reader to consider not just the legalities of means and methods of warfare but the broader implications of how we define and measure suffering in war. Throughout this book, I have sought to engage with the most relevant and contemporary scholarship while providing original inputs to the ongoing debates in this field. I am particularly indebted to the scholars and practitioners who have previously laid the groundwork in this area, and I hope that this work will serve as a meaningful continuation of that discourse. As such, this book is intended for international law scholars, practitioners in the field, and anyone interested in the intersection of law, ethics, and warfare. While the focus is on legal principles, the broader implications of this study extend into areas such as public health, international relations, and human rights.

I am deeply grateful to the many individuals and institutions that have supported me throughout this project. Their guidance, encouragement, and critical feedback have been invaluable. I would also like to acknowledge the thoughtful review of this book, which has pushed me to refine my arguments and strengthen the coherence of my analysis. It is my hope that this work will not only contribute to the academic field but also provoke thought and dialogue among its readers. As the nature of warfare continues to evolve, so too must our understanding of the laws that govern it. In this sense, the study of superfluous injury and unnecessary suffering remains as crucial today as it was over a century ago.

Nagasaki, Japan Jaroslav Krasny
20 May 2025

Table of Cases

Al Anfal, Case No. l/CSecond/2006, Judgment (Iraqi High Tribunal, 2007)	239
Case Concerning Military and Paramilitary Activities in and against Nicaragua (Merits) [1986] ICJ Rep 14	8, 13, 53
Corfu Channel (UK v Albania) (Merits) [1949] ICJ Rep 4	55
Finogenov and Others v Russia, Apps Nos 18299/03 and 27311/03, Judgment, ECHR 20 December 2011	85
Hostage Case, United States v List (Wilhelm) and Others, Case No 7, (1948) 11 TWC 757; (1950) 11 TWC 1230; (1948) 8 LRTWC 34; (1948) 15 ILR 632 (Nuremberg Military Tribunals)	45, 75
Isayeva v Russia, App No 57950/00, ECtHR, 24 February 2005	224–226, 241
JPK v Netherlands, CCPR/C/43/D/401/1990, UNHRC, 18 November 1991	227–228
Juan Carlos Abella v Argentina, Case 11.137, Inter-Am Comm HR, 13 April 1998 87	221–223, 225
Legality of the Threat or Use of Nuclear Weapons (Advisory Opinion) [1996] ICJ Rep 226	12, 54–55, 59, 87, 102, 115, 194, 207, 216
Legality of the Use of Force (*Yugoslavia v United States*), Dissenting Opinion of Judge Kreća, [1999] ICJ Rep 959	220
McCann v United Kingdom (1995) Series A No 324, ECtHR	85
Obligations concerning Negotiations relating to Cessation of the Nuclear Arms Race and to Nuclear Disarmament (*Marshall Islands v United Kingdom*) (Preliminary Objections) [2016] ICJ Rep	219
Prosecutor v Akayesu (Judgment) ICTR-96-4-A, 1 June 2001	9
Prosecutor v Tadić (Judgment) IT-94-1-A, 15 July 1999	80, 229
Ryuichi Shimoda et al. v State, Tokyo District Court, 7 December 1963	206, 208, 230–235, 237
The Lotus (*France v Turkey*) PCIJ Series A No 10	55
Vietnam Association for Victims of Agent Orange v Dow Chemical Co, 373 F Supp. 2d 7 (EDNY 2005)	230, 235–239

Table of Legislation

Convention for the Amelioration of the Condition of the Wounded and Sick in Armies in the Field, Geneva, 22 June 1865	3, 71–72
Convention for the Amelioration of the Condition of the Wounded in Armies in the Field (1906) (signed 6 July 1906, entered into force 09 August 1907) (1907) 1 AJIL Supp. 201	4, 72
Convention on the Prohibition of the Use, Stockpiling, Production and Transfer of Anti- Personnel Mines and on their Destruction (concluded 18 September 1997, entered into force 1 March 1999) 2056 UNTS 211 (Ottawa Convention)	125–126, 163, 180
Convention on Cluster Munitions (adopted 30 May 2008, entered into force 1 August 2010) (2009) 48 ILM 357 (Oslo Convention)	164, 182
Convention on the Prohibition of the Development, Production and Stockpiling of Bacteriological (Biological) and Toxic Weapons and on their Destruction (opened for signature on 10 April 1972, entered into force on 26 March 1975) 1015 UNTS 163	172
Convention on Prohibitions or Restrictions on the Use of Certain Conventional Weapons which may be Deemed to be Excessively Injurious or to have Indiscriminate Effects (adopted 10 October 1980, entered into force 2 December 1983) 1342 UNTS 137	99, 162–163, 169, 170, 179, 215
Convention on the Prohibition of the Development, Production, Stockpiling and Use of Chemical Weapons and on their Destruction (opened for signature 13 January 1993, entered into force 29 April 1997) 1974 UNTS 45	139, 163, 177
Declaration Renouncing the Use in Time of War of Explosive Projectiles Under 400 Grammes Weight 138 CTS 297 (entered into force 11 December 1868)	32, 37

UNSG Report on Chemical and Bacteriological (Biological) Weapons and the Effects of their Possible Use (August 1 1969) UN Doc. A/7575/Rev.1	172
UNGA Resolution A/RES/1(I), Establishment of a Commission to Deal with the Problems Raised by the Discovery of Atomic Energy, at para 5(c). (24 January 1946)	183
UNGA Resolution 1653 (XVI) Declaration on the Prohibition of the Use of Nuclear and Thermonuclear Weapons (24 November 1961)	183–184
UNGA Res. 1340 (XIV). Prevention of the Wider Dissemination of Nuclear Weapons (21 November 1959)	184
UNGA Resolution A/RES/3472 (XXX)A, Comprehensive study of the question of nuclear-weapon-free zones in all its aspects, at para. 5. (11 December 1975)	185
UNSC Res 984 (1995) Security Assurances against Use of Nuclear Weapons to Non-Nuclear-Weapon States (11 April 1995)	185
Vienna Convention on the Law of Treaties (concluded 23 May 1969, entered into force 27 January 1980) 1155 UNTS 331	22, 59, 196

Acknowledgments

An American philosopher and essayist, Ralph Waldo Emerson (1803–1882), once said: "It is the journey, not the destination." Besides the noble objective of contributing to knowledge in the relevant field, the journey of a researcher or scholar includes meeting extraordinary people who contribute to the study and enrich an individual. I was lucky to have met such people. Although the list is not exhaustive, I would like to express my gratitude to the following individuals.

First and foremost, my appreciation goes to Dr. Noriyuki Kawano of Hiroshima University, who tirelessly supervised my doctoral research on which this book is based, motivated me, and helped to stir the focus in the proper direction. His professional advice on the health effects of ionizing radiation is one of the cornerstones of this book. Dr. Yukio Takeshima of Hiroshima University Graduate School of Biomedical and Health Sciences, for his professional input and contribution regarding the long-term health effects of chemical agents. My sub-supervisors, Dr. Shinsuke Tomotsugu and Prof. Seiichi Koike, who offered their invaluable feedback in the context of international relations and politics. Many thanks also go to Dr. Osamu Yoshida, Dr. Tomoko Kakei, and Dr. Mari Katayanagi for their input and advice, which helped strengthen the argument presented in this book. Special appreciations go to Maj. Andrew Wilson of the Canadian Armed Forces, who offered his professional advice as a practitioner concerning particular weapons and ammunition. To the staff and experts at the International Committee of the Red Cross (ICRC), Mr. Romaric Ferraro, Mr. Magnus Lovold, Ms. Wen Zhou, Dr. Jan Romer, Ms. Margherita D'Ascanio and the ICRC archivist, Mr. Fabrizio Bensi.

To Dr. Gregory S. Gordon of the Faculty of Law, The Chinese University of Hong Kong, for his support and expertise. To Dr. William Boothby and Dr. Wolff Heintshel von Heinegg, who offered their perspectives regarding the principle of unnecessary suffering and its application. Great appreciation goes to the International Atomic Energy Agency (IAEA) and the Vienna Center for Disarmament and Non-Proliferation (VCDNP), Ms. Laura Rockwood, and Dr. Artem Lazarev for their professional input and advice. A special recognition has to be given to Ms. Katherine Bachner from the Brookhaven National Laboratory for offering her technical and professional input. Dr. Shahriar Khateri of the Organization for the Prohibition of Chemical Weapons (OPCW) who offered remarkable support concerning issues surrounding chemical weapons. The Tehran Peace Museum (TPM) and Ms. Elaheh Pooyandeh for facilitating interviews with the survivors of chemical weapons deployed by Iraq in the course of the Iran–Iraq War. To the Iranian Embassy in Tokyo and Dr. Sayed Banihashemi for offering documentary materials related to the use of chemical weapons during the war. To Mr. Alan Owen, the founder of LABRATS International, for kindly offering data concerning the so-called atomic veterans. I also want to thank all the atomic veterans, particularly Mr. Paul Griego. To Mr. Tomas Strnad for his valuable technical insights concerning military weapon systems and tactics. To all the veterans, survivors, and participants in the study affected by war and armed conflict. To my former seminar classmate and an excellent researcher, Ms. Vladisaya Bilyanova Vasileva. Last but not least, I thank my mother and my sister Martina for their continous support.

One of the key traits of research is the recognition that the work is never truly complete, as each discovery reveals how much more there is to explore. Needless to say, any errors or misinterpretations are entirely my own.

About the Book

This book aims to answer the question of what are the contentious points and why there is a substantial difference in the interpretation of the principle prohibiting superfluous injury or unnecessary suffering among legal scholars. Moreover, through jurisprudence, historical analysis, and medical data, it seeks to assess whether the principle encompasses health aspects for determining compliance or is merely balanced against military necessity. The book is structured chronologically, reflecting the evolution and codification of the law of armed conflict (LOAC). The framework of the content structure consists of focused lead-in material and literature in the field, and the subsequent core of the book provides necessary background materials according to the "need to know" rule so as not to overwhelm the reader with redundant concepts, since the law of armed conflict itself is an extensive field. This model provides background information before arriving at the original materials and analysis.

Accordingly, in Chap. 1, the author introduces the broader field of the law of armed conflict within its historical context and clarifies the essential differences between a right to use force or *jus ad bellum* from the law of war or *jus in bello*. Chapter 1 further positions the research within the current literature. The author has selected the literature of the most prominent advocates and scholars representing each interpretative legal position. A gap—or, rather, a difference in interpretation of the principle—becomes apparent through examining contemporary writings on the subject. This difference appears in the understanding of the nature of the principle as divided between, on the one hand, the predominant traditional interpretation that weighs military necessity with injury to, on the other hand, focus on specific health effects of particular weapons regardless of the military advantage such weapons may offer—an understanding of SIrUS known as effects-based approach. Chapter 2 then proceeds with a descriptive analysis of the historical evolution and codification of the "traditional" understanding of unnecessary suffering under LOAC. Continuing with this chronological order, Chap. 3 analyzes what Mathur (2017) defined as the "medicalization" of the principle by moving away from the traditional juxtaposition with military necessity to an increased focus on health effects. Chapter 4 forms the core of this interdisciplinary research in that it provides medical data and analysis of the health effects of controversial weapons, including interviews with the survivors. These selected interviews with survivors of notably chemical weapons represent a part of the original data acquired through field research. The weapons were selected based on their legal standing according to applicable agreements and negotiations leading to such agreements where States or a concerned civil society expressly referred to "unnecessary suffering" and particular health effects. Chapter 5 proceeds with a legal analysis of the treaties concerning the same weapons elaborated upon from the medical perspective in the preceding chapter. This analysis includes the reasoning behind the regulation or outright prohibition and whether SIrUS played any role during negotiations or *travaux preparatoires.*

Chapter 6 offers legal analysis of primary sources that invoke the principle of unnecessary suffering in judicial decisions of particular cases concerning the weapons discussed in Chaps. 4 and 5. It also examines archival materials of the International Committee of the Red Cross (ICRC) related to the bombing of Hiroshima to assess how the ICRC understood and applied SIrUS to the use of atomic bombs on Japan. While unnecessary suffering is a fundamental principle of LOAC, this body of law often lacks effective implementation mechanisms besides traditional "self-help" or the controversial notion of "reprisals." The author, therefore, looked for cases in Ad Hoc and international, regional, and national judicial and quasi-judicial bodies.

Before concluding this book, Chap. 7 offers a glimpse into the major challenges of applying the SIrUS, regardless of whether it is a traditional or effects-based interpretation. Such challenges lie mainly in the domains of naval warfare and new weapons technologies, including cyber and space warfare. Throughout the book, the author prefers to use the term the law of armed conflict (LOAC) instead of International Humanitarian Law (IHL), since the focus is placed on the nature of weapons and targeting as part of Hague law. Additionally, LOAC is a comprehensive term used to denote this field of public international law (PIL), encompassing IHL as its integral part. However, where appropriate, the author uses the term IHL to stress particular humanitarian features based on *Geneva law* regarding protected persons.

Contents

About the Author

Jaroslav Krasny is a professor at Nagasaki University, Research Center for Nuclear Weapons Abolition (RECNA). Previously, he worked as a researcher at the United Nations Institute for Disarmament Research (UNIDIR) in the Weapons of Mass Destruction Programme and with the Ministry of Interior of the Czech Republic, focusing on WMD non-proliferation and arms control measures. His research covers the law of armed conflict, weapons law, the law of targeting, arms control, and disarmament. Dr. Krasny has also held a research associate position at the Center for Peace at Hiroshima University, where he contributed to studies on the law of armed conflict and the long-term health effects of nuclear and chemical weapons on survivors. He holds a Ph.D. in Development Studies from Hiroshima University and a master's degree in international law in armed conflict from the Geneva Academy of International Humanitarian Law and Human Rights. Dr. Krasny's research contributes to ongoing global policy discussions on disarmament and arms control.

Abbreviations

ABCC	Atomic Bomb Casualty Commission
AO	Advisory Opinion
AP I	Additional Protocol I
AP II	Additional Protocol II
APL	Anti-personnel landmine
AVL	Anti-vehicle landmine
AWS	Autonomous Weapon Systems
BW	Biological Weapons
BWC	Biological Weapons Convention
CCW	Convention on Certain Conventional Weapons
CoH	Conduct of Hostilities
CW	Chemical Weapons
CWC	Chemical Weapons Convention
DoD	Department of Defense
ECtHR	European Court of Human Rights
GC	Geneva Conventions
HRC	Human Rights Council
IAC	International Armed Conflict
IAEA	International Atomic Energy Agency
ICC	International Criminal Court
ICCPR	International Covenant on Civil and Political Rights
ICESCR	International Covenant on Economic, Social and Cultural Rights
ICJ	International Court of Justice
ICL	International Criminal Law
ICRC	International Committee of the Red Cross
ICTY	International Criminal Tribunal for Former Yugoslavia
IHFFC	International Humanitarian Fact Finding Commission

IHL	International Humanitarian Law
IHRL	International Human Rights Law
IMT	International Military Tribunal
LOAC	Law of Armed Conflict
MoD	Ministry of Defense
NGO	Non-Governmental Organization
NIAC	Non-international Armed Conflict
NPT	Treaty on the Non-Proliferation of Nuclear Weapons
NSAG	Non-State Armed Group
NWS	Nuclear Weapon Stats
PCIJ	Permanent Court of International Justice
PIL	Public International Law
POW	Prisoner of War
PrepCom	Preparatory Committee
RERF	Radiation Effects Research Foundation
SIrUS	Superfluous Injury or Unnecessary Suffering
UN	United Nations
UNGA	United Nations General Assembly
UNSC	United Nations Security Council
UNSG	United Nations Secretary General
WMD	Weapons of Mass Destruction
WP	White Phosphorus WMD

CHAPTER 1

The Origins and Evolution of the Law of Armed Conflict

1.1 Law of War in Historical Context

Wherever there is society, there is law.[1] Rules, principles, regulations, and doctrines permeate all social activities. Rules and principles in public international law likewise delimit interactions between States. At first glance, armed conflict or war[2] appears to be a form of interstate interaction where the law is put on hold. Understandably, scholars question how we can reconcile such violent interstate interactions and the harsh realities of combat with international law while still accounting for its humanitarian principles. As Rousseau (2020) puts it, war "is not a relation between man and man, but a relation between State and State, in which individuals are enemies only by accident, not as men, nor even as citizens, but as soldiers."[3] Such a definition allows us to perceive combat as an impersonal engagement. However, with all the terrible violence, war breeds hate and

[1] *Ubi Societas Ibi Jus*, a Latin maxim meaning that law may be found in all forms of stable political organization arising from social collaboration. See Aaron X. Fellmeth and Maurice Horwitz, *Guide to Latin in International Law* (New York: Oxford University Press, 2009), 281.

[2] War, as a rather archaic term, contains a subjective element, i.e., it is the will to consider oneself at war. Robert Kolb and Richard Hyde, *An Introduction to the International Law of Armed Conflicts* (Portland: Hart Publishing, 2008), 11.

[3] Jean-Jacques Rousseau, *The Social Contract and the First and Second Discourses*, ed. Susan Dunn (New York: Yale University Press, 2020), 160.

J. Krasny, *War Injuries*,
https://doi.org/10.1007/978-3-032-00737-7_1

hunger for revenge among combatants as well as non-combatants. In other words, the conduct of those involved determines how strong these feelings of hatred and want for reprisals will be, making postwar reconciliation very challenging.

Rules related to the conduct of hostilities (CoH) have existed since ancient times. Rules of conflict between Sparta and Athens were recorded by Thucydides as early as the fifth century BCE.[4] Countless philosophical and religious concepts incorporate or, at some point, did incorporate rules regulating the conduct of war, including regulations on the use of particular weapons.[5] The Law of Armed Conflict (LOAC), also known as the Law of War or International Humanitarian Law (IHL),[6] besides its humanitarian side under Geneva Law, also places restrictions on the means and methods of warfare, that is, on weapons and the way they are used throughout the conduct of hostilities. This body of LOAC is traditionally referred to as the law of the Hague, or simply Hague law, and refers to the two Hague Conventions (1899/1907) and regulates the means and methods of warfare.[7] It is essential to highlight that LOAC is applicable only in situations of armed conflict, either international armed conflict (IAC) or non-international armed conflict (NIAC).[8] This means that LOAC does not take effect in all forms and cases of violence, such as sporadic internal disturbances and riots.[9] Such classification is essential when discussing particular weapons' legal standing. This is because certain

[4] John F. Lazenby, *The Peloponnesian War: A Military Study* (London: Routledge, 2004), 116.

[5] Stuart Casey-Maslen and Tobias Vestner, *A Guide to Disarmament Law* (New York: Routledge, 2019),4.

[6] The use of different terms often depends on the subject matter and organization. While humanitarians such as the ICRC prefer the notion of International Humanitarian Law (IHL), States prefer the Law of Armed Conflict (the United Kingdom) or even the traditional Law of War (the United States). However, the law of armed conflict is preferable since it is the wider term encompassing humanitarian law as its integral part. See Kolb and Hyde, *Introduction*, 16–17.

[7] See Stuart Casey-Maslen and Steven Haines, *Hague Law Interpreted: The Conduct of Hostilities under the Law of Armed Conflict* (New York: Hart, 2020).

[8] Specified in the scope of application of the 1977 Additional Protocols to Geneva Conventions of 1949. International Armed Conflict or IAC traditionally refers to the use of force between States according to Art.1(4) of the Additional Protocol I and in accordance with the UN Charter while application to non-international armed conflict is defined in Art.1(1) of the Additional Protocol II.

[9] 1977 Additional Protocol II to the Geneva Conventions of 1949, Art.1(2).

weapons, such as expanding bullets or tear gas, may be used in NIAC but not in an international armed conflict or IAC, as the author explains later.

Nevertheless, the codification of rules related to warfare in the modern sense can be traced back to the second half of the nineteenth century.[10] In 1859, a Swiss businessman and humanitarian, Henry Dunant, witnessed the horrors of the battle of Solferino, the greatest battle of the Italian War of Independence (1859–1861).[11] Dumbfounded by the tremendous suffering endured by the combatants and lack of medical help in the field, Dunant called for the codification of rules protecting those soldiers who were *hors de combat*,[12] a French expression in LOAC denoting those no longer capable of engaging in hostilities.[13] These early humanitarian efforts resulted in the First Geneva Convention on the Amelioration of the Conditions of the Wounded in the Field[14] and the formation of the International Committee of the Red Cross (ICRC) in 1864.[15] Headquartered in Geneva, Switzerland, the ICRC is an international organization *sui generis*, i.e., of its "own kind" or "unique." ICRC remains the "guardian" of the Geneva Conventions and its Additional Protocols to this day.

Following the first Geneva Convention of 1864, supplementary articles were added four years later. A convention of 1868 concerning maritime warfare[16] preceded an international conference of 1906, further expanding the original agreement of 1864. The protection of combatants who are *hors de combat* was significantly expanded by including provisions on

[10] William H. Boothby, *Weapons and the Law of Armed Conflict* (New York: Oxford University Press, 2016), 10.

[11] Charles Phillips and Alan Axelrod, eds., *Encyclopedia of Wars* (New York: Zenda, Inc, 2005), 617.

[12] A French expression used in the field of the law of armed conflict denoting combatants who are unable to continue engaging in combat due to wounds, sickness, or being captured, lit. "out of combat". See Geoffrey S. Corn et al., *The Law of Armed Conflict: An Operational Approach* (New York: Wolters Kluwer, 2012), 78.

[13] Dunant's experience is vividly described in his book, *A Memory of Solferino*.

[14] Convention for the Amelioration of the Condition of the Wounded in Armies in the Field (signed 22 August 1864, entered into force 22 June 1865) (1864) 129 CTS 361.

[15] See David P. Forsythe, *The Humanitarians* (Cambridge: Cambridge University Press, 2005).

[16] See ICRC. *Treaties, States Parties and Commentaries.* "Additional Articles relating to the Condition of the Wounded in War. Geneva, 20 October 1868." Accessed April 13, 2022. https://ihl-databases.icrc.org/applic/ihl/ihl.nsf/Treaty.xsp?documentId=ECB39EA050F80A5DC12563C002D6624&action=openDocument.

burial, transmission of information to the families, and recognition of voluntary humanitarian organizations.[17] The Geneva Convention of 1906 was further expanded through yet another Geneva Convention concerning the treatment of prisoners of war (POWs) of 1929.[18] The latest and final revision occurred in the aftermath of WWII, with the conclusion of the four Geneva Conventions (GC) of 1949. These four GCs were concerned with protected personnel on land (GC I),[19] seas (GC II),[20] POWs (GC III),[21] and civilians in the power of the enemy (GC IV).[22]

This evolution of Geneva Conventions, as apparent from the above chronology and their objectives, forms part of the so-called *Geneva law*—a body of law concerned with protected personnel, including combatants *hors de combat*. In the realm of means and methods of warfare—that is, weapons, weapon systems, and the way they are deployed—the Hague Conventions of 1899,[23] later revised in 1907,[24] codified certain customary rules concerning the conduct of hostilities on land and sea. These rules also partially addressed hostilities in the air by, for instance, prohibiting launching projectiles from balloons, as airplanes were still in their infancy.

The development of legal frameworks concerning weapons and methods of their use is best illustrated in air warfare. The first use of an airplane in warfare took place a few years after adopting the revised Hague

[17] Convention for the Amelioration of the Condition of the Wounded in Armies in the Field (1906) (signed 6 July 1906, entered into force 09 August 1907) (1907) 1 AJIL Supp 201.

[18] Convention relative to the Treatment of Prisoners of War (signed 27 July 1929, entered into force 19 June 1931) 118 LNTS 343.

[19] Geneva Convention for the Amelioration of the Condition of the Wounded and Sick in Armed Forces in the Field (adopted 12 August 1949, entered into force 21 October 1950) 75 UNTS 31 (Geneva Convention I).

[20] Geneva Convention for the Amelioration of the Condition of Wounded, Sick and Shipwrecked Members of Armed Forces at Sea (adopted 12 August 1949, entered into force 21 October 1950) 75 UNTS 85 (Geneva Convention II).

[21] Geneva Convention relative to the Treatment of Prisoners of War (adopted 12 August 1949, entered into force 21 October 1950)) 75 UNTS 135 (Geneva Convention III).

[22] Geneva Convention relative to the Protection of Civilian Persons in Time of War (adopted 12 August 1949, entered into force 21 October 1950) 75 UNTS 287 (Geneva Convention IV).

[23] Hague Convention with Respect to the Laws and Customs of War by Land and its Annex: Regulations respecting the Laws and Customs of War on Land (signed 29 July 1899, entered into force 4 September 1900) (1898–1899) 187 CTS 429.

[24] Hague Declaration Prohibiting the Discharge of Projectiles and Explosives from Balloons (done 18 October 1907, entered into force 27 November 1907) 100 BSP 455.

Convention in 1907. During the battle of Tripoli in 1911, the Italians flew over the Turkish positions as part of their reconnaissance mission, only to drop bombs directly from the airplane one week later.[25] The airplane as a means of combat was virtually unknown during the Hague proceedings and did not exist beyond the above-mentioned balloon-launched projectiles. WWI saw the ultimate evolution of air warfare and the industrialization of the war effort. This rapid development in means and methods of warfare included, among other things, the first extensive use of chemicals developed by the chemical industry as pest control or disinfectants as weapons of war, as the author discusses in Chap. 3. Nonetheless, by the end of WWI, the military recognized the potential of strategic air power. As French Marshal Ferdinand Foch (1851–1929) stated in 1922, "The potentialities of aircraft attacks on a large scale are almost incalculable, but it is clear that such attack, owing to its crushing moral effect on a Nation, may impress the public opinion to the point of disarming the Government and thus becoming decisive."[26]

Italian General Giulio Douhet (1869–1930) was even convinced it was sufficient to gain control over the air for an overall military victory. In his book, *The Command of the Air* (1921), Douhet identified the civilian population as the prime target, as dropping bombs on cities would make the surrender of the country inevitable. Both Foch and Douhet laid the foundations for what would become known as the strategic bombing theory that would ultimately destroy cities such as Dresden, Tokyo, Hiroshima, and Nagasaki. As Douhet maintained at the time,

> Any distinction between belligerents and non-belligerents is no longer admissible today either in fact or theory…when nations are at war, everyone takes a part in it: the soldier carrying his gun, the woman loading shells in a factory, the farmer growing wheat, the scientist experimenting in his laboratory…nowadays the offensive may reach anyone; and it begins to look as though the safest place may be the trenches.[27]

[25] John Andreas Olsen, ed., *A History of Air Warfare* (Washington: Potomac Books, 2010), 4.

[26] Noble Frankland and Charles Webster, *The Strategic Air Offensive Against Germany: 1939–1945*, Vol.4.(Uckfield: Naval & Military Press), 75.

[27] Giulio Douhet, *The Command of the Air*, trans. Dino Ferrari (Maxwell Air Force Base, Alabama: Air University Press, 2019), 175.

The link between the Geneva law and the development of aerial warfare and strategic bombardment is particularly noteworthy, especially regarding the protection of civilians and combatants no longer able to continue in combat. While these groups were protected under the Geneva Convention of 1906, it appears that the Hague law overshadowed these efforts and that military necessity or so-called advantage dictated the course—a now outdated and unlawful approach known as *kriegsraison*.[28]

At the Washington Conference on the Limitation of Armaments in 1921–1922, jurists drew up the 1923 Hague Draft Rules of Aerial Warfare; however, these were never adopted by the individual States.[29] Certainly, States have recognized the potential of an airplane as a decisive means of warfare. Therefore, at WWII outbreak, no particular black-letter agreements were regulating the war waged from above.[30] Despite this, Douhet's strategic bombing theory—considered an effective method—was somewhat flawed. Because of the rudimentary nature of the bombs and undeveloped targeting systems of the air force during WWII, the main damage was inflicted upon civilians, "resulting in just a terror without decisive effects and undermining the moral position of the attacker."[31]

Nevertheless, while air warfare remained unregulated and this lack of regulation resulted in tremendous suffering of civilians, the so-called Geneva Gas Protocol[32] was adopted in 1925 in the aftermath of WWI to prohibit poisonous and asphyxiating gases and altogether outlawing biological weapons as the whole category of weapons. This black-letter limitation on the use of chemicals carried over to WWII, as chemical weapons were never deployed on the battlefield on a large scale.[33] There are,

[28] From German "*Kriegsraison geht vor Kriegsmanier* "or "the necessities of war take precedence over the rules of war". See Yves Sandoz, Christophe Swinarski, and Bruno Zimmerman, eds., *Commentary on the Additional Protocols of 8 June 1977 to the Geneva Conventions of 12 August 1949* (Geneva: International Committee of the Red Cross, 1987), 391.

[29] William H. Boothby, *The Law of Targeting* (Oxford: Oxford University Press, 2012), 22.

[30] Boothby, *Law of Targeting*, 22.

[31] Thomas Hippler, *Bombing the People: Gulio Douhet and the Foundations of Air-Power Strategy, 1884–1939* (Cambridge: Cambridge University Press, 2013), 132.

[32] Protocol for the Prohibition of the Use in War of Asphyxiating, Poisonous or other Gases, and of Bacteriological Methods of Warfare (signed 17 June 1925, entered into force 8 February 1928) 94 LNTS 65.

[33] Chemical weapons and poisons were used by the Germans in concentration camps and developed by the Japanese under the infamous Unit 731, which partially deployed biological and bacteriological weapons during the Japanese occupation of China (1937–1945). See

however, numerous documented cases of the Japanese Imperial Army using chemical weapons during the occupation of China. One such instance is the 1941 "Inchang Incident" when the Imperial Army deployed a variety of shells filled with chemicals, including Sulphur mustard, to bomb Chinese positions, resulting in approximately 1600 casualties.[34]

The introduction of new unregulated weapon technologies onto the battlefield has often resulted in massive casualties, as witnessed by both World Wars.[35] Examples of new devastating means include the Gatling gun, airplanes, incendiaries, chemical warfare, and, of course, nuclear weapons. With Hague law and *kriegsraison* shaping attitudes toward warfare during the nineteenth and twentieth centuries, the consequence was incomprehensible human suffering. Following WWII, the Geneva Conventions were significantly expanded and revised in 1949 and the Geneva law concerning protected persons became dominant—that is, LOAC was increasingly referred to as International Humanitarian Law or IHL. Then, both bodies of LOAC (i.e., Hague and Geneva) later merged into the Additional Protocols I[36] and II[37] of 1977, and the distinction between Geneva and Hague laws was thus no longer necessary apart from academic discussion. Accordingly, the fundamental purpose of the LOAC is to protect civilians (non-combatants)[38] and alleviate the suffering of combatants through limiting the effects of armed conflict and reducing

Fukiko Aoki, *731: Ishii Shiro to Saikinsen Butai no Yami wo Abaku* [731: Exposing the darkness of Ishii Shiro and the bacteriological unit] (Tokyo: Shinchosha, 2005).

[34] Walter E. Grunden, "No Retaliation in Kind: Japanese Chemical Warfare Policy in World War II." In Friedrich Bretislav, Dieter Hoffman, Jurgen Renn, Florian Schmaltz, and Martin Wolf, *One Hundred Years of Chemical Warfare: Research, Deployment, Consequences* (Springer, 2018), 262.

[35] Paul Scharre, *Army of None: Autonomous Weapons and the Future of War* (New York: WW Norton, 2019), 38.

[36] Protocol Additional to the Geneva Conventions of 12 August 1949 and relating to the Protection of Victims of International Armed Conflicts (Protocol I) (adopted 8 June 1977, entered into force 7 December 1978) 1125 UNTS 3.

[37] Protocol Additional to the Geneva Conventions of 12 August 1949, and relating to the Protection of Victims of Non-International Armed Conflicts (Protocol II) (adopted 8 June 1977, entered into force on 7 December 1978) 1125 UNTS 609.

[38] Combatant and non-combatant are legal terms used in the law of armed conflict. These denote the right of combatants to participate in hostilities, i.e., combatants may not be punished for mere participation in hostilities. Civilians may become military objectives under specific circumstances. For instance, when directly participating in hostilities. See Nils Melzer, *Interpretive Guidance on the Notion of Direct Participation in Hostilities Under International Humanitarian Law* (Geneva: ICRC, 2009), 87.

unnecessary suffering, loss, and damage. Airpower became an effective means during Operation Desert Storm (1991), with more effective technological improvements and targeting resulting in precision strikes and significantly decreased collateral damage.[39] Such precise targeting with limited collateral damage ensures the swift accomplishment of military objectives. On the contrary, by ignoring distinction, strategic bombing is no longer a lawful method of warfare[40] and is often counterproductive, leading to prolonged hostilities.

1.2 *Jus in Bello* and *Jus Ad Bellum*

Unlike ***jus ad bellum*** ("right to war"), ***jus in bello*** ("law of war") is not concerned with the nature or origin of the conflict or attribution of guilt to the parties of a conflict. As such, the law of war, or LOAC, is rather pragmatic. It does not prevent States from gaining military advantage while aiming at the same time to alleviate the horrors of armed conflict on those affected by it. The conduct of hostilities is regulated mainly by customary law as general practice accepted by States, that is, ***opinio juris***[41] and ***usus (consuetudo)***,[42] and, as such, applies to all nations[43] as opposed to a treaty, convention, or any other agreement which only binds those who are a party to it.[44] However, a custom may be codified in a treaty or applied in parallel with a treaty to non-parties. Hence, a treaty can have a declaring, crystallizing, or generating effect on customary law.[45]

[39] John Andreas Olsen, *Strategic Air Power in Desert Storm* (New York: Routledge, 2006), 149.

[40] Additional Protocol I, Art.51(5)(a).

[41] Opinio iuris (sive necessitatis). Legal opinion (or else necessity). The belief by the international community as a whole that a norm is legally binding. Further confirmed by the jurisprudence in *Military and Paramilitary Activities in and Against Nicaragua (Nicaragua v. U.S.)*, 1986 I.C.J. Rep. 14, 108–109, ¶ 207 (quoting North Sea Continental Shelf Case (F.R.G. v. Den./F.R.G. v. Nether.), 1969 I.C.J. Rep. 3, 44, ¶ 77). See Fellmeth and Horwitz, 209.

[42] Long and consistent practice, "use" of the norm giving rise to the expectation of a continuation of the practice. See Fellmeth and Horwitz, 62.

[43] A State may be opposing the existence of a custom from its inception, this is known as "persistent objector" status and as such is often controversial and contested. See Shaw, *International Law*, 67.

[44] Anthony Aust, *Modern Treaty Law and Practice* (Cambridge: Cambridge University Press, 2013), 18–19.

[45] Giovanni Distefano, *Fundamentals of Public International Law: A Sketch of the International Legal Order* (Leiden: Brill Nijhoff, 2019), 376–391.

The Geneva Conventions of 1949 are a prime example of a custom-declaring treaty reaching universal participation and recognition;[46] moreover, its two Additional Protocols (AP I, II) adopted in the aftermath of the shock of the Vietnam War gained nearly universal participation, with a small number of provisions not yet attaining the status of customary law. Nonetheless, Additional Protocol I and, to a lesser extent, Additional Protocol II reflect a large number of customary rules, since both documents merge traditional Hague law concerned with the conduct of hostilities or CoH with revised Geneva law concerning protected persons.[47]

Customary rules of LOAC include the most fundamental principles related to the conduct of hostilities, that is, proportionality, distinction, necessity, precautions, and humanity.[48] The principle of humanity under LOAC is, in fact, rooted in the prohibition of "superfluous injury or unnecessary suffering" (SIrUS).[49] Interpretation of these principles has to be strictly separated from *jus ad bellum* and human rights law, which understand *proportionality* and *necessity* in restrictive terms.[50] Furthermore, to avoid confusion, the principles referred to throughout this book are interpreted strictly under the LOAC and, as such, will not be confused with and interpreted through the lens of International Human Rights Law (IHRL). In addition to the six most fundamental LOAC principles mentioned above, the ICRC conducted large-scale research and identified and published in 2005 a total of 161 customary rules applicable to international and non-international armed conflicts.[51] However, the study does not represent a source of law, and a number of the identified rules, principally those applicable to non-international armed conflict (NIAC), are

[46] *The Prosecutor v. Jean-Paul Akayesu (Trial Judgement)*, ICTR-96-4-T, International Criminal Tribunal for Rwanda (ICTR), 2 September 1998, Customary status of GC Common Art. 3. 608–609.

[47] Andrew Clapham and Paola Gaeta, eds., *The Oxford Handbook of International Law in Armed Conflict* (Oxford: Oxford University Press, 2014), 62.

[48] UK Ministry of Defence, *The Manual of the Law of Armed Conflict* (Oxford: Oxford University Press, 2004), 21.

[49] UK Ministry of Defence, *Manual*, 21.

[50] See Nobuo Hayashi, "Using Force by Means of Nuclear Weapons and Requirements of Necessity and Proportionality *Ad Bellum*." In *Nuclear Weapons Under International Law*, ed. Gro Nystuen, Stuart Casey-Maslen, and Annie G. Bersagel, 15–30 (Cambridge: Cambridge University Press, 2014).

[51] See Jean-Marie Henckaerts and Louise Doswald-Beck, eds. *Customary International Humanitarian Law*. Vol.1, *Rules* (Cambridge: Cambridge University Press, 2005).

repeatedly contested by States.[52] Nevertheless, the ICRC study is a well-respected reference on customary law applicable to situations of armed conflict[53] and represents the only comprehensive compilation of customary LOAC often referred to by most States.[54]

Therefore, the law of armed conflict or *jus in bello* has to be distinguished from the conditions to use force known as *jus ad bellum*,[55] the basic legal framework of which is outlined in the Charter of the United Nations (UN),[56] Resolutions of the UN Security Council (UNSC) and General Assembly (UNGA).[57] The use of force is generally prohibited under Art. 2(4) of the UN Charter, however, may be permitted under Chapter VII in self-defense or as authorized by the UNSC, provided that such use in self-defense complies with the principles of proportionality and necessity, as understood under *jus ad bellum*.[58] That is, "for a threat to be unlawful, it has to relate to a projected use of force that is unlawful, i.e., breach of the UN Charter."[59] In other words, the use of force, including a threat of such use, may be permitted if in conformity with Chapter VII of the UN Charter, as explained above.

[52] For instance, in the case of NIAC, combatant status is rejected by several States, particularly the United States. The US addresses this by its own term, "*unlawful combatant*." This is quite an oxymoron since a combatant has a lawful status in LOAC. Combatant is a protective status that allows participation in hostilities. Most States treat fighters in NIAC as criminals or terrorists without the right to protective prisoner of war status. See Marco Sassoli, *International Humanitarian Law: Rules, Controversies, and Solutions to Problems Arising in Warfare* (Cheltenham: Edward Elgar, 2019), 23.

[53] Boothby, *Weapons*, 21.

[54] See Database of the military law of war manuals of States, accessed August 3, 2022, https://ihl-databases.icrc.org/en/customary-ihl/src/iimima.

[55] "Law/Right relating to war. The international law governing when and how military action may lawfully be commenced by one State against another. See Fellmeth and Horwitz, 150.

[56] Rules governing the legitimacy of the use of force, i.e., *jus ad bellum* fall generally under the UN Charter Arts. 2(4), 51 and 42. Charter of the United Nations and the Statute of the International Court of Justice (signed 26 June 1945, entered into force 24 October 1945).

[57] Stuart Casey-Maslen, *Jus ad Bellum: The Law on Inter-State Use of Force* (New York: Hart, 2020), 13–15.

[58] These principles are different in *ad bellum* and *in bello*. This is because in *jus in bello*, unlike *jus ad bellum*, the use of force is not functionally linked to achieving a pre-determined goal, e.g., stopping the attack with a proportionate response. See Clapham and Gaeta, 336.

[59] Yoram Dinstein, *War, Aggression and Self-Defence*, 6th ed. (Cambridge: Cambridge University Press, 2017), 91.

However, as *jus ad bellum* concerns itself more with a "function of force rather than its form," it does not appear to offer a substantial argument that could be effectively used to proscribe the use of weapons.[60] It is thus crucial to separate *jus ad bellum* from *jus in bello*. In *jus in bello*, an armed conflict is a matter of fact. The law of war as a distinct body of public international law applies "regardless [of] the nature or origin of the conflict or the cause espoused by or attributed to the Parties."[61] It is, therefore, irrelevant whether a Party to a conflict (i.e., a belligerent) is the aggressor or defender; in turn, for weapons law, there is no such thing as an offensive or defensive weapon *de jure* category under LOAC. A weapon is a tool of war; the norms apply to any current and future weapons and weapon systems,[62] regardless of their military or other non-legal categorization. Likewise, assigning responsibility for starting armed conflict under LOAC would be counterproductive to its purposes, where, according to Dinstein (2017), the aggressor would lose any motivation to follow any of the rules.[63] Perhaps even leading to disregarding the responsibility of combatants for grave breaches of the Geneva Conventions,[64] which is a form of individual responsibility.

The same argument pertains to overzealous limitations on weapons and methods that could conflict with the purpose of the LOAC in general. Once overpowered and facing defeat, the belligerent could simply disregard all of these over-restrictive rules on weapons out of despair. Such conflicting logic is reflected in one of the conclusions of the Advisory Opinion (AO) on the Use or Threat of Use of Nuclear Weapons by the

[60] Gro Nystuen, Stuart Casey-Maslen, and Annie G. Bersagel, *Nuclear Weapons Under International Law* (Cambridge: Cambridge University Press, 2014), 30.

[61] Sandoz, Swinarski, and Zimmerman, 29.

[62] A weapons system is "a combination of one or more weapons with all related equipment, materials, services, personnel, and means of delivery and deployment (if applicable) required for self-sufficiency." See US Department of Defense, *DOD Dictionary of Military and Associated Terms* (Washington DC: The Joint Staff, 2019), 234.

[63] Dinstein, *War.*

[64] "...the following acts, if committed against persons or property protected by the Convention: willful killing, torture or inhuman treatment, including biological experiments, willfully causing great suffering or serious injury to body or health, and extensive destruction and appropriation of property, not justified by military necessity and carried out unlawfully and wantonly. Art.50 (GCI). Grave breaches in relation to other three Conventions are stipulated as follows: Art.51(GCII), Art.130(GCIII) and Art.147(GCIV). Art. 11 and Art. 85 (API).

International Court of Justice (ICJ),[65] which will be examined in later chapters. The fact that the rules and principles of LOAC apply equally is undisputed in the case of international armed conflict (IAC), where the belligerents are States, as opposed to non-international armed conflict (NIAC), where the situation and actors can be a bit more complex. Nonetheless, applying the principle prohibiting superfluous injury or unnecessary suffering, often referred to as SIrUS, on all belligerents in NIAC is not disputed.[66]

The strict distinction between *jus ad bellum* and *jus in bello* is relevant and important for yet another pragmatic reason: principles are interpreted differently. Hayashi (2014) points out that the principles of necessity and proportionality, which are relatively restrictive under *jus ad bellum* and IHRL, are permissive under *jus in bello*.[67] This means that while under *jus ad bellum*, force has to be proportionate to the threat, under *jus in bello*, any lawful force that is necessary to accomplish legitimate military objectives is allowed, regardless of the threat. Proportionality is then under *jus in bello*, assessed in consideration of collateral damage. This will be further explained in the next chapter.

As explained above, emerging from two historical sources, the LOAC was traditionally divided between the Hague and the Geneva law. Hague law is primarily concerned with the means and methods—that is, the conduct of hostilities. It applies limitations on weapons and regulates the actions of combatants. Geneva law is then concerned with protected personnel including combatants who are *hors de combat*[68] and their humane treatment. Both sources later merged in the 1977 Additional Protocols to the Geneva Conventions of 1949. Rules governing the conduct of hostilities (CoH) are, therefore, in current form enshrined in both Additional Protocols and customary law.

Regarding the categorization of armed conflict, IAC or NIAC, for weapons law, this affects the legality of deployment of certain categories of

[65] Legality of the Threat or Use of Nuclear Weapons (Advisory Opinion) [1996] ICJ Rep226.

[66] See ICRC, "Rule 70. Weapons of a Nature to Cause Superfluous Injury or Unnecessary Suffering" Accessed April 12, 2022. https://ihl-databases.icrc.org/customary-ihl/eng/docindex/v1_rul_rule70.

[67] Hayashi, "Using Force".

[68] Lit. "out of combat", a term used for wounded, shipwrecked or sick combatants and POWs. See Sassoli et al., "Hors de Combat" accessed April 12, 2022. https://casebook.icrc.org/glossary/hors-de-combat.

weapons, such as tear gas or expanding bullets.[69] This issue will be further explored in Chap. 3. In non-international armed conflict, the legal framework includes the Common Article 3 to the Geneva Conventions (GC)[70] of 1949, the 1977 Additional Protocol II (AP II) to GC of 1949, as well as custom, national law, and international human rights law or IHRL. The interaction between LOAC and IHRL in relation to IAC will be briefly explored later in Chaps. 3 and 6. It is imperative to stress that IHRL, although sometimes quite controversially,[71] applies both in peacetime, during IACs, and especially NIACs; as such, IHRL influences, through its own implementing mechanisms, the interpretation of principles of LOAC, including the prohibition of unnecessary suffering. It is, therefore, relevant to explore whether this influence affects the legal interpretation of the SIrUS principle.

In sum, it should be reiterated that customary norms regulating means and methods of warfare crystallize and evolve. This is especially true for rules pertaining to the conduct of hostilities. New weapons and weapon systems are being developed at an ever-increasing pace. Understanding the roots and traditional interpretation of the prohibition of superfluous injury or unnecessary suffering vis-à-vis a particular weapon is essential for assessing its relevance and importance. Especially today.

1.3 Previous Research and Methodology

This section positions the study within the recent literature and elaborates on the state of research concerning the interpretation and application of the principle prohibiting superfluous injury or unnecessary suffering (SIrUS). The predominant focus is on reviewing both the traditional understanding of the principle and the contemporary position of legal scholars. First, the traditional position strives to maintain the stringent distinction between the law of war and other fields of international law, particularly human rights law. This interpretative approach stresses a strict division between LOAC and IHRL, which Sassoli (2019) describes as

[69] The use of riot control agents (RCA) such as tear gas as a method of warfare in IAC is prohibited by the Chemical Weapons Convention, Art.1 (5). However, it is allowed in NIAC, and the United States has reserved the right to use RCAs in special military operations. See ICRC, IHL Database, "Rule 74."

[70] As reaffirmed by *Case Concerning Military and Paramilitary Activities in and against Nicaragua* (Merits), [1986] *ICJ Rep.* 14¶ 114.

[71] See Sassoli, 423–432.

representative of IHL supremacy.[72] This means that traditional scholars often argue that during armed conflict, LOAC forms *lex specialis*,[73] and as such takes precedence over other branches of PIL, particularly IHRL.[74] That is, the principles and rules have to be interpreted purely from the traditional and customary LOAC standpoint without including modern concepts and interpretations.

Increasingly, though, contemporary literature reveals a certain synthesis of IHRL and IHL, including but not limited to the conduct of hostilities. Since 1968, it has been reiterated at the Tehran Conference that human rights are applicable even in times of armed conflict.[75] As most modern conflicts are essentially mixed (IAC and NIAC) or non-international and urban in character, this position has gained further impetus. Nonetheless, considering the *lex specialis* argument, IHRL norms have to be interpreted through the lens of LOAC during armed conflict. This is essentially true when those rules and principles touch upon the conduct of hostilities (CoH)—that is, on weapons and targeting. While traditional LOAC interpretations of unnecessary suffering balance military advantage with injury, recent scholars increasingly emphasize the health impacts of particular weapons. Such focus on health is evident in scholars with human rights backgrounds. Traditionally, the prohibition of superfluous injury or unnecessary suffering falls under CoH, more precisely under weapons law as a specific subfield of LOAC. Currently, the principle prohibiting superfluous injury or unnecessary suffering is codified in the 1977 Additional Protocol I to the Geneva Conventions of 1949 in the following formulation: "It is prohibited to employ weapons, projectiles and material and methods of warfare of a nature to cause superfluous injury or unnecessary suffering" (Art. 35 [2], Part III, Means and Methods of Warfare, Combatant and Prisoner of War Status).

The law of armed conflict is primarily based on customs that have evolved through centuries of cultural, religious, and philosophical influences.[76] Today, according to Sassoli (2019), it might be nearly impossible

[72] Sassoli, 435.

[73] Law unique to a particular regime or applicable in specific scenarios. See Fellmeth and Horwitz, 176.

[74] Sassoli, 495.

[75] Respect for Human Rights in Armed Conflicts [1968] UNGA 58; A/RES/2444 (XXIII) (19 December 1968)

[76] Yoram Dinstein, *The Conduct of Hostilities Under the Law of International Armed Conflict* (Cambridge: Cambridge University Press, 2004), 5–9.

to amend or revise the Geneva Conventions of 1949 or its Additional Protocols.[77] However, the means and methods of warfare are constantly changing, and even if challenging, States are at least willing to accept new weapon-specific agreements rather than general prohibitions. Hence, rules of war will have to naturally keep pace with this fast-paced progress in weapons development. However, in the case of SIrUS, it is imperative to examine the traditional understanding before there may be any evolution, transformation, or normative crystallization through an international agreement.

Dinstein (2004) reiterates that the law of war as such is not concentrated on constraining the ultimate objective, i.e., submission of the enemy in victory, where overzealous efforts to restrict or "humanize" warfare and limit the use of weapons would lead to a simple reality of the rules being ignored.[78] Prohibition of unnecessary suffering has to be, therefore, understood in its original meaning—that is, suffering without military purpose. Accordingly, "a weapon is proscribed only if it causes injury or suffering that can be avoided, given the military constraints of the situation."[79] It is apparent that Dinstein (2004) disregards particular health effects and instead equates military advantages with generic injury. Unnecessary suffering is, therefore, a rather comparative rule, where, according to Dinstein (2004), the judgment has to be based on two essential criteria: "(a) whether an alternative weapon is available, causing less injury or suffering; (b) whether the effects produced by the alternative weapon are sufficiently effective in neutralizing enemy personnel."[80]

Therefore, a decision to deploy a particular weapon has to be made upon the availability of alternative means before making any judgments as to the health effects and injuries caused by such a weapon. Specific health effects, such as long-term health damage, do not play a role if alternative weapons are unavailable that could achieve the same legitimate objective. In the realm of LOAC, a military *objective* should not be confused with an *object*. While *objective* always refers to a military objective, objects are generally civilian.[81] Accordingly, a military objective denotes enemy combatants or structures that, by their nature, place, or purpose, effectively

[77] Sassoli, 44.
[78] Dinstein, *Conduct*, 2.
[79] Dinstein, *Conduct*, 59.
[80] Dinstein, *Conduct*, 60.
[81] Kolb and Hyde, 46.

contribute to military action.[82] Superfluous injury or unnecessary suffering evidently cannot apply to weapons designed to attack structures or platforms, such as warships,[83] or other equipment used by the military or, for that matter, foliage.

According to another representative of traditional interpretation, Dr. Boothby (2016), the intended weapon design plays an essential role in SIrUS. This is because any weapon can be misused in violation of LOAC rules, including unnecessary suffering. Boothby (2016) points out the principal debate between effects-based and design-purpose approaches in which the intention is associated with the effects that inevitably follow and are, as such, deliberate rather than those that occur in specific circumstances, such as weather conditions, partial damage of the device, or incorrect manipulation.[84] According to the traditional interpretation offered by Boothby (2016) and Dinstein (2004), the principle has to be evaluated *vis-à-vis* particular weapons based on whether such a weapon breaches the principle in all designated or intended applications and not whether it is capable of use in a way that would breach the principle.

Subsequently, if we accept Dienstein's (2004) interpretation, such weapons would have to be evaluated further according to the military advantage they offer. Therefore, its use would become unlawful only if there is a less injurious weapon capable of accomplishing the given military objective. The following four points, therefore, summarize the traditional position:

1. Combatants are a military objective. Therefore, SIrUS applies only to combatants. It does not apply to civilians, i.e., non-combatants protected under the rule of distinction.
2. Less injurious weapons capable of accomplishing such objectives are not available.
3. The weapon must cause particular *intended* effects [emphasis added].
4. These effects have to *always* follow its use [emphasis added].

The traditional interpretation and notion that suffering should not and cannot be measured in medical terms and should only be weighed against

[82] 1977 Additional Protocol I to the Geneva Conventions of 1949, Art. 52(2).

[83] Louise Doswald-Beck, ed., *San Remo Manual on International Law Applicable to Armed Conflicts at Sea* (Cambridge: Cambridge University Press, 1995), 118.

[84] Boothby, *Weapons*, 49.

the military advantage of a particular weapon is further supported by Solis (2016), who argues that "great suffering is not the measurement by which a weapon is banned."[85] To illustrate his point, Solis (2016) uses the examples of white phosphorus, napalm, or flamethrowers as causing tremendous suffering to combatants without being banned. He further argues that nuclear weapons are not covered by the prohibition of SIrUS as codified under API due to the difficulty in undergoing the weighing test of injury against necessity. Solis (2016) further concedes there is no black-letter rule in determining what exactly constitutes unnecessary suffering[86] and refers to the case of the US Army's review of the combat shotgun: "The degree of superfluous injury must be **clearly** disproportionate to the intended objective(s)" and that "the suffering must outweigh **substantially** the military necessity for the weapon" [emphasis added].[87] Indeed, such a litmus test might apply to mechanical weapons causing kinetic injuries. However, in cases of continuous long-term injuries caused by the use of projectiles with depleted uranium, effects of ionizing radiation, or toxic effects of napalm, such a test is highly unsatisfying. Solis (2016) further points out that since SIrUS applies to combatants, the permissible suffering and injuries standard is more permissive than the standard protecting non-combatants.[88] While this might be accepted by some based on a purely philosophical perspective, in reality, there is no such legal provision *lex lata* stipulating that combatants shall endure greater suffering than non-combatants, particularly when it comes to weapons. Moreover, the effects of certain chemicals or ionizing radiation go beyond the temporal scope of armed conflict and continue to affect combatants long after hostilities end, that is, long after a combatant ceases to be a combatant *de jure*.

In sum, Dinstein (2004), Boothby (2016), and Solis (2016) are the most prominent advocates for those legal scholars who vigorously oppose the interpretation of SIrUS through medical terms. Their approach is rather traditional and remains in the pure realm of LOAC as *lex specialis*. Their view can be summarized as follows: the higher the value of military objective, the higher the permitted degree of injury if no alternative weapon is available. Moreover, their interpretation of unnecessary

[85] Gary D. Solis, *The Law of Armed Conflict: International Humanitarian Law in War*, 2nd ed. (Cambridge: Cambridge University Press, 2016), 292.

[86] Solis, 291.

[87] Solis, 291.

[88] Solis, 292.

suffering is opposed to any efforts to examine injuries caused by particular weapons or weapon systems through medical science.

While the positions mentioned above mirror the traditional understanding of the principle postulated in the Hague Conventions of 1899/1907 in Article 23(e) and the contemporary codification in the 1977 Additional Protocol I (API) to the Geneva Conventions of 1949 under Article 35(2), such an interpretation is not without its critics. Challenges to the traditional interpretation arose with the emergence of International Human Rights Law (IHRL) in the late 1960s that introduced legal concepts such as "right to life" or "right to health" and the subsequent inevitable intertwining of human rights law (IHRL) and humanitarian law (IHL).[89] The interdependence of IHRL and IHL has advocates as well as harsh critics. However, such IHRL and IHL interaction is not the focus of this book; it will be pointed out only in cases that relate to the reinterpretation of SIrUS.

The gradual focus on the health effects of weapons is reflected by Casey-Maslen and Haines (2020), who argue that seeing unnecessary suffering merely through the lenses of military necessity is a relatively narrow view.[90] Casey-Maslen and Haines (2020) further argue that such necessity for intent, i.e., where the weapon manufacturer must possess the intent to develop such weapons that deliberately cause excessive injuries, as advocated by Boothby (2016) and the design-purpose interpretation, is "akin to a formulation of the *actus reus* [material element] of the corresponding war crime."[91] Therefore, by such observation, Casey-Maslen and Haines (2020) challenge the argument of Boothby (2016), who leans toward intent when deliberating on the effects of particular weapons concerning unnecessary suffering. Casey-Maslen and Haines (2020) admit that "a serious violation of the superfluous injury rule may amount to a war crime when the *actus reus* of the crime is committed with the requisite mens rea."[92] Indeed, unnecessary suffering involving *mens rea*[93] is found in the articles of the Statute of the International Criminal Tribunal for the

[89] William H. Boothby, *Conflict Law: The Influence of New Weapons Technology, Human Rights and Emerging Actors* (The Hague: T.M.C. Asser Press, 2014), 317–331.

[90] See Casey-Maslen and Haines, *Hague Law*, 214.

[91] Casey-Maslen and Haines, *Hague Law*, 214.

[92] Casey-Maslen and Haines, *Hague Law*, 221.

[93] "The mental guilt element of a criminal offense. Most crimes have both a conduct component or material element (*actus reus*) and a mental or intent component (*mens rea*)." See Fellmeth and Horwitz, 186.

Former Yugoslavia (ICTY).[94] The ICTY Statute includes causing unnecessary suffering under the prosecutable violations of the laws or customs of war: “employment of poisonous weapons or other weapons calculated to cause unnecessary suffering” (Art. 3[a], Violations of the laws or customs of war). The significant difference lies in exchanging the term “of a nature to” as codified in the API to “calculated to.” Though, this is a logical change. *Mens rea* is required for assessing individual criminal responsibility and is included in the Rome Statute[95] under Article 30.[96] However, a similar provision on *actus reus* is not included in the statute itself but, instead, in the Elements of Crimes.[97] Nevertheless, such a definition involving “intent” fits the field of international criminal law (ICL). As for the law of war, it is important to draw a distinction between LOAC and ICL. These are two distinct, albeit interplaying, branches of international law. The ICTY Statute differs from the codification in the API, where the subject matter is the nature of the weapon itself rather than a particular conduct, i.e., an individual or group of individuals developing or deploying such a weapon or the intent or even the lack of it. Therefore, Casey-Maslen and Haines (2020) refute Boothby’s (2016) argument that there has to be an intent in deploying or creating a weapon that may cause unnecessary suffering. Such intent is a feature of ICL, but it is not always required under LOAC.

In line with arguments presented by and comparable to Casey-Maslen and Haines (2020) and thus belonging to the same group of interpretation—that is, discussing modern interpretation and medicalization—O’Connor (2014) points out an essential temporal aspect of the rule, namely that specific effects of weapons may manifest themselves later, such as those caused by ionizing radiation.[98] As such, these cases reach beyond the temporal scope of application of the LOAC. Correspondingly, the fact

[94] UNSC ‘Statute of the International Criminal Tribunal for the Former Yugoslavia’ UNSC Res 827 (1993) (25 May 1993) SCOR 48th Year 29. Art. 3(a).

[95] Rome Statute of the International Criminal Court (adopted 17 July 1998, entered into force 1 July 2002) 2187 UNTS 90.

[96] William Schabas, *The International Criminal Court: A Commentary on the Rome Statute*, 2nd ed., (Oxford: Oxford University Press, 2016), 563.

[97] Schabas, *Rome Statute*, 630. Also, see Elements of Crimes (9 September 2002) Doc ICC- ASP/1/3 (Pt. II-B).

[98] Simon O’Connor, “Nuclear Weapons and the Unnecessary Suffering Rule.” In *Nuclear Weapons Under International Law*, ed. Gro Nystuen, Stuart Casey-Maslen, and Annie G. Bersagel, 128–147 (Cambridge: Cambridge University Press, 2014).

that the victims develop leukemia or cancer over their lifetime serves no military purpose and, therefore, no military objective.[99] Placing this fact alongside the traditionalist argument that a particular effect has to occur every time such a weapon is used reveals an important difference in the interpretation of the principle. What if such an effect reveals itself ten years after using such a weapon—long after an armed conflict has ended? Is a mere "risk," albeit significant, capable of violating the SIrUS rule?

Rietiker (2018) goes even further in his interpretation of the principle, which draws closer to a human rights interpretation. As such, his analysis reflects current trends and discussions regarding the interaction of IHRL with IHL. Linking the superfluous injury principle with the principles of *humanity* and *proportionality*, Rietiker (2018) contends that even weapons specifically designed to cause traumatic amputation of the foot or lower leg are not strictly necessary and, therefore, violate the principle.[100] Rather than *proportionality* in its traditional *jus in bello* meaning (i.e., the value of a military objective vs. the reasonably anticipated collateral damage), Rietiker (2018) positions the principle against other long-term injuries—that is, the health effects of a particular weapon, in this case, anti-personnel landmines:

> It is generally suggested that legally speaking, weapons that are specifically designed to cause traumatic amputations of, at least, the foot and lower leg cause more suffering than is strictly necessary to render soldiers unable to fight (hors de combat). Indeed, it is hard to see what military purpose is served by deliberately inflicting life-long disability on the combatants when wounding them less severely would be sufficient to remove them from the battle.[101]

An anti-personnel landmine has a particular military value as an area-denial weapon without many effective alternatives. However, rather than discussing an alternative area-denial weapon, Rietiker (2018) explores the health effects. As such, his view contrasts with Dinstein's (2004) position by excluding the discussion of "alternative" options, thus refusing the balancing of alternative weapons with similar effects vs. military objectives. Considering nuclear weapons, like O'Connor (2014), Rietiker (2018)

[99] O'Connor, 147.
[100] Daniel Rietiker, *Humanization of Arms Control: Paving the Way for a World Free of Nuclear Weapons* (New York: Routledge, 2018), 121–122.
[101] Rietiker, 121.

likewise associates unnecessary suffering with ionizing radiation due to long-term health effects. This is juxtaposed with the traditionalists mentioned above, according to whom ionizing radiation belongs instead to the secondary effects, and, as such, is contrary to the weapon design-purpose theorem. In other words, the primary intended effect of nuclear weapons is not to irradiate but rather to utilize massive blasts and heat. It should be mentioned that according to Mathur (2017), the medical experts at the International Committee of the Red Cross (ICRC) see the concept or idea of illegal or legal weapons as somewhat irrelevant since only the effects-based interpretation, i.e., medical or health effects approach, is what gives the discussion an adequately pragmatic tone when discussing weapons and their legality.[102]

Therefore, there is obviously a difference in how the principle and its nature should be understood, interpreted, and applied. Should the principle prohibiting superfluous injury or unnecessary suffering be interpreted strictly as balancing military advantage and injury without going into medical particularities? The higher the advantage gained, the broader the acceptable injury if there is no alternative weapon. Or should the perceived military advantage yield to particular health effects, and if so, what injuries would therefore be considered "unnecessary" or "superfluous"?

The key issue is why, when, and mainly, what has caused this interpretative difference. Rather than perceiving this division as a misunderstanding on either side, it is imperative to subsequently enquire whether the principle itself, to gain normative substance, maybe or even shall be interpreted in medical terms. There is no doubt that rules and laws could advance as custom may often crystallize in a treaty.[103] However, while the customary nature and fundamental character of SIrUS is not disputed, its interpretation is. Thus, one of this book's main objectives is to clarify why the interpretation has become divided between the rejection of the medical perspective while focusing exclusively on the balance of military necessity and advantage, and, on the other hand, an increased focus on the medical and health effects of weapons. In addition, the author examines

[102] Ritu Mathur, *Red Cross Interventions in Weapons Control* (London: Lexington Books, 2017), 11.

[103] "...this term acutely describes the customary process to the extent that it underlines its magmatic character as opposed to treaty law which is eventually hardened, and the content fixed, by its written transcription." Distefano, 378.

whether the principle can, in fact, be interpreted through medical terms, as suggested by this alternate health effects approach.

The book looks at how the SIrUS principle has been interpreted and applied since its first codification in 1868 until 2017, when it served as one of the cornerstones of the Treaty for the Prohibition of Nuclear Weapons, to resolve the perplexing disagreement regarding the interpretation, as illustrated by the above legal scholars. While the medical approach offers an interpretation based on health effects, it scarcely includes medical data in supporting the argument, or the data are deficient and incomplete. It is insufficient, for instance, to state that ionizing radiation causes cancer, which is then in breach of the principle. Such statements can and often are refuted for being too dubious.

The questions explored in this book are predominantly legal questions falling under the specific field of the law of armed conflict (LOAC). However, since the book examines the notions of "suffering" and "injury," the author refers to medical science when analyzing particular injuries and health effects. As such, the study embodies an interdisciplinary legal research that goes beyond the traditional "strictly normative analysis of international law."[104] The major focus is on the LOAC as a specific field of public international law (PIL) and is supported by medical science and data. The methodology respects the normative structure since significant emphasis is put on an explicit legal principle of LOAC—that is, the SIrUS principle. It is centered around the theory of the sources of international law as embodied by Art. 38 of the ICJ Statute (i.e., conventions, customary rules, and general principles of law). While there is no particular hierarchy between these sources, the author follows the rules of legal interpretations.[105] Interpretation of relevant treaties follows the rules of interpretation as laid down in Articles 31–33 of the Vienna Convention on the Law of Treaties 1969 (VCLT).[106] Furthermore, treaty interpretation methodology follows the works of Aust (2013)[107] and Gardiner (2017),[108]

[104] See Rossana Deplano and Nicholas Tsagourias, eds., *Research Methods in International Law: A Handbook* (Cheltenham: Edward Elgar Publishing Limited, 2021), 4.

[105] The Article 38 does not present the normative system in a hierarchical order but merely tells the Court its applicable law and where to look for it. Distefano, 247.

[106] Vienna Convention on the Law of Treaties (concluded 23 May 1969, entered into force 27 January 1980) 1155 UNTS 331.

[107] Aust, *Modern Treaty Law*.

[108] Richard Gardiner, *Treaty Interpretation*, 2nd ed. (Oxford: Oxford University Press, 2017).

with an emphasis on *travaux preparatoire* and the normative language of the convention as a supportive element. In this sense, the methodology follows legal positivism,[109] as the well-known jurist Lassa Oppenheim regarded positivism as concentrating on "careful elaboration of the existing rules, as well as on progressive codification of the law."[110]

Indeed, the frustration with the positivist school following major wars and the subsequent emphasis placed on natural law has partly affected the author's decision to pursue interdisciplinary legal research rather than a purely doctrinal positivist one. This is because discussions of natural law "rejected the emphasis on form and concentrated instead on the definition in terms of universal factors, physical, psychological, social and historical."[111] Certainly, unnecessary suffering is understood by some scholars and practitioners alike as a LOAC principle stemming from natural law.[112]

Examining the codification of unnecessary suffering as a norm has been an exercise in both legal schools. It started with codification during the nineteenth century as a positive norm that developed further into a natural law or, as introduced by Shaw, a norm of "behaviorist theory"—a modern legal theory emphasizing the government's responsibility toward its citizens.[113] In any event, in this interdisciplinary study, the author focuses primarily on the positivist approach; moreover, in addition to conventions, UN Resolutions can serve as a particular reflection of State practice.[114] In the area of LOAC, such State practice and *opinio juris* can be found in official State-issued military manuals concerned with the LOAC. The ICRC offers an online database of relevant military manuals.[115] As interdisciplinary legal research in the field of the LOAC, particular emphasis is placed on case studies and jurisprudence. Jurisprudence is examined and studied through the case law database found on worldcourts.com, which represents an extensive database source for case law often employed by

[109] The positive law, as it developed through nineteenth century, declared that law as it exists should be analyzed empirically, shorn of all ethical elements, i.e., a normative science. Malcolm Shaw, *International Law* (Cambridge: Cambridge University Press, 2017), 36–37.

[110] Deplano and Tsagourias, 11.

[111] Shaw, 39.

[112] Kneubuehl et al., *Wound Ballistics: Basics and Applications* (New York: Springer, 2008), 334.

[113] Shaw, 40–47.

[114] Deplano and Tsagourias, 89.

[115] See ICRC, IHL Database: Customary IHL. "Military Manuals." Accessed April 19, 2022. https://ihl-databases.icrc.org/customary-ihl/eng/docs/src_iimima.

legal researchers.[116] Indeed, methodologies of international law have come to be understood as a particular kind of argumentative practice different from social science.[117] However, as an argumentative practice, it is not all-encompassing. As Deplano and Tsagourias (2021) put it, "all participants share the same burden of presenting the best evidence in favor of one rule or another, while the system itself forecloses the possibility that any of those determinations can have absolute finality."[118]

References

Aoki, Fukiko. *731: Ishii Shiro to Saikinsen Butai no Yami wo Abaku* [731: Exposing the darkness of Ishii Shiro and the bacteriological unit]. Tokyo: Shinchosha, 2005.

Aust, Anthony. *Modern Treaty Law and Practice.* Cambridge: Cambridge University Press, 2013.

Boothby, William H. *Conflict Law: The Influence of New Weapons Technology, Human Rights and Emerging Actors.* The Hague: T.M.C. Asser Press, 2014.

Boothby, William H. *The Law of Targeting.* Oxford: Oxford University Press, 2012.

Boothby, William H. *Weapons and the Law of Armed Conflict.* New York: Oxford University Press, 2016.

Casey-Maslen, Stuart. *Jus ad Bellum: The Law on Inter-State Use of Force.* New York: Hart, 2020.

Casey-Maslen, Stuart, and Steven Haines. *Hague Law Interpreted: The Conduct of Hostilities under the Law of Armed Conflict.* New York: Hart, 2020.

Casey-Maslen, Stuart, and Tobias Vestner. *A Guide to Disarmament Law.* New York: Routledge, 2019.

Clapham, Andrew, and Paola Gaeta, eds. *The Oxford Handbook of International Law in Armed Conflict.* Oxford: Oxford University Press, 2014.

Corn, Geoffrey S., Victor Hansen, Richard Jackson, M. Christopher Jenks, Eric Talbot Jensen, and James A. Schoettler. *The Law of Armed Conflict: An Operational Approach.* New York: Wolters Kluwer, 2012.

Deplano, Rossana, and Nicholas Tsagourias, eds. *Research Methods in International Law: A Handbook.* Cheltenham: Edward Elgar Publishing Limited, 2021.

Dinstein, Yoram. *The Conduct of Hostilities Under the Law of International Armed Conflict.* Cambridge: Cambridge University Press, 2004.

Dinstein, Yoram. *War, Aggression and Self-Defence.* 6th ed. Cambridge: Cambridge University Press, 2017.

[116] See World Courts, accessed October 12, 2021, http://www.worldcourts.com/.

[117] Deplano and Tsagourias, 18.

[118] Deplano and Tsagourias, 25.

Distefano, Giovanni. *Fundamentals of Public International Law: A Sketch of the International Legal Order.* Leiden: Brill Nijhoff, 2019.

Doswald-Beck, Louise, ed. *San Remo Manual on International Law Applicable to Armed Conflicts at Sea.* Cambridge: Cambridge University Press, 1995.

Douhet, Giulio. *The Command of the Air.* Translated by Dino Ferrari. Maxwell Air Force Base, Alabama: Air University Press, 2019.

Fellmeth, Aaron X., and Maurice Horwitz. *Guide to Latin in International Law.* New York, Oxford University Press, 2009.

Frankland, Noble, and Charles Webster. *The Strategic Air Offensive Against Germany: 1939 – 1945.* Vol. 4. Uckfield: Naval & Military Press, 2006.

Forsythe, David P. *The Humanitarians.* Cambridge: Cambridge University Press, 2005.

Gardiner, Richard. *Treaty Interpretation.* 2nd ed. Oxford: Oxford University Press, 2017.

Grunden, Walter E. "No Retaliation in Kind: Japanese Chemical Warfare Policy in World War II. In Friedrich, Bretislav, Dieter Hoffmann, Jürgen Renn, Florian Schmaltz, and Martin Wolf. *One Hundred Years of Chemical Warfare: Research, Deployment, Consequences.* Springer, 2018.

Hayashi, Nobuo. "Using Force by Means of Nuclear Weapons and Requirements of Necessity and Proportionality *Ad Bellum.*" In *Nuclear Weapons Under International Law*, edited by Gro Nystuen, Stuart Casey-Maslen, and Annie G. Bersagel, 15–30. Cambridge: Cambridge University Press, 2014.

Henckaerts, Jean-Marie, and Louise Doswald-Beck, eds. *Customary International Humanitarian Law.* Vol.1, *Rules.* Cambridge: Cambridge University Press, 2005.

Hippler, Thomas. *Bombing the People: Gulio Douhet and the Foundations of Air-Power Strategy, 1884–1939.* Cambridge: Cambridge University Press, 2013.

ICRC. "Rule 70. Weapons of a Nature to Cause Superfluous Injury or Unnecessary Suffering." Accessed April 12, 2022a. https://ihl-databases.icrc.org/customary-ihl/eng/docindex/v1_rul_rule70.

Kneubuehl, Beat P., Robin M. Coupland, Markus A. Rothschild, and Michael J. Thali. *Wound Ballistics: Basics and Applications.* New York: Springer, 2008.

Kolb, Robert, and Richard Hyde. *An Introduction to the International Law of Armed Conflicts.* Portland: Hart Publishing, 2008.

Lazenby, John F. *The Peloponnesian War: A Military Study.* London: Routledge, 2004.

Mathur, Ritu. *Red Cross Interventions in Weapons Control.* London: Lexington Books, 2017.

Melzer, Nils. *Interpretive Guidance on the Notion of Direct Participation in Hostilities Under International Humanitarian Law.* Geneva: ICRC, 2009.

Nystuen, Gro, Stuart Casey-Maslen, and Annie G. Bersagel, eds. *Nuclear Weapons Under International Law.* Cambridge: Cambridge University Press, 2014.

O'Connor, Simon. "Nuclear Weapons and the Unnecessary Suffering Rule." In *Nuclear Weapons Under International Law*, edited by Gro Nystuen, Stuart Casey-Maslen, and Annie G. Bersagel, 128–147. Cambridge: Cambridge University Press, 2014.

Olsen, John Andreas. *Strategic Air Power in Desert Storm*. New York, Routledge, 2006.

Olsen, John Andreas, ed. *A History of Air Warfare*. Washington: Potomac Books, 2010.

Phillips, Charles, and Alan Axelrod, eds. *Encyclopedia of Wars*. New York: Zenda, Inc, 2005.

Rietiker, Daniel. *Humanization of Arms Control: Paving the Way for a World Free of Nuclear Weapons*. New York: Routledge, 2018.

Rousseau, Jean-Jacques. *The Social Contract and the First and Second Discourses*. Edited by Susan Dunn. New York: Yale University Press, 2020.

Sandoz, Yves, Christophe Swinarski, and Bruno Zimmerman, eds. *Commentary on the Additional Protocols of 8 June 1977 to the Geneva Conventions of 12 August 1949*. Geneva: International Committee of the Red Cross, 1987.

Sassoli, Marco. *International Humanitarian Law: Rules, Controversies, and Solutions to Problems Arising in Warfare*. Cheltenham: Edward Elgar, 2019.

Marco Sassoli et al., "Hors de Combat." Accessed April 12, 2022. https://casebook.icrc.org/glossary/hors-de-combat.

Schabas, William. *The International Criminal Court: A Commentary on the Rome Statute*. 2nd ed. Oxford: Oxford University Press, 2016.

Scharre, Paul. *Army of None: Autonomous Weapons and the Future of* War. New York: WW Norton, 2019.

Shaw, Malcolm. *International Law*. Cambridge: Cambridge University Press, 2017.

Solis, Gary D. *The Law of Armed Conflict: International Humanitarian Law in War.* 2nd ed. Cambridge: Cambridge University Press, 2016.

ICRC. IHL Database: Customary IHL. "Military Manuals." Accessed April 19, 2022b. https://ihl-databases.icrc.org/customary-ihl/eng/docs/src_iimima.

ICRC. Treaties, States Parties and Commentaries. "Additional Articles relating to the Condition of the Wounded in War. Geneva, 20 October 1868." Accessed April 13, 2022c. https://ihl-databases.icrc.org/applic/ihl/ihl.nsf/Treaty.xsp?documentId=ECB39EA050F80A5DC12563CD002D6624&action=openDocument.

UK Ministry of Defence. *The Manual of the Law of Armed Conflict*. Oxford: Oxford University Press, 2004.

US Department of Defense. *DOD Dictionary of Military and Associated Terms*. Washington DC: The Joint Staff, 2019.

CHAPTER 2

Traditional Interpretation

2.1 Introduction

Unlike International Human Rights Law or IHRL, the law of armed conflict (LOAC)—that is, the rules and regulations applicable to the conduct of hostilities (CoH)—is not a modern concept. Contemporary LOAC has evolved in stages to address advances in weapons technology and transformations in the nature of combat and armed conflict. Indubitably, these rules have been deeply influenced by the great wars of the twentieth century; however, their roots are ancient. Limitations concerning the conduct of hostilities are found in Christian, Buddhist, Muslim,[1] Hindu, and African cultures.[2] Most well-known among these ancient texts and doctrines are *The Art of War* by Sun Tzu (fifth century BCE), the Japanese codex of bushido,[3] and the Bible.[4] These are just a few well-known examples that discuss the means and methods of warfare.

[1] See Ahmed Al-Dawoody, *The Islamic Law of War*: Justifications and Regulations (New York: Palgrave Macmillan, 2011).

[2] Geoffrey Darnton, *Nuclear Weapons and International Law: From the London Nuclear Warfare Tribunal Via the International Court of Justice Advisory Opinion to Contemporary Developments*, 2nd ed., (Bournemouth: Requirements Analytics, For Peace Analytics, 2015), 183–184.

[3] Bushido as codex was largely unwritten. The first comprehensive written reference is from Nitobe Inazo. See Nitobe Inazo, *Bushido: The Soul of Japan* (New York: Kodansha, 2002).

[4] Deuteronomy 20, "Going to War."

J. Krasny, *War Injuries*,
https://doi.org/10.1007/978-3-032-00737-7_2

Not only were restrictions placed on methods concerning the conduct of hostilities, such as a general abhorrence of targeting civilian populations, but gradually, the means of warfare or weapons were likewise regulated. An ancient story in the Mahabharata describes the prohibition of "*pashupatastra*," an exceedingly devastating weapon and, as such, considered dishonorable and out of conformity with religious values, including the rules of war.[5] Besides mythology, early historical cases are found in the book of Manu (second century BCE to third century CE), containing the prohibition of hooked spikes or poisoned arrows.[6] In Europe, the 1139 Second Lateran Council tried to restrict the use of the crossbow with its armor-piercing capabilities as "socially subversive where a mere commoner could now butcher knights on horseback who typically hailed the ranks of nobility."[7] The concern with a crossbow is similar to that expressed about poison, which, as explained in later chapters, was perceived as a weapon of the weak, who could then slay even the king. It would, therefore, be naïve to suggest that weapons were banned or restricted because of their injurious effects; instead, the common denominator was the availability or lack of defensive countermeasures.

Later, the fathers of international law deliberated upon the question regarding limitations on the means and methods of warfare. To illustrate just a few, Hugo Grotius in *De iure praedae commentarius* (Commentary on the Law of Prize and Booty) argued that captured ships are a lawful prize in a just war.[8] Emer de Vattel in *The Law of Nations* discussed the rights of nations in war and deliberated whether poison, among other weapons, could be used as a means of warfare.[9] It is, nonetheless, critical

[5] See Sanskriti. "Pashupatastra: Weapon of Lord Shiva" accessed April 12, 2022 https://www.sanskritimagazine.com/indian-religions/hinduism/pashupatastra-weapon-of-lord-shiva/.

[6] 16.3.11: Honor in Battle: "When he fights with his foes in battle, let him not strike with weapons concealed (in wood), nor with (such as are) barbed, poisoned, or the points of which are blazing with fire. [v.7.90.]." See George Buhler, *The Laws of Manu* (Pinnacle Press, 2017).

[7] Michael S. Bryant, *A World History of War Crimes: From Antiquity to the Present*, 2nd ed., (New York: Bloomsbury Academic, 2021), 161.

[8] Randall Lesaffer, "Grotius on the Use of Force. Perfect, Imperfect and Civil Wars: An Introduction" *Grotiana 41*, no. 2 (2020): 255–262. https://doi.org/10.1163/18760759-41020001.

[9] See Bela Kapossy and Richard Whatmore,eds., *Emer de Vattel: The Law of Nations, Or, Principles of the Law of Nature, Applied to the Conduct and Affairs of Nations and Sovereigns, with Three Early Essays on the Origin and Nature of Natural Law and on Luxury* (Indianapolis: Liberty Fund, 2008), 574.

to reflect that the objective of LOAC is not to impose unrealistic or overtly ambitious restrictions or to "humanize" warfare through utopian limitations. The concept of *jus in bello* upholds the fact that armies need to achieve legitimate objectives. As such, this particular body of law has traditionally imposed limits on the cruelest means and methods that serve no military purpose whatsoever. This theoretical deliberation of balancing military necessity with humanity goes back as far as the Thirty Years' War (1618–1648) with Grotius's *De jure belli ac pacis* (1625).[10] Under the traditional law of war, limitations on weapons and the methods of their deployment consist primarily of customary rules and principles rather than treaties or conventions.[11]

Whereas the contemporary LOAC is formed by both the Hague and Geneva laws, as previously explained, the focus in this chapter is principally on the Hague law—that is, the rules and principles related to the conduct of hostilities and the means and methods of warfare. Integral components of this body of law are rules pertaining to weapons and targeting. The main difference lies in the subject matter. Weapons law, as a subfield of the LOAC, is concerned with the sole nature of a particular weapon, such as whether the mere existence of such weapon with its attributes is lawful or not, and thereby regulates the development of such weapons.[12] Targeting law as an additional distinct subfield then pertains to and regulates the use or deployment of weapons.[13] This distinction is significant since even a lawful weapon can be misused and thus breach the LOAC. The most straightforward example is a machine gun used to gun down civilians.

After reflecting on this process of codification of the prohibition of unnecessary suffering and superfluous injury (SIrUS) in conventional sources—principally the 1868 St. Petersburg Declaration,[14] the Hague Conventions of 1899/1907, and the so-called Geneva Gas

[10] See Hugo Grotius, *The Rights of War and Peace*, (Vol. I–III), ed. Richard Tuck (Indianapolis: Liberty Fund, 2005).

[11] Frits Kalshoven and Liesbeth Zegveld, *Constraints on the Waging of War*, 4th ed. (Cambridge: Cambridge University Press, 2011).

[12] William H. Boothby, *Weapons and the Law of Armed Conflict* (New York: Oxford University Press, 2016), 3–5.

[13] William H. Boothby, *The Law of Targeting* (Oxford: Oxford University Press, 2012) 4.

[14] Declaration Renouncing the Use in Time of War of Explosive Projectiles Under 400 Grammes Weight 138 CTS 297 (entered into force 11 December 1868).

Protocol[15]—the author proceeds to discuss the notion of military necessity and examine five fundamental customary principles concerning the conduct of hostilities, namely distinction, precautions, proportionality, and humanity before arriving at the core principle of the prohibition of unnecessary suffering or superfluous injury. This chapter, therefore, examines the traditional understanding of the so-called SIrUS principle as a balance between military necessity and injury without medical explanation and establishes the groundwork for the later modern, alternate interpretations explored in the subsequent chapter.

2.2 Hague Law and the Conduct of Hostilities

Studies and literature that probe the detailed nuances of Hague law are relatively scarce, as acknowledged by Casey-Maslen and Haines (2020).[16] This is quite surprising given the deep historical roots of this body of law, as introduced above. This so-called Hague law, named after the two Hague conferences of 1899 and 1907, regulates the conduct of hostilities—that is, the means and methods of warfare, weapons, targeting, and methods of deployment as well as, to a certain extent, the legitimacy of particular tactics and strategy. Hague law, as embodied in the Hague conventions, was already regarded as customary during the criminal proceedings at Nuremberg[17] and Tokyo.[18] The founders of the ICRC, H. Dunant and G. Moynier, already raised the problem of weapons development, their use, and the resultant suffering during the 1863 Geneva Congress that led to the adoption of the first Geneva Convention.[19]

[15] Protocol for the Prohibition of the Use in War of Asphyxiating, Poisonous or other Gases, and of Bacteriological Methods of Warfare (signed 17 June 1925, entered into force 8 February 1928) 94 LNTS 65.

[16] Stuart Casey-Maslen and Steven Haines, *Hague Law Interpreted: The Conduct of Hostilities under the Law of Armed Conflict* (New York: Hart, 2020).

[17] Charter of the [Nuremberg] International Military Tribunal (8 August 1945) 82 UNTS.

[18] Charter of the International Military Tribunal for the Far East (19 January 1946) 4 Bevans

[19] See Angela Bennett, *Geneva Convention: The Hidden Origins of the Red Cross* (Cheltenham: The History Press, 2006).

2.3 The Law of Targeting

The law of targeting is not identical to the law of weaponry. This might not be apparent at first glance. Any weapon can be misused in violation of LOAC rules. These unlawful misuses include, for example, simple alterations such as carving crosses or X symbols with knives on the top of bullets to make them expand upon impact, thus branding a primitive "dum-dum" bullet;[20] indiscriminate bombardment by lawful explosives; and using disproportionately large ammunition or serrated knives for anti-personnel purposes.[21] Particular weapons deemed inherently in violation of LOAC are then restricted under specific agreements, which are explored in Chap. 5.

Amid ongoing conflicts in regions such as the Middle East and Ukraine, media outlets, including commentators on social networks, frequently offer their views on the actions of warring parties, often without even a basic understanding of the laws of war. This lack of knowledge leads to public confusion and fuels heightened emotions by promoting misleading narratives. Often, such a misleading narrative stems from ignorance of the rules and definitions rather than a hidden agenda. Definitions are, therefore, crucial starting points for approaching weapons law and the law of targeting. *Concise Oxford English Dictionary* defines a target as a "person, object, or a place selected as the aim of an attack."[22] Thus, targeting is defined in layman's terms as aiming or directing the attack. However, in military practice, targeting is much more complex. As Boothby (2012) explains:

> [W]hen applied to the military context, targeting is a broad process encompassing planning and execution including the consideration of prospective targets of attack, the accumulation of information to determine whether the attack of a particular object, person, or group of persons will meet military, legal, and other requirements, the determination of which weapon and method should be used to prosecute the target, the carrying out of attacks,

[20] See Marco Sassoli, Antoine Bouvier, Anne Quintin, and Julia Grignon "Dum-dum Bullets" accessed March 14, 2022. https://casebook.icrc.org/glossary/dum-dum-bullets.

[21] "Each of these war crimes demands either deliberate intent (*dolus directus*) or recklessness (*dolus eventualis*)." Casey-Maslen and Haines, *Hague Law*, 129.

[22] Maurice Waite, ed., *Paperback Oxford English Dictionary* (Oxford: Oxford University Press, 2012), 746.

including those decided upon at short notice and with minimal opportunity for planning, and other activities.[23]

Accordingly, the official US Department of Defense (DoD) *Dictionary of Military and Associated Terms* defines targeting as "The process of selecting and prioritizing targets and matching the appropriate response to them, considering operational requirements and capabilities."[24] The term attack, in its general term and meaning, is defined in the *Oxford English Dictionary* as "to take violent action against [something or somebody]."[25] As Boothby (2012) clarifies, "the importance of targeting lies in the direct and fundamental relationship between the use of force and accomplishment of the strategic goals of the military operation."[26] This is because the conduct of hostilities takes place against the backdrop of public perception, and it is, therefore, in the national interests of belligerents that any use of force is seen as legitimate in the eyes of the public. Therefore, the law of targeting has to be separated from the law of weaponry, which focuses simply on the nature of weapons and not how belligerents use them in combat. However, as will be explained later, the design and purpose of weapons can play a significant role in determining their legitimacy.

2.4 Weapons Law

Weapons law concerns the nature of arms and weapons, which Boothby (2016) defines as any objects designed to kill, injure, or damage.[27] There is a plethora of means of warfare, including "a device, system, munition, implement, substance, object, or piece of equipment that is used, that it is intended to use, or that has been designed for use to apply the offensive

[23] Boothby. *Law of Targeting*, 4.

[24] US Department of Defense, *DOD Dictionary of Military and Associated Terms* (Washington DC: The Joint Staff, 2019), 215.

[25] Waite, 39.

[26] Boothby, *Law of Targeting*, 4.

[27] Bowyer defines arms merely as synonymous with "weapons." See Richard Bowyer, *Dictionary of Military Terms*, 3rd ed. (London: A&C Black, 2007), 15. On the other hand, Waite (2012), in the *Paperback Oxford Dictionary*, defines arms or armaments as "military weapons or equipment," 33. It can thus be inferred that a weapon is anything that can be used to harm or kill, while an arm is factory-produced military equipment. However, for the purposes of this book, both terms are treated as synonyms.

capability, usually causing injury or damage to an adverse party to an armed conflict."[28] The Air and Missile Warfare Manual[29] defines a weapon as "instruments used to cause, in the course of armed conflict, (i) the death of, or injury to, individuals; or (ii) damage to, destruction of, objects."[30] Therefore, the determination of "whether a weapon is lawful per se or whether an intended use of a particular weapon complies with the law applicable to that weapon falls under weapons law."[31]

States are generally reluctant to give up a weapon already in their arsenal and deemed effective for particular objectives. As Boothby (2016) points out, "Ad hoc initiatives have often produced new weapons law treaties while processes based on consensus have not yielded such tangible results."[32] While such a statement is factually correct, it is also typical for the traditional interpretation of unnecessary suffering revolving around the military advantage offered by a specific weapon rather than seeking a general, all-encompassing definition. The process of SIrUS codification is reflective of this balancing litmus test.

2.4.1 The Lieber Code of 1863

Clapham and Gaeta (2014) fittingly reiterated that, "A soldier is not a bandit and must not behave like one."[33] The codification of adequate conduct during hostilities began in the second half of the nineteenth century. Notwithstanding the diverse cultural or religious concepts briefly introduced above, the prohibition of excessive injury without military necessity was first codified in an instrument of soft law, the Lieber Code[34] (1863). An army manual for those engaged in what today would be classified as a non-international armed conflict (NIAC). This was an important milestone that inspired subsequent law of war agreements. Written during the

[28] Boothby, *Weapons*, 346.

[29] Program on Humanitarian Policy and Conflict Research at Harvard University, *HPCR Manual on International Law Applicable to Air and Missile Warfare* (Cambridge: Cambridge University Press, 2013).

[30] Program, *HPCR Manual*, 31.

[31] Boothby, *Weapons*, 5.

[32] Boothby, *Weapons*, 197.

[33] Andrew Clapham and Paola Gaeta, eds., *The Oxford Handbook of International Law in Armed Conflict* (Oxford: Oxford University Press, 2014), 92.

[34] Instructions for the Government of Armies of the United States in the Field, *US Army General Order No. 100*, 24 April 1863.

American Civil War (1861–1865) at the request of President Abraham Lincoln,[35] its author, Francis Lieber, emphasized what we now define as justifiable military necessity.[36] Article 15 of the code stipulates that military necessity: "…admits of all direct destruction of life or limb of armed enemies, and of other persons whose destruction is incidentally unavoidable in the armed contests of the war." As pointed out above, military necessity in *jus in bello* is a permissive principle that allows all *lawful* [emphasis added] means necessary to achieve the objective; only unavoidable incidental destruction that is proportionate to the value of the target may be permitted. All other acts are prohibited in war, including, of course, looting, rape, arbitrary killing (i.e., murder), or meaningless destruction. Such a rule is articulated in Article 16 of the code:

> Military necessity does not admit of cruelty—that is, the infliction of suffering for the sake of suffering or for revenge, nor of maiming or wounding except in fight, nor of torture to extort confessions. It does not admit of the use of poison in any way, nor of the wanton devastation of a district. It admits of deception, but disclaims acts of perfidy; and, in general, military necessity does not include any act of hostility which makes the return to peace unnecessarily difficult.[37]

At first glance, Articles 15 and 16 of the Code might appear in stark contrast, since Art. 15 addresses "all direct destruction" as permitted. However, Lieber did identify as unlawful acts of violence for wanton reasons, that is, with the only purpose of increasing suffering or wounding for the sake of suffering. Hence, an infliction of suffering cannot become a military objective. Going beyond military necessity would thus breach the accompanying principle of unnecessary suffering. Therefore, the roots of this principle and its idea can be traced back to the Lieber Code. For its period, the Lieber Code represented a document or military manual ahead of its time.

[35] Jenny Gesley, "The 'Lieber Code' – the First Modern Codification of the Laws of War." Library of Congress blog. April 24, 2018. https://blogs.loc.gov/law/2018/04/the-lieber-code-the-first-modern-codification-of-the-laws-of-war/.

[36] Clapham and Gaeta, 93.

[37] Instructions for the Government of Armies of the United States in the Field, *US Army General Order No. 100*, 24 April 1863. Art.16.

Indeed, the lingering question is why such a provision was even included. The answer relates to Francis Lieber's experiences in Europe[38] and in the course of the American Civil War, which was plagued by guerrilla warfare, where pointless violence was returned with the same senseless ferocity.[39] Lieber's objective was thus to instruct the Union army to follow basic rules of the law of war to alleviate at least the suffering of soldiers that was not strictly necessary to ensure reciprocity from the enemy. This underlying idea of proscribing meaningless cruelty was picked up again in the St. Petersburg Declaration of 1868—one of the first agreements to outlaw specific means of warfare and the first international agreement to prohibit unnecessary suffering.

2.4.2 St. Petersburg Declaration of 1868

In 1868, Tsar Alexander II of Russia organized an International Military Conference to initiate negotiations into the prohibition of hollow rifle bullets that expand easily upon impact.[40] This type of ammunition caused severe and often untreatable injuries, rendering the death of affected troops almost inevitable. The Russian Empire subsequently developed bullets filled with explosives against artillery (i.e., inanimate targets).[41] Recognizing the potential impact of such ammunition, the Russian Empire was willing to forsake its military advantage if other States in the international community did the same. The concern was that, in the heat of the battle, a soldier could use these bullets against enemy combatants, causing unnecessarily large, in most cases, lethal wounds. Indeed, to believe that the St. Petersburg Declaration[42] was inspired purely by noble

[38] Much like Henry Dunant, Lieber was appalled by excessive suffering without any military justification and was even wounded during his taking part in the Napoleonic wars in Europe. Holquist, "Lieber Code to Brussels."

[39] See Gary W. Gallagher, et al., *The American Civil War: This Mighty Scourge of War* (Oxford: Osprey Publishing, 2003), 251.

[40] Natalia Jevglevskaja, "St. Petersburg, 1868: First International Agreement Prohibiting the Use of Certain Weapons," in *Online Atlas on the History of Humanitarianism and Human Rights*. Accessed April 9, 2022. https://hhr-atlas.ieg-mainz.de/articles/jevglevskaja-st_petersburg.

[41] Scott Keefer, "Explosive Missals: International Law, Technology, and Security in Nineteenth-Century Disarmament Conferences" *War in History* 21, no. 4 (2014): 445–464 accessed May 11, 2022. http://www.jstor.org/stable/26098618.

[42] Declaration Renouncing the Use in Time of War of Explosive Projectiles Under 400 Grammes Weight 138 CTS 297 (entered into force 11 December 1868).

humanitarian reasons would be naïve. As Keefer (2014) points out, the British insistence on including the clause on reciprocity signals that the agreeing parties intended the use of such munition against nations they considered "uncivilized."[43] Nevertheless, from the perspective of SIrUS interpretation, the focal point is the Preamble of the Declaration:

> That the only legitimate object which States should endeavor to accomplish during war is to weaken the military forces of the enemy;
>
> That for this purpose it is sufficient to disable the greatest possible number of men;
>
> That this object would be exceeded by the employment of arms which uselessly aggravate the sufferings of disabled men, or render their death inevitable;
>
> That the employment of such arms would, therefore, be contrary to the laws of humanity. Its humanitarian subtext is ostensible.

Contrary to the Lieber Code, the wording highlights several essential and distinctive aspects. No longer does the language include "destruction of the enemy," but rather "weakening" of its military forces through disabling or neutralizing[44] the greatest possible number of men. However, the following reference to weapons is crucial. Arms that *uselessly* [emphasis added] aggravate the suffering of disabled men or render their death inevitable. The interdependence between military necessity and unnecessary suffering becomes self-evident through the word "uselessly." Hence, it is not difficult to reflect upon exploding bullets as unnecessary for accomplishing a military objective of disabling the enemy's forces and rendering them *hors de combat*. Regular bullets can achieve this objective. Also, these excessively injurious bullets put an additional strain on medical services in the field. A certain resemblance emerges with the prohibition of hooked spikes mentioned in Chap. 1, where simple spikes are enough to put a combatant out of the battle. Who would argue that disemboweling an enemy combatant is militarily necessary? Indeed, ballistic vests increasingly protect soldiers, and the scope of permissible injury is redefined in a way consistent with such developments in protective gear. Therefore, it is prudent to follow the progress and application of this rule concerning particular weapons and defensive countermeasures.

[43] Keefer, "Explosive Missals," 458.

[44] The military uses the term "to neutralize" [the enemy]. According to the US DoD *Dictionary of Military and Associated Terms,* 157, to neutralize means, *inter alia,* to: "render enemy personnel or materiel incapable of interfering with a particular operation."

2.4.3 *Brussels Declaration of 1874 and the Hague Conventions of 1899 and 1907*

The Brussels Declaration[45] that emerged from the 1874 conference, convened on the initiative of, yet again, Tsar Alexander II, pronounced a set of rules that served as an important cornerstone for subsequent Hague Conferences.[46] Although the declaration is not legally binding, as it was not adopted and did not enter into force, it nonetheless represents progress in the formulation of the law. It can be interpreted as an expression of the opinion of States.[47] Of particular interest are Art. 12 and Art. 13. Article 12 stipulates: "The laws of war do not recognize in belligerents an unlimited power in the adoption of means of injuring the enemy." Subsequent Article 13 specifies that it is especially forbidden to: "(e) employ arms, projectiles or material calculated to cause unnecessary suffering, as well as the use of projectiles prohibited by the Declaration of St. Petersburg of 1868." The concept of unnecessary suffering is articulated more precisely than in the preamble of the St. Petersburg Declaration. In particular, the prohibition of "projectiles or material calculated to cause…" is worded carefully. This wording was later adopted by the International Criminal Tribunal for the former Yugoslavia or ICTY in its statute as one of the prosecutable crimes. Nevertheless, the wording "calculated to" lies at the core of subsequent disputes over applying and interpreting the SIrUS principle.[48] The debate over the interpretation of this principle's fundamental nature has traditionally revolved around intent and intended design purpose, as opposed to the "nature" of the weapon.

Following the Brussels Declaration, the first Hague Conference convened in 1899 on the initiation of Tsar Nicolas II intended to curb uncontrolled military buildup and reaffirm rules applicable during warfare. While primarily focusing on alleviating the financial strain of military spending, the conferences did serve as a reaffirmation of customary prohibition of particular means, such as poison and poisoned weapons, and expanding bullets, albeit only among European nations.[49] The conference was the

[45] Project of an International Declaration concerning the Laws and Customs of War (27 August 1874) (1907) 1 AJIL Supp 96.

[46] Boothby, *Law of Targeting*, 15.

[47] Boothby, *Law of Targeting*, 16.

[48] Boothby, *Weapons*, 49.

[49] Keefer, 459–460.

first of its kind with 26 delegations, even including non-European countries, and it was successful in its focus on arms control, military budgets, and the implementation of regulations prohibiting unnecessary suffering, such as the St. Petersburg Declaration concerning exploding and expanding bullets.[50] The result was the 1899 Hague Convention that codified the rules and principles applicable during hostilities. Due to the large number of attached specific regulations, the Hague Convention of 1899 is often called the Hague Regulations.

As a result of the worsening international situation—particularly the Boer War (1899–1902)[51] and the Russo-Japanese War (1904–1905)[52]—a second conference was convened in 1907 with 43 delegations, enlarging the number of non-European States with the main purpose of deliberating on the peaceful settlement of disputes.[53] The conventions further reaffirmed the customary status and codified the SIrUS principle in its final document, although the discrepancy regarding the language would form the basis of different interpretations to the present day. Another conference that could potentially clarify this difference was proposed in 1914. Unfortunately, this effort did not materialize due to the outbreak of WWI.[54] The two Hague Conferences regulated multiple issues, such as air warfare, land warfare, and prisoners of war, established the court of arbitration, and ultimately codified the rules of the conduct of hostilities.[55] The Hague Conferences are crucial when interpreting superfluous injury or unnecessary suffering (SIrUS) for two reasons.

First, the Hague Conference of 1899 codified the principle of the prohibition of weapons "of a nature to" cause unnecessary suffering; second,

[50] Stanislas Jeannesson, "The International Hague Conferences of 1899 and 1907." *Encyclopedie d'histoire numerique de l'Europe*. June 22, 2020. https://ehne.fr/en/node/12230.

[51] Charles Phillips and Alan Axelrod, eds., *Encyclopedia of Wars* (New York: Yenda, Inc., 2005), 194.

[52] Phillips and Axelrod, 973–976.

[53] Freya Baetens. "Hague Conferences (1899, 1907)" in *Oxford Bibliographies*. November 21, 2012. https://www.oxfordbibliographies.com/view/document/obo-9780199743292/obo-9780199743292-0115.xml#obo-9780199743292-0115-bibItem-0012.

[54] Joseph H. Choate, *The Two Hague Conferences* (Princeton: Princeton University Press, 1913), 84.

[55] William I. Hull, *The Two Hague Conferences and Their Contributions to International Law* (Boston: For International School of Peace, Ginn, 1908).

the 1907 conference codified the principle of the prohibition of weapons "calculated to" cause unnecessary suffering, thus going back to the wording of the Brussels Declaration. This discrepancy, which is the backbone of the difference in interpretation, will be explained in Sect. 2.6 concerning superfluous injury or unnecessary suffering. However, it is essential to mention the first document outlawing an entire category of weapons—the Geneva Gas Protocol of 1925.

2.4.4 Protocol for the Prohibition of the Use in War of Asphyxiating, Poisonous, or Other Gases, and of Bacteriological Methods of Warfare of 1925

The aftermath of WWI is often incorrectly pinpointed as the beginning of the formation of the norm prohibiting the use of chemical weapons. During WWI, the French army employed non-lethal agents such as lachrymators (tear gas) on several occasions, arguing that the 1907 Hague Convention[56] effectively prohibits only the most toxic gases (i.e., lethal poisons).[57] The Battle of Ypres in Flanders, on April 22, 1915, witnessed the first large-scale deployment of chemical weapons on the battlefield when the Germans deployed large numbers of chlorine gas canisters.[58] The reaction to these new means and methods of war, after the dissipation of the first shock accompanying the use of any new weapon, was that gas is not an exceptionally cruel weapon or notably worse than a bayonet or an explosive. The British casualties due to gas were around 1% of all the casualties during WWI.[59] Many, as documented by several soldiers and military theorists, such as B.H. Liddell Hart, who himself experienced a gas attack in WWI, considered gas as more "humane" than being torn

[56] Hague Conventions respecting the Laws and Customs of War on Land and its Annex: Regulations concerning the Laws and Customs of War on Land, Art.23(a).

[57] Richard M. Price, *The Chemical Weapons Taboo* (New York: Cornell University Press, 1997), 53.

[58] National Geographic, *Visual History of the World* (Washington DC; National Geographic Society, 2005), 441.

[59] Edgar Jones. "Terror Weapons: The British Experience of Gas and Its Treatment in the First World War" *War in History* 21, no. 3 (2014): 355–375. https://doi.org/10.1177/0968344513510248.

apart by a bayonet or a grenade.[60] This picture of gas being perceived as somewhat preferred is further evidenced by the resistance of multiple WWI veteran organizations in the United States, who initially opposed the 1925 Geneva Gas Protocol.[61]

On the contrary, soldiers, civilians, and commentators who were not exposed to gas "were susceptible to the same kinds of fear of unknown that had caused such fear among soldiers when gas was first introduced."[62] These "unaffected" portions of the public, including combatants, were unable to draw distinctions between lethal and incapacitating gas as they feared any use of chemicals. This fear would epitomize "the most important interpretive continuity reinforced silently through political and military practice."[63] Artists and poets such as Wilfred Owen (1893–1918), with his graphic description of a gas attack in "Dulce et decorum est," helped further instigate the fear of the unknown, i.e., fear of the gas in the general public.[64]

The widespread use of chemical weapons and the subsequent pressure by the unaffected public prompted States to conduct further negotiations. The strategy of the chemical industry, eager to get lucrative chemical weapons defense contracts, accentuated and actively often exaggerated the dangers of chemical weapons, spurring fear of this new weapon among the lay public, which ultimately backfired on the US.[65] As Price (1997) wittingly points out, the "continuing presence of fears of hypothesized gas attacks on civilians was the crucial enabling condition for gas to be depicted as unacceptable."[66] Therefore, civilians who suffered relatively few casualties formed the core of those calling for the prohibition of the gas. These factors behind the ban on chemical weapons are essential to understanding the initial driving forces behind the regulation of weapons and why certain weapons are deemed excessive or causing unnecessary suffering. Such calls are not always grounded on medical data, pragmatic considerations, or derived from battlefield experiences. Therefore, the testimony of those with direct experience—soldiers and combatants—is of key significance to

[60] Price, 66.

[61] Price, 79.

[62] Price, 66.

[63] Price, 67–68.

[64] See Kenneth Simcox, "Poetry Critique: Dulce Et Decorum Est" accessed August 8, 2022. http://www.wilfredowen.org.uk/poetry/dulce-et-decorum-est.

[65] Price, 73.

[66] Price, 96.

ensure any regulation or disarmament is pragmatic and practical. The chemical weapons taboo and a general abhorrence regarding the use of chemicals for combat remain to this day, however, and was exacerbated by the Iran–Iraq War, as discussed in Chap. 4.

Following the end of WWI, Art. 171 of the Treaty of Versailles[67] further added yet another foundational layer of normative proscription against chemical weapons besides a general prohibition of poison under the Hague Conventions: "The use of asphyxiating, poisonous or other gases and all analogous liquids, materials or devices being prohibited... The same applies to materials specially intended for the manufacture, storage, and use of the said products or devices.." Article 171 adds asphyxiating and "other" analogous gases and liquids to poison. The adjective "other" refers to gases with similar asphyxiating properties that result in difficulty of breathing without being directly a choking agent such as yperite, which is a vesicant.[68]

The Washington Naval Conference (1921–1922) on the limitation of naval armaments "marked an important move from attempts to limit certain uses of a new weapon to a blanket prohibition on any use."[69] Certain uses in the context of the preceding Treaty of Versailles meant releases from cylinders, a method deployed mainly during WWI and distinct from weapons with the sole purpose of releasing poison banned by Hague Regulations of 1899. Therefore, Art. V of the Treaty on the Use of Submarines and Noxious Gases in Warfare[70] formed a necessary cornerstone for the subsequent agreement, the 1925 Geneva Gas Protocol.

> The use in war of asphyxiating, poisonous, or other gases, and all analogous liquids, materials, or devices, having been justly condemned by the general opinion of the civilized world and a prohibition of such use having been declared in treaties to which a majority of the civilized Powers are parties. The Signatory Powers, to the end that this prohibition shall be universally accepted as a part of international law binding alike the conscience and prac-

[67] Treaty of Peace between the Allied and Associated Powers and Germany (signed 28 June 1919, entered into force 10 January 1920) (1919) 225 CTS 188 (Versailles Peace Treaty).

[68] Boothby, *Weapons*, 107–111.

[69] Price, 84–99.

[70] Treaty regarding the Use of Submarines and Noxious Gases in Warfare (signed 6 February 1922, never entered into force) 25 LNTS 2020. The treaty did not enter into force, since Art. 6 required all victorious nations of WWI to ratify it, but France did not ratify the document.

> tice of nations, declare their assent to such prohibition, agree to be bound thereby as between themselves and invite all other civilized nations to adhere thereto.[71]

Hence, the proscription was built on an already institutionalized tradition of abhorrence toward gas.[72] This is evident from the wording of the article, "having been justly condemned by the general opinion of the civilized world." The Geneva Conference was thus, in a way, a "confirmation" of existing international law. The 1925 Geneva Conference, convened under the auspices of the League of Nations, in the Protocol regarding poisoned gas, adopted a comprehensive prohibition on "asphyxiating, poisonous, or other gases, all analogous liquids, materials, or devices, and further included prohibitions on bacteriological methods of warfare."[73]

No longer was it just a prohibition of certain uses or weapons with the sole purpose of diffusing poison; this time, the ban was all-encompassing, excluding reprisals. The addition of bacteriological warfare was quite a step ahead for the international community, since viruses or bacteria were not yet weaponized on an industrial scale, and biological weapons did not yet exist. The success of the 1925 Geneva Gas Protocol stemmed from several factors. Among the lay public, chemical weapons were associated with poison, fear, and certain death, whereas bacteriological warfare is viewed as both unfamiliar and inherently repulsive. Thus, unnecessary suffering was not the primary motivation for the prohibition. This would, however, change in the aftermath of the Iran-Iraq War (1980–1988), as discussed in Chaps. 4 and 5.

2.5 Military Necessity and Customary Principles

This section discusses the concept of military necessity as the primary balancing principle in relation to the five fundamental rules of LOAC: distinction, precautions, proportionality, humanity, and unnecessary suffering. While certain rules of armed conflict might be controversial or even disputed, such as the right to reprisals,[74] countless manuals include

[71] Art. 5, Treaty on the Use of Submarines and Noxious Gases in Warfare.

[72] Price, 91.

[73] Boothby, *Weapons*, 16.

[74] There is no consensus on the legality of reprisals, Clapham and Gaeta, *The Oxford Handbook*, 136. However, reprisals are referred to as at times the only "practical" means of coercing the enemy to stop violation of IHL, and as such is included in the manual of the law

the abovementioned principles as the fundamentals of the law of war.[75] While not a formal source of law, State-issued military manuals of the law of war may also serve as a reliable indicator of *opinio juris* or legal opinion of States.[76] Every manual of major powers and militarily significant states includes the abovementioned principles. As such, "[t]he foundational principles of military necessity and humanity undergird IHL in the sense that every IHL general principle and rule on the conduct of hostilities reflects a balancing by States of these foundational principles as they create, interpret, and apply individual operative norms."[77]

In the *United States v. Wilhelm List (1949)*,[78] the military tribunal at Nuremberg refuted the historical notion of military necessity interpreted by *kriegsraison*. As the tribunal stated, military necessity has to be lawful, i.e., in compliance with the law of war:

> (ix) Military necessity has been invoked by the defendants as justifying the killing of innocent members of the population and the destruction of villages and towns in the occupied territory. Military necessity permits a belligerent, *subject to the laws of war* (emphasis added), to apply any amount and kind of force to compel the complete submission of the enemy with the least possible expenditure of time, life and money.[79]

Besides, relying on superior orders by the defendants, disregards and diminishes the counterbalancing of the customary law, particularly the principle of distinction and military necessity against the ultimate objective of military victory. In its reasoning leading to the definitive rejection of *kriegsraison,* the military tribunal deliberated that:

of armed conflict of the United Kingdom. See UK Ministry of Defense, *The Manual of the Law of Armed Conflict* (Oxford: Oxford University Press, 2004), 421. In any way, reprisals are prohibited against protected persons, e.g., non-combatants (AP I, Art. 20).

[75] See ICRC, "Practice Relating to Rule 70. Weapons of a Nature to Cause Superfluous Injury or Unnecessary Suffering" accessed April 12, 2022. https://ihl-databases.icrc.org/customary-ihl/eng/docindex/v2_rul_rule70.

[76] Boothby, *Weapons*, 21.

[77] Ben Saul and Dapo Akande, eds., *The Oxford Guide to International Humanitarian Law* (Oxford: Oxford University Press, 2020), 148.

[78] Hostage Case, United States v List (Wilhelm) and ors, Trial Judgment, Case No 7, (1948) 11 TWC 757, (1950) 11 TWC 1230, (1948) 8 LRTWC 34, ICL 491 (US 1948), (1948) 15 ILR632, 19th February 1948, International Military Tribunal [IMT]; Nuremberg Military Tribunal [NMT].

[79] UN War Crimes Commission, *Law Reports of Trials of War Criminals.*1949, Vol. VIII, London.

> It is further charged that these defendants participated in a deliberate scheme of terrorism and intimidation wholly unwarranted and unjustified by military necessity by the murder, ill-treatment and deportation to slave labor of prisoners of war and members of the civilian populations in territories occupied by· the German Armed Forces, by plundering and pillaging public and private property, and wantonly destroying cities, towns and villages for which there was no military necessity...[80]

Hence, the tribunals at Nuremberg and correspondingly in Tokyo refuted the argument that in pursuing military objectives, efficiency—that is, the accomplishment of military missions with the least amount of expenses—trumps the fundamental rules of war, including distinction. Therefore, the principles of distinction and humanity were reaffirmed as balancing principles when considering military necessity. Indeed, they are even above military necessity. Necessity under *jus in bello* is a permissive rule. All necessary means should, therefore, be read as all necessary *lawful* means. As the military tribunal at Nuremberg further pointed out:

> There has been complete failure on the part of the nations' of the world to limit or mitigate the practice by conventional rule. This requires us to apply customary law. That international agreement is badly needed in this field is self-evident...they [the Germans] invoke the plea of military necessity, a term which they confuse with convenience and strategical interests [*sic*].[81]

Military necessity is nearly impossible to define precisely, fitting every combat situation, and thus, formulating a general definition that would fit all forms of armed conflict and situations is not realistic. However, it is a principle that, according to the United States Department of Defense (DoD) Manual of the Law of War, refers to "the use of all measures needed to defeat the enemy as quickly as efficiently as possible and are not prohibited by the law of war."[82] The United Kingdom Manual of the Law of Armed Conflict interprets the principle in a bit more restrictive terms than their US counterparts in the sense that necessity, as understood by the law of armed conflict, "permits the use of only that degree and kind of force not otherwise prohibited by the law of armed conflict to achieve legitimate

[80] UN War Crimes Commission, 35.

[81] UN War Crimes Commission, 63.

[82] Michael A. Newton, ed., *The United States Department of Defense: Law of War Manual Commentary and Critique* (Cambridge: Cambridge University Press, 2018), 116.

purpose... complete or partial submission of the enemy at the earliest possible moment with the minimum expenditure of lives and resources."[83] This means that weapons not explicitly banned are lawful, given their use does not violate the fundamental principles of LOAC.[84] That, of course, does not mean a weapon must be prohibited by a treaty. Such an effective disarmament treaty is rare, with only two successful examples being the conventions banning chemical and biological weapons discussed in later chapters.

A weapon under the law of armed conflict may be unlawful by its nature, even without a treaty, by custom, or by violating the fundamental principles of LOAC. Poison[85] was, as explained in preceding paragraphs, disfavored long before it was prohibited by black letter law. "Concrete military operations and conduct of hostilities are predominantly ruled by customary law and principles in the sense that the use of means of warfare which are not specifically prohibited by a treaty are still subject to other fundamental principles which have to be in most instances balanced against military necessity."[86]

2.5.1 *Precautions*

Throughout the conduct of hostilities, constant care needs to be taken by the commander in order to prevent or at least minimize accidental harm to civilian populations and objects. Precaution as a customary principle is codified in the Additional Protocol I (API) in Articles 57 and 58. "In the conduct of military operations, constant care shall be taken to spare the civilian population, civilians and civilian objects" (Additional Protocol I, Art.57(1)). Article 58 places constraints on the defending belligerent as well as not to place military objectives near civilian objects. Obligations are therefore placed on all belligerents.

[83] UK Ministry of Defense, 21–22.

[84] Jaroslav Krasny and Noriyuki Kawano, "Use of Nuclear Weapons in Armed Conflict" *Hiroshima Peace Science* 41, (2019): 73–84. https://doi.org/10.15027/49035.

[85] The Oxford English dictionary defines poison as a "substance that causes death or injury when swallowed or absorbed by living organism" (Waite, 554). Not all chemical weapons are poisons, meaning they cause death or injury; some have temporary effects, such as irritants (e.g., tear gas). Therefore, it is essential not to confuse these two terms, poison and chemical weapons. While all poisons can be regarded as chemical weapons, not all chemical weapons are poisons.

[86] Krasny and Kawano, "Use of Nuclear Weapons."

An obvious example would be placing a school near a military base or an ammunition depot near the hospital. Consequently, an essential aspect is that care should be constant, i.e., before, during, and after the military operation(s). Therefore, such care is more than evaluating the situation on the ground before commencing an attack and then re-evaluating it after the operation. Doing everything "feasible" to verify whether an objective is military or civilian vis-à-vis weapons is essentially enshrined in the second paragraph of Article 57, which states that belligerents shall: "take all feasible precautions in the choice of means and methods of attack to avoid, and in any event minimizing, incidental loss of life, injury to civilians and damage to civilian objects" (API, Art.57(2)(ii)). It is, then, obligatory that an attacker does everything in his power to avoid harm to protected persons by selecting the least injurious weapon capable of accomplishing the objective. Still, as precautions have to be weighed against military necessity as well, an attacker can only do such actions that are "reasonable" under the given circumstances.[87] We can interpret "feasibility" as a standard requiring the attacker to take measures to avoid collateral damage, i.e., measures that are practical or practically possible.[88] This includes under continuing paragraphs of Art.57 of AP I to:

2. Effective advance warning shall be given of attacks which may affect the civilian population, unless circumstances do not permit. Art.57(2)(c).
3. In the conduct of military operations at sea or in the air, each Party to the conflict shall, in conformity with its rights and duties under the rules of international law applicable in armed conflict, take all reasonable precautions to avoid losses of civilian lives and damage to civilian objects. Art.57(4).

Undeniably, Additional Protocol I, Art.57 lays down "general" obligations requiring interpretation and adaptation to a concrete situation and circumstances. Circumstances are different for a commander of artillery or air force, who might not have clear visual contact with the target, unlike, for instance, an infantry commander. In any case, the United Kingdom Manual on the Law of Armed Conflict indicates specific factors that such commanders need to consider:

[87] Saul and Akande, 167.
[88] Saul and Akande, 167.

a. whether he [the commander] can personally verify the target;
b. instructions from higher authority about objects which are not to be targeted;
c. intelligence reports, aerial or satellite reconnaissance pictures, and any other information in his possession about the nature of the proposed target;
d. any rules of engagement imposed by higher authority under which he is required to operate;
e. the risk to his own forces necessitated by target verification.[89]

It would be insufficient to place restrictions merely upon attacking the Party. As stated above, both or all belligerents are required to take precautionary measures when engaging in hostilities. The defending Party is required to:

a. without prejudice to Article 49 of the Fourth Convention, endeavor to remove the civilian population, individual civilians, and civilian objects under their control from the vicinity of military objectives;
b. avoid locating military objectives within or near densely populated areas; and
c. take the other necessary precautions to protect the civilian population, individual civilians, and civilian objects under their control against the dangers resulting from military operations. (Article 58, API)

These requirements shall be reasonable for both belligerents. Taking practical precautionary measures ensures the effectiveness of the operation on the side of the attacker while protecting civilian infrastructure on the side of the defending Party. The ICRC study of customary law identifies precaution under Rule 17 as: "Each party to the conflict must take all feasible precautions in the choice of means and methods of warfare with a view to avoiding and in any event to minimizing, incidental loss of civilian life, injury to civilians and damage to civilian objects."[90] The principle of precautions thus involves selecting a weapon that, on the one hand, accomplishes a given military objective but, on the other hand, does not cause unnecessary harm or destruction.

[89] UK Ministry of Defense, 82.
[90] Rule 17. Jean-Marie Henckaerts and Louise Doswald-Beck, eds., *Customary International Humanitarian Law, Vol.I, Rules* (Cambridge: Cambridge University Press, 2005), 56–57.

2.5.2 *Distinction*

"States must always differentiate between military objectives and civilian objects when engaged in hostilities. The rule of distinction constitutes part of *jus cogens* or peremptory norms where no derogation is permitted."[91] Further, military necessity cannot outweigh the distinction between combatants and non-combatants, i.e., non-combatants may never be made the objective of an attack under any circumstances. This is the most fundamental rule and *raison d' etre* of international humanitarian law (IHL).[92] The definition of a military objective is contained in Article 52(2) of the Additional Protocol I.

It states that "military objectives are objects which by their nature, location, purpose or use make an effective contribution to military action or whose total or partial destruction, capture or neutralization in the circumstances ruling at the time offers a definite military advantage. Article 52 further elaborates that: "The destruction of the object—in whole or in part—capturing it or neutralizing it must show a specific military advantage. Hence, attacks resulting in solely unspecified or potential advantage are prohibited." Consequently, it is imperative that tangible intelligence, which is as detailed as realistically possible given the circumstances in the field, provides all the necessary information regarding the object of attack (defines concretely the significance of the military objective). The value of the target must be evaluated continuously on all levels: tactical, operational, and strategic.

The distinction lies at the core of the law of armed conflict and LOAC. It refers to a distinction between military objectives and civilian objects, between combatants and non-combatants. While combatants are legitimate military objectives and targetable, non-combatants are protected persons under LOAC and, therefore, cannot become *the target* [emphasis added]. The term civilian can be confusing; a civilian, under specific circumstances, may become a military objective. For example, if he or she is directly participating in hostilities (DPH), he or she may lose his or her protective status and may become a military objective.[93] Indirect

[91] Henckaerts and Doswald-Beck, 56–57.

[92] Clapham and Gaeta, 296.

[93] See Nils Melzer, *Interpretative Guidance on the Notion of Direct Participation in Hostilities Under International Humanitarian Law* (Geneva: ICRC, 2009).

participation in hostilities, such as transportation of ammunition, may, at times, be controversial. However, the military objective would be the transportation truck or ammunition depot, not the driving non-combatant in such cases.[94] When there is expected collateral damage, the anticipated military advantage must be weighed against proportionality. That is, the value of the target has to outweigh the anticipated harm to civilians or civilian objects. This is, of course, impossible to determine in quantitative terms and has to be evaluated depending on a particular and concrete combat situation.

Distinction represents the heart of LOAC. However, it doesn't mean absolute, unconditional protection of non-combatants from the effects of war. In case collateral damage is unavoidable, it has to be proportionate. Non-combatants may not become the *intended* [emphasis added] target.[95] For instance, attacking civilians and combatants alike out of fear of guerilla attacks, i.e., situations where combatants wear plain clothes and hide among civilians, would constitute an indiscriminate attack. Indiscriminate attacks, including deploying an inherently indiscriminate weapon, are unlawful and constitute a grave breach of the Geneva Conventions. An inherently indiscriminate weapon is such that it has a rudimentary targeting system or cannot be targeted at all, such as the first generation of SCUD missiles or German V2 rockets during WWII.[96] Indiscriminate attacks are defined in Additional Protocol I as:

a. those which are not directed at a specific military objective;
b. those which employ a method or means of combat which cannot be directed at a specific military objective; or
c. those which employ a method or means of combat the effects of which cannot be limited as required by this Protocol; and consequently, in each such case, are of a nature to strike military objectives and civilians or civilian objects without distinction. (API, Article 51(4))

[94] Clapham and Gaeta, 93.
[95] Clapham and Gaeta, 122.
[96] Boothby, *Weapons*, 220.

In its customary law study, the ICRC puts distinction as its first rule applicable in international armed conflict (IAC) and non-international armed conflict (NIAC). "The parties to the conflict must always distinguish between civilians and combatants. Attacks may only be directed against combatants. Attacks must not be directed against civilians."[97] While certainly the rule is aimed at protecting non-combatants, it is somewhat controversial whether in NIAC there exists a status of a combatant as understood by IHL.[98] Governments are generally quite reluctant to consider rebels as combatants with a protective status of prisoner of war or POW to anyone taking a weapon against them.

2.5.3 Proportionality

Proportionality serves as a balancing principle between military necessity and collateral damage. It is practically impossible and morally questionable to quantify permissible collateral damage. How many incidental deaths are acceptable given a particular military objective? Thus, proportionality has to be considered, along with precautions. This means that excessive damage to civilian objects and civilians should be avoided and, if not feasible, minimized. Article 51(5)(b) of AP I defines proportionality under LOAC as: "An attack which may be expected to cause incidental loss of civilian life, injury to civilians, damage to civilian objects, or a combination thereof, which would be excessive in relation to the concrete and direct military advantage anticipated." The rule is further identified as customary in the ICRC study.[99]

Assessment of proportionality may not be conducted *ex post facto*; it has to be continuously assessed whether an attack is proportionate from all available sources. The French Military Operation Serval of 2013 is a brilliant real-world case study of proportionality and precautions. Below are five real-life examples of commanders' and officers' assessment of the circumstances in accordance with the LOAC principles, including proportionality and distinction. The following cases of proportionality and

[97] Henckaerts and Doswald-Beck, 3–8.

[98] Marco Sassoli, *International Humanitarian Law: Rules, Controversies, and Solutions to Problems Arising in Warfare* (Cheltenham: Edward Elgar, 2019), 22.

[99] Henckaerts and Doswald-Beck, 46–50.

precautions are retrieved from the project IHL in Action,[100] which documents compliance with the rules of international humanitarian law:

(Case 1) In the city of Gao, a force Commander of the French military decides to use 30-mm shells instead of a helicopter armed with HOT[101] missiles to destroy a police station under the control of the enemy, judging that using Hot missiles in an urban area was too great of a risk to harm civilians.[102]

(Case 2) U.S. Air Forces carry out a collateral damage estimate using a computer model to determine the weapon, fuse, attack angle, and time of day to ensure maximum effect on a target with minimum civilian casualties. Defense Secretary Donald Rumsfeld reportedly had to personally authorize all targets that had a collateral damage estimate of more than thirty civilian casualties. Asked how carefully the U.S. Air Force reviewed strikes in Iraq for collateral damage, a senior U.S. Central Command [CENTCOM] official responded, "with excruciating pain."[103]

(Case 3) Two Canadian CF-18 fighter jets took part in a mission over Libya on Tuesday morning but returned to base without attacking their target because the risk of collateral damage was too great.[104]

(Case 4) Both the United States and the United Kingdom deployed new types of cluster munitions in Iraq that are designed to reduce the dud rate. The U.S. Air Force dropped the CBU-105 Sensor Fused Weapon for the first time in combat. This weapon, 88 of which were used, employs the Wind-Corrected Munitions Dispenser. It contains ten BLU-108 submunitions, each releasing four skeet warheads, the size of hockey pucks, with

[100] See IHL in Action, "About the Project" accessed April 20, 2022. https://ihl-in-action.icrc.org/about.

[101] Haut subsonique Optiquement Téléguidé Tiré d'un Tube or High Subsonic, Optical, Remote-Guided, Tube Launched. See "HOT Missile," Britannica, accessed May 12, 2022, https://www.britannica.com/technology/HOT-missile.

[102] See IHL in Action, "Mali, France's Operation Serval, Minimising Civilian Casualties," accessed April 20, 2022. https://ihl-in-action.icrc.org/case-study/mali-frances-operation-serval-minimising-civilian-casualties.

[103] See IHL in Action, "Iraq, Computer Modelling in Collateral Damage Estimates and Choice of Weapons." Accessed April 20, 2022. https://ihl-in-action.icrc.org/case-study/iraq-computer-modelling-collateral-damage-estimates-and-choice-weapons.

[104] See IHL in Action, "Libya, Canada's Operation Mobile and the Principles of Proportionality and Precautions in Attack." Accessed April 20, 2022. https://ihl-in-action.icrc.org/case-study/libya-canadas-operation-mobile-and-principles-proportionality-and-precautions-attack.

infrared sensors. To reduce the dud rate, the submunitions have self-destruct mechanisms.[105]

As apparent, even strict observation of LOAC norms does not impede the operation but ensures its effectiveness. For example, Operation Serval resulted in zero collateral damage, thus ensuring the legitimacy of the military action in the eyes of the local population.[106] On the other hand, during the high-intensity phase of fighting, the specific military rules of engagement are interpreted rather widely to protect combatants and ensure the integrity of the force. In contrast, during the low-intensity, strict interpretation ensures the prevention of violation and prevents alienating the population.[107] This, in turn, ensures the legitimacy of the operation. Proportionality in the law of armed conflict is therefore interpreted as a balance between collateral damage and the military value of the target. Observing the rule as strictly as possible prevents the conflict from spiraling into tic-for-tac violations.

2.5.4 *Humanity*

The principle of humanity was identified by the International Court of Justice Advisory Opinion on the Legality of the Use or Threat of Use of Nuclear Weapons as one of the fundamental principles regarding future weapons technology.[108] In its present form, it is codified in AP I, Art. 1(2): "In cases not covered by this Protocol or by other international agreements, civilians and combatants remain under the protection and authority of the principles of international law derived from established custom, from the principles of humanity and from the dictates of public conscience."

It first appeared in the so-called Martens Clause included in the preamble of the 1899 Hague Convention, expressing the idea that a conflict between belligerents shall be ruled by "the laws of humanity, and the dictates of public conscience." The fact that the clause does not offer any concrete example for interpretation should not constrain the general rule

[105] See IHL in Action, "Iraq."

[106] See Sergei Boeke, *Transitioning from Military Interventions to Long-Term Counter Terrorism Policy: The Case of Mali (2013–2016)*. (Leiden: Leiden University-Institute of Security and Global Affairs, 2016), 41.

[107] See IHL in Action, "Mali."

[108] Legality of the Threat or Use of Nuclear Weapons (Advisory Opinion) [1996] ICJ Rep 226.¶ 79.

that all treaties shall be interpreted in "good faith" and in intended meaning. That is, unlike domestic law, international law looks more at the substance than the form.[109] The father of the Martens Clause is Fyodor Fyodorovich Martens (1848–1909), representing the Russian Empire at the Hague Conference of 1899, who included what would become known as the Martens Clause in the preamble of the 1899 Hague Convention II regulating land warfare:[110]

> Until a more complete code of the laws of war has been issued, the High Contracting Parties deem it expedient to declare that, in cases not included in the Regulations adopted by them, the inhabitants and the belligerents remain under the protection and the rule of the law of nations, as they result from the usages established among civilized peoples, from the laws of humanity and the dictates of public conscience.

Initially understood as a diplomatic statement made by Martens to address the disagreement between large occupying states and smaller ones, the clause is a mixture of positive and natural law.[111] Accordingly, "the clause serves as a reminder that an act is not just yet permissible when an act of war is not expressly prohibited by international law or customary law."[112] As such, it starkly contrasts the *Lotus* principle: "Whatever is not explicitly prohibited by international law is permitted."[113]

The success of the clause in protecting combatants and non-combatants is open to debate. Indeed, several humanitarian documents and judicial decisions refer to the clause in cases when a concrete norm is missing. All four Geneva Conventions embodying humanitarian law, in addition to the Hague Regulation II of 1899 and the Hague Convention IV of 1907, refer to humanity as a norm of IHL.[114] In addition to the operative Art.

[109] Illustrated by the approach of the members of the United Nations when two members of the Security Council, the Republic of China and the Union of Soviet Socialist Republics, changed their names, whose original names are mentioned in the UN Charter and were not changed. See Anthony Aust, *Modern Treaty Law and Practice* (Cambridge: Cambridge University Press, 2013), 160–161.

[110] Evan Trigt, "The Martens Clause: A New Research Guide" Peace Palace Library blog, August 31, 2017. https://peacepalacelibrary.nl/blog/2017/martens-clause-new-research-guide.

[111] Trigt.

[112] Trigt.

[113] *The 'Lotus' (France v Turkey)*. PCIJ Series A No. 10.

[114] GCI, Art.63, GC II, Art.62, GC III Art. 142, GC IV Art. 152

1(2) of API stated above, the preambular paragraph 4 of APII and the preambular paragraph 4 of the Convention on Certain Conventional Weapons, which is discussed in Chap. 5, all refer to humanity as a specific norm under the law of war. Humanity is unquestionably a customary principle of LOAC or IHL, as confirmed in well-known judicial decisions, including the *Corfu Channel* case of 1949[115] and the *Nicaragua* case of 1986.[116] The ICJ Advisory Opinion (AO) on nuclear weapons further refers to the principle of humanity as fundamental under the IHL and effective in addressing new weapons technologies.[117]

However, this broad interpretation is not immune to criticism. Although it helps to fill the void in IHL, Dinstein (2017) has interpreted the rule in a relatively narrow sense as *humane treatment,* such as humane treatment of non-combatants under enemy occupation and of prisoners of war.[118] It is helpful to recall that the POW status is not a punishment; instead, it is a protective status because a combatant shall not be punished for participating in hostilities.[119] From the perspective of positive law, this rather narrow interpretation is easier to grasp than deliberating on what humanity in warfare actually means. Nevertheless, the real difficulty undeniably arises when the principle of humanity is applied to weapons. As Trigt (2017) discussed: "Opinions about the legal significance of the Martens clause differ. In the opinion of some jurists, this clause has had its best days; they consider the Martens clause as superfluous, vague, out of date, and ineffective. Other scholars, however, still emphasize the importance of the Martens clause for international humanitarian law." Boothby (2016) has argued that to take the clause as "comprising of morality stemming from the words *dictates of public conscience* [emphasis added] would constitute another unwarranted distinct puzzling norm of the law of armed conflict."[120] According to Boothby (2016), a safer interpretation would be

[115] Corfu Channel (*United Kingdom of Great Britain and Northern Ireland v Albania*) (Merits) [1949] ICJ Rep 4., p.22.

[116] Case Concerning Military and Paramilitary Activities in and against Nicaragua (Merits), [1986] ICJ Rep. 14 ¶114. Particularly in correlation with common article 3 of the Geneva Conventions.

[117] Legality of the Threat or Use of Nuclear Weapons (Advisory Opinion) [1996] ICJ Rep 226.¶ 78

[118] Yoram Dinstein, *War, Aggression and Self-Defence*, 6th ed. (Cambridge: Cambridge University Press, 2017).

[119] Sassoli, 20–21.

[120] Boothby, *Weapons*, 351.

that "the dictates of public conscience drive the evolution of custom, and perhaps of the other major source of law, by inspiring treaty negotiations."[121]

Based on such interpretation, humanity should be understood not as a separate constitutive norm of international law of armed conflict but rather as a supportive principle that leads to more concrete traditional interpretations subsequently codified in an international agreement. Dinstein (2004) argued that while considerations of humanity may explain the development of LOAC, humanity's influence on weapons law is rather limited.[122] Distefano (2019) added that the Martens Clause might eventually impact secondary norms as they, in turn, impact the production of primary norms.[123] However, as international agreements regulating the most injurious weapons are relatively rare, such definitions are unsatisfactory and, in many ways, do not reflect the reality where many States refer to the principle of humanity as a LOAC norm when negotiating arms treaties. It is because humanity has its roots in the principle prohibiting superfluous injury or unnecessary suffering, which is in no way a secondary norm.

2.6 Superfluous Injury or Unnecessary Suffering (SIrUS)

Continuous State practice confirms that "the use of means and methods of warfare which are of a nature to cause superfluous injury or unnecessary suffering is prohibited" not only by a treaty—e.g., Additional Protocol I—but also by a custom.[124] The SIrUS is in its contemporary form codified in Additional Protocol I, Art.35(2) as such: "It is prohibited to employ weapons, projectiles and material and methods of warfare of a nature to cause superfluous injury or unnecessary suffering." The customary nature of the rule stems from the above sources, namely the St. Petersburg Declaration of 1868 and the Hague Conventions of 1899 and 1907.

The St. Petersburg Declaration already regulates specific means of warfare—i.e., exploding bullets— without deliberating on the general health effects of weapons. The underlying issue, therefore, is that exploding

[121] Boothby, *Weapons*, 14.

[122] Yoram Dinstein, *The Conduct of Hostilities Under the Law of International Armed Conflict* (Cambridge: Cambridge University Press), 57.

[123] Giovanni Distefano, *Fundamentals of Public International Law: A Sketch of the International Legal Order* (Leiden: Brill Nijhoff, 2019), 630.

[124] Henckaerts and Doswald-Beck, 237–244.

bullets are unnecessary. Should they be indispensable to penetrate body armor, for instance, they may as well be lawful according to the traditional view, which, in a sense, relativizes the application of the prohibition by such interpretation. Such approach represents the dominant design purpose focus in traditionalist interpretation. The major difference between the St. Petersburg Declaration and the Hague Conventions is that the former applies the principle to a concrete weapon, such as exploding bullets. The codification in the Hague Conventions and, later, in API is thus more general without reference to specific weapons.

The St. Petersburg wording prohibiting useless suffering was carried onto the Brussels Declaration of 1874. The idea of banning excessive injuries was codified under Art. 13(e): "The employment of arms, projectiles or material calculated to cause unnecessary suffering, as well as the use of projectiles prohibited by the Declaration of St. Petersburg of 1868."[125] This phrasing inspired the Hague Convention of 1899 under Art. 23(e) prohibits: "To employ arms, projectiles, or material of a nature to cause superfluous injury."[126] The most significant difference with the Brussels Declaration is the wording, which shifts from "calculated to"— denoting intent—to a more wide-ranging "of a nature to." The subsequent revision in the Hague Regulations of 1907 under Art.23(e), however, returned to the original wording of the 1874 Brussels Declaration, which prohibited: "To employ arms, projectiles, or material calculated to cause unnecessary suffering."[127] Thus, the most notable difference between the 1899 and 1907 Hague Conferences lies in the terms "of a nature to" and "calculated to," respectively.

The final codification in the 1977 API does not follow the wording of the preceding 1907 Hague Convention. Instead, it follows the 1899 Hague Convention's "of a nature to." This phrase apparently stems from an English translation of the original French text that prohibits: "*…d'employer des armes, des projectiles ou des matières propres à causer des*

[125] Project of an International Declaration concerning the Laws and Customs of War (27 August 1874) (1907) 1 AJIL Supp 96.

[126] Hague Convention with Respect to the Laws and Customs of War by Land and its Annex: Regulations respecting the Laws and Customs of War on Land, 29 July 1899 187 CTS 429 (entered into force 4 September 1900.

[127] Hague Conventions respecting the Laws and Customs of War on Land and its Annex: Regulations concerning the Laws and Customs of War on Land,18 October 1907, entered into force 26 January 1910) 205 CTS 277.

maux superflus [emphasis added]."[128] The French phrase *propres à causer* could be translated as "likely to cause" or "to belong to, to be unique to."[129] This "discrepancy" is at the core of the subsequent dichotomy between traditional and alternate views in relation to the principle's interpretation and application. These views disagree about whether there must be an intent to cause harm or whether the sole nature of a weapon is sufficient. The contentious interpretation "calculated to," as opposed to "of a nature to," further supports the underlying idea of the design purpose of a particular weapon vis-à-vis unnecessary suffering.

Hence, the wording "calculated to" necessarily involves *mens rea* and *actus reus* on the side of those developing or deploying a particular weapon because any weapon, by its nature, can cause unnecessary suffering if misused. The traditional view, therefore, appears inclined toward the 1907 wording, which denotes intent. A weapon must be specifically designed, created, or "modified" to cause unnecessary suffering. A dictate that requires the intent to cause excessive injuries on the side of those that deploy the weapon rather than the inherent characteristics of such a weapon. This is contrary to the current wording "of a nature to" that emphasizes characteristics of such weapons. The question, of course, is what happened in the course of the two Hague Diplomatic Conferences. Why had the wording changed?

Boothby (2016) argues that the language was deliberately changed in 1907 to encompass the required intent to focus on specific weapon design rather than all-encompassing "of a nature to."[130] The ICRC, however, has offered a more straightforward explanation: a mistake in translation. The original text is French, and there is no difference in the French phrasing of the original documents of 1899 and 1907. The ICRC insists that the correct translation is "of a nature to," which is why it was finally codified correctly in the 1977 API but incorrectly as "calculated to" in the 1907 Hague Convention.[131]

[128] Boothby, *Weapons*, 48.

[129] See "Propre à," French-English at Collins Dictionary, accessed April 20, 2022, https://www.collinsdictionary.com/dictionary/french-english/propre-%C3%A0.

[130] Boothby, *Weapons*, 49.

[131] See Roger S. Clark, "Methods of Warfare That Cause Unnecessary Suffering or Are Inherently Indiscriminate: A Memorial Tribute to Howard Berman" *California Western International Law Journal* 28, no. 2 (1997): Article 4. https://scholarlycommons.law.cwsl.edu/cwilj/vol28/iss2/4.

Nevertheless, the restrictive notion of "calculated to" was abandoned in the English translation for more inclusive "of a nature to," which is also the final phrasing used and codified in Art. 35(2) API. Accordingly, as Judge Weeramantry observed in his dissenting opinion in the International Court of Justice (ICJ) Advisory Opinion or AO on the threat or use of nuclear weapons, regarding the reference to the terms "of a nature to" or "calculated to": "It is, moreover, a literal interpretation which does not take into account the spirit and underlying rationale of the provision—a method of interpretation particularly inappropriate to the construction of a humanitarian instrument."[132]

The Vienna Convention on the Law of Treaties further supports this understanding. According to Art. 31—on the general rules of interpretation, which largely reflect customary law—it is the "ordinary meaning of the terms in the context of the object and purpose of an agreement."[133] Therefore, what matters is the effects of weapons, regardless of whether they are intended or not. Because Art. 35(2) codifies customary law and forms a *jus cogens* norm, the wording of the custom for States not party to API follows the "of a nature to" phrasing.[134] Thus, preventing any misguided interpretations. The term "calculated to" shall, therefore, be disregarded or confined to the specific purposes of the International Criminal Tribunal for Former Yugoslavia (ICTY), which used the term in its Statute solely for the purposes of criminal prosecution. It is thus crucial to distinguish between the specific purposes of the ad hoc ICTY and the overall rules and principles of LOAC. Superfluous injury or unnecessary is a comparative principle that must be weighed against military advantage and the value of the objective.

According to the traditional interpretation, the higher the advantage gained by using a particular weapon, the higher the threshold for unnecessary suffering, exclusive of deliberations on specific health effects.[135] This means that, according to the traditionalists, what counts are the

[132] *Legality of the Threat or Use of Nuclear Weapons* (Advisory Opinion), (Dissenting Opinion of Judge Weeramantry), 1996, 499.

[133] Vienna Convention on the Law of Treaties, 23 May 1969 1155 UNTS 331 (entered into force 27 January 1980).

[134] Legality of the Threat or Use of Nuclear Weapons (Advisory Opinion) [1996] ICJ Rep 226.¶ 79. Also, in the declaration of President Bedjaoui unnecessary suffering forms a part of peremptory norms or *jus cogens*. *Legality of the Threat or Use of Nuclear Weapons (Advisory Opinion) (Dissenting Opinion of Judge Weeramantry)* [1996] ICJ ¶21

[135] Dinstein, *Conduct,* 59–60.

intended primary effects and not secondary or unintended ones. O'Connor (2014) countered such logic by using the example of nuclear weapons, stating that "although nuclear weapons, and particularly ionizing radiation, do not give the attacker or defender any military advantage, they do unnecessarily aggravate the suffering of affected personnel."[136] This argument shifts the balance toward the dominance of long-term injury and health rather than military necessity. The medicalization of the principle is an alternative interpretation and, as such, one refuted by traditionalists, who sternly oppose any inclusion of medical means into the assessment of weapon effects. Furthermore, regarding nuclear weapons, the United Kingdom, for instance, argues that ionizing radiation is a secondary effect and that it shall not be considered in the assessment of a weapon, according to LOAC.[137] As will be explained later, such an argument is indeed flawed while not based in reality.

In sum, the traditionalist interpretation requires intent to inflict unnecessary injury. Moreover, such injury is only unnecessary if exceeding the force needed to accomplish a particular military objective. Such understanding, while traditional, is inherently vague. This leaves a wide opportunity for interpretation by the military and States that may benefit from such vagueness in circumventing the norm. What exactly unnecessary suffering and superfluous injury mean thus remains without tangible substance. Thus, with such vagueness, scholars and practitioners are even debating whether the term also includes psychological harm, as contained in the word "suffering," as opposed to physical harm, contained in the word "injury."[138] In 1997, the ICRC attempted to define the term by medical means in the ill-fated SIrUS Project, which will be discussed in the subsequent chapter.[139]

[136] Simon O'Connor, "Nuclear Weapons and the Unnecessary Suffering Rule" in *Nuclear Weapons Under International Law*, ed. Gro Nystuen, Stuart Casey-Maslen, and Annie G. Bersagel, 128–147 (Cambridge: Cambridge University Press, 2018), 146–147.

[137] Letter Dated 16 June 1995 from the Legal Adviser to the Foreign and Commonwealth Office of the United Kingdom of Great Britain and Northern Ireland, together with Written Comments of the United Kingdom, p. 48.

[138] Sassoli, 382.

[139] See Robin M. Coupland, ed., "The SIrUS Project: Towards a Determination of Which Weapons Cause Superfluous Injury or Unnecessary Suffering" 1997 last access on June 5, 2023, https://www.loc.gov/collections/military-legal-resources/?q=RC_SIrUS-project.html.

2.7 Conclusion

Violating one of the fundamental principles of the law of armed conflict usually leads to the parallel violation of others. In many cases, these violations give rise to individual criminal responsibility and form what is known as a grave breach of the Geneva Conventions. The SIrUS principle is weighed merely against military necessity in its traditional interpretation. The infliction of unnecessary wounds through needlessly cruel means, such as hooked spikes, hollow bullets, or explosive projectiles, is considered superfluous not because of health effects, but rather because the same military objective—to put combatant *hors de combat*—could be accomplished by less injurious weapons. The ultimate goal is not to kill soldiers but to neutralize them and to put them out of combat by making them incapable of fighting. The traditional interpretation of the principle still relies on an understanding from the end of the nineteenth century, when field medical service was very rudimentary and blood transfusion was almost impossible.

Consequently, using prohibited weapons often meant certain death to those affected. Weapons, as such, were rudimentary arms relying on the transfer of kinetic energy, causing usually deadly wounds. Both World Wars intensified the development of weapons whose complexity exceeded expectations. Healthcare, including combat medicine, evolved as well. Nevertheless, this does not mean that prohibited weapons, such as dumdums or hooked spikes, would become lawful because there was an available medical remedy. Although combatants' lives are increasingly spared in twentieth- and twenty-first-century combat, thus decreasing the number of combat casualties, long-term injuries are becoming more evident.[140] A shift in focus toward the long-term health effects of particular weapons has occasionally culminated in restrictions or outright prohibitions based on humanitarian concerns to protect non-combatants and combatants alike.

Following this chronological evolution, the following chapter shifts the focus from Hague law—that is, from the dominion of the conduct of hostilities with means and methods—to Geneva law. As a representative body of humanitarian law under the broader context of LOAC, Geneva law protects persons caught in armed conflict, not by regulating weapons or

[140] "The absolute number of war deaths has declined after 1945." See Max Roser, Joe Hasell, Bastian Herre, and Bobbie Macdonald "War and Peace After 1945" *Our World in Data*, accessed April 12, 2022. https://ourworldindata.org/war-and-peace.

their use. Hence, exploring the logic behind this humanitarian approach under international humanitarian law (IHL) is essential. Moreover, we cannot disregard the impact of international human rights law or IHRL, which firmly entered the field of armed conflict in the middle of the twentieth century. IHRL further centered the focus of legal protection on the individual, albeit predominantly by protecting individuals from their governments.[141] Nevertheless, it was universally agreed that IHRL would not cease during hostilities; it would apply in parallel with LOAC to offer maximum protection.[142] Finally, around the same time human rights entered the realm of armed conflict, the health impact of warfare and the effects of weapons gained increased attention.

After briefly discussing the interaction between LOAC and IHRL—focusing predominantly on the difference between the prohibition of unnecessary suffering and the right to life—I will proceed to define the difference between the injuries that are frequently inflicted in combat and those that are deemed unacceptable. The final section of the following chapter will elaborate on the ICRC's attempt to define unnecessary suffering in medical terms via the so-called SIrUS Project. Ultimately, the goal of the following chapter is to explore the emerging trends and alternative interpretations that focus increasingly on defining the notions of injuries, pain, and suffering in medical terms.

References

Al-Dawoody, Ahmed. *The Islamic Law of War: Justifications and Regulations.* New York: Palgrave Macmillan, 2011.

Aust, Anthony. *Modern Treaty Law and Practice.* Cambridge: Cambridge University Press, 2013.

Baetens, Freya. "Hague Conferences (1899, 1907)." Oxford Bibliographies. Last modified November 21, 2012. https://www.oxfordbibliographies.com/view/document/obo-9780199743292/obo-9780199743292-0115.xml#obo-9780199743292-0115-bibItem-0012.

Bantekas, Ilias, and Lutz Oette. *International Human Rights: Law and Practice.* 3rd ed. Cambridge: Cambridge University Press, 2020.

[141] See Illias Bantekas and Lutz Oette, *International Human Rights: Law and Practice*, 3rd ed., (Cambridge: Cambridge University Press, 2020).

[142] Respect for Human Rights in Armed Conflicts [1968] UNGA 58; A/RES/2444 (XXIII) (19 December 1968)

Bennett, Angela. *The Geneva Convention: The Hidden Origins of the Red Cross.* Cheltenham: The History Press, 2006.

Boeke, Sergei. *Transitioning from Military Interventions to Long-Term Counter Terrorism Policy: The Case of Mali (2013-2016).* Leiden: Leiden University – Institute of Security and Global Affairs, 2016.

Boothby, William H. *The Law of Targeting.* Oxford: Oxford University Press, 2012.

———. *Weapons and the Law of Armed Conflict.* New York: Oxford University Press, 2016.

Bowyer, Richard. *Dictionary of Military Terms.* 3rd ed. London: A&C Black, 2007.

Bryant, Michael S. *A World History of War Crimes: From Antiquity to the Present.* 2nd ed. New York: Bloomsbury Academic, 2021.

Buhler, George. *The Laws of Manu.* Pinnacle Press, 2017.

Casey-Maslen, Stuart, and Steven Haines. *Hague Law Interpreted: The Conduct of Hostilities under the Law of Armed Conflict.* New York: Hart, 2020.

Clapham, Andrew, and Paola Gaeta, eds. *The Oxford Handbook of International Law in Armed Conflict.* Oxford: Oxford University Press, 2014.

Choate, Joseph H. *The Two Hague Conferences.* Princeton: Princeton University Press, 1913.

Clark, Roger S. "Methods of Warfare That Cause Unnecessary Suffering or Are Inherently Indiscriminate: A Memorial Tribute to Howard Berman," *California Western International Law Journal* 28, no. 2 (1997): Article 4. https://scholarlycommons.law.cwsl.edu/cwilj/vol28/iss2/4.

Coupland, Robin M, ed. *The SIrUS Project: Towards a Determination of Which Weapons Cause "Superfluous Injury or Unnecessary Suffering."* Geneva: ICRC, 1997. https://www.loc.gov/collections/military-legal-resources/?q=RC_SIrUS-project.html.

Darnton, Geoffrey. *Nuclear Weapons and International Law: From the London Nuclear Warfare Tribunal Via the International Court of Justice Advisory Opinion to Contemporary Developments.* 2nd ed. Bournemouth: Requirements Analytics, for Peace Analytics, 2015.

Dinstein, Yoram. *The Conduct of Hostilities Under the Law of International Armed Conflict.* Cambridge: Cambridge University Press, 2004.

———. *War, Aggression and Self-Defence.* 6th ed. Cambridge: Cambridge University Press, 2017.

Distefano, Giovanni. *Fundamentals of Public International Law: A Sketch of the International Legal Order.* Leiden: Brill Nijhoff, 2019.

Gallagher, Gary W., Stephen D. Engle,Robert K. Krick, and Joseph T. Glatthaar. *The American Civil War: This Mighty Scourge of War.* Oxford: Osprey Publishing, 2003.

Gesley, Jenny. "The 'Lieber Code' – the First Modern Codification of the Laws of War." Library of Congress blog. April 24, 2018. https://blogs.loc.

gov/law/2018/04/the-lieber-code-the-first-modern-codification-of-the-laws-of-war/.

Grotius, Hugo. *The Rights of War and Peace*. (Vol. I–III). Edited by Richard Tuck. Indianapolis: Liberty Fund, 2005.

Henckaerts, Jean-Marie, and Louise Doswald-Beck, eds. *Customary International Humanitarian Law*. Vol.1, *Rules*. Cambridge: Cambridge University Press, 2005.

Holquist, Peter. "The Laws of War: From the Lieber Code to the Brussels Conference." Accessed April 12, 2022. https://www.americanacademy.de/the-laws-of-war/.

Hull, William I. *The Two Hague Conferences and Their Contributions to International Law*. Boston: For International School of Peace, Ginn, 1908.

Inazo, Nitobe. *Bushido: The Soul of Japan*. New York: Kodansha, 2002.

ICRC. "Practice Relating to Rule 70. Weapons of a Nature to Cause Superfluous Injury or Unnecessary Suffering." Accessed April 12, 2022. https://ihl-databases.icrc.org/customary-ihl/eng/docindex/v2_rul_rule70.

IHL in Action. "About the Project." Accessed April 20, 2022a. https://ihl-in-action.icrc.org/about.

———. "Iraq, Computer Modelling in Collateral Damage Estimates and Choice of Weapons." Accessed April 20, 2022b. https://ihl-in-action.icrc.org/case-study/iraq-computer-modelling-collateral-damage-estimates-and-choice-weapons.

———. "Libya, Canada's Operation Mobile and the Principles of Proportionality and Precautions in Attack." Accessed April 20, 2022c. https://ihl-in-action.icrc.org/case-study/libya-canadas-operation-mobile-and-principles-proportionality-and-precautions-attack.

———. "Mali, France's Operation Serval, Minimising Civilian Casualties." Accessed April 20, 2022d. https://ihl-in-action.icrc.org/case-study/mali-frances-operation-serval-minimising-civilian-casualties

Kalshoven, Frits, and Liesbeth Zegveld. *Constraints on the Waging of War*. 4th ed. Cambridge: Cambridge University Press, 2011.

Jeannesson, Stanislas. "The International Hague Conferences of 1899 and 1907." *Encyclopedie d'histoire numerique de l'Europe*. June 22, 2020. https://ehne.fr/en/node/12230.

Jevglevskaja, Natalia. "St. Petersburg, 1868: First International Agreement Prohibiting the Use of Certain Weapons." *Online Atlas on the History of Humanitarianism and Human Rights*. Accessed April 9, 2022. https://hhr-atlas.ieg-mainz.de/articles/jevglevskaja-st_petersburg

Jones, Edgar. "Terror Weapons: The British Experience of Gas and Its Treatment in the First World War." *War in History* 21, no. 3 (2014): 355–375. https://doi.org/10.1177/0968344513510248

Kapossy, Bela, and Richard Whatmore, eds. *Emer de Vattel: The Law of Nations, Or, Principles of the Law of Nature, Applied to the Conduct and Affairs of Nations and Sovereigns, with Three Early Essays on the Origin and Nature of Natural Law and on Luxury*. Indianapolis: Liberty Fund, 2008.

Keefer, Scott. "'Explosive Missals: International Law, Technology, and Security in Nineteenth-Century Disarmament Conferences." *War in History* 21, no. 4 (2014): 445–464. Accessed May 11, 2022. http://www.jstor.org/stable/26098618.

Krasny, Jaroslav, and Noriyuki Kawano. "Use of Nuclear Weapons in Armed Conflict." *Hiroshima Peace Science* 41, (2019): 73–84. https://doi.org/10.15027/49035.

Lesaffer, Randall. Grotius on the Use of Force. Perfect, Imperfect and Civil Wars: An Introduction. *Grotiana* 41, no. 2 (2020): 255–262. https://doi.org/10.1163/18760759-41020001.

Melzer, Nils. *Interpretive Guidance on the Notion of Direct Participation in Hostilities Under International Humanitarian Law*. Geneva: ICRC, 2009.

National Geographic. *National Geographic Visual History of the World*. Washington, DC: National Geographic Society, 2005.

Newton, Michael A., ed. *The United States Department of Defense: Law of War Manual Commentary and Critique*. Cambridge: Cambridge University Press, 2018.

O'Connor, Simon. "Nuclear Weapons and the Unnecessary Suffering Rule." In *Nuclear Weapons Under International Law*, edited by Gro Nystuen, Stuart Casey-Maslen, and Annie G. Bersagel, 128–147. Cambridge: Cambridge University Press, 2014.

Phillips, Charles, and Alan Axelrod, eds. *Encyclopedia of Wars*. New York: Zenda, Inc, 2005.

Price, Richard M. *The Chemical Weapons Taboo*. New York: Cornell University Press, 1997.

Roser, Max, Joe Hasell, Bastian Herre, and Bobbie Macdonald. "War and Peace After 1945." Our World in Data. Accessed April 12, 2022. https://ourworldindata.org/war-and-peace.

Sanskriti. "Pashupatastra: Weapon of Lord Shiva." Accessed April 12, 2022. https://www.sanskritimagazine.com/indian-religions/hinduism/pashupatastra-weapon-of-lord-shiva/.

Sassoli, Marco. *International Humanitarian Law: Rules, Controversies, and Solutions to Problems Arising in Warfare*. Cheltenham: Edward Elgar, 2019.

Sassoli, Marco, Antoine Bouvier, Anne Quintin, and Julia Grignon. "Dum-dum Bullets." Accessed March 14, 2022. https://casebook.icrc.org/glossary/dum-dum-bullets.

Saul, Ben, and Akande, Dapo, eds. *The Oxford Guide to International Humanitarian Law*. Oxford: Oxford University Press, 2020.

Simcox, Kenneth. "Poetry Critique: Dulce Et Decorum Est." 2000. Accessed August 8, 2022. http://www.wilfredowen.org.uk/poetry/dulce-et-decorum-est.

Trigt, Evan. "The Martens Clause: A New Research Guide." Peace Palace Library blog, August 31, 2017. https://peacepalacelibrary.nl/blog/2017/martens-clause-new-research-guide.

US Department of Defense. *DOD Dictionary of Military and Associated Terms.* Washington DC: The Joint Staff, 2019a.

Waite, Maurice, ed. *Paperback Oxford English Dictionary.* Oxford: Oxford University Press, 2012.

Program on Humanitarian Policy and Conflict Research at Harvard University. *HPCR Manual on International Law Applicable to Air and Missile Warfare.* Cambridge: Cambridge University Press, 2013.

UN War Crimes Commission, *Law Reports of Trials of War Criminals.* 1949, Vol. VIII, London.

US Department of Defense. *DOD Dictionary of Military and Associated Terms.* Washington DC: The Joint Staff, 2019b.

UK Ministry of Defence. *The Manual of the Law of Armed Conflict.* Oxford: Oxford University Press, 2004.

CHAPTER 3

Health Effects–Based Interpretation

3.1 Introduction

This chapter expands on the part of the broader law of armed conflict known as international humanitarian law (IHL), otherwise known as Geneva law, and a modern humanitarian approach that emphasizes the health effects of weapons rather than their military usefulness. Humanitarian law is increasingly becoming a prominent portion of the international law of armed conflict (LOAC), with a focus shifting from regulating the conduct of hostilities toward alleviating the suffering of combatants and protecting non-combatants. It was in the aftermath of WWII's brutalities that the international community realized what was at stake and recognized the need for an extensive re-evaluation of the norms related to protecting persons during hostilities.[1]

This chapter examines Geneva law as it is embodied in the four Geneva Conventions (GCs) of 1949, which enjoy universal ratification to this day and reflect customary LOAC norms. In 1977, the Hague and Geneva laws merged into Additional Protocols (APs) with near-universal ratification and reflected many customary rules. The GCs, on the other hand, contain detailed rules for specific situations related to protected persons—for instance, GC III applies to POWs, while GC IV applies to personnel in the

[1] Boyd Van Dijk, *Preparing for War: The Making of the Geneva Conventions* (Oxford: Oxford University Press, 2022), 253.

J. Krasny, *War Injuries*,
https://doi.org/10.1007/978-3-032-00737-7_3

power of the enemy, that is, under occupation. After discussing Geneva law and Additional Protocols, this chapter will examine the applicability of human rights law in armed conflict. In 1968, at the Tehran Conference, the UNGA reaffirmed in Resolution 2444 (XXIII) that international human rights law (IHRL) applies in times of armed conflict.[2] Although such applicability is undoubtedly understandable in non-international armed conflict (NIAC), there are several contentious issues in the case of international armed conflict (IAC). Legal scholars specializing in LOAC indeed concur with the International Court of Justice (ICJ) statement in the Advisory Opinion (AO) on the threat or use of nuclear weapons that human rights norms in IAC must be interpreted through the lenses of LOAC as a specialized body of public international law (PIL) concerned with armed conflict.[3] A maxim known as *lex specialis derogati lex generali* or *lex specialis.*[4]

It is, therefore, worth examining whether IHRL has any effect on the interpretation of the prohibition on unnecessary suffering. IHRL and IHL both apply in conflict, but how is the right to life under human rights law compatible with unnecessary suffering, a principle specific to LOAC? It would be too simplistic to conclude that the right to life applies to non-combatants and that unnecessary suffering protects combatants. Yet, some legal experts— including Judge Shahabuddeen, who wrote a dissenting opinion regarding the ICJ Advisory Opinion on the threat or use of nuclear weapons—are of the opinion that unnecessary suffering may also apply to non-combatants, i.e., civilians.[5] Thus, how the right to life and unnecessary suffering interact helps to clarify the changes in the interpretation of the principle.

Later, this chapter provides a general discussion concerning weapon injuries. Because every weapon is capable of causing injuries, it is vital to understand the basics of what these injuries are, how they can be categorized, what the most common wounds on the battlefield are, and where the line between the acceptability of particular wounds is drawn. Rather than medical examination, the chapter offers essential information about

[2] Respect for Human Rights in Armed Conflicts [1968] UNGA 58; A/RES/2444 (XXIII) (19 December 1968).

[3] Legality of the Threat or Use of Nuclear Weapons (Advisory Opinion) [1996] ICJ Rep 226.¶25.

[4] Special law trumps general law or simply "Special Law." "Law unique to a particular regime or applicable to specific scenarios." See Aaron X. Fellmeth and Maurice Horwitz, *Guide to Latin in International* (New York: Oxford University Press, 2009), 176.

[5] Legality of the Threat or Use of Nuclear Weapons (Advisory Opinion) (Dissenting Opinion of Judge Shahabuddeen) [1996] ICJ, p.182

the most common instantaneous field injuries, such as blast and shot wounds, and juxtaposes them against delayed and long-term wounds. Finally, the chapter concludes with a discussion of the International Committee of the Red Cross's (ICRC's) SIrUS project, which endeavored to medically assess which injuries are superfluous and thereby determine the definition of unnecessary suffering based on medical data. Although the SIrUS Project and its conclusions were withdrawn in 2002, they are of particular interest because the Project is constantly referred to in the literature, a fact that hints that the project may not be as dead as it seems.

3.2 Geneva Law and Additional Protocols of 1977

Alleviating suffering—including that of combatants *hors de combat*—has been one of the underlying *raisons d'être* of IHL ever since Henry Dunant's vivid description of wounded soldiers screaming in agony on the battlefield of Solferino.[6] IHL, or Geneva law, was first codified in 1864 in the Geneva Convention on the Amelioration of the Condition of the Wounded in Armies in the Field.[7] The convention's objectives are best illustrated by its very first article: "Officers and soldiers and other persons officially attached to the armed forces who are wounded or sick shall be respected and protected in all circumstances; they shall be treated with humanity and cared for medically, without distinction of nationality, by the belligerent in whose power they may be." The underlying idea is that combatants who can no longer fight shall not be targets of added attacks that would exacerbate their injuries. In contrast to Hague law—which regulates the conduct of hostilities, weapons, and targeting—the objectives of Geneva law are humanitarian. In other words, they strive to guarantee the humane treatment of those no longer engaged in combat. In addition to the first article, which sets the treaty's objective, subsequent articles include protections for medical formations, personnel, buildings, and materials, and address transporting and caring for the deceased. Geneva law also introduced the symbol of a red cross on a white background to represent the most well-known aid society, the ICRC.[8] The ICRC, founded by Henri

[6] Henry Dunant, *A Memory of Solferino* (Geneva: ICRC, 1959).

[7] Convention for the Amelioration of the Condition of the Wounded in Armies in the Field (signed 22 August 1864, entered into force 22 June 1865) (1864) 129 CTS 361.

[8] Convention for the Amelioration of the Condition of the Wounded in Armies in the Field (signed 22 August 1864, entered into force 22 June 1865) (1864) 129 CTS 361, Art. 7.

Dunant, was the major driving force behind the negotiations of the 1864 Geneva Conventions.[9] The indescribable suffering of combatants, which was so vividly described in *A Memory of Solferino*, impacted Dunant, who, therefore, set out to establish a humanitarian organization that would alleviate the suffering of injured soldiers.

Additional articles to the convention were introduced in 1868 to extend the application of the GCs to naval forces.[10] The final document, "Additional Articles relating to the Conditions of the Wounded in War, 1868" was, however, never adopted. Still, belligerents agreed to abide by its provisions[11] on several occasions, including the Franco-Prussian War (1870–1871).[12] The humanitarian rules of naval warfare codified in the additional articles were adopted in the 1899 Hague Convention on naval warfare (i.e., Hague III).[13] After 1899, the international community agreed to revise and expand the protections offered to sick and wounded combatants.[14] Consequently, the first Geneva Convention of 1864 and its articles were further revised during an international conference in 1906 when provisions on the burial of the dead or the transmission of information were added.[15] The final evolution of Geneva law before 1949 was the Geneva Convention of 1929, which expanded on the treatment of prisoners of war (POWs) because the provisions contained in the Hague Regulations proved insufficient after the experiences of WWI.[16] The war

[9] One of the founders of the ICRC, besides Dunant, is also "a self-effacing lawyer," Gustav Moynier. See Angela Bennett, *The Geneva Convention: The Hidden Origins of the Red Cross* (Cheltenham: The History Press, 2006).

[10] See ICRC, Treaties, States Parties and Commentaries. "Additional Articles relating to the Condition of the Wounded in War. Geneva, 20 October 1868" Accessed April 13, 2022. https://ihl-databases.icrc.org/applic/ihl/ihl.nsf/Treaty.xsp?documentId=ECB39EA050F80A5DC12563CD002D6624&action=openDocument.

[11] ICRC, Treaties, "Additional Articles."

[12] Charles Phillips and Alan Axelrod, eds., *Encyclopedia of Wars* (New York: Zenda, Inc., 2005), 465.

[13] Hague Convention for the Adaptation to Maritime Warfare of Principles of the Geneva Convention of 22 August 1864 (1907) 1 AJIL Supp 159 (1899 Hague Convention III).

[14] See ICRC, Treaties, "Convention for the Amelioration of the Condition of the Wounded and Sick in Armies in the Field. Geneva, 6 July 1906" accessed April 13, 2022. https://ihl-databases.icrc.org/applic/ihl/ihl.nsf/Treaty.xsp?documentId=C64C3E521F5CC28FC12563CD002D6737&action=openDocument.

[15] Convention for Amelioration, Arts. 3–4.

[16] See ICRC, Treaties, "Convention Relative to the Treatment of Prisoners of War, Geneva, 27 July 1929" accessed April 13, 2022. https://ihl-databases.icrc.org/applic/ihl/ihl.nsf/INTRO/305?OpenDocument.

was a major shock to the humanitarian law and efforts with extensive legal violations, particularly regarding the treatment of POWs.[17]

The most blatant and shocking violations of the rules and customs of war, including those of humanitarian law, happened during WWII. The horrors of WWII, and particularly the indiscriminate attacks on civilians, accelerated the revision of the 1906 and 1929 GCs.[18] War could no longer be accepted as a continuation of "politics by other means."[19] From the shock and ashes of the war rose a new world order that was embodied in the establishment of the United Nations (UN) and the growing importance of a humanitarian law centered around the protection of an individual, even during hostilities. The Geneva Conference took place on August 12, 1949. It resulted in four GCs that form the basis of contemporary IHL or Geneva law. GC I of 1949 applies to the sick and wounded in the field. This revision of the GC from 1906 expands on protecting wounded soldiers, medical personnel, and units.[20] GC II contains articles protecting the sick and wounded and shipwrecked combatants at sea. It replaced the Hague Convention of 1907 with the Adaptation to Maritime Warfare of the Principles of the Geneva Convention.[21] GC III regulates the treatment of POWs, and according to Art. 41 of GC III, the text of the convention shall be available to POWs in camps.[22] Finally, GC IV protects civilians in the power of the enemy, i.e., under occupation.

On the one hand, the fourth convention rose from the horrendous treatment of civilians during WWII. On the other hand, as discussed in the introductory chapter, it arose in response to the insufficient protection and regulation of air warfare. Due to Anglo-American opposition to regulating air warfare in 1949, the ICRC focused on endorsing mandatory safe and neutral zones; thus, the convention does not address air operations.[23]

[17] Van Dijk, 257.

[18] Van Dijk, 67–96.

[19] Carl Von Clausewitz, *On War*, Transl. Michael Howard and Peter Paret (Oxford: Oxford University Press, 1976), 28.

[20] Dietrich Schindler and Jiri Toman, eds., *The Laws of Armed Conflict: A Collection of Conventions, Resolutions and Other Documents* (Leiden: Martinus Nijhoff Publishers, 2004), 459.

[21] Schindler and Toman, 485.

[22] "In every camp the text of the present Convention and its Annexes and the contents of any special agreement provided for in Article 6, shall be posted, in the prisoners' own language, at places where all may read them. Copies shall be supplied, on request, to the prisoners who cannot have access to the copy which has been posted." Art. 41, (1). (GC III).

[23] Van Dijk, 227.

As such, it is important to stress that GC IV does not regulate the protection of civilians during the conduct of hostilities. The fourth convention is interpreted to protect civilians in the power of the enemy—for instance, under the conditions of occupation.[24] The protection of civilians during the conduct of hostilities is regulated under the Hague law and in the 1977 Additional Protocols.

As stated in the preceding paragraphs, Hague law (conduct of hostilities) and Geneva law (protected persons) merged in 1977 into two Additional Protocols to the GCs of 1949. Four international conferences held from 1974 to 1977 recognized the insufficient protection of civilians during hostilities when combat is ongoing. After the experiences of the Vietnam War and colonial struggles for independence, the ICRC developed the draft protocols adopted by the international conference convened by the Swiss government.[25] These were Additional Protocol I (API),[26] applicable to IAC, and Additional Protocol II (APII),[27] regulating non-international armed conflict or NIAC.[28] For States not parties to the protocols, customary law and the Hague Conventions of 1907 still apply. Accordingly, AP I and AP II reflect a large number of these customary rules.[29]

[24] Robert Kolb and Richard Hyde, *An Introduction to the International Law of Armed Conflicts* (Portland: Hart Publishing, 2008), 222.

[25] Schindler and Toman, 699.

[26] Protocol Additional to the Geneva Conventions of 12 August 1949 and relating to the Protection of Victims of International Armed Conflicts (Protocol I) (adopted 8 June 1977, entered into force 7 December 1978) 1125 UNTS 3.

[27] Protocol Additional to the Geneva Conventions of 12 August 1949 and relating to the Protection of Victims of Non- International Armed Conflicts (Protocol II) (adopted 8 June 1977, entered into force 7 December 1978) 1125 UNTS 609.

[28] The term "civil war" is somewhat archaic and confusing and is not used anymore in the field of LOAC (IHL). "Civil wars were not recognized as real wars, thus falling within domestic jurisdiction." Instead, the term "internal conflict" or, better yet, "non-international armed conflict (NIAC)" is more suitable for modern battlefields. Traditional civil wars denote a conflict between the State and *recognized* armed groups within the State. NIAC, on the other hand, denotes a much more complex situation with citizens of different States taking part in hostilities, supplies of weapons via international borders, humanitarian help, etc. Ben Saul and Dapo Akande, eds., *The Oxford Guide to International Humanitarian Law* (Oxford: Oxford University Press, 2020), 30.

[29] The United States, Israel, Iran, Pakistan, India, and Turkey signed but not ratified, signaling their intention to abide by the rules and objectives. See ICRC, Treaties, "Protocol Additional to the Geneva Conventions."

Arts. 35–36 of API are crucial when it comes to weapons law. Art. 35(1) reaffirms the customary rule that the means and methods of warfare are not unlimited: "In any armed conflict, the right of the Parties to the conflict to choose methods or means of warfare is not unlimited." The underlying idea behind this customary rule was already introduced in the St. Petersburg Declaration of 1868, discussed in the previous chapter. The declaration stipulated that the employment of arms causing unnecessary suffering would constitute a legal excess—hence, means are not unlimited. The norm against unlimited weapons choice was later reaffirmed in Article 22 of the Hague Conventions of 1907; it represents customary law and is intertwined with military necessity and SIrUS. As confirmed by the IMT in the *Wilhelm List case (1949)* discussed in the previous chapter, military necessity cannot be invoked to allow a belligerent to derogate from this rule.[30] In other words, LOAC does not permit a derogation unless it is expressly allowed; belligerents, however, enjoy freedom of action within the boundaries of the law.[31] Limitation on means and methods is not only customary but also part of fundamental IHL norms of *jus cogens*, as confirmed by the International Law Commission.[32] Consequently, it can be modified only by norms with the same standing, i.e., *jus cogens.*[33] This is also affirmed in Article 53 of the Vienna Convention on the Law of Treaties of 1969. The rule is found in official military manuals on the rules of war, which again indirectly confirms its customary status.[34] Concerning weapons law, the norm represents the basic idea that only lawful means may be used to accomplish military objectives. Article 35(1) of AP I, limiting the use of arms, is further interlinked with the subsequent one, Art.35(2), or the prohibition of weapons of a nature to cause superfluous injury or unnecessary suffering.

[30] UN War Crimes Commission, *Law Reports of Trials of War Criminals.*1949, Vol. VIII, London, 35.

[31] Yves Sandoz, Christophe Swinarski, and Bruno Zimmerman, eds., *Commentary on the Additional Protocols of 8 June 1977 to the Geneva Conventions of 12 August 1949* (Geneva: ICRC, 1987), 393.

[32] See International Law Commission. Annual Reports. *Report on the Work of the Seventy-First Session (2019).* Last updated December 10, 2019. https://legal.un.org/ilc/reports/2019/, 161.

[33] UN Office of Legal Affairs, *Yearbook of the International Law Commission* 1980, Vol. II/2. New York: UN, 1981, last access June 6, 2022, https://legal.un.org/ilc/publications/yearbooks/english/ilc_1980_v2_p2.pdf.

[34] See for example the US Department of Defense, *Law of War Manua* (Washington DC: General Counsel of the Department of Defense, 2016), 67.

The St. Petersburg Declaration of 1868 and the Hague Convention of 1899 had one thing in common: they affected specific weapons such as exploding bullets or dum-dum bullets. Then, the Hague Convention of 1907 codified a general rule against unnecessary suffering that was rather vague; this vagueness had to be resolved for the codification in API of 1977.[35] The *travaux preparatoires* began in 1971, when the ICRC convened two conferences of government experts. One focused on IAC and the other focused on NIAC, which would eventually be regulated under API and APII.

The diplomatic conferences that ultimately led to the adoption of Additional Protocols to the GC in 1977 took place over four official sessions[36] and included an Ad Hoc committee on weapons that had the task of elaborating, analyzing, and codifying the final form of the SIrUS principle, as explained below. Although the principle and its application were never contested, its scope of application concerning the general means of combat remained unclear.[37] The Ad Hoc Committee on Weapons recognized "the difficulty of going beyond a very general study as long as certain problems concerning definitions, especially that of 'unnecessary suffering,' had not been resolved."[38] Of particular interest is Volume XVI of the *travaux preparatoires*, which contains the work of the Ad Hoc Committee on Conventional Weapons.[39] The committee's final report also served as the basis for negotiating the Convention on Conventional Weapons, or CCW, adopted in 1980, which is discussed in Chap. 5.

The members of the Ad Hoc Committee generally agreed that the discussion should be constrained to conventional weapons because nuclear weapons serve deterrent purposes and because conventional weapons are actually used in conflict; the most controversial of these weapons were, therefore, incendiaries.[40] The deliberation of individual diplomats on the notion of SIrUS was wide ranging. The representatives discussed issues

[35] Sandoz, Swinarski, and Zimmerman, 402.

[36] February 20–March 1974 (Session I), February 3–April 18, 1975 (Session II), April 21–June 11, 1976 (Session III), March 17–June 10, 1977 (Session IV).

[37] Sandoz, Swinarski, and Zimmerman, 403.

[38] *Summary Record of the Organizational Meeting held on Friday*, March 8 1974. Examination and Adoption of Agenda, Doc. CDDH/IV/1., para.3.

[39] *Official Records of the Diplomatic Conference*, Volume XVI.

[40] AdHoc Committee on Conventional Weapons Report, CDDH/47/Rev.1, Paras. 5–6.

such as flechettes and high-velocity bullets.[41] In discussing specific health effects, the diplomats relied heavily on the ICRC report on weapons that may cause unnecessary suffering or have indiscriminate effects.[42] However, there was no universal agreement regarding the contents of the report and its applicability. A statement from the Polish representative, H.E. Flemming, is particularly noteworthy. He declared that unnecessary suffering should be defined "not from the viewpoint of those who inflict it, but rather from the viewpoint of the victims."[43] This narrative focuses on health effects and stands at odds with the traditional understanding of the principle requiring the attacker to juxtapose SIrUS with military necessity. During the sixth meeting, the representative of Sweden, H.E. Blix, proposed that the Conference of Government Experts should study unnecessary suffering from technical, operational, and medical viewpoints.[44] That is, Blix considered medical science as an essential element for determining SIrUS. Such development of a holistic, multi-dimensional approach leaves the traditional balancing of a target value vis-à-vis weapons. Instead, it turns to how such use affects combatants and their health, giving the principle and its application a strong substance.

The committee deliberated on various types of weapons, such as incendiaries, small-caliber projectiles, blast weapons, fragmentation weapons, and even weapons that might be developed in the future. However, the legal criteria for SIrUS were still inconclusive. Of particular interest is the position of H.E. Scheetz of the United States, a country that sternly opposed any attempts at medicalization. On the subject of fuel-air explosives (FAEs), Scheetz stated that: "[The US] also questioned whether death from fuel-air explosives was especially cruel or caused unusual or unnecessary suffering as compared to other conventional weapons and that evidence demonstrated that death would be rapid and caused by air embolism to the heart and brain following lung rupture due to the overpressure effect."[45] Based on animal experiments, the United States further opined that:

[41] Swedish delegation, page 12, Summary Record of the Third Meeting, March 15, 1974. CDDH/IV/SR.3, at para 23.

[42] See ICRC, *Weapons That May Cause Unnecessary Suffering or Have Indiscriminate Effects: Report on the Work of Experts* (Geneva: ICRC, 1973) last access April 22, 2022 https://www.loc.gov/item/2011525354/.

[43] Para.27 Summary Record of the First meeting, March 13, 1974 CDDH/IV/SR.1

[44] Summary Record of the Sixth Meeting, March 22, 1974, para 3. CDDH/IV/SR.6.

[45] Summary Record of the Forty second (closing) meeting, Tuesday 24, 1977, para. 19.

> [T]he blast effect of FAE, in the lethal area, caused rupture of the lung tissue with subsequent release of air bubbles into the blood circulation...Casualties surviving the blast had hemorrhage of varying degrees within the lung tissue. Some of those casualties would require support with mechanical ventilatory apparatus...the lung hemorrhages would resolve in a matter of a few weeks with no lasting effects.[46]

The statement reflects that the representatives were willing and frequently discussed the health effects of weapons on combatants. Mentioning a concern of lasting effects is also noteworthy, particularly given the discussion concerning nuclear weapons and ionizing radiation, where States prefer to dismiss this effect as secondary to the blast, as I will explain later. This is a rather new development from the traditional approach that weighs SIrUS with military advantage. Such progress was undoubtedly possible, thanks to the ICRC activities and reports being widely cited during the conferences.

It thus becomes apparent in the late 70s that the traditional interpretation of SIrUS was not sufficient, and detailed deliberations on health were ongoing, albeit vis-à-vis specific weapons such as the above-mentioned FABs. The Working Group III worked on Art. 33 that would finally become the Art. 35(2), codifying the final version of SIrUS—noted that the phrase "superfluous injury or unnecessary suffering" was a translation of the French original "*maux superflus*"; as such, it included both physical and mental injury.[47] Such interpretation would indeed point toward the long-term effects of weapons, which often encompass psychological suffering on the survivors that have to live and die with ongoing detrimental effects of weapons on their health.

The final codification in API Art.35(2) and *travaux preparatoires* did not offer a conclusive interpretation and definition of SIrUS. It, however, reaffirmed that the principle is understood to mean the employment of force that is in excess of what is needed to put a combatant out of combat and unnecessarily aggravates suffering.[48] The conference, however, included extended deliberations and discussions of specific health effects and discussions of injuries from the medical perspective. As noted above, the representatives deliberated on SIrUS in medical terms. These

[46] Summary Record of the Forty-First meeting, May 19, 1977. CDDH/IV/SR.41. para11.

[47] Report to Committee III on the Work of the Working Group Submitted by the Rapporteur, April 3–9, 1975. Article. 33. CDDH/III/293.

[48] See *Official Records of the Diplomatic Conference*, Volume XIV.

deliberations became essential for concluding the Convention on Conventional Weapons (CCW)—an LOAC treaty, with the prohibition of weapons causing unnecessary suffering as its ultimate objective. The CCW is discussed in Chap. 5, as it relates to specific weapons.

The diplomats never contested the applicability of the principle in the case of the second Additional Protocol, APII, regulating non-international armed conflict (NIAC), albeit it is not included verbatim in the provisions.[49] As explained above, LOAC applies during IAC or NIAC; only a few provisions are applicable in peacetime.[50] Accordingly, the four Geneva Conventions of 1949 apply only to IAC. Common Article 3 of GCs is the only provision applicable to NIAC. Consequently, all these agreements specify conditions that must be fulfilled to trigger the application.[51] Classifying and separating IAC and NIAC is essential in identifying which rules are or are not applicable to regulate weapons and their use. The rules for war between States are not identical to those for armed conflict between a state and an armed group.[52] States, i.e., governments, rarely want to grant combatant status to those taking weapons against them. This is quite a controversial issue, however. If a rule is missing in NIAC, it is possible to apply a rule of IAC. Customary rules are nearly the same for both forms of combat, albeit with few exceptions—for instance, a combatant's status in NIAC, as mentioned above.[53] Why is this important for interpreting and applying the prohibition of unnecessary suffering? Simply because, without the combatant status, unnecessary suffering does not apply. Prohibition of unnecessary suffering traditionally applies only to combatants who are *hors de combat*. As the author discusses in Chap. 6, the ICJ has recognized the customary and *jus cogens* status of the norm. Although the norm is not included in APII and its application has not been

[49] *Official Records of the Diplomatic Conference*, Volume VII, CDDH/SR.53, P.157.

[50] Saul and Akande, 368–375.

[51] GC I – IV (Common Article 2 in IAC and Common Article 3 in NIAC). AP I (Art.1) and AP II (Art.1).

[52] An Armed group is defined in Art. 1 of APII as an organized armed group having responsible command, exercising control over a territory, and being able to sustain and concentrate military operations and implement the Protocol.

[53] Marco Sassoli, *International Humanitarian Law: Rules, Controversies, and Solutions to Problems Arising in Warfare* (Cheltenham: Edward Elgar, 2019), 219–224.

contested,[54] it is uncertain how the prohibition of SIrUS can be applied if there is no recognized combatant status.

The definition of a combatant in NIAC was discussed in the famous *Tadic case* before the International Criminal Tribunal for the Former Yugoslavia (ICTY).[55] Paragraph 96 of the Tadic judgment deserves particular attention.

> This body of law [international humanitarian law] is not grounded on formalistic postulates. It is not based on the notion that only those who have the formal status of State organs, i.e., are members of the armed forces of a State, are duty bound both to refrain from engaging in violations of humanitarian law as well as—if they are in a position of authority—to prevent or punish the commission of such crimes. Rather, it is a realistic body of law, grounded on the notion of effectiveness and inspired by the aim of deterring deviation from its standards to the maximum extent possible. It follows, amongst other things, that humanitarian law holds accountable not only those having formal positions of authority but also those who wield de facto power.[56]

LOAC norms are applicable in non-international armed conflict through analogy with the norms applicable in IAC.[57] Hence, the applicability of SIrUS in NIAC is not contested if a fighter or rebel in NIAC has a combatant status. Furthermore, as the *Tadic case* confirmed, weapons that are indiscriminate or that cause unnecessary suffering in IAC are also prohibited in NIAC.[58] This comes out of pure logic that the effects of weapons do not change based on the categorization of a particular situation. What matters is whether or not the affected victim, or, better say, survivor, has the legal status of a combatant. Yet again, why is such

[54] *Legality of the Threat or Use of Nuclear Weapons* (Advisory Opinion) [1996] ICJ Rep 226¶78.

[55] "…militias or paramilitary groups or units may be regarded as legitimate combatants if they form 'part of [the] armed forces' of a Party to the conflict (Article 4A(1)) or 'belong […]' to a 'Party to the conflict' (Article 4A(2)) and satisfy the other four requirements provided for in Article 4A(2). It is clear that this provision is primarily directed toward establishing the requirements for the status of lawful combatants." Prosecutor v Tadic (Judgment) IT-94-1-A ¶92.

[56] Prosecutor v Tadic (Judgment) IT-94-1-A, para.96.

[57] Sassoli, 224–230.

[58] Prosecutor *v Tadić (Decision on the Defence Motion for Interlocutory Appeal on Jurisdiction)* IT-94-1-AR72 (2 October 1995) ¶127 and 134.

deliberation on IAC or NIAC necessary? The diplomatic conferences to negotiate the Additional Protocols took place after the Korean War (1950–1953), and wars raged in Vietnam (1956–1975) and Cambodia (1970–1975). Conflicts were becoming increasingly non-international, which further presented challenges for SIrUS, its interpretation, and application.[59] Negotiations were increasingly politicized, with States unwilling to discuss weapons they were actually using, albeit controversially and often with accompanying public backlash, on the battlefields.

Against this backdrop, a novel branch of international law emerged in the late 1960s: international human rights law (IHRL). IHRL is not State-centered but individual-centered. Examining the evolution of IHRL is beyond the scope of this book, but the effect of this human-centered approach on the SIrUS norm cannot be ignored. The focus turns to how war affects an individual. There is inevitable, at times, friction between LOAC and IHRL because of their different objectives and how they define combatants, POWs, or judicial proceedings during hostilities.

Nevertheless, countless scholars, and even the ICRC, see IHRL and LOAC as complementary rather than contradictory.[60] This is to offer maximum protection to individuals caught up in hostilities. Even so, the idea that these two fields are complementary is not universally accepted. During times of combat, both might seek the same objective: the protection of the individual. At different times, however, they seek different goals.[61] For instance, IHRL and LOAC uphold different views on using the death penalty for particularly grave breaches of the law during hostilities. This book cannot elaborate on the interplay between IHRL and IHL, which is an issue in itself. However, for further understanding, it is imperative to discuss the application of human rights in armed conflict briefly. This brief discussion will explore whether there is a particular interaction between IHL and IHRL principles that could shed light upon the modern interpretation of SIrUS and the use of weapons in the course of armed conflict.

[59] For a specific number of IACs and NIACs, see *The Rule of Law Project* (RULAC) of the Geneva Academy, https://www.rulac.org/.

[60] Andrew Clapham and Paola Gaeta, eds., *The Oxford Handbook of International Law of Armed Conflict* (Oxford: Oxford University Press, 2014), 198–202.

[61] 22nd Bruges Colloquium, "Same Law, New Wars: The Enduring Relevance of International Humanitarian Law and the Importance of the Updated ICRC Commentaries," October 22, 2021 (held online).

3.3 International Human Rights Law and the Law of Armed Conflict

While LOAC, as *lex specialis,* regulates the use of any weapon during armed conflict, this does not mean that other bodies of public international law do not apply. Legal scholars stress the increasing relevance of IHRL during the conduct of hostilities; furthermore, human rights law is an integral part of disarmament law.[62] Concerning the nature and use of weapons, there are, however, substantial differences. While expanding bullets—so-called dum-dums—are unlawful under LOAC in the course of international armed conflict, IHRL does not prohibit the use of expanding bullets as part of law enforcement operations if such use may save the victim's life; for example, expanding bullets may be effective in hostage situations.[63] As police professionals note: "the [expanding] bullet has slightly skewed stability, so after the impact, it remains in the first target and does not tend to continue as military ammunition does. Ideal for crowds or hostage situations."[64] The Czech Republic, France, the United States, and Switzerland are just a few of the States that allow expanding bullets for police operations.[65] Regular police operations sometimes continue, even during armed conflict, particularly with localized hostilities. This can sometimes create an inevitable friction between LOAC and IHRL.

The UNGA Resolution 2444 (XXIII) at the Tehran Conference of 1968 affirmed that human rights apply in peacetime, during internal disturbances, and armed conflict.[66] The resolution restates the 1965 ICRC's own Resolution On the Protection of Civilian Populations Against the Dangers of Indiscriminate Warfare.[67] As explained above, the rules or

[62] Daniel Rietiker, *Humanization of Arms Control: Paving the Way for a World Free of Nuclear Weapons* (New York: Routledge, 2018), 279.

[63] Robert Arnold and Noelle N.R. Quenivet, eds., *International Humanitarian Law and Human Rights: Towards a New Merger in International Law* (Leiden: Martinus Nijhoff Publishers, 2008), 591.

[64] Interview with a police officer of the Czech Republic Police Force, Warrant Officer Libor Zlamal (ret.), Service Preparation Dept., Weapons training, [in-person] May 19, 2020.

[65] Samuel Longuet, "Permitted for Law Enforcement Purposes but Prohibited in the Conduct of Hostilities: The Case of Riot Control Agents and Expanding Bullets" *International Review of the Red Cross* 98, no. 901 (2016): 249–274. https://doi.org/10.1017/S1816383117000108.

[66] UNGA Res 2676 (XXV) 'Respect for Human Rights in Armed Conflict' (9 December 1970).

[67] Schindler and Toman, 349–350.

principles of LOAC cannot be derogated from or limited unless explicitly provided for in the Geneva Conventions or the Protocols; this is true even in circumstances of military necessity.[68] That is, military necessity cannot justify any derogation. In contrast, certain norms of IHRL may be limited or suspended—if they include a derogation clause.[69] The limitations of IHRL are usually related to freedoms, such as the rights to privacy, family life, expression, assembly, association, movement, or religion. These limitations must be based on law, contain an explicit and legitimate aim, and be necessary and proportionate to achieve whatever they are supposed to achieve.[70]

The seemingly same principles of proportionality and necessity appear in LOAC and IHRL. Nevertheless, caution is necessary because these terms are interpreted very differently from IHRL. Whereas LOAC interprets these principles in a permissive manner—that is, as all lawful means necessary to achieve a military objective and proportionality in terms of collateral damage—human rights law is restrictive; it holds that derogation must not surpass what is strictly necessary and appropriate to the fulfillment of a legitimate goal.[71] In other words, IHRL allows only those measures that are necessary, only for a necessary time period, and only in proportion to the threat or danger they seek to mitigate. The case of *Zakharov v. Russia* (2015) illustrates the distinction between different understandings of proportionality.[72]

In this case, the Russian State defended the surveillance of Roman Zhakarov as a limitation on the right to privacy based on national security reasons. However, the mere existence of legislation may not serve as grounds for interference, in this case, limitation of rights. The European Court of Human Rights (ECtHR) ruled that necessary safeguards against the misuse of limitations on the right to privacy were insufficient, thereby calling into question the proportionality of such a limitation on the right

[68] Such as Art.5 of GCIV, see Marco Sassoli et al., "Derogations" accessed April 21, 2022. https://casebook.icrc.org/glossary/derogations.

[69] For instance, Art.4 of the International Covenant on Civil and Political Rights (adopted 16 December 1966, entered into force 23 March 1976) 999 UNTS 171.

[70] Illias Bantekas and Lutz Oette, *International Human Rights: Law and Pracice*, 3rd ed. (Cambridge: Cambridge University Press, 2020), 406.

[71] Bantekas and Oette, 82.

[72] European Court of Human Rights. *Roman Zakharov v. Russia* [GC] - 47143/06 Judgment 4.12.2015 [GC].

to privacy.[73] Thus, IHRL conducts a proportionality assessment as a balancing act between the gravity of the threat and the measures taken.[74]

On the other hand, derogations depend upon exceptional states of emergency, such as threats to the nation's existence. A measure may be implemented only to the extent that is strictly required.[75] Derogations include specific measures that are temporary in nature, limited geographically in scope, and include safeguards against abuse.[76] Indeed, the right to life as such is non-derogable. Nonetheless, right to life is not an absolute right. As affirmed in the International Covenant on Civil and Political Rights (ICCPR) General Comment 36, "the use of lethal force consistent with the law of armed conflict is not arbitrary, nor does it violate Art. 6 of the ICCPR, which protects individuals against arbitrary killing."[77]

3.3.1 *Right to Life and Unnecessary Suffering*

Under IHRL, the right to life is codified in Art. 6 of the ICCPR.[78] This negative right prohibits the arbitrary deprivation of life, including severe restrictions on capital punishment in States that have not abolished it. The Human Rights Committee's (HRCtee) General Comment 36 further elaborates on Art. 6 of the ICCPR.[79] In its General Comment 36, 2018, the HRCtee defines the right to life as a supreme right, albeit not an absolute one.[80] The right to life is also found in regional human rights law instruments, such as in Art. 4 of the American Convention on Human Rights[81] and Article 4 of the African Convention on Human Rights.[82] The

[73] *Roman Zakharov v. Russia*, at *Merits*, para. (b)(v).

[74] Olivier de Schutter, *International Human Rights Law: Cases, Materials, Commentary* (Cambridge: Cambridge University Press, 2010), 316–321.

[75] Schutter, 514.

[76] Schutter, 536.

[77] UN HRC 'General Comment No. 36: The Right to Life (Art. 6)' (27 July 1982) GAOR 37th Session Supp. 40 ¶ 64.

[78] International Covenant on Civil and Political Rights (adopted 16 December 1966, entered into force 23 March 1976) 999 UNTS 171.

[79] UN HRCtee 'General Comment No. 36: The Right to Life (Art. 6)' (27 July 1982) GAOR 37th Session Supp. 40 ¶ 93.

[80] General comment 36 to ICCPR, paragraph 2.

[81] American Convention on Human Rights (signed 22 November 1969, entered into force 18 July 1978) 1144 UNTS 123 (Pact of San José).

[82] African Charter on Human and Peoples' Rights (adopted 27 June 1981, entered into force 21 October 1986) 1520 UNTS 217 (Banjul Charter).

European Convention of Human Rights[83] includes the right to life under Art. 2, although Art. 2(2) contains a more precise set of circumstances for the lawful deprivation of life.[84]

In *McCann v. UK* (1995), the European Court of Human Rights, or ECtHR, reaffirmed that "the use of force under IHRL must be absolutely necessary" and that it can be applied only after the exhaustion of other non-lethal means.[85] General Comment no. 36 of HRCtee further points out that force must be strictly necessary given the threat posed by an attacker; moreover, "lethal force must be a measure of last resort" that is used only when facing an "imminent threat to life" or the possibility of serious injury.

An illustrative jurisprudence is found in the case of *Finogenov v. Russia* (ECtHR).[86] During the so-called Moscow theater siege, a decision was made to storm the theater since a severe and immediate threat to the hostages gave reason to believe that the use of force was absolutely necessary.[87] In such circumstances, as ruled by the ECtHR, the use of gas (fentanyl)[88] was not, per se, disproportionate to the threat. The right to life, although a negative obligation of a State to refrain from interfering, also, to a certain extent, includes positive obligations in such situations. That is, the State must provide subsequent medical care, supply sufficient information about the chemical agent to medical staff to facilitate

[83] Council of Europe 'Convention for the Protection of Human Rights and Fundamental Freedoms' (signed 4 November 1950, entered into force 3 September 1953) 213 UNTS 221 (European Convention on Human Rights).

[84] (a) in defence of any person from unlawful violence; (b) in order to effect a lawful arrest or to prevent the escape of a person lawfully detained; (c) in action lawfully taken for the purpose of quelling a riot or insurrection. No derogation is allowed only in case of lawful acts of war, Art. 15(2). Further, the ECHR does not prohibit death penalty for war crimes under Protocol No. 6, Art. 2.

[85] *McCann v UK (1995),* para.147.

[86] *Finogenov v. Russia (2010),* paras. 217–236.

[87] See Chemical and Biological Weapons Nonproliferation Program "The Moscow Theater Hostage Crisis: Incapacitants and Chemical Warfare" James Martin Center for Nonproliferation Studies, November 4, 2002. https://nonproliferation.org/the-moscow-theater-hostage-crisis-incapacitants-and-chemical-warfare/.

[88] Fentanyl is an incapacitant, a psychotomimetic agent or BZ. Ramesh C. Gupta, ed., *Handbook of Toxicology of Chemical Warfare Agents*, 2nd ed. (Oxford: Academic Press, 2015), 139.

treatment, and provide adequate means of transport to hospitals for the victims.[89]

Accordingly, under IHRL, the use of force is seen as a last resort, and proportionality is linked to the magnitude of the threat. Under LOAC, in contrast, necessity refers to all lawful means necessary to accomplish a military objective, and proportionality is related to the scope of incidental harm and damage. Yet another point to note is that such use of chemical gas as a weapon of war is prohibited under LOAC, while it might be permitted under IHRL in NIAC. Categorization of a particular situation is crucial when discussing whether SIrUS applies or not and to whom.

Thus, concerning an armed conflict, the right to life ensures protection against arbitrary killing, the deliberate targeting of non-combatants, the killing of those combatants who are *hors de combat*, and the wanton killing of individuals during police operations that take place even in the course of armed conflict, particularly NIAC. In comparison, LOAC is concerned with obligations rather than rights. Common Art. 3 of the GCs of 1949 prohibits violence against life and against people who are not or who are no longer participating in hostilities. According to ICRC commentary, this article underlines the respect for life in NIAC.[90] It does not protect the lives of combatants or those participating in hostilities. That is to say, LOAC does not include or explicitly recognize combatants' right to life, as IHRL does not recognize unnecessary suffering as a norm.

The matter, therefore, is whether, under the law of armed conflict (not human rights), non-combatants have a right to life in armed conflict. Ex-combatants in the power of the enemy are protected by GCIII of 1949. Similarly, non-combatants are protected during the conduct of hostilities insofar as *direct* [emphasis added] attacks against them are prohibited.[91] Indiscriminate attacks are not permitted, but, as stated in the Hague law section, incidental or collateral damage is not entirely proscribed.[92]

[89] See *Finogenov and Others v. Russia* - 18299/03 and 27311/03 Judgment 20.12.2011 [Section I].

[90] See ICRC, Treaties, "Commentary of 2016. Article 3: Conflicts Not of an International Character" accessed April 13, 2022. https://ihl-databases.icrc.org/ihl/full/GCI-commentaryArt3.

[91] Art. 51(2) of AP I which stipulates that civilians: "...shall not be made the object of...[attack]."

[92] Art. 51(5)(b) of AP I: "an attack which may be expected to cause incidental loss of civilian life...excessive in relation to the concrete and direct military advantage...".

Further prohibitions indirectly protect the right to life by banning "attacks on objects that are indispensable to the survival of the civilian population."[93]

Hence, the fundamental difference would lie in applying the right to life as a norm of IHRL during the conduct of hostilities through the lenses of LOAC, that is, prohibiting *the arbitrary* and *intended* killing of non-combatants as well as combatants *hors de combat*. Additionally, the right to life would apply principally to law enforcement activities during an armed conflict. During the special police operations that might take place in the course of hostilities, the use of force by law enforcement is still a last resort; law enforcement officers must capture rather than kill or escalate, and they must avoid incidental casualties as far as the circumstances of the police operation allow.[94] Under IHRL, lethal force should be avoided as much as possible. Unlike soldiers or combatants, police officers are legally obliged to protect a perpetrator's life.[95]

Hence, the concept of unnecessary suffering or excessive injury does not—and, by its own rationale, cannot—exist in IHRL beyond the scopes of necessity and proportionality.[96] Because the right to life was envisaged mostly for peacetime, its implementation during armed conflict must be interpreted through LOAC as *lex specialis*.[97] Such application ensures the realistic and pragmatic application of norms in armed conflict and strengthens the protection of individuals without any impractical or idealistic concepts.

As a distinct LOAC rule, unnecessary suffering is directly intertwined with military objectives and military necessity. As stated above, the right to life in LOAC is only ensured for non-combatants, who cannot be made

[93] Art. 54 of AP I and Art. 14 of AP II.

[94] See Stuart Casey-Maslen, ed., *Weapons Under International Human Rights Law* (Cambridge: Cambridge University Press, 2014).

[95] Casey-Maslen, *Weapons*, 33. Also see in this regard the *Basic Principles on the Use of Force and Firearms by Law Enforcement Officials* adopted by the Eighth United Nations Congress on the Prevention of Crime and the Treatment of Offenders, Havana, Cuba, 27 August to 7 September 1990, at para. 5(b).

[96] According to the Inter-American Commission of Human Rights regarding human rights instruments: "Although one of their purposes is to prevent warfare, none of these human rights instruments was designed to regulate such situations and, thus, they contain no rules governing the means and methods of warfare." *Juan Carlos Abella v. Argentina*, Case 11.137, Report N° 55/97, Inter-Am.C.H.R., OEA/Ser.L/V/II.95 Doc. 7 rev. at 271 (1997)¶158.

[97] Legality of the Threat or Use of Nuclear Weapons (Advisory Opinion) [1996] ICJ Rep 226.¶24–25.

the objects of an attack, and for combatants *hors de combat*. However, what if a weapon causes injuries that persist long-term, even after LOAC ceases to apply? This scenario stretches beyond the temporal boundaries of an armed conflict when IHRL is once again the dominant legal framework and when the right to life and health apply to ex-combatants, i.e., former soldiers.

As codified in Art. 12 of the International Covenant on Economic, Social and Cultural Rights (ICESCR),[98] the right to health is an obligation for the State to provide; it is a so-called positive obligation.[99] Of course, it is challenging to ensure the enforcement of this obligation during hostilities. The ability to do so would depend on sufficient medical care, the availability of medical material, and the existence of post-conflict medical rehabilitation and help.

In this case, a combatant suffering from a weapon's long-term health effects would exist in two paradigms. In the first paradigm, the effect of a particular weapon whose use fell under LOAC norms is still continuously causing harm. In the second paradigm, i.e., peacetime, IHRL ensures that the State guarantees the right to life and health. The implication is that weapons that violate the principle of unnecessary suffering codified under API Art.35(2) would likely violate the right to life under the ICCPR, Art.6. Although SIrUS does not exist in IHRL, IHRL judicial or quasi-judicial mechanisms address the issue through their norms. This important point will be explored further in Chap. 6. First, however, it is essential to discuss what particular health effects exist and occur on the battlefield and how to categorize them to assess which effects might be deemed excessive under LOAC. Through such examination, the effects of long-term injuries on the application of SIrUS will become apparent.

3.4 Health Effects and Medicalization

Health effects and the medicalization of SIrUS reflect an increased focus on how armed conflict impacts individuals, whether or not they are combatants. As explained earlier, any weapon can either be used indiscriminately or altered in such a way as to violate the SIrUS rule. Thus, to clarify what constitutes unnecessary suffering, it is crucial to consider a weapon's

[98] International Covenant on Economic, Social and Cultural Rights (adopted 16 December 1966, entered into force 3 January 1976) 993 UNTS 3.

[99] Bantekas and Oette, 443.

intended and designed uses in addition to its specific characteristics.[100] Weapons that are specifically designed to attack particular platforms—such as warships, vehicles, tanks, or aircraft—cannot understandably cause unnecessary suffering. Only weapons designed against live power are capable of such a violation. Whereas traditionalists see unnecessary suffering only as a balancing principle, alternative views and the view of the ICRC often assess SIrUS by medical means.

According to Mathur (2017), an effects-based approach to weapons is based on testimonialization from the victims, medicalization through medical science, and legalization via the customary and conventional sources of LOAC. The ICRC employs medical science that strives to balance the demands of military necessity and unnecessary suffering by regulating and prohibiting particular weapons.[101] In her study, Mathur (2017) was particularly successful in re-counting the prevailing opinion of the ICRC regarding suffering and superfluous injury. The ICRC endeavors to medically define these terms to give SIrUS a more substantial normative weight. As Mathur (2017) argues: "The medical professionals [at the ICRC] justify their efforts to classify and codify the sufferings endured by the victims as a scientific endeavor to give meaning to concepts such as unnecessary suffering."[102]

Because ICRC medical staff often work in the combat environment, they have established an extensive data collection regarding wounds from particular weapons.[103] On February 8, 1918, the ICRC issued a public appeal against using poisonous and asphyxiating gases. The ICRC invoked unnecessary suffering based on testimonies from its medical staff[104]—this is an illustration of testimonialization. This moment was the organization's first diplomatic intervention to address weapons problems.[105] The ICRC medical staff members' testimony and the medicalization of the

[100] Jaroslav Krasny and Noriyuki Kawano, "Weapons of Mass Destruction and the Principle of Unnecessary Suffering: The Use of Nuclear Weapons in an Armed Conflict" *Hiroshima Peace Science* 36, (2014): 101–116. https://doi.org/10.15027/38055.

[101] Ritu Mathur, *Red Cross Interventions in Weapons Control* (London: Lexington Books, 2017), 18–19.

[102] Mathur, 55

[103] See the ICRC Archives, accessed August 3, 2022, https://www.icrc.org/en/archives.

[104] See ICRC, "World War I: The ICRC's Appeal Against the Use of Poisonous Gases. 8 February 1918" accessed April 13, 2022, https://www.icrc.org/en/doc/resources/documents/statement/57jnqh.htm.

[105] Mathur, 35–36.

subject helped to facilitate the conclusion of the Geneva Gas Protocol of 1925, which prohibited the use of asphyxiating and poisonous gases. We can positively argue that this success stems, inter alia, from the application of victim testimonies and medical data to the discussion of unnecessary suffering, not in general terms but vis-à-vis a particular weapon. Similar to the call for a ban on poison in 1918, the ICRC issued an appeal against the use of nuclear weapons on April 5, 1950.[106] The organization once again argued against a specific weapon using medical terms such as burns, delayed effects, and long-term effects of ionizing radiation. The ICRC maintained that "the suffering caused by atomic bombs is disproportionate to strategic necessity."[107] At the Oslo Conference in May 1954, Dr. Junod and Dr. Suzuki proposed a ban on nuclear weapons to the ICRC based on the observations from Hiroshima and Nagasaki and the effects of the bombs on the victims.[108]

All these efforts helped to cultivate a health-based approach and plant the seeds of the subsequent medicalization of SIrUS. Against the backdrop of harrowing wars and the use of incendiary weapons in Southeast Asia, the ICRC adopted a number of resolutions condemning the effects of such weapons during International Conferences in Vienna (1965),[109] Istanbul (1969),[110] and Tehran (1973).[111] The ICRC set up an International Conference of Experts to study the question of unnecessary suffering concerning particular conventional weapons used during the conflicts in East and Southeast Asia.[112] In 1973, as part of the preliminary meetings for the conference, the ICRC published a report titled "Weapons That May Cause

[106] See ICRC, "Atomic Weapons and Non-Directed Missiles: ICRC Statement, 1950. 05-04-1950 Article, International Review of the Red Cross, - Supplement, Vol. III, No. 4," accessed April 13, 2022. https://www.icrc.org/en/doc/resources/documents/article/other/5kylur.htm.

[107] ICRC, "Atomic Weapons."

[108] Mathur, 72.

[109] See *XXth International Conference of the Red Cross*, accessed May 10, 2022, https://international-review.icrc.org/sites/default/files/S002086040000890la.pdf.

[110] See *XXIst International Conference of the Red Cross*, accessed May 10, 2022, https://international-review.icrc.org/sites/default/files/S0020860400063555a.pdf.

[111] See *XXIInd International Conference of the Red Cross*, accessed May 10, 2022, https://international-review.icrc.org/sites/default/files/S0020860400004605a.pdf.

[112] See ICRC, "Conference of Government Experts On Weapons Which May Cause Unnecessary Suffering or Have Indiscriminate Effects" *International Review of the Red Cross*. Accessed April 22, 2022. https://international-review.icrc.org/sites/default/files/S002086040001604la.pdf, 538–539.

Unnecessary Suffering or Have Indiscriminate Effects."[113] The report further confirmed the basic principles of customary international law, including prohibiting unnecessary suffering. Moreover, it included an additional requirement "to refrain from weapons whose effects cannot be controlled or that are unnecessary to accomplish military objectives"[114]—in other words, weapons whose effects are excessively injurious and extend beyond the control of those using it. To follow up on this development and to keep the momentum, in April 1974, the ICRC declared at the Diplomatic Conference on Humanitarian Law—which concluded with the adoption of the two Additional Protocols—that it was ready to convene a specialized conference on conventional weapons.[115]

The Conference took place in the Swiss city of Lucerne next month on May 17, 1974, and the program included discussions of criteria that could be used to assess the lawfulness of particular weapons. These criteria included terms revolving around unnecessary suffering. Particular discussions occurred about incendiaries, small-caliber projectiles, blast weapons, fragmentation weapons, delayed action weapons, new weapons, and other categories of weapons. The discussions were divided into the following subcategories: "(a) discussion of the weapon category, (b) military value and possible less injurious alternatives to the weapons, (c) accuracy of the weapons, (d) medical effects of the various weapons, the degree of suffering or injury."[116] Before further examining these diplomatic deliberations, it is imperative to examine how the Committee defined what constitutes excessive suffering or pain.

Generally, pain is "a signal transmitted by nociceptors to the central nervous system (CNS), which includes the spinal cord and the brain."[117] In the 1973 report, the ICRC introduced three criteria to assess excessive injury and suffering. These criteria represented the factors in determining when defining SIrUS, namely: "a) degree of pain, b) degree of permanent disability or injury, c) probability of death."[118] The 1973 ICRC report

[113] ICRC, *Weapons That May Cause Unnecessary Suffering or Have Indiscriminate Effects: Report on the Work of Experts* (Geneva: ICRC, 1973), available at https://www.loc.gov/item/2011525354/.

[114] ICRC, *Weapons That May*, 17.

[115] ICRC, "Conference of Government Experts", 538–541.

[116] See ICRC, "Conference of Government Experts."

[117] British Medical Association, *Illustrated Medical Dictionary*, 1st ed. (London: Dorling Kindersley, 2002), 430.

[118] ICRC, *Weapons That May*, 25.

determines the probability of death by: "localization of the wound, the time lag between injury and treatment, and the state of physical resistance of the wounded person."[119] According to the ICRC, "injuries to the CNS usually result in permanent damage."[120] Numerous CWs—especially nerve agents such as sarin, which was used in the course of the Iran–Iraq War and in the 1995 Tokyo subway attack—cause injuries to the CNS.[121]

It is important to note that the report did not discuss unnecessary suffering in general terms. Instead, it assessed the criteria against specific weapons listed above, including incendiaries, blast weapons, fragmentation weapons, and delayed weapons. As such, the report provided a general framework for interpreting SIrUS in medical terms, not just military necessity. It also provided a specific framework for applying SIrUS concerning selected weapons. As such, the report formed a solid groundwork for the CCW.

Therefore, it was the use of chemical and nuclear weapons that triggered the true medicalization of the SIrUS rule, which was subsequently expanded due to the Vietnam War and the use of incendiaries. However, the main question remains: where is the borderline between acceptable and unacceptable injury and pain? Does it lie in the availability of medical care, in a military alternative to a particularly injurious weapon, or in a degree of pain? To identify injuries that might be excessive in medical terms, the following subsection of this chapter categorizes and discusses the general types of wounds that combatants may experience on the battlefield.

3.4.1 *Instantaneous Health Effects*

To better understand how a particular weapon affects combatants, I have divided health effects into three sequential categories: instantaneous effects that manifest themselves immediately after the use of a specific weapon, delayed effects that appear after a limited period but within the temporal scope of armed conflict, and long-term effects that impact combatants for the rest of their lives. According to a study conducted in 2010,

[119] ICRC, *Weapons That May*, 25–28.

[120] ICRC, *Weapons That May*, 29.

[121] N. Yanagisawa, H. Morita, and T. Nakajima, "Sarin Experiences in Japan: Acute Toxicity and Long- term Effects" *Journal of the Neurological Sciences* 249, no. 1 (2006): 76–85. https://doi.org/10.1016/j.jns.2006.06.007.

the most common injuries on modern battlefields occur due to explosive devices (70%) and gunshot wounds.[122] Accordingly, the most common causes of death are "chest or abdominal injuries (40%) and traumatic brain injuries (35%)."[123] Instantaneous injuries, therefore, could be categorized as blast, bullet, or fragment wounds. Fragments, also in the form of shrapnel, are the most common cause of injury on contemporary battlefields.[124] Even in the course of active hostilities, a gunshot wound is not always lethal. In a statistical analysis of casualty numbers in four different wars (WWII, the Korean War, the Vietnam War, and the Persian Gulf War), the number of battle deaths steadily decreased; the one exception was the Vietnam War, in which the number of fatalities exceeded that of the Korean War.[125]

Urban warfare yields an added number of fatalities with increased hit injuries to the head, neck, and extremities, and decreased injuries to the abdomen and thorax. These patterns emerge due to improved body protection technology and equipment.[126] Due to the combatants' improved armor and protection, it is understandably more difficult to put a combatant hors de combat on the modern battlefield than in the late nineteenth century, when the St. Petersburg Declaration was concluded. In the contemporary offense–defense parallel, since the nineteenth century, ammunition companies have continuously developed new highly penetrative projectiles.[127]

Mortality is significantly increased when combatants use expanding, exploding, or poisoned bullets that cause extensive tissue damage and bleeding.[128] Because the first prohibitions dealt with projectiles such as exploding projectiles—which were banned by the St. Petersburg

[122] Achatz, G. R. Lechner, T. Hauer, H.G. Palm, A. Lieber, and C. Willy, *Verletzungsmuster und-ursachen in modernen Kriegen* [Patterns and causes of injuries in a contemporary combat environment]. *Unfallchirurg* 113, no. 2 (2010):106–113. https://doi.org/10.1007/s00113-009-1732-9.

[123] Lechner et al., "Patterns."

[124] Beat P. Kneubuehl, Robin M. Coupland, Markus A. Rothschild, and Michael J. Thali. *Wound Ballistics: Basics and Applications* (New York: Springer, 2008).

[125] Amir Khorram-Manesh, Krzysztof Goniewicz, Fredereick M. Burkle, and Yohan Robinson, "Review of Military Casualties in Modern Conflicts – The Re-Emergence of Causalities From Armored Warfare" *Military Medicine* 187, no. 3–4 (2022): e313–e321. https://doi.org/10.1093/milmed/usab108.

[126] Khorram-Manesh et al., 317.

[127] Kneubuehl et al., 325.

[128] Kneubuehl et al., 312.

Declaration—and dum-dum bullets, it is essential to explore the basics of ballistics and how the principle of unnecessary suffering relates to the kinetic wounds associated with projectiles that cause such instantaneous injuries. In its elemental form, the principle of unnecessary suffering is best illustrated through the example of excessively injurious bullets. To understand the issues behind the injurious effects of particular gunshots, it is necessary to briefly discuss the basics of ballistics as a field of mechanics concerned with projectiles and bullets. This scientific field includes a plethora of bullets and designs:

> Bullets are designed mainly for flight. Pistol bullets are flatter because they are slower than the speed of sound. Rifle bullets go faster than the speed of sound, so are they pointed. Damage for either is based on kinetic energy, and rifle bullets do more damage based on kinetic energy. Armor also slows the bullet down and effectively expands the cross-sectional area by the time the body is affected.[129]

A cross-sectional area (CSA) or cross-sectional density (CSD), i.e., a nail point, causes deep body penetration and has little potential for localized damage. A smaller density causes little penetration but has a significant potential for local destruction. Hence, a small cross-sectional area assures deeper penetration, even against armor.[130] This applies to small-caliber ammunition of up to 15mm and large-caliber weapons of more than 60mm. Such bullets transfer kinetic energy to the body; the projectiles deform and physically affect bones and vessels.[131] Accordingly, injuries from bullets have damaging effects on tissues and vessels and differ between soft tissues, such as muscles and organs, and bones, including tubular bones, bone plates, and skulls.

From the perspective of LOAC, it is vital to point out that non-expanding (NEX) bullets create a relatively small entrance wound and lodge inside the body, where they form a cavity and a treatable wound.[132] NEX shots have short track lengths and are, therefore, easier to treat. They often enter and leave the body. Expanding (EX) bullets, such as those used for hunting, flatten easily upon contact with human tissue and

[129] Interview with Maj. Andrew Wilson of the Canadian Armed Forces, Ammunition Specialist, December 9, 2019, in Geneva.

[130] Kneubuehl et al., 202.

[131] Kneubuehl et al., 27.

[132] Kneubuehl et al., 20

expand in a way that causes large wounds at the entrance and through the body until the bullets lose energy.[133] The seriousness of a shot wound depends on the amount of energy transferred. EX bullets transfer a high amount of energy early. NEX bullets transfer a high amount of energy late. Bone shots with EX bullets behave like shrapnel and often lead to amputations, which could cause unnecessary suffering since such amputation is not necessary as far as the effects of bullets are concerned.

The St. Petersburg Declaration banned explosive bullets, while the Hague Declarations—as part of the 1899 convention—banned semi-jacketed, expanding bullets, also known as dum-dums.[134] In both cases, the ban concerned enormous wounds after the impact on the body since dum-dums behave similarly to shrapnel. Therefore, it is not challenging to understand the basic concept of unnecessary suffering explained through projectiles and bullets. It is sufficient to neutralize a combatant with regular bullets that also retain the chance of the combatant's survival and treatment. Altered bullets, or the aforementioned EX bullets, do not offer additional military advantage. Still, they uselessly aggravate the combatant's injuries and subsequent treatment, thereby increasing the chances of a combatant's death due to large injuries accompanied by extensive bleeding. Current rifle bullets with a smaller CSA have enough power to penetrate body armor and to render a combatant *hors de combat*. Expanding bullets are often used for hunting or law enforcement purposes in hostage situations.[135] The concerning issue, however, is that current conventions do not reflect recent or future developments in ammunition; instead, they apply to the types of bullets used when the conventions were formulated.[136] That is, the modern technology of ammunition and legal framework based on the technology of the nineteenth century are in stern chronological imbalance.

Explosive weapons—such as mortar shells, rockets, artillery shells, cluster munitions, grenades, and air-delivered bombs—cause blast and

[133] Kneubuehl et al., 312.

[134] Hague Declaration concerning Expanding Bullets (done 29 July 1899, entered into force 4 September 1900) 91 BSP 1017.

[135] The purpose is to kill the animal by inflicting a large wound and also pinpointing the wound area. In rifle bullets, the projectile would lodge inside the animal, hard to find. In law enforcement operations, expanding bullets eliminate the perpetrator and do not endanger the hostage by passing further through the perpetrator's body.

[136] Kneubuehl et al., 340.

fragmentation injuries.[137] These injuries take the form of fragment (shrapnel) wounds, as mentioned above wounds. In addition, such injuries also include blast damage, in which the ears and lungs are often damaged, and burns that occur due to combustion when the device explodes.[138] Compared to injuries to infantry, injuries to combatants inside or around armored vehicles are less frequent as they are under partial cover; nonetheless, these combatants experience increased mortality, more burns, and a higher incidence of amputations.[139] Explosive weapons eject fragments that assume a perpendicular position to the direction of their travel; because fragments have no stabilizing mechanisms, they pass through the tissue while oscillating.[140] Usually, the wound they cause is "largest at the point of entry, and progressively smaller as the fragment penetrates the body."[141] Whereas expanding and exploding bullets are controversial projectiles, thermobaric or fuel-air bombs (FABs) are somewhat controversial explosives. Their energy output is more significant than regular conventional weapons, producing a massive shockwave, though they also make fewer fragments. Thus, their deployment in increasingly urbanized warfare can be problematic from the perspective of distinction, proportionality, and necessity.

3.4.2 *Delayed and Long-Term Health Effects*

There is no official internationally recognized classification of delayed effects. Understandably, armed forces are interested in neutralizing the enemy not weeks or years after an attack but during the military operation. Thus, most weapons produce instantaneous effects that armies often refer to as primary effects, and little thought is given to the effects that appear later. These effects are usually associated with particularly toxic weapons and tools of war, such as white phosphorus, depleted uranium projectiles, defoliants, and napalm. Delayed and long-term effects are particularly

[137] UN Institute for Disarmament Research, "European Action on Small Arms and Light Weapons and Explosive Remnants of War: Final Report," Geneva: UNIDIR, 2006, available at https://unidir.org/publication/european-action-small-arms-and-light-weapons-and-explosive-remnants-war-final-report, 4.

[138] Thomas E. Bowen, ed. *Emergency War Surgery* (Collingdale, PA: Diane Publishing Co., 2005), 1.3–35.

[139] Bowen, 1.9–40.

[140] Kneubeuhl et al., 232.

[141] Kneubeuhl et al., 232.

problematic from the perspective of LOAC's temporal scope of application. Therefore, categorizing delayed and long-term health effects is critical.

The term delayed effects is predominantly associated with nuclear weapons. Hence, ionizing radiation serves as the best example to illustrate these long-term consequences. The author distinguishes between delayed and long-term health effects. This categorization is based on victims' experiences in the atomic bombings of Hiroshima and Nagasaki. Whereas the effects caused by shockwaves, heat, and large doses of radiation appeared almost instantaneously, health effects of radiation doses that were not as but still very high appeared over several months after the bombings. These delayed health effects plagued survivors following the bombings. An unexpected disease that kept reappearing took the lives of even those who appeared to have fully recovered from the initial effects.

"Ionizing radiation accounts for roughly 17% of the overall energy distribution during the nuclear explosion" of a uranium-type bomb.[142] By lowering resistance to infections, "ionizing radiation substantially complicates the healing process of thermal injuries."[143] The first two weeks are the most life-threatening for the victim, where within a radius of 1km, those affected usually died in 7–10 days "from cerebral symptoms including convulsions and delirium."[144] After the first two weeks, "the second stage of acute radiation followed, producing a fatality rate of about one-tenth of those exposed."[145] By the end of the fourth month after the bombing, the victims' health conditions generally showed improvement.[146] Nevertheless, the symptoms kept reappearing, further generating anxiety and fear among survivors. Like the sword of Damocles, no one knew whether they were next, and a cure was non-existent. Thus, overall health improvement beyond the fourth-month threshold was in no way indicative of the overall mortality rate that accompanied exposure to ionizing radiation from a nuclear explosion. Delayed effects followed instantaneous injuries and, in the case of ionizing radiation, for about four

[142] Los Alamos Scientific Laboratory and Norris E. Bradbury, *The Effects of Atomic Weapons* (Whitefish, MT: Literary Licensing, 2013), 21.

[143] Committee for the Compilation of Materials on Damage Caused by the Atomic Bombs in Hiroshima and Nagasaki, *Hiroshima and Nagasaki: The Physical, Medical and Social Effects of the Atomic Bombings* (Tokyo: Iwanami Shoten, 1981), 115.

[144] Committee, *Hiroshima and Nagasaki,* 131.

[145] Committee, *Hiroshima and Nagasaki,* 114.

[146] Committee, *Hiroshima and Nagasaki,* 114.

months after the bombings. Beyond four months, long-term effects continue for years afterward. Among those exposed to a single high dose of radiation, effects will persist for the rest of their lives.

According to the Radiation Effects Research Foundation (RERF), long-term health effects of ionizing radiation "include blood disorders (e.g., various forms of leukemia), solid cancers, ocular lesions, and cataracts and even developmental disorders for those exposed *in utero* between weeks 8–15 of pregnancy."[147] These may result in "lowered IQ, decreased academic performance, and microcephaly."[148] RERF is still studying the late effects of radiation among the survivors of Hiroshima and Nagasaki. According to RERF, the effects are dose-dependent. In the case of Hiroshima, the estimated doses, as measured according to the distance from the hypocenter, are approximately 42 Gray or Gy (within 500m), 4.5 Gy (within 1 km), 0.6 Gy (within 1.5 km), and 0.01 Gy (at 2 km). *LD*50[149] is estimated to be between 3 and 5 Gy.[150] The risk of leukemia peaks 5–10 years after exposure, while the risk of solid cancers gradually increases after the tenth year.[151] "Thyroid cancer manifested earlier than other types. Other malignancies include lung, stomach, breast, colorectal, and liver tumors. The brain and CNS were also affected by a significant risk of tumors, particularly schwannoma, a type of cancer also detected in the so-called atomic veterans."[152] Atomic veterans are usually military employees and soldiers working in the proximity of atmospheric nuclear tests or involved in the ensuing cleanup.[153] Symptoms of exposure typically

[147] Radiation Effects Research Foundation, *A Brief Description* (Hiroshima: RERF, 2016), 30.

[148] RERF, *Brief Description*, 31.

[149] Lethal Dose or LD when 50% of the affected die within one month. See "Lethal Dose" definition, US Nuclear Regulatory Commission, "Lethal Dose (LD)" last updated March 9, 2021. https://www.nrc.gov/reading-rm/basic-ref/glossary/lethal-dose-ld.html.

[150] Tetsuji Imanaka, "Casualties and Radiation Dosimetry of the Atomic Bombings on Hiroshima and Nagasaki" in *Radiation Risk Estimates in Normal and Emergency Situations,* edited by Arrigo A. Cigna and Marco Durante, 149–156. Dordrecht: Springer, 2006. https://doi.org/10.1007/1-4020-4956-0_15.

[151] Itsuzo Shigematsu, Mitoshi Akiyama, Hideo Sasaki, Chikato Ito, and Nanao Kamada, eds. *Genbaku hoshasen no jintai eikyo* [Effects of A-bomb radiation on the human body] (Tokyo: Bunkodo, 1995), 17–20.

[152] Krasny and Kawano, "Use of Nuclear Weapons."

[153] See National Association of Atomic Veterans, accessed August 4, 2022, https://www.naav.com/, or LABRATS International, accessed August 4, 2024, https://www.labrats.international/.

appear close to 0.2 Gy, and reduced lymph cells appear with a dose of 0.5 Gy. $LD_{90/100}$ begins from approximately 10 Gy and above.[154] In a similar manner, chemical weapons (CW), particularly mustard gas, often cause long-term health effects.

In these CW cases, "carcinogenicity is defined by an increased risk of upper and lower respiratory tract cancers (e.g., oral cavity, nasopharynx, larynx, and lung cancers)."[155] The risk depends on the length of time a person was exposed to the chemical agent. The relative risk for cancer among the exposed is estimated to be "4.02 times higher than among the unexposed; mortality is 1.44 times higher."[156] Inai (2012) further points out that although there is an "increased rate of malignancies in exposed individuals, no exact relationship was found between single-acute exposure to sulfur mustard and a particular type of cancer."[157] Similar to the difficulty in linking radiation exposure to specific types of cancer, it is challenging to definitely associate exposure to certain chemicals or radiation with particular malignant tumors. Thus, we talk about probability. However, efforts are ongoing to identify which cancers are caused by exposure.

3.5 The SIrUS Project

In 1997, the ICRC embarked on an ambitious project to qualitatively define the substance of superfluous injury or unnecessary suffering. The goal was to clarify the interpretation of the norm to enhance its practical application. This was the so-called SIrUS Project. The authors correctly note that "injury and suffering are health issues."[158] In light of the organization's previous activities, which deliberated the nature of unnecessary suffering in proceedings before the CCW,[159] the ICRC proposed that

[154] Norman E. Bolus, "Basic Review of Radiation Biology and Terminology" *Journal of Nuclear Medicine Technology* 45, no. 4 (2017): 259–264. https://doi.org/10.2967/jnmt.117.195230.

[155] Kouki Inai, *Atlas of Mustard Gas Injuries: Building Bridges Between Iran and Japan Through the Relief of Victims Exposed to Mustard Gas.* Hiroshima: MOCT, 2012), 50.

[156] Inai, 51.

[157] Inai, 53.

[158] Coupland, *The SIrUS Project*, 14.

[159] Convention on Prohibitions or Restrictions on the Use of Certain Conventional Weapons which may be Deemed to be Excessively Injurious or to have Indiscriminate Effects (adopted 10 October 1980, entered into force 2 December 1983) 1342 UNTS 137.

"what constitutes superfluous injury or unnecessary suffering [should] be determined by design-dependent, foreseeable effects of weapons when they are used against human beings."[160] Hence, through such an approach, the ICRC became an advocate of medicalization and a medical effects-based approach when deliberating on the legality of particular weapons.

Through the SIrUS Project, the ICRC defined unnecessary suffering in medical terms and specified four criteria for determining whether a weapon violates the principle. These criteria include, inter alia, whether a weapon causes a specific disease or abnormal physiological condition, field mortality of more than 25%, or "Grade 3 wounds as measured by the Red Cross wound classification, or effects for which there is no well-recognized and proven treatment."[161] Because any weapon can be misused, as I have mentioned before, the design dependency of a particular weapon is central to the study. The study did not distinguish between weapons' primary or secondary effects. There is no need to draw such a distinction; the reality is that a weapon affects a combatant's health in a certain way. It doesn't matter to the combatant, and even for legal analysis, whether such effects are primary or secondary. Such distinction or argument is, therefore, inherently flawed.

Drawing from the ICRC's large database, the project's authors attempted to use acquired field medical data to define which wounds would be in breach of SIrUS specifically. This was the first scientific attempt to medicalize a particular LOAC rule. The four criteria set by the project depended on weapon design and foreseeable effects; therefore, they were summarized in the SIrUS Project as follows:

Criterion 1

Specific disease, specific abnormal physiological state, specific abnormal psychological state, specific and permanent disability, or specific disfigurement.[162]

According to the ICRC SIrUS Project, this criterion would be fulfilled in two instances. First, a weapon does not produce any physical harm but

[160] Robin M. Coupland., ed., *The SIrUS Project: Towards a Determination of Which Weapons Cause "Superfluous Injury or Unnecessary Suffering."* Geneva: ICRC, 1997, available at https://www.loc.gov/collections/military-legal-resources/?q=RC_SIrUS-project.html. 8.

[161] Coupland, *The SIrUS Project,* 25.

[162] Coupland, *The SIrUS Project,* 8.

induces an exceptional physiological state. Here, the ICRC experts do not refer to extreme stress or fear. As the study observes, fear accompanies all combat situations. Therefore, such a state would arise from weapons that disorient, confuse, or cause seizures or psychosis.[163] This means that such effects are intended, and the weapon is designed to produce them.

The second instance, the physical perspective, refers to specific injuries that would also cause tremendous constraints on medical help. In other words, they would require large blood banks, which may be very challenging to establish in an active combat zone, or they would cause wounds that require multiple operations. The ICRC states that an average battle injury requires a maximum of three operations.[164]

Criterion 2
Field mortality of more than 25% or hospital mortality of more than 5%.

The second criterion separates field and hospital mortality. It is based upon the effects of weapons, notably incendiary weapons, that may cause death after days or weeks.[165] That is, producing delayed effects. The ICRC accounts for the availability of resources and medical personnel, which affect the percentage of "acceptability." This calculation of "acceptability" of 25% and 5% is based on field data and, as the ICRC explains, represents a "conservative baseline."[166] Whether or not someone agrees with this percentage, this baseline helps form a tangible criterion and gives the prohibition of unnecessary suffering a more tangible form.

Criterion 3
Grade 3 wound as measured by the Red Cross wound classification (such as the location of the wound, nature of the wound, including depth and size, need for transfusion or complex medical operation).[167]

An important aspect of Criterion 3 is its focus not on the bullet's technological elements, but rather on the injuries it causes. Expanding bullets and dum-dums are already prohibited, and, as the ICRC observes,

[163] Coupland, *The SIrUS Project*, 23.
[164] Coupland, *The SIrUS Project*, 24.
[165] Coupland, *The SIrUS Project*, 24.
[166] Coupland, *The SIrUS Project*, 24.
[167] Coupland, *The SIrUS Project*, 24.

"conventional weapons produce less than 10% of Grade 3 wounds."[168] Grade 3 wounds are the most serious—threatening life or limb.[169] Such wounds may be similar to those caused by dum-dums or expanding bullets.

Criterion 4
Effects for which there is no well-recognized and proven treatment.

This criterion is self-explanatory. Blinding lasers that damage eyes are not responsive to medical treatment. Therefore, this criterion is closely linked to Criterion 1, which addresses weapons that produce specific and unusual long-term injuries. As the ICRC states, medical help is not readily available to treat the wounds that such weapons cause. In this case, blindness is caused by lasers. In addition, these weapons produce tremendous injury that not only makes reintegration into society difficult but also puts a heavy burden on healthcare resources.[170] Even following the cessation of hostilities.

Those opposing and rejecting the results of the SIrUS project claim that its figures rely primarily on wounded civilians who lack appropriate protection or training and that most conflicts are non-international and confined to an underdeveloped region where medical care is still rather rudimentary.[171] The major criticism that the project "emphasizes unnecessary suffering and superfluous injury to the near exclusion of military necessity" was raised at the ICRC Meeting of Experts on the SIrUS Project in Geneva, which convened on May 10–11, 1999.[172] Two years later, the ICRC announced the withdrawal of the SIrUS project at the Expert Meeting on Legal Reviews of Weapons and the SIrUS Project, which was held at Jongny-sur-Vevey from January 29 to 30, 2001. The project was withdrawn due to the backlash from State representatives that the study was undermining the applicability of the SIrUS principle by

[168] Coupland, *The SIrUS Project*, 24.

[169] See Robert M. Coupland, *The Red Cross Wound Classification*. Geneva: ICRC, 2020, available at *https://www.icrc.org/en/publication/0498-red-cross-wound-classification*.

[170] Coupland, *The SIrUS Project*, 24.

[171] Marie Donna Verchio, "Just Say No! The SIrUS Project: Well-Intentioned, But Unnecessary and Superfluous" *Air Force Law Review* 51, (2001): 183–228, 200.

[172] Verchio, 259.

excluding the balancing principle of military advantage and necessity as understood by LOAC.[173]

As discussed above, defining military necessity in objective terms is a near-impossible task that depends upon too many variables. Necessity is likely to be determined on the battlefield by commanders and combatants based on circumstances at the time. Nevertheless, according to Crawford (2013), military necessity can be understood in at least two ways. One of these is restrictive—necessity involving only so much force as is required to achieve a particular objective. The other is expansive or permissive: "an action considered militarily necessary can excuse a breach in the law of war or is defined so that it is legal."[174] Thus, we have to be very careful as not to confuse a legal excess in the law of war with military necessity nor be blind to it.

The permissive concept of military necessity was reflected in the ICJ Advisory Opinion of 1996 on the threat or use of nuclear weapons, in which the Court essentially argued that military necessity in the form of the protection of the State's survival could justify the breach of fundamental IHL principles.[175] Notwithstanding what State survival means, vis-à-vis government survival is unclear; such an interpretation runs contrary to the evolution, development, and trends in military technology developing yet more efficient and precise ammunition. Further, LOAC does not allow suspension of its norms, even under extreme circumstances.

Yet, it is commendable that the ICRC has endeavored and taken up the challenge to define unnecessary suffering to strengthen the term's normative effect. In the author's view, this effort was successful and greatly helped with the overall interpretation and understanding of the norm against unnecessary suffering. Continuous references to the SIrUS project in the relevant literature reflect the reality that the idea or spirit behind the project is not entirely gone. Scholars even suggest the SIrUS project could

[173] See ICRC, "Expert Meeting on Legal Reviews of Weapons and the SIrUS Project. 30-06-2001 Article, International Review of the Red Cross, No. 842" accessed April 13, 2022. https://www.icrc.org/en/doc/resources/documents/article/other/57jr5z.htm.

[174] Neta Crawford, *Accountability for Killing: Moral Responsibility for Collateral Damage in America's Post-9/11 Wars* (Oxford: Oxford University Press), 2013, 174–175.

[175] "...the Court cannot conclude definitively whether the threat or use of nuclear weapons would be lawful or unlawful in an extreme circumstance of self-defence, in which the very survival of a State would be at stake;" *Legality of the Threat or Use of Nuclear Weapons (Advisory Opinion)* [1996] ICJ Rep 226.¶ 105(2)(E).

have been successfully recalibrated or restarted rather than "binned."[176] The time may come when the ICRC begins to work on the SIrUS Project 2.0.

3.6 Conclusion

The purpose of this chapter is to introduce humanitarian efforts under the umbrella of Geneva law. These efforts stem from observers who witnessed the horror of injuries on the battlefield. Methods of warfare, which evolved from ancient times, began to yield to the requirements of humanity by the end of the nineteenth century and intensified after WWII. This intensification was triggered not by a sudden and mystical progress of civilization, but rather by observers who witnessed the horrors caused by technical progress in warfare—that is, by humanitarians and medical professionals who experienced the development and use of yet more lethal means of killing without parallel developments in the field of combat medical care. Even with ensuing advancements in medical care, particular weapons and ammunition caused such gruesome wounds that they were perceived as unnecessary to accomplish any legitimate military objective. It is sufficient to put combatants *hors de combat* without making their deaths inevitable through exploding, expanding, or poisoned bullets. Therefore, weapons and ammunition that inflict wounds greater than those required to neutralize a combatant are prohibited.[177] Such referencing of wounds and injuries marks a novel development in SIrUS interpretation through medical terms.

In the aftermath of WWII, it was apparent that new codifications regulating armed conflict were necessary. A new approach centered on individuals' human rights began to gain momentum. As IAC became less frequent, NIAC increased. This increase helped to make human rights more prominent. The importance of human rights increased because LOAC was predominantly applicable to interstate conflicts; it left NIAC largely unregulated. After all, under traditional LOAC, non-international armed conflict was seen as a domestic issue of sovereign States. Inevitably,

[176] Stuart Casey-Maslen and Steven Haines, *Hague Law Interpreted: The Conduct of Hostilities under the Law of Armed Conflict* (New York: Hart, 2020), 215.

[177] Louis Maresca and Stuart Maslen, *The Banning of Anti-Personnel Landmines: The Legal Contribution of the International Committee of the Red Cross* (Cambridge: Cambridge University Press, 2000), 178.

the law of war started to interact with IHRL, but this interaction has not been without controversies. Although IHRL ensures the right to life, the law of war admits a certain level of collateral damage. While IHRL protects combatants against arbitrary killing or the death penalty, LOAC admits a death penalty under specific conditions, and combatants who are not engaged in hostilities (e.g., those who are taking a break at the base) are still legitimate targets, although under protection against unnecessary suffering.

The importance of the principle in the wake of the Vietnam War as the least of the least to protect combatants assured its codification during Diplomatic Conferences of 1974–1977 that adopted two Additional Protocols, which today, with Geneva Conventions, form the basis of the codified law of armed conflict. The codification, while general in meaning, ensued while discussing specific weapons, such as incendiaries, and their health effects. Whereas traditionalists sternly oppose medicalization, the ICRC has promoted arguments for interpreting SIrUS in medical terms. Suffering has been connected to the medical treatment of wounds since the St. Petersburg Declaration. Suffering and injury are, ultimately, medical terms. In the nineteenth century, however, it was much easier to assess excessive injury. With the advent of chemical and nuclear weapons, making such an assessment became problematic. Hence, for interpretation purposes, the author divides injuries according to their temporal scope: instantaneous, delayed, and long-term, with the latter being particularly problematic concerning SIrUS.

To further focus the argument by going from general to specific health effects, the following chapter explores five particularly controversial weapons. It includes two case studies: the bombings of Hiroshima and Nagasaki and the Iran–Iraq War. In other words, it examines the use of nuclear and chemical weapons. The author selected these case studies because they inspired the first attempts to medicalize weapon-induced injuries. As explained above, the ICRC had argued for the prohibition of poison gas to promote the 1925 Geneva Gas Protocol and, in the 1950s, actively campaigned to ban nuclear weapons based on their health effects, particularly ionizing radiation. In addition to these case studies, the next chapter discusses antipersonnel landmines and incendiaries. These weapons are included because debates about their legality often employ unnecessary suffering to argue for their prohibition. It is important to keep in mind that the law of armed conflict does not know the terms "conventional" or "unconventional" weapon. Only lawful, unlawful, and regulated means and methods of warfare.

References

Arnold, Roberta, and Noelle N. R. Quenivet, eds. *International Humanitarian Law and Human Rights: Towards a New Merger in International Law*. Leiden: Martinus Nijhoff Publishers, 2008.

Bantekas, Ilias, and Lutz Oette. *International Human Rights: Law and Practice*. 3rd ed. Cambridge: Cambridge University Press, 2020.

Bennett, Angela. *The Geneva Convention: The Hidden Origins of the Red Cross*. Cheltenham: The History Press, 2006.

British Medical Association. *Illustrated Medical Dictionary*. 1st ed. London: Dorling Kindersley, 2002.

Bolus, Norman E. "Basic Review of Radiation Biology and Terminology." *Journal of Nuclear Medicine Technology* 45, no. 4 (2017): 259–264. https://doi.org/10.2967/jnmt.117.195230.

Bowen, Thomas E., ed. *Emergency War Surgery*. Collingdale, PA: Diane Publishing Co., 2005.

Casey-Maslen, Stuart,ed. *Weapons Under International Human Rights Law*. Cambridge: Cambridge University Press, 2014.

Casey-Maslen, Stuart, and Steven Haines. *Hague Law Interpreted: The Conduct of Hostilities under the Law of Armed Conflict*. New York: Hart, 2020.

Chemical and Biological Weapons Nonproliferation Program. "The Moscow Theater Hostage Crisis: Incapacitants and Chemical Warfare." James Martin Center for Nonproliferation Studies, November 4, 2002. https://nonproliferation.org/the-moscow-theater-hostage-crisis-incapacitants-and-chemical-warfare/.

Clausewitz, Carl von. *On War*. Translated by Michael Howard and Peter Paret. Oxford: Oxford University Press, 1976.

Clapham, Andrew, and Paola Gaeta, eds. *The Oxford Handbook of International Law in Armed Conflict*. Oxford: Oxford University Press, 2014.

Coupland, Robin M., ed. *The SIrUS Project: Towards a Determination of Which Weapons Cause "Superfluous Injury or Unnecessary Suffering."* Geneva: ICRC, 1997. https://www.loc.gov/collections/military-legal-resources/?q=RC_SIrUS-project.html.

Coupland, Robin M.. *The Red Cross Wound Classification*. Geneva: ICRC, 2020. https://www.icrc.org/en/publication/0498-red-cross-wound-classification.

Crawford, Neta. *Accountability for Killing: Moral Responsibility for Collateral Damage in America's Post-9/11 Wars*. Oxford: Oxford University Press, 2013.

Committee for the Compilation of Materials on Damage Caused by the Atomic Bombs in Hiroshima and Nagasaki. *Hiroshima and Nagasaki: The Physical, Medical and Social Effects of the Atomic Bombings*. Tokyo: Iwanami Shoten, 1981.

Dunant, Henry. *A Memory of Solferino*. Geneva: International Committee of the Red Cross, 1959.

Fellmeth, Aaron X., and Maurice Horwitz. *Guide to Latin in International Law*. New York, Oxford University Press, 2009.
Gupta, Ramesh C., ed. *Handbook of Toxicology of Chemical Warfare Agents*. 2nd ed. Oxford: Academic Press, 2015.
ICRC. *Weapons That May Cause Unnecessary Suffering or Have Indiscriminate Effects: Report on the Work of Exper*ts. Geneva: ICRC, 1973a. https://www.loc.gov/item/2011525354/.
ICRC. "Conference of Government Experts On Weapons Which May Cause Unnecessary Suffering or Have Indiscriminate Effects." *International Review of the Red Cross*. Accessed April 22, 2022a. https://international-review.icrc.org/sites/default/files/S0020860400016041a.pdf.
———. "Commentary of 2016. Article 3: Conflicts Not of an International Character." Accessed April 13, 2022b. https://ihl-databases.icrc.org/ihl/full/GCI-commentaryArt3.
———. "Convention for the Amelioration of the Condition of the Wounded and Sick in Armies in the Field. Geneva, 6 July 1906." Accessed April 13, 2022c. https://ihl-databases.icrc.org/applic/ihl/ihl.nsf/Treaty.xsp?documentId=C64C3E521F5CC28FC12563CD002D6737&action=openDocument.
———. "Convention Relative to the Treatment of Prisoners of War. Geneva, 27 July 1929." Accessed April 13, 2022d. https://ihl-databases.icrc.org/applic/ihl/ihl.nsf/INTRO/305?OpenDocument.
———. "Expert Meeting on Legal Reviews of Weapons and the SIrUS Project. 30-06-2001 Article, International Review of the Red Cross, No. 842." Accessed April 13, 2022e. https://www.icrc.org/en/doc/resources/documents/article/other/57jr5z.htm.
——— Treaties, States Parties and Commentaries. "Additional Articles relating to the Condition of the Wounded in War. Geneva, 20 October 1868." Accessed April 13, 2022f. https://ihl-databases.icrc.org/applic/ihl/ihl.nsf/Treaty.xsp?documentId=ECB39EA050F80A5DC12563CD002D6624&action=openDocument.
ICRC. "Atomic Weapons and Non-Directed Missiles: ICRC Statement, 1950. 05-04-1950 Article, International Review of the Red Cross, - Supplement, Vol. III, No. 4." Accessed April 13, 2022. https://www.icrc.org/en/doc/resources/documents/article/other/5kylur.htm.
ICRC, *Weapons That May Cause Unnecessary Suffering or Have Indiscriminate Effects: Report on the Work of Exper*ts (Geneva: ICRC, 1973b), available at https://www.loc.gov/item/2011525354/.
ICRC. "World War I: The ICRC's Appeal Against the Use of Poisonous Gases. 8 February 1918." Accessed April 13, 2022g. https://www.icrc.org/en/doc/resources/documents/statement/57jnqh.htm.

Imanaka, Tetsuji. "Casualties and Radiation Dosimetry of the Atomic Bombings on Hiroshima and Nagasaki. In *Radiation Risk Estimates in Normal and Emergency Situations,* edited by Arrigo A. Cigna and Marco Durante, 149–156. Dordrecht: Springer, 2006. https://doi.org/10.1007/1-4020-4956-0_15.

Inai, Kouki. *Atlas of Mustard Gas Injuries: Building Bridges Between Iran and Japan Through the Relief of Victims Exposed to Mustard Gas.* Hiroshima: MOCT, 2012.

International Law Commission. Annual Reports. *Report on the Work of the Seventy-First Session (2019).* Last updated December 10, 2019. https://legal.un.org/ilc/reports/2019/.

Khorram-Manesh, Amir, Krzysztof Goniewicz, Fredereick M. Burkle, and Yohan Robinson. "Review of Military Casualties in Modern Conflicts – The Re-Emergence of Causalities From Armored Warfare." *Military Medicine* 187, no. 3–4 (2022): e313–e321. https://doi.org/10.1093/milmed/usab108.

Kneubuehl, Beat P., Robin M. Coupland, Markus A. Rothschild, and Michael J. Thali. *Wound Ballistics: Basics and Applications.* New York: Springer, 2008.

Kolb, Robert, and Richard Hyde. *An Introduction to the International Law of Armed Conflicts.* Portland: Hart Publishing, 2008.

Krasny, Jaroslav, and Noriyuki Kawano. "Weapons of Mass Destruction and the Principle of Unnecessary Suffering: The Use of Nuclear Weapons in an Armed Conflict." *Hiroshima Peace Science* 36, (2014): 101–116. https://doi.org/10.15027/38055.

Lechner, R., G. Achatz, T. Hauer, H.G. Palm, A. Lieber, and C. Willy. Verletzungsmuster und-ursachen in modernen Kriegen [Patterns and causes of injuries in a contemporary combat environment]. *Unfallchirurg* 113, no. 2 (2010):106–113. https://doi.org/10.1007/s00113-009-1732-9

Longuet, Samuel. "Permitted for Law Enforcement Purposes but Prohibited in the Conduct of Hostilities: The Case of Riot Control Agents and Expanding Bullets." *International Review of the Red Cross* 98, no. 901 (2016): 249–274. https://doi.org/10.1017/S1816383117000108.

Los Alamos Scientific Laboratory and Norris E. Bradbury. *The Effects of Atomic Weapons.* Whitefish, MT: Literary Licensing, 2013.

Maresca, Louis, and Stuart Maslen. *The Banning of Anti-Personnel Landmines: The Legal Contribution of the International Committee of the Red Cross.* Cambridge: Cambridge University Press, 2000.

Mathur, Ritu. *Red Cross Interventions in Weapons Control.* London: Lexington Books, 2017.

Phillips, Charles, and Alan Axelrod, eds. *Encyclopedia of Wars.* New York: Zenda, Inc, 2005.

Rietiker, Daniel. *Humanization of Arms Control: Paving the Way for a World Free of Nuclear Weapons.* New York: Routledge, 2018.

Radiation Effects Research Foundation. *A Brief Description.* Hiroshima: RERF, 2016.

Saul, Ben, and Akande, Dapo, eds. *The Oxford Guide to International Humanitarian Law.* Oxford: Oxford University Press, 2020.

Sandoz, Yves, Christophe Swinarski, and Bruno Zimmerman, eds. *Commentary on the Additional Protocols of 8 June 1977 to the Geneva Conventions of 12 August 1949.* Geneva: International Committee of the Red Cross, 1987.

Sassoli, Marco. *International Humanitarian Law: Rules, Controversies, and Solutions to Problems Arising in Warfare.* Cheltenham: Edward Elgar, 2019.

Sassoli et al., "Derogations" accessed April 21, 2022. https://casebook.icrc.org/glossary/derogations.

Schindler, Dietrich, and Jiri Toman, eds. *The Laws of Armed Conflict: A Collection of Conventions, Resolutions and Other Documents.* Leiden: Martinus Nijhoff Publishers, 2004.

Schutter, Olivier de. *International Human Rights Law: Cases, Materials, Commentary.* Cambridge: Cambridge University Press, 2010.

Shigematsu, Itsuzo, Mitoshi Akiyama, Hideo Sasaki, Chikato Ito, and Nanao Kamada, eds. *Genbaku hoshasen no jintai eikyo* [Effects of A-bomb radiation on the human body]. Tokyo: Bunkodo, 1995.

UN Institute for Disarmament Research. *European Action on Small Arms and Light Weapons and Explosive Remnants of War: Final Report.* Geneva: UNIDIR, 2006. https://unidir.org/publication/european-action-small-arms-and-light-weapons-and-explosive-remnants-war-final-report.

UN Office of Legal Affairs. *Yearbook of the International Law Commission* 1980, Vol. II/2. New York: UN, 1981. https://legal.un.org/ilc/publications/yearbooks/english/ilc_1980_v2_p2.pdf.

UN War Crimes Commission, *Law Reports of Trials of War Criminals.* 1949, Vol. VIII, London.

US Department of Defense. *Law of War Manual.* Washington, DC: General Counsel of the Department of Defense, 2016.

US Nuclear Regulatory Commission. "Lethal Dose (LD)." Last updated March 9, 2021. https://www.nrc.gov/reading-rm/basic-ref/glossary/lethal-dose-ld.html.

Van Dijk, Boyd. *Preparing for War: The Making of the Geneva Conventions.* Oxford: Oxford University Press, 2022.

Verchio, Donna Marie. "Just Say No! The SIrUS Project: Well-Intentioned, But Unnecessary and Superfluous." *Air Force Law Review* 51, (2001): 183–228.

XXth International Conference of the Red Cross. Accessed May 10, 2022, https://international-review.icrc.org/sites/default/files/S0020860400008901a.pdf.

XXIst International Conference of the Red Cross. Accessed May 10, 2022, https://international-review.icrc.org/sites/default/files/S0020860400063555a.pdf.

XXIInd International Conference of the Red Cross. Accessed May 10, 2022, https://international-review.icrc.org/sites/default/files/S0020860400004605a.pdf.

Yanagisawa, N., H. Morita, and T. Nakajima. "Sarin Experiences in Japan: Acute Toxicity and Long- term Effects." *Journal of the Neurological Sciences* 249, no. 1 (2006): 76–85. https://doi.org/10.1016/j.jns.2006.06.007.

CHAPTER 4

Weapons Use and Health Effects

4.1 Introduction

The preceding chapter introduced a general discussion about the effects of weapons on the human body. This chapter further concretizes that theme by discussing selected weapons, their deployment, and the particular health effects they produce. Because this book focuses on weapons law, the particular reasons behind the targeting or deployment of these weapons—including the legitimacy of their deployment in specific situations—are excluded. Thus, the author is not going to discuss whether using napalm in Vietnam or dropping atomic bombs on Japan were lawful actions per se. The focus is on these weapons' particular health effects and their role when interpreting the superfluous injury or unnecessary suffering principle. This chapter shows that the prohibition of SIrUS is the underlying idea behind these weapons' projected regulation or outright ban. The author selected the weapons in question based on their ambiguous legal status and because they are part of ongoing controversies in weapons law and "disarmament."[1]

[1] The North Atlantic Treaty Organization (NATO) defines disarmament as: "...the act of eliminating or abolishing weapons (particularly offensive arms) either unilaterally or reciprocally. It may refer either to reducing the number of arms, or to eliminate entire categories of weapons." See NATO, accessed April 14, 2024, https://www.nato.int/cps/en/natohq/topics_48895.htm.

J. Krasny, *War Injuries*,
https://doi.org/10.1007/978-3-032-00737-7_4

This chapter explores medical data on the injuries these selected weapons inflict on the human body. Where appropriate, it discusses United Nations mechanisms and their roles in connecting particular weapons with unnecessary suffering. These mechanisms include the UN General Assembly (UNGA) and the United Nations Security Council (UNSC) Resolutions, often following the use of particular weapons. The limited role of civil societies cannot be entirely dismissed and will be included where relevant. The first selected case study is the strategic bombings of Hiroshima and Nagasaki. It is important to reiterate that, in the wake of the bombings, nuclear weapons were considered conventional, albeit special, weapons of tremendous power. Needless to say, LOAC makes no distinction between conventional and unconventional weapons. It applies to all weapons used in armed conflict.

Studies of radiation effects were only beginning in 1945. Still, it is vital to explore how the atomic bombings were perceived and whether the provisions of LOAC, including SIrUS, were already being raised. The SIrUS element will also be examined in the context of anti-personnel landmines (APL) and incendiaries such as napalm, which was used in the course of the Vietnam War. Finally, the Iran–Iraq war (1980–1988) serves as this chapter's important second case study. The prohibition of chemical weapons (CWs) is one of the few successes in disarmament law and the global prohibition of particular weapons. As stated above, the use of CWs represents one of the very first instances when the International Committee of the Red Cross (ICRC) medicalized the unnecessary suffering principle to achieve a ban on their use. Of course, this ban would be followed by a ban on nuclear weapons.

4.2 Nuclear Weapons

Nuclear weapons are not weapons of one category and yield. The yield differs, and so does the purpose of their use, be it in its very basic categorization, tactical or strategic. Given the later development of small tactical nuclear weapons and their use against remote targets, it is not particularly difficult for States to argue for nuclear weapons' non-violation of the LOAC principle of distinction.[2] "In their statements before the

[2] See Paul C. Robinson, *A White Paper: Pursuing a New Nuclear Weapons Policy for the 21st Century.* Sandia National Laboratories White Paper, March 22, 2001 available at https://www.sandia.gov/media/whitepaper/2001-04-Robinson.htm.

International Court of Justice (ICJ), nuclear States have opined that customary law would not necessarily render the use of nuclear weapons innately illegal. For instance, the United States has argued that the legality of use would depend upon the specific circumstances surrounding the weapons' deployment."[3]

As such, the US has considered different types of weapons and a variety of locations for their deployment, including—but not limited to—the high seas or remote military bases where such use could be lawful. While possibly not violating the principles of distinction and proportionality, such use would still be incompatible with the prohibition of unnecessary suffering. In its Advisory Opinion (AO), the ICJ confirmed that "there exists no conventional law either allowing or prohibiting the use of nuclear weapons."[4] The ICJ then contradicted itself by stating that the use of nuclear weapons would generally be "contrary to the principles of international humanitarian law," with the following paragraph concluding that it is unable to decide whether such use would be unlawful under "extreme circumstances where survival of a State is at stake."[5] This is an unfortunate argument from the perspective of LOAC because, as opposed to the specific norms of IHRL, LOAC cannot be derogated from or limited unless expressly provided for under the relevant article. This is true even when the survival of a State is at stake, whatever this "survival of a State" means. Current warfare of the twenty-first century usually does not end in a total annihilation of a nation. Certainly, the ICJ did not mean the survival of a government; that would be absurd. Unfortunately, the ICJ did not offer any more clarity into the debate about nuclear weapons' legality or the applicability of the SIrUS principle. The Court did reaffirm, however, that the general principles of the LOAC would apply to the use of nuclear weapons.[6]

While global large-scale nuclear exchange is certain to violate fundamental norms of LOAC, could limited deployment of low-yield weapons result in limited collateral damage? The author intentionally neglects the

[3] See *Statement of the United States of the June 20, 1995 to the ICJ on the legality of the threat of use of nuclear weapons*, accessed on April 14, 2022, https://www.icj-cij.org/en/case/95/written-proceedings.

[4] Legality of the Threat or Use of Nuclear Weapons (Advisory Opinion) [1996] ICJ Rep 226.¶57.

[5] Legality of the Threat or Use of Nuclear Weapons (Advisory Opinion) [1996] ICJ Rep. 226. *Dispositif E.*

[6] Legality of the Threat or Use of Nuclear Weapons (Advisory Opinion) [1996] ICJ Rep

likelihood of escalation as this does not fall under the scope of the law of weapons and targeting or LAOC in general. To distinguish low from high-yield nuclear weapons is certainly a challenge. What precise yield would mark the distinction? There is no consensus on what constitutes a low-yield nuclear weapon.[7] Given that the yields of current nuclear arsenals reach into megatons, it is reasonable for legal analysis to consider the yields of the Hiroshima and Nagasaki bombs (16kt and 20kt, respectively) to be low-yield. It is crucial to remember that some currently deployed nuclear weapons could have significantly lower yields than those of Hiroshima or Nagasaki. Such an example would be the W72-2 warhead, presently deployed on the USS Tennessee. W72-2 has a yield of 5–7kt,[8] or one-third that of the Hiroshima yield. Alternatively, "the B61-Mod 12 gravity bomb has a yield of up to 50Kt, and it includes an operational option to select lower yields."[9] While the Treaty on the Prohibition of Nuclear Weapons (TPNW) has been in force since January 2021, none of the nuclear weapon States (NWS) have ratified or signed the agreement. So far, it seems that this status quo will remain unchanged for the foreseeable future.[10] Therefore, the Hague Regulations of 1907, Geneva Conventions of 1949, and Additional Protocols of 1977, as reflecting particularly the customary principles of LOAC applicable to all weapons used during armed conflict, would also apply to any use of nuclear weapons.[11]

[7] The US Doctrine for Joint Theater Nuclear Operations of 1996 recognizes five categories of nuclear yield: very low (less than 1kt), low (1kt to 10kt), medium (over 10 to 50), high (over 50 to 500), and very high (over 500kt). This is, however, not a recognized international standard for yield categorization. See US Air Force, *Doctrine for Joint Theater Nuclear Operations,* February 9, 1996, available at https://www.nukestrat.com/us/jcs/JCS_JP3-12-1_96.pdf.

[8] William M. Arkin and Hans M. Kristensen, "US Deploys New Low-Yield Nuclear Submarine Warhead" Federation of American Scientists, January 29, 2020 available at https://fas.org/blogs/security/2020/01/w76-2deployed/.

[9] Hans M. Kristensen and Matt Korda, "United States Nuclear Forces, 2020" *Bulletin of the Atomic Scientists* 76, no. 1 (2020): 46–60. https://doi.org/10.1080/00963402.2019.1701286.

[10] The Treaty on the Prohibition of Nuclear Weapons (TPNW) entered in force on January 22, 2021. However, the treaty is binding only for States which have ratified the document. None of the five major nuclear States or States under the nuclear umbrella have ratified or even signed the treaty as of April 2022. See the number of signatories and ratifications, accessed September, 2024, https://www.icanw.org/signature_and_ratification_status.

[11] The UK and France made statements during the Diplomatic Conferences to negotiate the API that the rules of the protocol do not apply to nuclear weapons. UK Ministry of Defense, *The Manual of the Law of Armed Conflict* (Oxford: Oxford University Press, 2004), 117. This, however, does not matter since SIrUS as explained above is a customary rule of LOAC.

Setting aside the other fundamental principles of *jus in bello, that is*, the law applicable during armed conflict, to examine the medicalization of SIrUS, it is first vital to explore the health effects of a nuclear explosion that would affect combatants.

4.2.1 Hiroshima and Nagasaki (1945)

A nuclear explosion differs from a conventional one in how it releases energy. Whereas conventional explosives generally use a chemical reaction, a nuclear explosion releases energy through either nuclear fission or fusion.[12] In nuclear fission, atoms of fissile material—uranium or plutonium (U^{235} or Pu^{239})—are hit and split by fast-moving neutrons. This process produces fission fragments in an excited state and neutrons that hit and split further atoms. The process is known as an "explosive chain reaction," and it is accompanied by a release of energy.[497] Released energy is distributed unevenly between thermal radiation, shockwave, and ionizing radiation. These effects interact in a complex manner. Although shockwave and thermal radiation (i.e., blast and heat) are not specific to nuclear weapons, thermal radiation acts differently from the heat generated by a conventional explosion.[13] The difference is in a nuclear explosion's production of infrared rays.[14] Depending on one's distance from the hypocenter, shielding and bright-colored clothing can significantly reduce the burns caused by thermal radiation. The worst effects of the Hiroshima and Nagasaki bombings impacted victims who were in the proximity of the explosion, facing toward the hypocenter and wearing simple Japanese clothes.[15] Generally speaking, thermal injuries are not specific to nuclear

[12] Nuclear fusion is required in thermonuclear reactions, that is, hydrogen bombs. However, fusion is initiated by nuclear fission. Therefore, the hydrogen bomb is a two-stage device containing a lower yield fission bomb to initiate fusion reaction through massive energy release. Richard Rhodes, *Dark Sun: The Making of the Hydrogen Bomb* (New York: Simon & Schuster, 2005), 253–254.

[13] Including near-ultraviolet ray, visible ray, and infrared rays. Committee for the Compilation of Materials on Damage Caused by the Atomic Bombs in Hiroshima and Nagasaki, *Hiroshima and Nagasaki: The Physical, Medical and Social Effects of the Atomic Bombings* (Tokyo: Iwanami Shoten, 1981), 30–36.

[14] Committee for Compilation, 30–36.

[15] Los Alamos Scientific Laboratory and Norris E. Bradbury, *The Effects of Atomic Weapons* (Whitefish, MT: Literary Licensing, 2013), 204.

weapons. Incendiary weapons such as napalm, magnesium-based bombs, or white phosphorus can cause widespread fires that produce severe and often fatal burns.[16] Moreover, it is difficult to extinguish a fire caused by such incendiaries.

The Tokyo bombardment by incendiary bombs in March 1945 resulted in a death toll ranging from 87,793 to 124,711.407 people. Many incendiary weapons are still in the arsenal of some States. Although there is, and should be, a general reluctance to use these weapons, they remain legal to use, providing that specific precautionary measures and regulations are met.[17]

The Japanese scientists delved into the studies of the effects of a nuclear explosion practically immediately after the bombings of Hiroshima and Nagasaki. However, it was not until 1947 that President Truman gave the order to establish the Atomic Bomb Casualty Commission (ABCC) in Hiroshima.[18] The ABCC's objective was to study the acute and long-term health effects of a nuclear explosion, especially those of ionizing radiation, and thereby to improve defenses against a nuclear attack and to provide proper treatment to any possible future victims.[19] The purpose of the ABCC was not to provide medical treatment to the victims of the Hiroshima and Nagasaki bombings. This was one of the reasons why many Japanese residents initially distrusted and criticized the Commission. In March 1975, the ABCC dissolved and transformed into the Radiation Effects Research Foundation (RERF). RERF is a joint US-Japanese organization with research centers in both Hiroshima and Nagasaki.[20]

The Hiroshima and Nagasaki bombings certainly provide tragic, however, indispensable case studies for the LOAC analysis of nuclear weapons. Nevertheless, it is imperative to remember the very different social, economic, and medical circumstances in 1945 from modern times. Most of

[16] See Katsumoto Saotome, *Tokyo Daikuushuu: Showa Nijyuunen Sangatsu Tooka no Kiroku* [The Great Tokyo Air Raid: A Memory of March 10, 1945] (Tokyo: Iwanami-Shinsho, 2015).

[17] Ben Saul and Dapo Akande, eds. *The Oxford Guide to International Humanitarian Law* (Oxford: Oxford University Press, 2020), 267.

[18] William J. Schull, *Effects of Atomic Radiation: A Half-Century of Studies from Hiroshima and Nagasaki* (New York: Wiley-Liss, 1995), 19.

[19] See RERF, "Historical Materials" accessed April 14, 2022. https://www.rerf.or.jp/en/about/history_e/.

[20] See RERF, "About RERF" accessed April 14, 2022. https://www.rerf.or.jp/en/about/establish_e/.

the houses were wooden, making them easily combustible. The lack of medicine and the prevalence of general malnutrition among the populace further contributed to an increased number of fatalities. According to Bradbury (Los Alamos, 2013), countermeasures in the form of relatively light shielding or a certain positioning of the body can substantially reduce the injuries sustained by shockwave and heat.[21] Modern medicine can treat many injuries sustained from blasts and heat. In the 1946 Report of the British Mission to Japan, the United Kingdom argued that, due to differences in buildings and urban environments, the same Hiroshima and Nagasaki-type bombs would cause a lower—albeit still very significant—number of casualties. For the UK, instant casualties were estimated at 50,000, as compared to 15 by V2 rockets.[22] More importantly, the report stated that: "The problem of providing against and of treating gamma ray casualties in particular is exceptionally grave and difficult."[23] In sum, countermeasures against highly penetrative ionizing radiation are difficult to enact, and the effects complicate the healing of any wounds sustained from the explosion's blast and heat. The UK thus recognized the "exceptionally grave" effects of ionizing radiation which are in no way secondary.

A nuclear explosion generates ionizing radiation consisting of gamma rays, neutrons, alpha particles, and beta particles. Because of their short range, alpha particles do not pose a significant hazard in an air burst. Not many fission products release beta particles; depending on the material they hit, these particles do not travel far.[24] The simple shielding provided by a wooden house, for instance, serves as sufficient protection. Also, alpha particles are not highly penetrative; proper clothing offers further protection. Therefore, gamma rays and neutrons cause the most damage, especially in the first moments of the explosion.[25] The radiation from a nuclear explosion is divided between the initial release, which occurs within the first minute, and a residual release 1 minute after the explosion.[26]

Residual radiation is induced by scattered neutrons that hit atoms in certain materials in buildings or soil. It also includes fission products and fissile material that did not undergo fission, rose into the air with the

[21] Los Alamos Lab and Bradbury, 200–201.

[22] *The Effects of the Atomic Bombs at Hiroshima and Nagasaki: Report of the British Mission to Japan*, (London: His Majesty's Stationery Office, 1946), para. 87.

[23] *Report of the British Mission*, para. 88.

[24] Los Alamos Lab and Bradbury, 220.

[25] Los Alamos Lab and Bradbury, 220.

[26] Los Alamos Lab and Bradbury, 248.

fireball, and descended in the fallout.[27] The fission itself results in approximately 60 atomic fragments representing 34 different isotopic elements that are also undergoing decay and are, therefore, radioactive.[28] However, these are scattered across a relatively wide area during an airburst, and they undergo decay relatively fast.[29] Regardless, tens of thousands of inhabitants of Hiroshima and Nagasaki suffered radiation poisoning.

The Committee for the Compilation of Materials on Damage Caused by the Atomic Bombs in Hiroshima and Nagasaki identified four stages of exposure, which were included in the Report of Investigation of Atom Bomb Casualties that both cities sent to the UN in 1976.[30] Stage I, the early or initial stage, ranges from the moment of the explosion to the end of the second week. During this period, thermal radiation, burns, and the blast caused most of the fatalities. Stage II, the intermittent stage, ranges from the third to the eighth week after the explosion. This period is the demarcation between the acute and recovery phases, in which survivors show signs of recuperation. Stage III, the late stage, ranges from the third to the end of the fourth month after the explosion—until December 1945. In most cases, this period was characterized by recovery. Stage IV includes delayed effects, which appeared after five months. The designation of the temporal stages differs from the terms the author used in Chap. 3. This is because the Committee focused specifically on atomic bombs and ionizing radiation. In contrast, the author discussed all weapons and their general effects. In this context, Stages I–III can be understood to contain delayed effects, while Stage IV marks the beginning of long-term health effects. Overall, by the end of December 1945 (i.e., by the end of the delayed effects stage), approximately 140,000 of 327,457 lives in Hiroshima and 70,000 of 286,702 in Nagasaki were lost.[31]

As for the delayed effects of acute radiation poisoning, the Japanese Army medical school observed and classified radiation injuries into three chronological stages: Stage I (August 6–17), Stage II (from August 18 to

[27] These materials rose into the air with the fireball and then fell back in a "fallout." The yield of Little Boy was approx. 15kt and contained around 60kg of U^{235}. One kg of fissile material produces approx. 20kt of energy release. Therefore, only a tiny portion of the material underwent fission. See Los Alamos Lab and Bradbury,13.

[28] Los Alamos Lab and Bradbury, 250.

[29] Los Alamos Lab and Bradbury, 220.

[30] Committee for Compilation, 113–114.

[31] Committee for Compilation, 348.

early September), and Stage III (from early to late September).[32] From a medical standpoint, Stage I was characterized by high doses of radiation that resulted in vomiting; diarrhea; nausea; hemorrhaging from the mouth, rectum or urethra; convulsions; delirium with epilation; purpura;[33] and death, which permeated all three chronological stages.[34] The three primary symptoms of acute, high doses of radiation illness—whose onset was delayed after the explosion— were epilation, purpura, and oropharyngeal lesions; the incidence of these symptoms was the highest within one kilometer or 0.6 miles of the hypocenter.[35]

It is challenging to determine how many fatal cases occurred as a result of acute radiation illness until the end of December 1945. A lack of medicine, poor nutrition, and infections inhibited the recovery of fatal cases during a period terminating 40 days after the bombing—this period accounted for 10% of all fatalities.[36] Regarding secondary radiation, during the first hour after the explosion, staying near the hypocenter for five hours would result in a dose of approximately 0.2Gy. The next day, people who stayed for eight hours received half of this dose, or 0.1 Gy.[37] As explained above, the observable dose-effect threshold is 1 Gy, with LD_{90} ranging from 7–10 Gy. For a non-shielded dose, Young and Kerr (2005) estimate that people at a distance of approximately one kilometer from the hypocenter would receive a total dose (gamma rays and neutrons) of around 6.82 Gy, while those finding themselves at a distance of 1.5 kilometers would receive a total dose of around 0.617 Gy.[38]

[32] Committee for Compilation, 130.

[33] "Any of a group of disorders characterized by purplish or reddish-brown areas or spots of discoloration, caused by bleeding within skin or mucous membranes. Purpura also refers to the discolored areas themselves. There are many different types and causes of purpura. Common (senile) purpura mostly affects middle-aged or elderly women. Large discolored areas, caused by thinning of the tissues supporting blood vessels under the skin, appear on the thighs or the back of the hands and forearms. Purpura can also occur as a result of thrombocytopenia. In addition, it can be associated with septicemia." British Medical Association, *Illustrated Medical Dictionary*, 1st ed., (London: Dorling Kindersley, 2002), 473.

[34] Committee for Compilation, 130–131.

[35] Committee for Compilation, 136

[36] Committee for Compilation, 146.

[37] Committee for Compilation, 149.

[38] Robert W. Young and Geroge D. Kerr, *Reassessment of the Atomic Bomb Radiation Dosimetry for Hiroshima and Nagasaki. Dosimetry System 2002. DS02. Volume 1* (Hiroshima: RERF, 2005).

Schull (1995) has observed that, according to the estimates of The Joint Commission for the Investigation of the Effects of the Atomic Bombing in Japan, more than half of all casualties succumbed to burns.[39] Thirty percent to ionizing radiation and 18% were attributed to the blast or shockwave. In the years following the bombings, information gathered on the survivors included their location, shielding, and activity after the explosions. This information and the development of dosimetry allowed for more precise and reliable data. One important fact to point out is that the Joint Commission presented radiation as the bombs' second main injurious effect. Therefore, yet again, the argument that radiation is a secondary effect of atomic bombs (with the primary effects being heat and shockwave) and that it should not be considered under the design-purpose interpretation of SIrUS—as proclaimed by the United States and others—is not supported by scientific evidence.[40] In reality, radiation is one of the major lethal effects of nuclear weapons. By its nature, it is in no way secondary.

The RERF divides the energy output of the Hiroshima bomb as follows: 50% blast, 35% heatwave, and 15% radiation.[41] The readers should not confuse this with the information in the above paragraph, which discusses the percentage of casualties, not the energy output. The intense heat and high doses of radiation instantly killed people within 500m of the hypocenter. As described above, those who survived would develop delayed radiation symptoms depending on the absorbed dose. $LD_{50/60}$ was calculated at distances around 1000–1200m with a dose of about 2.9.–3.3 Gy.[42] Doses of 4–6 Gy represent $LD_{95/60}$, clearly offering an unlikely chance of survival.[43] The threshold dose, which marks observable effects, was therefore set at approximately 1 Gy.

For this reason, the RERF focuses predominantly on studying the delayed effects of ionizing radiation. The Foundation confirms Schull's (1995) observation that late radiation effects are rarely specific to

[39] Schull, 12.

[40] Letter dated 20 June 1995 from the Acting Legal Adviser to the Department of State, together with Written Comments of the Government of the United States of America - 20 June 1995, 24.

[41] RERF, 2016, 2.

[42] RERF, 2016, 4. The term LD50 stands for Lethal Dose for 50% of the population. See Gupta, 115.

[43] Schull, 126.

radiation.[44] As clarified above, it is difficult to distinguish whether a malignant tumor originates from a person's physical predisposition, lifestyle, or exposure to ionizing radiation. After conducting numerous surveys and collecting the data of survivors in the 1950s, the RERF established its Life Span Study (LSS) in 1955.[45] The cohort consists of four groups. Group 1 includes people exposed within 2000m, and Group 2 includes those exposed between 2000 and 2499m. Group 3 contains those exposed between 2500 and 9999m, and finally, Group 4 contains those exposed beyond 10km; these are, therefore, regarded to have been outside the Hiroshima city.[46] This last group also included those who entered the city within 30 days of the bombing. Concerning the dose-response analysis, the LSS included only people who had a known initial dose of radiation since the LSS was set up by the RERF nearly ten years after the bombings. Therefore, it was practically impossible to acquire data on individuals' locations and the duration of their stays throughout Hiroshima. As explained above, however, the doses of residual radiation were almost negligible. Measurements of residual radiation began almost immediately after the explosions, and they continued until November 1945. In other words, data were obtained before global contamination by atmospheric nuclear testing.[47] The estimate of the maximum dose received through residual radiation ranges from 10 to 100 mGy.[48] Threshold doses of about 1 to 4 Gy show a clear radiation-dose response. However, obtaining the same dose-response data is incredibly challenging for doses around 10–100mGy.

According to RERF (2016), there is no scientific data basis for concluding that internal exposure is more dangerous than external exposure. Internal exposure refers, for instance, to swallowing radioactive particles in dust, smoke, or rain. Both internal and external exposure contribute to the development of cancer. Even so, the location of the radioactive particle in the body is important insofar as it reflects the different responses of internal organs to radioactive particles.[49]

Among the most significant long-term health effects of radiation exposure is an increased risk of leukemia. Of this cancer's four

[44] Schull, 162–167.
[45] For detailed description of these studies see Schull, *Effects*.
[46] RERF, *A Brief Description* (Hiroshima: RERF, 2016), 5.
[47] RERF, *A Brief Description*, 13.
[48] RERF, *A Brief Description*, 20.
[49] RERF, *A Brief Description*, 4.

subtypes— "acute myelogenous leukemia, acute lymphatic leukemia, chronic myelogenous leukemia, and chronic lymphatic leukemia—all were detected in survivors."[50] The risk of developing leukemia began about two years after the bombings and reached its peak 7–8 years after radiation exposure.[51] The risk never disappears entirely, however. For survivors, the threat of the disease is permanent. This is especially true among those exposed to radiation before adulthood. The Relative Risk (RR) for leukemia at 1Gy is exceptionally high; it measures 4.92, or almost five times higher than it is among those not exposed to 1Gy, followed by the RR of 2.00 and 2.02 for breast and bladder cancers, respectively.[52]

The RR for solid cancers at 1Gy is calculated at 1.29, meaning the cancer incidence is more than 1 times higher than it is among unexposed. According to a RERF study, the Excess Relative Risk for 1Gy is "more significant for leukemia, while the estimated excess number of cases is higher for solid cancers."[53] That is, "within the cohort, solid cancers constitute a more considerable impact of radiation than leukemia."[54] Although leukemia is "strongly associated with radiation, it is less common than solid cancers."[55]

The risk is higher among those exposed in early childhood, suggesting continued risk throughout life.[56] Overall, however, the so-called F1 study of the second-generation survivors is inconclusive.[57] It does not present evidence of an increased risk for the children of atomic bomb survivors; they do not seem to suffer genetic effects.[58] However, the fact that the second generation does not suffer effects at the moment does not mean the risk is not present. Many of the second generation of hibakusha are

[50] RERF, *A Brief Description*, 19–20.

[51] Itsuzo Shigematsu, Mitoshi Akiyama, Hideo Sasaki, Chikato Ito, and Nanao Kamada, eds. *Genbaku hoshasen no jintai eikyo* [Effects of A-bomb radiation on the human body] (Tokyo: Bunkodo, 1995), 45–50.

[52] Y. Shimizu, H. Kato, and William J. Schull. "Studies of the Mortality of A-bomb Survivors. 9. Mortality, 1950–1985: Part 2. Cancer Mortality Based on the Recently Revised Doses (DS86)." *Radiation Research* 121, no. 2 (1990): 120–141.

[53] See RERF, *A Brief Description*. Excess Relative Risk, or ERR, refers to the difference between the observed relative risk and 1, the value expected without an effect. Schull, 134.

[54] RERF, *A Brief Description*.

[55] RERF, *A Brief Description*, 23.

[56] RERF, *A Brief Description*, 25.

[57] See RERF, "Children of Atomic Bomb Survivors (F1) Study" accessed April 14, 2022, https://www.rerf.or.jp/en/programs/research_activities_e/outline_e/progf1-en/.

[58] RERF, *A Brief Description*, 37.

now reaching the age where many of the diseases described above appear. Notwithstanding, constant anxiety and fear are prevalent regarding health conditions among the second-generation hibakusha.

Regarding atomic veterans, while the United States adopted the Radiation Exposure Compensation Act (RECA), the United Kingdom lacks such legislation with direct compensation programs and attribution of medical benefits. In 2021, the UK was still the only Western nuclear-testing country that did not officially recognize its nuclear veterans.[59] Medical research has proven that the United Kingdom's atomic veterans suffer from long-term health effects related to their exposure to significant doses of ionizing radiation as a result of nuclear tests, including tests of hydrogen bombs.[60] Among these long-term health effects are an increased risk of leukemia, which peaks 2–3 years after exposure, and a risk of solid cancer, which increases ten years after exposure. Such risks also adversely affect nuclear veterans' children. Among these atomic test veterans, still-births and miscarriages are at high levels of (29.2%) within their respective communities.[61] On average, 90% experience at least one health condition attributable to exposure, with 61.6% constantly taking medication.[62]

4.3 Antipersonnel Landmines

Mines can be defined as explosives designed to maim rather than kill.[63] Anti-personnel landmines (APLs) are usually small explosive devices concealed under the ground so that victims will step on them and trigger the

[59] See Chris Wood, "Nuclear Test Veterans: 'My Dad Was Treated Like a Guinea Pig" BBC, May 30, 2021 available at https://www.bbc.com/news/uk-wales-57157476.

[60] Susie Boniface, "Nuclear Heroes Betrayed by Ministry of Defence Pen-Pushers Over Medals." *Mirror*, December 10, 2020 available at https://www.mirror.co.uk/news/uk-news/nuclear-heroes-betrayed-pen-pushers-23149346?fbclid=IwAR2bVUGg_Et6Rh9qRWtrj2Z36awq1Vbpzvf4nZ7PFEdGLZYM8UYwIsDdx8g.

[61] Alan Owen, "Global Health Survey 2020" LABRATS International Health Survey 2020 available at https://www.labrats.international/healthsurvey, 34.

[62] Owen, 34.

[63] UN Institute for Disarmament Research, *European Action on Small Arms and Light Weapons and Explosive Remnants of War: Final Report*, (Geneva: UNIDIR, 2006) available at https://unidir.org/publication/european-action-small-arms-and-light-weapons-and-explosive-remnants-war-final-report.

explosion.[64] Mines are of two basic categories: antipersonnel and antivehicle. The latter are used against tanks or other armored vehicles.[65] Antivehicle mines require a heavier pressure weight, usually 100–300kg, to trigger the explosion; consequently, they are rarely triggered by a single person.[66] Their intended use is against platforms (i.e., vehicles) rather than humans. Mines designed for use against combatants are defined in the Ottawa Convention[67] as follows:

> Anti-personnel mine means a mine designed to be exploded by the presence, proximity or contact of a person and that will incapacitate, injure or kill one or more persons. Mines designed to be detonated by the presence, proximity or contact of a Vehicle as opposed to a person, that are equipped with anti-handling devices, are not considered anti-personnel mines as a result of being so equipped.[68]

Anti-tank mines that are misplaced or placed inappropriately may accidentally affect noncombatants in civilian vehicles. Such unintentional effects are, however, a question of distinction and precautions. In terms of injuries to combatants, the subsequent explosion would not differ significantly from that of any other conventional explosive, such as a rocket-propelled grenade. Nevertheless, a contentious issue lies in the use of APLs against combatants and whether such use violates the prohibition of unnecessary suffering by causing needless damage to human health. APLs are used as area-denial weapons and, as such, are still in the armory of a number of States. This is because their function as area-deniers is difficult to substitute with other area-denial weapons.

Nevertheless, it is pertinent to explore the issue of landmines through the lens of unnecessary suffering because this principle was raised during

[64] "Mine means a munition designed to be placed under, on or near the ground or other surface area and to be exploded by the presence, proximity or contact of a person or a vehicle." The Ottawa Convention, Art.2, (2).

[65] The Ottawa Convention, Art.2, (2).

[66] See ICRC, *Anti-Personnel Landmines: Friend or Foe? A Study of the Military Use and Effectiveness of Anti-Personnel Mines.* (Geneva: ICRC, 1996) available at https://www.icrc.org/en/publication/0654-anti-personnel-landmines-friend-or-foe-study-military-use-and-effectiveness-anti, 10.

[67] Convention on the Prohibition of the Use, Stockpiling, Production and Transfer of Anti-Personnel Mines and on their Destruction (concluded 18 September 1997, entered into force 1 March 1999) 2056 UNTS 211 (Ottawa Convention).

[68] Ottawa Convention, Art.2(1).

the campaign to ban such means of warfare.[69] Under the Ottawa Treaty, the ICRC specifically raised the incompatibility of APLs with the legal norm prohibiting superfluous injury caused by landmines. However, many States that possess anti-personal landmines do not share such a view due to the utility of APLs. The lack of a clear definition of unnecessary suffering "reinforced the logic of military necessity, which led to the unchecked proliferation and use of conventional weapons, especially landmines."[70] Therefore, the case of APLs again shows the necessity to define unnecessary suffering and provide for yet a more precise litmus test.

The blast causes injuries from anti-personnel landmines and includes fragments—pieces of the mine, such as metal or plastic, which cause additional mechanical injuries to the victim.[71] When triggered by an adult, APLs are not always lethal, but they often cause lifelong injuries. Victims may die from the blast due to a sudden loss of blood; survivors usually suffer amputation.[72] A special type of landmine called a bounding fragmentation mine explodes and fragments at waist height, causing severe injuries to the abdomen.[73] Indeed, if placed with care and properly marked, the military later collects these landmines. As mentioned above, APLs serve their purpose as area deniers, for example, when placed around a military base with a proper warning sign. However, with the urbanization of conflict or the use of mines in areas with dense foliage, these weapons' subsequent collection might become difficult. This difficulty has been proven during conflicts in Southeast Asia and the ongoing conflict between the Russian war against Ukraine. Arguably, Russian commanders gave little care when deploying these weapons. An incident that occurred during the conflict between Ukraine and Russia involved the use of PFM-1 anti-personnel landmines.[74] The Russian military air-dropped this type of land-

[69] Louis Maresca and Stuart Maslen, *The Banning of Anti-Personnel Landmines: The Legal Contribution of the International Committee of the Red Cross* (Cambridge: Cambridge University Press, 2000), 569.

[70] Maresca and Maslen, 583.

[71] Maresca and Maslen, 261.

[72] See International Campaign to Ban Landmines, "What is a Landmine?" accessed April 29, 2022. http://www.icbl.org/en-gb/problem/what-is-a-landmine.aspx.

[73] Maresca and Maslen, 261.

[74] See David Hambling, "Russia Accused of Using Air-Dropped Butterfly Mines to Block Ukrainian Evacuation Route" *Forbes,* last accessed March 10, 2022, https://www.forbes.com/sites/davidhambling/2022/03/10/russia-reportedly-blocks-ukrainian-evacuation-route-with-air-dropped-butterfly-mines/?sh=165e514a1a32.

mine by airplane without marking their location. These types are difficult to detect and are often mistaken by children for toys. On the subject of landmines, and particularly the use of PFM-1, a statement by the explosives and ammunition expert Maj. Wilson of the Canadian Armed Forces deserves to be quoted in full:

> These are particularly nasty due to their ease of deployment either through artillery or aerial munitions. This means that there can be lots of them in an area. Because these are deployed at a distance and without precision, no one is at the location to properly mark the hazard area. Plus, with the low metal content, they are highly difficult to clear. All this together means an almost certain probability of civilian casualties over many years, including post-conflict. Using such a weapon indicates a lack of concern for non-participants [in hostilities]. Out of all the anti-personnel landmines out there, these are among the worst.[75]

This statement is important to the legal analysis of weapons for several reasons. First, the use of mines must be subject to certain conditions, such as placement markers, subsequent cleanup by the military, and restrictions on places without noncombatants. In other words, the issue behind landmines is, according to the expert quoted above, an issue of distinction, not of unnecessary suffering. There are voices, particularly among the military, defending their use and acknowledging their effectiveness in particular situations. To understand such voices, it is important to keep in mind that only if properly marked on a map, and adequately recorded for post-conflict remediation can these weapons serve their purpose without indiscriminately affecting non-combatants:

> Anti-personnel landmines serve basically as a barrier. There are three tasks for a barrier: to encourage the enemy to move to a place marked as a kill zone (KZ) - a KZ is a technical term to denote an area where you have sited interlocking weapons. The second task is to make them [the enemy] do something you want them to do. Task number three: you can slow the enemy down in a KZ.[76]

[75] Online interview by the researcher with a military professional and an explosives and ammunition expert, Maj. Andrew Wilson of the Canadian Armed Forces. March 07, 2022

[76] Ibid.

The most notorious case of landmine use comes from Southeast Asia. Cambodia spiraled into a non-international armed conflict (NIAC) or "civil war" from 1970–1975.[77] This conflict was characterized by a massive deployment of APLs that continues to haunt Cambodians to this day due to the weapons' inconsiderate and often unlawful placement.[78] Cambodia is one of the countries that has been most affected by landmines. The Cambodian Mine Action and Victim Assistance Authority estimates that, during the period from 1979–2022, there were about 64,984 victims of mines, including 51,157 casualties, 36,098 wounded, and 9073 amputees.[79] Around 4% of blindness cases in Cambodia are caused by ocular trauma due to landmines.[80] An ICRC study included in the final document of the SIrUS Project confirms the observation that the injuries caused by landmines put tremendous constraints on medical and surgical supplies, especially blood banks.[81] The ICRC study confirms predictable disability from three different patterns of injury. Pattern 1 results from standing on a buried mine, and Pattern 2 results from a fragment of a nearby mine explosion; this has a lower chance of amputation but a higher possibility of injuries to the neck or chest due to flying fragments. Finally, Pattern 3 injuries result from handling the mine; these include injuries to the face, eyes, and neck.[82]

Direct effects of a mine in Pattern 1 usually require significant blood donations, multiple visits to the surgical table, and a complex operation that includes surgeries to save even the leg that was not in direct contact

[77] Charles Phillips, and Alan Axelrod, eds, *Encyclopedia of Wars.* (New York: Zenda, Inc, 2005), 277–279.

[78] See Cambodian Self-Help Demining, "About CSHD" accessed April 14, 2022, https://www.cambodianselfhelpdemining.org/about/.

[79] Cambodian Mine Action and Victim Assistance Authority, "Monthly Report."

[80] Heather Jackson, "Severe Ocular Trauma due to Landmines and Other Weapons in Cambodia" *Community Eye Health Journal* 10, no. 23 (1997): 37–39. https://www.cehjournal.org/article/severe-ocular-trauma-due-to-landmines-and-other-weapons-in-cambodia/.

[81] Robin M. Coupland, ed., *The SIrUS Project: Towards a Determination of Which Weapons Cause "Superfluous Injury or Unnecessary Suffering."* (Geneva: ICRC, 1997), 24, available at *https://www.loc.gov/collections/military-legal-resources/?q=RC_SIrUS-project.html.*

[82] Robin M. Coupland and Adriaan Korver, "Injuries From Antipersonnel Mines: The Experience of the International Committee of the Red Cross." *British Medical Journal* 303, no. 6816 (1991): 1509–1512. https://doi.org/10.1136/bmj.303.6816.1509.

with the APL.[83] As for the second pattern—indirect injuries from a landmine that detonates nearby—the wounds that it causes can be referred to as fragmentation injuries. Usually, these more extensive, irregularly shaped wounds require several operations to remove fragments, and they entail the danger of massive bleeding.[84] Pattern 3 usually occurs when demining professionals try to handle or defuse a mine. Their facial areas are in proximity to the weapon, resulting in injuries to the eyes and face, often including the danger of losing an upper limb.

Therefore, Patterns 1 and 3 result from direct contact with the mine, while Pattern 2 results from indirect contact. This means that the ICRC observes a violation of the principle of unnecessary suffering above all in Pattern 1; it perceives this violation not merely because of the danger involved with amputation but also due to the surgical difficulties that result from other objects such as dust, fragments, and stones, all of which are propelled upwards to wound the legs and extremities. As pointed out by Maresca and Maslen (2000):

> The surgical task is to cut away all the dead and severely damaged tissue and remove the debris and dirt. In principle it is easy, in practice not so. In the case of a traumatically amputated limb the blast pushes debris far up into the leg, which necessitates a higher amputation than is apparent to the inexperienced surgeon or untutored observer. Unwise attempts to preserve tissue and poor techniques of amputation result in much unnecessary suffering with multiple operations and poor stumps for the fitting of prostheses. Without physiotherapy and provision of a functional prosthesis a lower-limb amputee is sentenced to permanent in-capacity and loss of the potential to be independent and self-supporting in society. Double lower-limb amputees are usually confined to wheelchairs, if available; otherwise many become beggars.[85]

In addition to suffering a traumatic amputation of a foot or leg, the victims of a Pattern 1 injury—if they survive—have "a high chance of contralateral upper and lower limb injury as well as a lower chance of genital and central injuries."[86] The observation that Pattern 1 injuries are the

[83] Thomas E. Bowen, ed. *Emergency War Surgery*. Collingdale, PA: Diane Publishing Co., 2005.

[84] Bowen, 1.4.

[85] Maresca and Maslen, 261.

[86] Coupland and Korver.

most severe is confirmed by the fact that they are "the greatest drain on surgical and transfusion resources."[87] ICRC hospitals observe that "of all patients, those with limb injuries resulting from mines require the most blood."[88]

Landmines are, therefore, the prime example of instantaneous injuries. While effects might include life-long amputation, these shall be distinguished from the long-term effects discussed in relation to nuclear weapons. While amputations undoubtedly impact a victim's quality of life, the injury is often immediate and confined to a specific moment in time, keeping in mind that we are considering combatants, not civilians since the norm against SIrUS does not apply to them. However, the long-term injuries addressed in this book present a more insidious reality. These injuries arise from weapons whose effects continue to inflict damage long after their initial use, actively deteriorating the victim's health over their entire lifespan. Unlike instantaneous injuries, these lingering effects make recovery elusive and pose a continuous burden on the physical and psychological well-being of the victims, as if the weapon is still being used against them.

4.4 Incendiaries

Fire and poison have always incited panic and repulsion in people's minds. Germany, or the German Empire at that time, first used flamethrowers on the battlefield of Verdun in 1915, triggering horror among enemy troops.[89] Countless explosives cause burns and trigger fires as secondary effects to a blast. This is especially true of antivehicle weapons.[90] Incendiary weapons, however, differ from these. Incendiaries are designed to burn as a primary effect—that is, they are "substances which oxidize with a powerful exothermic effect."[91] Various oil and magnesium-based explosives, such as those used during the bombardment of Tokyo in March 1945,[92] belong to this category of weapons. One such example is the E-46 bomb, which consists of several small incendiary tubes filled with oil and other highly

[87] Coupland and Korver.

[88] Coupland and Korver, 149.

[89] Robert M. Neer, *Napalm: An American Biography*. (Cambridge: Belknap Press of Harvard University Press, 2013), 23.

[90] Bowen, 9.

[91] SIPRI, *A Monograph: Incendiary Weapons* (Cambridge, MA: MIT Press, 1975), 87.

[92] M-17, M-69, M-19. Katsumoto Saotome, *Toukyo Daikuushuu: Zusetu* [Great Tokyo Air Raid: Illustrated] (Tokyo: Kawade Shobo Shinsha, 2015), 94.

flammable materials. The most used incendiary during the bombardment of Tokyo was the AN-M69 oil incendiary contained in the E-46 bundle.[93] Around 325 combat airplanes deployed incendiaries. Official records show 87,793 deaths and 40,918 injuries, meaning about 18% of Tokyo's industrial district and almost two-thirds of its commercial district were destroyed.[94] The most notorious incendiary weapon is napalm, which gained infamy in the course of the Korean War (1950–1953) and the Vietnam War (1956–1975). The iconic picture of a burned little girl, Kim Phuc, running away from an incinerated village created strong associations of incendiaries with brutality, inhumanity, and suffering. Mrs. Kim Phuc eventually became an activist against napalm and a peace advocate.[95]

Napalm and other incendiaries have been often used against supply dumps, troop concentrations, and vehicles.[96] By becoming more urbanized, modern warfare has changed the battlefield's terrain. Although incendiaries are restricted, and although the CCW has decreed that they may not be used in densely populated areas, they may be deployed—and they occasionally are deployed—against shielded combatants.[97] Therefore, it is vital to examine incendiaries and the injuries that they cause, particularly in the context of the shock and anger they generated in the world during the Vietnam War.

Louis Fieser invented napalm in 1942, and the weapon gained infamy with its extensive use in the course of the Vietnam War.[98] Attacks were usually conducted with low-flying planes, leaving victims with little time to escape. The first case of napalm use was already controversial, and the Americans tried to hide its deployment due to the controversy sprouting from the French use of napalm in Indochina.[99] The initial hiding and informational embargo concerning the use of napalm may hint at the US Army's realization that the weapon was capable of causing excessive and

[93] See Bryan R. Swopes, "9–10 March 1945: Operation Meetinghouse." This Day in Aviation, accessed March 9, 2022, https://www.thisdayinaviation.com/tag/an-m69-incendiary-bomblet/.

[94] Neer, 80.

[95] See www.kimfoundation.com for her projects and activities, accessed August 14, 2024.

[96] Neer, 57.

[97] The United States deployed napalm in 2003 during the operation Iraqi Freedom. Neer, 194.

[98] Neer, 124.

[99] See UQAM, Faculte des sciences humaines, "Napalm" La Guerre d'Indochine, 1945–1956. accessed April 14, 2022. https://indochine.uqam.ca/fr/le-dictionnaire/940-napalm.html.

abhorrent injuries, and its legal status could be ambiguous. In 1963, South Vietnamese planes increasingly began to deploy napalm; by the end of the year, such use was routine.[100] The US military increasingly considered napalm to be a regular, not particularly horrendous, weapon, even though the appearance of photos of burned civilians, especially children, caused horror among the civilian population in the United States. Therefore, the issue of napalm use appeared to be related to distinction rather than unnecessary suffering of combatants, and "by 1966, napalm was an integral part of the war effort. Fighter-bombers dropped around 4,500 tons per month in Indochina."[101] Overall, "about 388,000 tons of US napalm bombs fell on Indochina in the decade from 1963–1973, compared to 32,357 tons used on Korea in just over 3 years and 16,500 tons dropped on Japan in 1945."[102] According to Neer (2013), the United States found the psychological effect of napalm to be irreplaceable.[103]

The inherent human fear of fire and burning alive often incites dread and distress in the enemy. As the engagement in Vietnam intensified in 1965–1966, so did debates in the United States. Countless university movements inspired a nationwide crusade against DOW Chemicals, the manufacturer of napalm and the infamous defoliant known as Agent Orange.[104] Members of the Stanford Committee for Peace in Vietnam argued that international law prohibited war crimes and, as such, the indiscriminate use of napalm.[105] This, however, doesn't mean that napalm was perceived as inherently unlawful, breaching the norm against unnecessary suffering. As pointed out above, in fact, the issue was distinction. Although, it is debatable how much the public was and is aware that such norm even exists. News articles describing the incendiary effects helped to change the perspective of the public, which, apart from the students as mentioned above, had often considered napalm not as a particularly cruel weapon, but as a necessity of war. This opinion was reinforced by armed forces referring to military necessity and the advantages of napalm.[106]

[100] Neer, 110.
[101] Neer, 111.
[102] Neer, 233.
[103] Neer, 95.
[104] Neer, 114.
[105] Stanford Libraries, "Stanford Oral History Collections" accessed April 24, 2022, https://exhibits.stanford.edu/oral-history.
[106] Neer, 113.

In January 1967, the *Ramparts* magazine published 15 full-color photographs of burn victims, children, and busy hospitals.[107] These photographs and images, especially those of burned children, shocked the population, as the author of the article, William Pepper—the director of Mercy College Children Institute for Advanced Study and Research in New York—has described.[108] Pepper rejected the United States' claims of military necessity by stressing that causing such injuries to children put responsibility directly upon the US government. Although abhorrence to using napalm against noncombatants was particularly strong, even its use against combatants caused disgust and contempt; the public did not differentiate between combatants and noncombatants. The involvement of physicians and medical professionals in Vietnam played an important part in vilifying the weapon. As Mathur (2017) points out, testimonialization inculcates a sense of realism.[109] The pictures from *Ramparts* magazine were used in the February 1967 demonstrations, in which thousands of women's strike groups protested outside of the Pentagon.[110] Such calls could not go without a governmental response. Nevertheless, that response is a question of disarmament law. For the purpose of unnecessary suffering, it is important to understand that, due to public pressure during the Vietnam War, a shift of focus from military necessity to medicalization began to intensify.

As stated above, napalm is not a mere fire weapon. It is a substance that sticks to the surfaces it touches and burns relentlessly. In addition to being extremely difficult to extinguish, it is toxic. Drawing on multiple case studies from WWI to the Vietnam War, Lumsden offered medical insight into the specific health effects of incendiary weapons.[111] In his analysis, he referred to the medical aspect as a valid argument in the debate between military necessity and humanitarian priorities that would induce unnecessary suffering.[112] Medical characteristics thus began to be employed as an

[107] Neer, 126.

[108] Neer, 126.

[109] Ritu Mathur, *Red Cross Interventions in Weapons Control* (London: Lexington Books, 2017), 74.

[110] Mathur, 130.

[111] Malvern Lumsden held the position of senior peace researcher at Peace Research Institute Oslo (PRIO) between 1994–1997. His research work focused on the humanitarian aspects of antipersonnel weapons. See https://www.prio.org/people/5054, accessed August 14, 2024.

[112] SIPRI, *A Monograph: Incendiary Weapons*, 122.

essential point of any discussion about the legitimacy of incendiary weapons. Lumsden (SIPRI, A Monograph: Incendairy Weapons, 1975b) raised even the principle of combatants' unnecessary suffering vis-à-vis incendiaries and maintained that medical science should determine the principle. A 1975 Stockholm International Peace Research Institute (SIPRI) study on incendiaries by Lumsden provides yet another confirmation of the shift of focus toward the health issues of antipersonnel weapons in the late 1960s and 1970s. This shift was influenced by the extensive use of napalm and by civil society movements that publicized the horrible injuries that this weapon caused.[113]

Because napalm is essentially a fire weapon, its mortality rate is related to the degree of burns. This is also true of thermobaric bombs, for instance, in which the air is consumed by the fire, and the subsequent vacuum causes asphyxiation.[114] Napalm—and, for that matter, white phosphorus, which is pyrophoric (i.e., self-igniting)—is not an ordinary fire weapon. It typically uses a mixture of highly flammable compounds, including magnesium, gasoline, or oil. The vapor and smoke is toxic due to carbon monoxide and carbon dioxide production.[115] The burns it causes usually leave deep scars, and victims may develop keloids.[116] About 5% of those who recover from napalm injuries experience secondary effects related to carbon monoxide poisoning.[117] Such exposure to carbon monoxide may cause lasting effects in the form of brain damage and Parkinsonism.[118] Napalm's primary effects are burns, which are categorized into three degrees depending on the level of damage to the tissue. Deep third-degree burns are not exceptionally painful due to the destruction of nerves; the skin, however, grows more sensitive, and even daily changes of clothes become extremely painful. Lumsden (SIPRI, A Monograph: Incendairy

[113] SIPRI, *A Monograph: Incendiary Weapons,* 122.

[114] Gregory T. Guldner and Curtis Knight, *Napalm Toxicity*, Treasure Island, FL: StatPearls Publishing, 2021, accessed March 20, 2022, https://www.ncbi.nlm.nih.gov/books/NBK537127/#:~:text=Napalm%20burns%20result%20in%20severe,to%20napalm%20may%20be%20severe.

[115] Guldner and Knight.

[116] Guldner and Knight.

[117] ICRC, *Weapons That May Cause Unnecessary Suffering or Have Indiscriminate Effects: Report on the Work of Experts* (Geneva: ICRC, 1973), 63, available at https://www.loc.gov/item/2011525354/.

[118] See NHS, "Carbon Monoxide Poisoning" accessed April 10, 2019. https://www.nhs.uk/conditions/carbon-monoxide-poisoning/#:~:text=Prolonged%20exposure%20to%20carbon%20monoxide%20can%20cause%20memory%20problems%20and,tremors%2C%20stiffness%20and%20slow%20movement.

Weapons, 1975b) has compared these burns to "the act of tearing off the outer, insensitive layer of the skin from the inner, sensitive layer."[119] The second factor affecting the overall survival rate is, of course, the extent of burns. This factor affects the victim's overall suffering and mortality; fatalities often occur when burns exceed 60% of the body's surface area.[120] Often, first aid classes offer the rule of nines as a rudimentary estimate of burn extensity. According to this rule, the arms represent 9%, the legs 18%, the front 18%, the back 18%, and the head 9% of the body surface area and the palms can serve as an indicator in localized burns because a palm represents 1% of surface area in the so-called rule of nine.[121]

According to the Lumsden (SIPRI, A Monograph: Incendairy Weapons, 1975b) study, burns that cover 5% of the body are regarded as light; those that cover "more than 10%, or first- and second-degree burns that cover more than 30%, are regarded as severe," especially if they cover the face, hands, feet, and genitalia.[122] According to the ICRC study on weapons that may cause unnecessary suffering, burns that cover up to 40% of the body's surface leave the victim with a reasonable chance of survival.[123] The initial phase of a napalm burn wound is defined as the shock phase. This term refers to the hypovolemic shock caused by a reduction in the volume of blood.[124] This reduction may result in cardiac arrest. Burns may cause kidney damage due to decreased circulating blood volume that passes through the kidneys.[125] Similarly, white phosphorus may cause liver damage due to phosphorus absorption through the skin.[126]

The most important aspect of this discussion is the risk of potential long-term health effects. As mentioned above, incendiaries may cause pulmonary damage if victims inhale steam from fire, which has "a thermal capacity 4,000 times higher than that of normal air."[127] The casualty effects of napalm include heatstroke, pulmonary burns, carbon monoxide

[119] SIPRI, *A Monograph: Incendiary Weapons*, 128.

[120] ICRC, *Weapons That May*, 61.

[121] Czech Red Cross, "First Aid Course for Emergency Services," attended by the author. March 17–19, 2017. Prague [on-site], the Czech Republic.

[122] SIPRI, *A Monograph: Incendiary Weapons*, 129.

[123] ICRC, *Weapons That May*, 61.

[124] An abnormally low volume of blood. British Medical Association, 297.

[125] Guldner and Knight.

[126] Guldner and Knight.

[127] SIPRI, *A Monograph: Incendiary Weapons*, 142.

poisoning, oxygen starvation, and shock.[128] Two-thirds of napalm burn victims suffer a total burn area of up to 25% of the body's surface—that is, close to the most severe third-degree burns.[129] Further complications certainly include infections. Such as septicemia, where bacterial toxins are present directly in the blood[130] which is one of the main life-threatening complications. Medical treatment is therefore costly and difficult. Victims do not die immediately. They may live for hours, days, or weeks; "even a burn that causes a large area of damage to the skin does not have the immediate impact of a bullet wound."[131] This extended agony underscores the ethical imperative to reconsider the use of such weapons, as they inflict unnecessary and prolonged suffering beyond the immediate effects of warfare.

White phosphorous (WP) is particularly controversial within the category of incendiaries. WP is a compound used either as an illuminant or as camouflage. Mortars or shells can also deploy white phosphorus to produce smoke to provide cover, firebomb the enemy, or burn without killing.[132] Tanks and other armored vehicles or artillery, such as howitzers, deploy WP to constrain visibility.[133] WP was used effectively during the Allied campaign in Mosul, Iraq (2016–2017). The coalition forces deployed WP as a camouflage to support civilians fleeing the area.[134] As an illuminant, WP is deployed from planes to illuminate areas before an attack. In one case, WP was deployed during the Nagorno-Karabakh conflict.[135] A reconnaissance plane flying over a wooded area deployed WP to

[128] SIPRI, *A Monograph: Incendiary Weapons*, 152.

[129] SIPRI, *A Monograph: Incendiary Weapons*, 153.

[130] British Medical Association, 504–505.

[131] SIPRI, *A Monograph: Incendiary Weapons*, 185.

[132] U.S. Department of Health and Human Services, *Toxicological Profile for White Phosphorus* (Atlanta, GA: Agency for Toxic Substances and Disease Registry, 1997), 15.

[133] Timothy M. Laur and Steven L. Llanso, *Encyclopedia of Modern U.S. Military Weapons* (New York: The Army Times Publishing Company, 1995), 176–184.

[134] Alison Meuse, "U.S. – Led Coalition Has Used White Phosphorus In Fight For Mosul, General Says." *NPR*, accessed August 1, 2022, https://www.npr.org/sections/parallels/2017/06/13/532809626/u-s-led-coalition-has-used-white-phosphorous-in-fight-for-mosul-general-says#:~:text=Press-,White%20Phosphorus%20Used%20Against%20Islamic%20State%20In%20Mosul%2C%20Coalition%20General,to%20get%20civilians%20out%20safely.%22.

[135] Asbarez Staff, "Use of White Phosphorus Bombs by Azerbaijan Confirmed" *Asbarez*, accessed October 30, 2020. https://asbarez.com/use-of-white-phosphorous-bombs-by-azerbaijan-confirmed/.

increase visibility, causing severe injuries to refugees who were hiding in the forest below.[136] The Israeli military asserts that there are vital uses for WP and that it is not meant to be used against personnel.[137] Armed Forces often maintain that White Phosphorus is great for illumination, revealing the enemy, and subsequently neutralizing them with other weapons. While the author sees nothing particularly problematic with such use, deploying WP directly against personnel is despicable and unlawful. The military often employs the traditionalist view of design-purpose. Weapons that are not designed to be used against personnel cannot, by their nature, cause unnecessary suffering according to the military logic. Instead, it is because of their misuse that they cause excessive injuries. Hence, Art. 35(2) of Additional Protocol I (API) does not apply to misuses.

Massive ordnance air blasts (MOABs), or so-called thermobaric bombs or fuel-air bombs (FABs), remain in use even today.[138] MOABs are a controversial issue. First, it is quite challenging to define them as incendiary weapons because their primary effect is the production of massive shockwave. Nevertheless, their incendiary properties are not negligible.[139] The deployment of thermobaric bombs on contemporary battlefields is usually followed by a public outcry that mistakenly considers them to be unlawful. If thermobaric bombs should be regarded as incendiaries, however, then their use would not be prohibited under the CCW's Protocol III; instead, it would merely be restricted.[140] This legal framework is discussed in the following chapter. The military considers the use of thermobaric bombs to be particularly advantageous. As Maj. Wilson of the Canadian Armed Forces notes: "Shock waves are great against structures. The design of the munition is a tradeoff. There's less fragmentation damage. We complain about these being used against humans, but a regular high-explosive bomb

[136] Asbarez.

[137] *Yoav Hess et al v. Chief of Staff*, HCJ 4146/11, Supreme Court, 09 July 2013.

[138] See Marco Sassoli, Antoine Bouvier, Anne Quintin, and Julia Grignon "Afghanistan/US, 'Mother of All Bombs.' " *How Does Law Protect in War?* Geneva: ICRC, 2014 accessed April 14, 2022. https://casebook.icrc.org/case-study/afghanistanus-mother-all-bombs.

[139] See ICRC, *Weapons That May*, 40.

[140] Due to the primary thermal and blast effects of thermobaric munition, the author classifies these weapons as incendiaries. See Center For Arms Control and Non-Proliferation, "Fact Sheet: Russia's Use of Thermobaric Weapons in Ukraine" accessed March 1, 2022 https://armscontrolcenter.org/fact-sheet-russias-use-of-thermobaric-weapons-in-ukraine/.

against those same humans is similarly effective. Shock waves are bad for people too, but flying bits of metal are really, really bad."[141]

This perspective refers to the fact that conventional explosives cause fragmentation injuries, as explained in Chap. 3. Although MOABs' blasts and burns might shock the population, other explosives produce similar effects. Moreover, being dismembered by a flying fragment is no less traumatic and injurious to combatants than pulmonary damage through amplified shockwave. Therefore, it is challenging to argue that MOABs violate SIrUS, particularly when compared to other weapons with injuries produced through burns, such as napalm. Indeed, the 1973 ICRC and 1975 Lumsden studies helped to set the cornerstone for subsequent restrictions designed to spare civilian populations under the CCW and stir the discussion from the advantage offered by incendiaries to the horrendous long-term injuries such weapons cause.

4.5 Chemical Weapons

As defined by Art. II (1)(b) of the Chemical Weapons Convention of 1997, chemical weapons or CWs utilize the toxic properties of chemical compounds, including their precursors, to inflict damage on living organisms.[142] The primary effect of these weapons—be it suffocation, blisters, or paralysis of the central nervous system (CNS)—is usually instant. Unlike biological weapons, CWs have no incubation period.[143] Once they are deployed, control over their effects is limited and depends largely on weather conditions. This property distinguishes them from rockets or missiles, which can be targeted at specific military objectives and sometimes even controlled in midair by an attacker.[144]

Historically, as during the outbreak of WWI, gas weapons have rarely been lethal.[145] The exception is poison. It is important to remember that

[141] Interview with Maj. Andrew Wilson, Canadian Armed Forces, April 14, 2022 [online]

[142] Convention on the Prohibition of the Development, Production, Stockpiling and Use of Chemical Weapons and on their Destruction (opened for signature 13 January 1993, entered into force 29 April 1997) 1974 UNTS 45.

[143] See Joshua Lederberg, ed., *Biological Weapons: Limiting the Threat* (Cambridge, MA: MIT Press, 1999).

[144] See US Department of Defense, Missile Defense Agency, "The Ballistic Missile Defense System (BMDS)" accessed April 14, 2022 https://www.mda.mil/system/system.html.

[145] About 91,000 deaths are recorded as due to lethal gas. See James Patton, "Gas in the Great War." *Medicine in the First World War* accessed April 14, 2022. https://www.kumc.

not all CWs are designed to cause fatalities. The most commonly used gas in WWI was sulfur mustard, an irritant and a blister agent with a low mortality rate of about 2–3%.[146] Because Germany had the most developed chemical industry, it pioneered researching chemicals for use in war. Proponents of CWs, such as Fritz Haber, considered gas (aerosol or vapor) the ultimate weapon despite its high dependence on weather conditions and the rapid improvement of adversaries' antichemical defense capabilities.[147] With the outbreak of WWI, efforts to develop a reliable delivery system accelerated. The issue, however, was that the Hague Declaration of 1907—discussed in Chap. 2—explicitly prohibited the use of poison and poison only.[148] To circumvent this prohibition, gas advocates argued that these weapons were not of a poisonous character; poison was secondary to the primary explosive effect of the shell.[149] This illustrates the inherently vague and tricky character of the design-purpose argument of those who maintain that only primary effects matter when assessing the lawfulness of a weapon.

At first, as explained above, the Germans mixed toxic substances with regular explosives and thus circumvented also the Hague Declarations of 1899, which prohibited shells with the "sole objective of diffusing asphyxiating gases."[150] Subsequently, Haber proposed the deployment of respiratory agents—including chlorine and, later, phosgene—which would either be placed inside projectiles and shot at the enemy or buried in cylinders along the front line and released.[151] Dispersal would be carried out by the winds, spreading the agent across the battlefield. Chlorine thus became the first CW to be successfully used. The German Army used it against the

edu/school-of-medicine/academics/departments/history-and-philosophy-of-medicine/archives/wwi/essays/medicine/gas-in-the-great-war.html#:~:text=The%20minimal%20immediate%20effects%20are,%2C%20diphosgene%20(trichloromethane%20chloroformate).

[146] Jaroslav Krasny and Noriyuki Kawano, "Weapons of Mass Destruction and the Principle of Unnecessary Suffering: The Use of Nuclear Weapons in an Armed Conflict" *Hiroshima Peace Science* 36, (2014): 101–116. https://doi.org/10.15027/38055.

[147] SIPRI, *The Problem of Chemical and Biological Warfare: The Rise of CB Weapons* (Stockholm: SIPRI, 1971) 28.

[148] SIPRI, *Problem*, 27.

[149] George Bunn, "Banning Poison Gas and Germ Warfare: Should the United States Agree?" *Wisconsin Law Review*, no. 2 (1969): 375–420, 305.

[150] Hague Declaration to Prohibit the Use of Projectiles, the Only Object of Which is the Diffusion of Asphyxiating or Deleterious Gases (signed 29 July 1899, entered into force 4 September 1900) (1907) 1 AJIL Supp 155 (1899 Hague Declaration III).

[151] SIPRI, *Problem*, 30.

French in the battle at Ypres (Belgium) on April 22, 1915. During this battle, the Germans deployed approximately 180 tons of chlorine contained inside 5730 cylinders buried across the border of the front.[152] According to British medical history, the result was 7000 casualties, including 350 fatalities.[153]

The military's attempt to utilize gas was refocused on developing lethal gases rather than irritants. At the battle of Ypres, Germany introduced yet another weapon that would later be used extensively. This was *bis (2chloroethyl) sulfide*, or sulfur mustard, sometimes incorrectly referred to as mustard gas or "yperite" based on the first place of its use. This substance is a sticky liquid (or vapor) that causes painful blisters analogous to chemical burns.[154] After its introduction by Germany, this oily liquid (or dark solid) vesicant was used until the end of the war. Most of these CWs were, in reality, nothing more than enhanced industrial chemicals. Although these substances did not play a strategic or decisive role during the war, their psychological and physiological effects gained recognition.[155]

Following WWI, Dr. Schrader was searching for new insecticides in 1935.[156] During this endeavor, he prepared a new range of organophosphorus compounds. Due to its toxicity, one stood out: *ethyl NN-dimethylphosphoramidocyanidate* or tabun. A few years later, Schrader began researching fluorine-containing organophosphorus compounds. These compounds "inhibit cholinesterase enzyme in the nerve synapse responsible for the breakdown of the neurotransmitter acetylcholine resulting in respiratory failure and death."[157] Thus, his research led to another variation: a form of *isopropyl methylphosphonofluoridate*, the infamous sarin. However, these substances were barely used during WWII.[158] Tabun, sarin, and—later—soman became known as a new category of

[152] SIPRI, *Problem,* 29.

[153] SIPRI, *Problem,* 31.

[154] Ramesh C. Gupta, ed., *Handbook of Toxicology of Chemical Warfare Agents,* 2nd ed, (Oxford: Academic Press, 2015), 69–70.

[155] Edgar Jones, "Terror Weapons: The British Experience of Gas and Its Treatment in the First World War" *War in History* 21, no. 3 (2014): 355–375. https://doi.org/10.1177/0968344513510248.

[156] Gupta, 11–12.

[157] Gupta, 11.

[158] SIPRI, *Problem,* 71.

chemical weapons. They were the first generation of nerve agents or G- agents.[159]

In the 1950s, after the war, the United Kingdom also engaged in studies of organophosphate compounds. Dr. Ranajith Ghosh studied their characteristics to use them, yet again, as pesticides. This research led to the discovery of another category of nerve agents: V-agents.[160] Among the best- known V-agents (V for "venomous") are VE, VG, and VM. The most commonly produced V-agent is VX.[161] VX is a nerve agent with a lethal dose of approximately 7mg.[162] V-agents produce effects rapidly when absorbed through the lungs, but they work much faster when absorbed through the skin. Moreover, they can spread across vast land areas depending on the weather.[163] A single warhead filled with sarin could create a dangerous dosage in the area of 20–40ha.[164]

Thus, organophosphates, or nerve agents, are the most lethal category of CWs. Gupta (2015) has defined nerve agents as those that block the primary neurotransmitters, such as acetylcholine, and thus threaten the central nervous system with the likelihood of long-term effects. Historical instances of large-scale CW and particularly nerve agents used on the battlefield are, fortunately, limited. There are two outstanding examples: WWI and the Iran–Iraq War. In particular, the Iran–Iraq War offers a recent case study that illustrates how CWs affect combatants compared to other means of war.

4.5.1 Iran-Iraq War (1980–1988)

The prolonged war between Iran and Iraq undoubtedly hastened negotiations to achieve a comprehensive prohibition of CWs. This armed conflict witnessed extensive use of chemicals, predominantly sulfur mustard, but also nerve agents such as sarin and tabun. These chemicals were weaponized and deployed as missiles, mortars, and bombs on battlefields and

[159] G for "German" agents, since this class was discovered by German researchers. Gupta, 12.

[160] SIPRI, *Problem*, 74.

[161] Gupta, 13.

[162] Lethal Concentration time (LCt50) for 70kg man breathing 10 liters/min for 10 mins. Gupta, 94.

[163] SIPRI, *Problem*, 85.

[164] Steve Fetter, "Ballistic Missiles and Weapons of Mass Destruction: What is the Threat? What Should be Done?" *International Security* 16, no. 1 (1991): 5–42. 10.2307/2539050.

against civilian populations in various Iranian cities, towns, and villages bordering Iraq. Chemical companies from Spain, Egypt, Germany, Belgium, Denmark, the Netherlands,[165] and the United States provided material support and chemical precursors for the development of Iraqi CW capabilities, including the ability to manufacture nerve agents.[166]

In 1931, Iraq joined the 1925 Geneva Gas Protocol with reservations. Iraq reserved the right to respond with chemicals if CWs were used against it.[167] As Iraq began to suffer the ramifications of Iranian human wave attacks in 1982, Iraqi leaders began to consider the use of lethal CWs.[168] Following a common pattern, the first use of CWs included the deployment of irritants and vomiting agents in small initial attacks on the towns of Helaleh and NeyKhazar in 1981. The first extensive use of CWs occurred in March 1984 at Majnoon Island. This attack included the use of sulfur mustard as well as nerve agents.[169] Upon the request of the Iranian government, the first UN mission was dispatched to Iran by the UN Secretary-General (UNSG) on May 21–26, 1983, to inspect civilian areas subjected to military attacks by Iraq. The UN report did not refer to the use of chemical weapons.[170] Following the Majnoon chemical attacks, the Iranian government requested another UN mission. Mr. Javier Perez de Cuellar, who was the UNSG at the time, appointed a mission from March 13–19, 1984, to investigate Iran's allegations that Iraq had used chemical weapons.[171] The mission confirmed the use of sulfur mustard and

[165] See in this matter the appeal at the ECHR *Frans Cornelis Adrianus van Anraat v. The Netherlands (2010),* at the International Crimes Database https://www.internationalcrimes-database.org/Case/869/Van-Anraat/, accessed August 4, 2022.

[166] Pierre Razoux, *The Iran-Iraq War*, transl. Nicholas Elliott (Cambridge, MA: Belknap Press of Harvard University Press, 2015), 298.

[167] See ICRC, Treaties, "Protocol for the Prohibition of the Use of Asphyxiating, Poisonous or Other Gases, and of Bacteriological Methods of Warfare Geneva, 17 June 1925" accessed April 24, 2022. https://ihl-databases.icrc.org/applic/ihl/ihl.nsf/States.xsp?xp_viewStates=XPages_NORMStatesParties&xp_treatySelected=280.

[168] Richard M. Price, *The Chemical Weapons Taboo.* (New York: Cornell University Press, 1997), 137.

[169] Inai, Atlas of Mustard Gas, 19.

[170] UN Secretary-General Report, Mission to Inspect Civilian Areas in Iran and Iraq Which Have Been Subject to Military Attack, UN Document, S/15834.

[171] Letter Dated 14 February 1984 From the Permanent Representative of the Islamic Republic of Iran to the United Nations Addressed to the Secretary-General, UN Doc. S/16340 (14 February 1984).

tabun in the form of aerial bombs.[172] The report was transmitted to the UNSC on 26 March 1984. On March 30, 1984, the UNSC issued a statement condemning the use of CWs and calling for belligerents to adhere strictly to the 1925 Geneva Gas Protocol.[173] In the following year— from April 1–5, 1985—the UNSG was concerned by continuous allegations of the ongoing use of CWs. The Secretary-General dispatched a team to hospitals around Europe—including those in Belgium, Germany, and the United Kingdom—which were already admitting and treating Iranian victims who had suffered exposure to toxic chemicals. At the same time—April 7–9, 1985—the UNSG personally visited both Tehran and Baghdad with an 8-point proposal to address severe violations of humanitarian law, including indiscriminate attacks and the use of chemical weapons.

During this visit, Iraq's Foreign Minister, Tariq Aziz, demanded the complete withdrawal of Iranian troops that had gained positions in its territory. He also requested the complete exchange of POWs and a comprehensive adherence to a ceasefire. In contrast, Iran maintained its position that the UNSC had failed to condemn Iraq as the war's aggressor.[174] The condemnation of Iraq as the perpetrator of a war of aggression would, of course, trigger State responsibility for wrongful acts.[175] Overall, Iran questioned the UNSC's impartiality, insisted on the condemnation of Iraq as the aggressor, and demanded reparations payments for the ceasefire to be effective. This report was transmitted to the UNSC on April 24, 1985.[176] Iraq justified its reintroduction of CWs with Iran's counter-offensive and its incursions into Iraqi territory on February 9, 1986, using human wave attacks. In light of these intensified hostilities, the UNSC finally adopted Resolution 582 on February 24, 1986. This resolution confirmed and

[172] UN Security Council Report of the Specialists Appointed by the Secretary-General to Investigate Allegations by the Islamic Republic of Iran Concerning the Use of Chemical Weapons, UN Doc. S/16433, (26 March 1984).

[173] Note by the President of the Security Council, UN Doc., S/16454 (30 March 1984).

[174] Report of the Secretary-General on His Visit to Iran and Iraq, UN Doc. S/17097 (12 April 1985).

[175] UN ILC 'Draft Articles on Responsibility of States for Internationally Wrongful Acts' (2001) GAOR 56th Session Supp 10, 43.

[176] Letter Dated 17 April 1985 From the Secretary-General Addressed to the President of the Security Council, UN Doc. S/17127 (24 April 1985).

condemned the use of CWs in a legally binding document.[177] Nevertheless, the UNSC neither declared Iraq to be the aggressor nor declared that Iraq had violated the 1925 Geneva Gas Protocol.[178]

Then again, in light of new allegations about the use of chemical agents, a third UN investigation mission was dispatched from February 26 to March 3, 1986. The resulting report was transmitted to the UNSC on March 6, 1986.[179] The UNSC repeated its strong condemnation of the use of chemical weapons through a Note of the President of the UN Security Council.[180] According to this note, Iran possessed a limited CW capability, but there were no reliable indications that it had actually deployed chemical weapons against Iraq. Thus, most of Iran's CW capabilities had been developed for defensive purposes.[181] These purposes included deploying neutralization solutions using vehicles in areas affected by chemical weapons.

Iran had been a party to the 1925 Geneva Protocol without reservations to use chemical weapons in retaliation; therefore, it was under absolute legal obligation not to deploy chemical gas. The permanent representative of the Islamic Republic to the UN, H. E. Said Rajaie-Khorassani, criticized the UNSC's lack of action. In particular, he condemned the body's inaction following an extensive chemical attack against the Iranian city of Sardasht, which marked the first time that chemical weapons attacked an entire town. Khorassani explicitly compared this attack to the bombings of Hiroshima and Nagasaki, stressing the suffering of its residents.[182] However, since such an attack was predominantly ruled by distinction, he did not explicitly refer to SIrUS. Furthermore, Khorassani warned of possible setbacks to the negotiations of the convention set to entirely prohibit chemical weapons without a possibility for reservations—later to become the chemical weapons convention—which

[177] UNSC Resolution 582 (1986) 'Iraq-Islamic Republic of Iran' (24 February 1986).

[178] Protocol for the Prohibition of the Use in War of Asphyxiating, Poisonous or other Gases, and of Bacteriological Methods of Warfare.

[179] Report of the Mission Dispatched by the Secretary-General to Investigate Allegations of the Use of Chemical Weapons in the Conflict Between the Islamic Republic of Iran and Iraq, UN Doc. S/17911 (12 March 1986).

[180] Note by the President of the Security Council, UN Doc. S/17932 (21 March 1986).

[181] Razoux, 300–301.

[182] Letter dated 10 August 1987 from the Permanent Representative of the Islamic Republic of Iran to the United Nations addressed to the Secretary-General, UN Doc. S/19029.

was already "reaching final stages."[183] Due to the likelihood of these set-backs, the UNGA issued a resolution calling for an urgent acceleration of negotiations for the absolute prohibition of chemical weapons.[184]

Following the release of particularly distressing information about the influx of chemical weapons and their use against civilian populations, the UNSG decided to dispatch a specialist, Dr. Manuel Dominiquez, who had also been a member of all previous missions.[185] His objective was to conduct further investigations in Iran and Iraq because on April 5, Iraq has, in turn, accused Iran of using chemical weapons against its troops in the Halabja sector.[186] This accusation was an attempt to confuse Western nations further and to conceal the Iraqi use of nerve agents against its domestic Kurdish population. Dominiquez submitted his findings to the UNSC on April 14, 1988. The findings confirmed the intensified and widespread use of CWs against the civilian population of Iran and Iraqi Kurds.[187] Dominiquez reported on what would later become known as the Halabja Massacre of March 16, 1988. An event that claimed more than 5000 civilian victims, including many women and children.[188] This distressing report resulted in the UNSC's unanimous adoption of Resolution 612, which finally affirmed the urgent need to observe the 1925 Geneva Gas Protocol, stressing the indiscriminate nature of chemical weapons.[189]

On May 19, 1988, Iran published a letter accusing Iraq of continuous use of CWs against a number of Iranian villages despite the UNSC resolution calling for an execution of Art. V, which should have bound the

[183] Letter dated 10 August 1987, para. 7.

[184] UNGA Res. 42/37 regarding 'Chemical and bacteriological (biological) weapons (30 November 1987). UN Doc. A/RES/42/37.

[185] See Michael J. Berlin, "U.N. Team Says Chemical Agents Used in Gulf War" *Washington Post,* March 27, 1984, accessed March 22, 2022, https://www.washingtonpost.com/archive/politics/1984/03/27/un-team-says-chemical-agents-used-in-gulf-war/a515ae16-5d8b-4d2c-ae0f-7d33eb45d07f/.

[186] Letter Dated 4 April 1988 From the Permanent Representative of Iraq to the United Nations Addressed to the Secretary-General, UN.Doc. S/19730 (5 April 1988).

[187] Report of the Mission Dispatched by the Secretary-General to Investigate Allegations of the Use of Chemical Weapons in the Conflict Between the Islamic Republic of Iran and Iraq. UN Doc. S/19823 (25 April 1988).

[188] See ANHA Hawar News Agency, "Halabja…Massacre Whose Effects Still Linger Today" accessed March 16, 2020, http://www.hawarnews.com/en/haber/halabjamassacre-whose-effects-still-linger-today-h15286.html.

[189] UNSC Res 612 (1988) 'Iraq-Islamic Republic of Iran' (9 May 1988).

UNSC to take effective punitive and preventive measures against Iraq for a violation of the UNSC Resolution, a severe breach of a binding resolution and, as such, international law.[190] Hence, mere weeks after the adoption of the UN Resolution 612, the UNSG dispatched another mission, which submitted its report to the UNSC on July 8, 1988.[191] Pursuant to Resolution 612, and considering the seriousness of the situation, the UNSC requested the UNSG on August 5, 1988, that any new allegations be promptly investigated. Throughout all these investigative missions and resolutions, no particular reference was made to unnecessary suffering, as understood by LOAC. The contentious issues were predominantly related to indiscriminate warfare, that is, violation of the rule of distinction. Although the UNSC resolutions arguably helped to end the Iran–Iraq War, they failed to deter attacks using CWs. Iraq deployed CWs against an adversary that lacked deterrent capability, and it did so within a legal vacuum. That legal vacuum was defined by the absence of comprehensive agreements prohibiting CWs and these weapons' ambiguous status under LOAC. The Iraqi regime deployed CWs against military objectives and civilians. The most affected border areas were Sardasht (1987), Marivan (1988), and the Iraqi city of Halabja. The Anfal Campaign of March 16, 1988, ended in the massacre of more than 5000 civilians.[192] More than a decade later, a United Nations Monitoring, Verification, and Inspection Commission (UNMOVIC) report estimated that 1800 metric tons of sulfur mustard, 140 tons of tabun, and more than 600 tons of sarin were used against Iran.[193] As a result, more than a million Iranian combatants and civilians were exposed to a variety of chemical agents. In 2011, more than 20 years after the end of the war, approximately 65,000 Iranians were still registered as recipients of care for chronic CW injuries; a further

[190] Letter Dated 19 May 1988 From the Charge D'Affaires A.I. of the Permanent Mission of the Islamic Republic of Iran to the United Nations Addressed to the Secretary-General, UN Doc.S/19892 (19 May 1988).

[191] Report of the Mission Dispatched by the Secretary-General to Investigate Allegations of the Use of Chemical Weapons in the Conflict Between the Islamic Republic of Iran and Iraq, UN Doc. S/20060 (20 July 1988).

[192] Kouki Inai, *Atlas of Mustard Gas Injuries: Building Bridges Between Iran and Japan Through the Relief of Victims Exposed to Mustard Gas* (Hiroshima: MOCT, 2012), 21–23.

[193] Unresolved Disarmament Issues Iraq's Proscribed Weapons Programmes, Working Document (6 March 2003), at 145.

45,000 Iranians were not officially registered even though they suffered long-term health effects.[194]

Sulfur mustard is a carcinogenic compound with long-term effects, including various forms of cancer as well as injuries to the respiratory tract and the eyes; these injuries can result in blindness or decreased vision that is accompanied by an extreme sensitivity to light, known as photophobia.[195] As part of testimonialization, a term coined by Mathur (2017), of the effects of chemical weapons and their distinctive features when compared to conventional explosives, it is appropriate to illustrate them in actual cases. As one of the war veterans, Mr. MohammadReza Taghipoor, who was seriously injured, losing both his legs and several fingers, puts it: "My legs will not grow back; I had to make my peace with it, learn to live with it. However, chemical weapons keep affecting health continuously, causing injuries and health problems. It is still attacking the affected veterans."[196] It is appropriate to add that Mr. Taghipoor himself was not affected by CWs. However, many of his compatriots and friends were.

Mr. Hamid Salehi has been suffering for almost 40 years from the continuous effects of mustard gas.[197] He was 15 years old when he volunteered to join and defend his country from Iraqi aggression. Mr. Salehi was a part of Operation Val-Fajr 8 right around the time when large-scale chemical attacks against Iranian troops were intensifying. In the course of the war, Mr. Salehi was wounded several times by bullets as well as shrapnel and, according to his own words, usually recovered within 10 to 15 days. However, his last injury was caused by an attack with mustard gas. During the attack, the chemical agent was combined with conventional explosives (a method used by Germans in WWI to circumvent the Hague Regulations). Due to this concealment method, at first, Mr. Salehi did not realize this was a chemical attack and did not take any preventive countermeasures. After 3–4 hours, his skin started to burn and itch unbearably. Simultaneously, his eyes started to swell so much that he could not open them anymore. His fear of the unknown and not knowing how exactly these chemicals work was insufferable. He knew blood agents (nerve agents) act quickly, and if it were a nerve agent, he would already be dead.

[194] Inai, 25.

[195] Inai, 99–119.

[196] Interview with the Iran-Iraq war veteran Mr. MohammadReza Taghipoor at the Tehran Peace Museum, March 11, 2018.

[197] Interview with the Iran-Iraq war veteran Mr. Hamid Salehi at the Tehran Peace Museum, March 11, 2018.

However, the exact course of effects of mustard gas was only heard of but unknown. The fear of this weapon was so intense that it resulted in psychosomatic effects because of which the body, to prevent possible injury and loss of blood, concealed the veins so the field medical staff could not inject him with proper medicine to mitigate the effects and had to cut open his arm to get to the vain directly. All this happens in total blindness. Mr. Salehi ended up being hospitalized for four months, and for 25 days, he could not see and open his eyes. The doctors were using eyedrops to treat his eye injuries due to the gas, which Mr. Salehi describes as feeling like needles being stuck in the eyes. He developed large blisters all over his body that caused large wounds resembling chemical burns.

Therefore, his body was in constant pain due to his skin being peeled off daily. Every day, he had to change his bandages, which took almost five hours. Again, all this is happening in total darkness. Gradually, his eyesight returned but did not heal. To this time, he already had three corneal transplants, and each time, his body refused the transplant. Finally, he says he can't take the operations and transplants anymore. The medicine for this transplant has serious side effects. Indeed, his lungs and skin are also severely affected. As Mr. Salehi puts it: "Unlike conventional explosives used during the war, chemical weapons affected my mind and soul; I am not at peace, I can't rest, I am nervous, irritated." He compared it to a virus continuously affecting the body: if his eyes get better, his lung condition worsens; if his lungs get better, his heart condition worsens. This is an illustrative case of how some weapons keep affecting even after a person ceases to be a combatant after the end of hostilities.

Mr. Asadollah Mohammadi was hit by the mustard gas southwest of Iran. He describes the experience as smelling a garlic-like odor at first.[198] Since he was instructed that if he smelled garlic, he should immediately put on his gas mask, and he acted swiftly. However, then, after just 15 minutes, followed the onset of symptoms such as burning eyes, difficulty breathing, convulsions, and nausea. He started vomiting heavy yellowish liquid very heavily, which finally knocked him unconscious. Mr. Mohammadi was then taken to the hospital. Like Mr. Salehi, he could not see what was happening around him, and being blind caused him great torment. During his stay in the hospital, his eyes were discharging lots of secretion; he kept vomiting, coughing, and losing consciousness. Each

[198] Interview with the Iran-Iraq war veteran Mr. Asadollah Mohamadi at the Tehran Peace Museum, March 11, 2018.

time he lost consciousness he stopped breathing. His family members by his bed were instructed to tap his back, which prompted him to breathe whenever he lost consciousness. Ultimately, he could not open his eyes for almost a month. However, even after opening them, he couldn't see well. As long-term health effects, he still suffers severe pulmonary problems and photophobia, and his skin that was damaged by the mustard had to be removed several times. Until his eventual death, he has to use medications and antibiotics and have regular doctor visits. His doctor has instructed him to live near a humid place since even a tiny smog or a small catch of cold can mean a death sentence.

To further illustrate these long-term effects, a slight cough developed into a severe infection nearly a year after the exposure. Mr. Mohammadi was hospitalized again for months as his body is even today still very susceptible to infections due to the damage caused by the chemical. When he coughs, it is not an ordinary cough. His body discharges phlegm, and for this reason, he has to use a piece of specialized medical equipment that vaporizes the liquid in his throat and lungs to gas, allowing him to breathe. He has to keep taking medications four times a day, including a drug, to reduce the possibility of infections, which are deadly to him, together with using three kinds of eye drops daily. As his doctors told him, there is no chance of ever stopping the use of medication. He has had to change the machine three times already and is in line for cornea transplantation because of the scar on his cornea, similar to Mr. Salehi's. Mr. Mohammadi suffers continuous pain in his eyes and lungs with heavy coughing. Such unending reliance on medicine causes further psychological problems, anxiety, depression, and loss of will to live among the survivors. Whenever they go to a new place and start coughing, people look at them with repugnance, thinking they have an infectious disease. One can only imagine how difficult and dangerous was the COVID-19 pandemic for these survivors and how it further exacerbated their suffering. As Mr. Mohammadi puts it:

> Air pollution bothers me the most; it affects my body and mind and causes lung and respiratory infections. If I hear there is going to be air pollution, this already triggers anxiety. With the metal in my throat, I am always careful not to cough. Even if I have a common cold and cough, it might misplace too much, and I have to go to surgery again. This causes further pain to my family.[199]

[199] Interview with the Iran-Iraq war veteran Mr. Asadollah Mohamadi at the Tehran Peace Museum, March 11, 2018.

The metal that Mr. Mohammadi refers to is a special device that keeps his throat and his trachea open so he can breathe. Without it, his trachea shrinks too much due to the chemical injuries. As apparent also from the medical data discussed below, mustard gas is a carcinogenic compound that causes different types of cancers. Predominantly gastrointestinal and blood cancers, that is, leukemia. Several of Mr. Mohammadi's friends have already passed away from cancer. However, the primary fear and anxiety is due to respiratory failure. Many of the survivors suddenly stop breathing and pass away. Mr. Mohammadi points out the difference with conventional explosives, "it depends which part of the body is exposed, for instance, if eyes or lungs, these are vital organs and the gas keeps affecting them. If you lose your leg or hand, it is difficult, but you can live and learn to live with it."

Mr. Mohammadi is in no way trivializing injuries caused by conventional explosives. However, he points out an essential aspect of "unacceptability," which is continuous suffering. The experiences and injuries of the body are further accompanied by social stigma and psychological problems when the survivors realize there is no way to treat this and be free from the continuous medication. They lose their hope and will to live. The prevalent societal impression was that they are very sick, as Mr. Salehi recalls his experience: "I couldn't marry for a long time because the family of the girl I liked told me I was affected by CWs and as such they did not know if I will live, survive and they were worried about my psychological injuries due to the exposure." There were worries that those exposed could not have children, die soon, or have children with asthma. The overall mortality is higher among those exposed to chemical weapons with lower life expectancy as Ms. Pooyandeh of the Tehran Peace Museum points out: "The quality of life is significantly lower in chemical weapons survivors as opposed to those affected by conventional weapons."[200]

These experiences are far too similar. While the Iranian war veterans, combatants by status, can accept war injuries due to conventional weapons, such as shrapnel wounds, bullet wounds, and even losing a limb, effects that continue "attacking" them are intolerable. The constant threat

[200] Interview with the International Affairs Officer Ms. Elaheh Pooynadeh at the Tehran Peace Museum, March 11, 2018.

of deadly disease and cancer is lingering. There is indeed a specific correlation with hibakusha. In 2016, Mr.Salehi offered his testimony at the 21st Conference of State Parties to the Chemical Weapons Convention at the OPCW in the Hague, further pointing out these health effects and their incompatibility with the principles of the law of armed conflict and its humanitarian norms.

In addition, Dr. Takeshima has studied the pathology of genetic alterations among workers at the Okunoshima CW factory in Japan. From 1929–1945, this factory produced a variety of chemical agents, including the aforementioned sulfur mustard, lewisite, and phosgene, all used during WWI.[201] Although such exposure was chronic and long-term as opposed to acute single high dose, it nevertheless correlates with the exposure of Iranian war veterans. Such chronic exposure induces cancer of the respiratory tract, where the possible influence of smoking is negligible.[202] This further included severe clinical symptoms of bronchitis among heavily exposed workers compared to unexposed ones.[203] As Inai and Takeshima (1995) point out, "Lung cancer is the most prevalent cancer with malignant tumors ranging throughout the stomach, liver, skin, and colorectal system."[204] Sulfur Mustard's toxic effects are predominantly linked to DNA alkylation, a process that is likely responsible for the mutagenic outcomes following cellular exposure.[205]

Exposure to chemical weapons often induces crippling anxiety about the deterioration of one's health. The appearance of lung cancer usually follows a latent period that lasts for an average of 22 years.[206] Research on sulfur mustard exposure also indicates that genetic abnormalities, such as mutations in the p53 gene, may arise during the early stages of carcino-

[201] Kouki Inai and Yukio Takeshima, "Pathology of Respiratory Tract in Former Workers in Mustard Gas Factory: A Review" *Journal of Toxicologic Pathology* 8, no. 4 (1995): 343–353. https://doi.org/10.1293/tox.8.343.

[202] Y. Nishimoto, M. Yamakido, T. Shigenobu, K. Onari, and M. Yukutake, "Long-term observation of poison gas workers with special reference to respiratory cancers" *Journal of UOEH* 5 Suppl, (1983): 89–94.

[203] Nishimoto, Y, Burrows, B, Miyanishi, M, Katsuta, S, Shigenobu, T, Kettel LJ: "Chronic obstructive lung disease in Japanese poison gas workers." Am Rev Resp Dis 102:173–179, 1970, as cited by Inai and Takeshima, 347.

[204] Tokuoka et al., as cited by Inai and Takeshima, 348–349.

[205] Inai and Takeshima, 345.

[206] Inai and Takeshima, 347.

genesis.[207] This means that exposure to sulfur mustard can cause changes in DNA, specifically in a gene called p53, which normally helps protect the body from developing cancer. The p53 gene plays a critical role in regulating cell growth and repairing damaged DNA. When this gene mutates or gets damaged early on, it can lead to the uncontrolled growth of cells, that is, development of cancer.

Sarin is yet another chemical agent that Iraq used widely against Iran during the war. Furthermore, it was an agent used by a doomsday cult in Japan in the 1995 Tokyo subway attack. Sarin's properties are quite different because sarin is a nerve agent. As such, it primarily affects the CNS. Sarin has specific long-term effects. There was a follow-up study ten years after the subway incident, during which 5500 people were exposed. Those who were severely affected "suffered neuropathy with dysesthesia and a decrease in vibration sense."[208] This usually means severe apathy and depression, including extreme fatigue and low concentration. Therefore, unlike ionizing radiation, depending on the category of the chemical agent, the pathophysiology of long-term health effects varies.

4.6 Conclusion

This chapter examined the SIrUS principle's medicalization development and further illustrated this process with concrete events and weapons. Using the examples of the most controversial weapons, the author discussed how they impacted combatants' health, focusing predominantly on CWs (mustard gas) and nuclear weapons. There are several reasons behind this specific focus.

First, as stated above, LOAC does not differentiate between conventional or unconventional weapons; it applies to any use of any weapon. Second, the long-term effects these weapons cause illustrate prolonged suffering that exceeds the temporal scope of the application of LOAC. That is to say, the weapons continue to affect combatants until their deaths, even when LOAC is no longer applicable to them. Whereas weapons such as landmines and, to a certain extent, incendiaries cause horrendous injuries, their controversies originate from the violation of the principle of

[207] Inai and Takeshima, 351.

[208] N. Yanagisawa, H. Morita, and T. Nakajima. "Sarin Experiences in Japan: Acute Toxicity and Long-term Effects." *Journal of the Neurological Sciences* 249, no. 1 (2006): 76–85. https://doi.org/10.1016/j.jns.2006.06.007, 82.

distinction, not that of unnecessary suffering. Blasts, burns, and heat are common to many of the explosives used today. In contrast, carcinogenicity and a significantly increased lifelong risk of leukemia are not. Fire has always been a part of warfare, but—given the progress of civilization and the fact that injuries can prevent human beings from returning to ordinary life—its restriction under CCW is a welcome development.

The use of landmines remains controversial to this day. If deployed carefully and recorded correctly for subsequent collection, their limited use may be acceptable in light of the unavailability of other weapons; there is simply no alternative to landmines in the form of a different, less injurious area-denier. Although the ICRC argues that landmine injuries put tremendous strain on field surgeons and medical material, it is difficult to say that they cause unnecessary suffering as such. Many explosives cause injuries similar to those incurred by mines. Indeed, using the examples and data referring to the development of leukemia and solid cancers as health effects illustrates that long-term injuries, rather than instantaneous injury, represent continuous unnecessary suffering for victims.

Long-term risks and the constant worry about one's health—including the potential effects on one's children— incur a heavy psychological burden. Nevertheless, should policymakers decide that such risk is acceptable and in conformity with LOAC, those affected by ionizing radiation would become collateral damage after they pass away from the diseases caused by such weapons long after an armed conflict ends. This is unacceptable and legally flawed. As such, long-term health effects far exceed the scope of the applicability of the norms of the law of armed conflict. The next chapter then explores a legal framework concerning the aforementioned weapons. It maintains a concurrent focus on CWs and nuclear weapons, and it turns to the operational articles and issues behind the legal agreements. Its purpose is to examine whether SIrUS was raised and discussed during negotiations and whether the trend of medicalization and testimonialization examined in preceding chapters affected the conclusion of these agreements.

References

ANHA Hawar News Agency. "Halabja…Massacre Whose Effects Still Linger Today." March 16, 2020. http://www.hawarnews.com/en/haber/halabjamassacre-whose-effects-still-linger-today-h15286.html.

Arkin, William M., and Hans M. Kristensen. "US Deploys New Low-Yield Nuclear Submarine Warhead." Federation of American Scientists, January 29, 2020. https://fas.org/blogs/security/2020/01/w76-2deployed/.

Asbarez Staff. "Use of White Phosphorus Bombs by Azerbaijan Confirmed." *Asbarez*, October 30, 2020. https://asbarez.com/use-of-white-phosphorous-bombs-by-azerbaijan-confirmed/.

Berlin, Michael J. "U.N. Team Says Chemical Agents Used in Gulf War." *Washington Post*, March 27, 1984. https://www.washingtonpost.com/archive/politics/1984/03/27/un-team-says-chemical-agents-used-in-gulf-war/a515ae16-5d8b-4d2c-ae0f-7d33eb45d07f/.

Boniface, Susie. "Nuclear Heroes Betrayed by Ministry of Defence Pen-Pushers Over Medals." *Mirror*, December 10, 2020. https://www.mirror.co.uk/news/uk-news/nuclear-heroes-betrayed-pen-pushers-23149346?fbclid=IwAR2bVUGg_Et6Rh9qRWtrj2Z36awq1Vbpzvf4nZ7PFEdGLZYM8UYwIsDdx8g.

Bowen, Thomas E., ed. *Emergency War Surgery*. Collingdale, PA: Diane Publishing Co., 2005.

British Medical Association. *Illustrated Medical Dictionary*. 1st ed. London: Dorling Kindersley, 2002.

Bunn, George. "Banning Poison Gas and Germ Warfare: Should the United States Agree?" *Wisconsin Law Review*, no. 2 (1969): 375–420.

Cambodian Mine Action and Victim Assistance Authority. "Monthly Report of February 2022." Accessed May 2, 2022. https://www.cmaa.gov.kh/detail/content/rzlUAsxfrSDhHmGktDHP.

Cambodian Self-Help Demining. "About CSHD." Accessed April 14, 2022. https://www.cambodianselfhelpdemining.org/about/

Center For Arms Control and Non-Proliferation. "Fact Sheet: Russia's Use of Thermobaric Weapons in Ukraine." March 1, 2022. https://armscontrolcenter.org/fact-sheet-russias-use-of-thermobaric-weapons-in-ukraine/.

Committee for the Compilation of Materials on Damage Caused by the Atomic Bombs in Hiroshima and Nagasaki. *Hiroshima and Nagasaki: The Physical, Medical and Social Effects of the Atomic Bombings*. Tokyo: Iwanami Shoten, 1981.

Coupland, Robin M., ed. *The SIrUS Project: Towards a Determination of Which Weapons Cause "Superfluous Injury or Unnecessary Suffering*." Geneva: ICRC, 1997. https://www.loc.gov/collections/military-legal-resources/?q=RC_SIrUS-project.html.

Coupland, Robin M., and Adriaan Korver. "Injuries From Antipersonnel Mines: The Experience of the International Committee of the Red Cross." *British*

Medical Journal 303, no. 6816 (1991): 1509–1512. https://doi.org/10.1136/bmj.303.6816.1509.

Fetter, Steve. "Ballistic Missiles and Weapons of Mass Destruction: What is the Threat? What Should be Done?" *International Security* 16, no. 1 (1991): 5–42. https://doi.org/10.2307/2539050.

Guldner, Gregory T., and Curtis Knight. *Napalm Toxicity*. Treasure Island, FL: StatPearls Publishing, 2021. https://www.ncbi.nlm.nih.gov/books/NBK537127/#:~:text=Napalm%20burns%20result%20in%20severe,to%20napalm%20may%20be%20severe.

Gupta, Ramesh C., ed. *Handbook of Toxicology of Chemical Warfare Agents*. 2nd ed. Oxford: Academic Press, 2015.

Hambling, David. "Russia Accused of Using Air-Dropped Butterfly Mines to Block Ukrainian Evacuation Route." *Forbes*, March 10, 2022. https://www.forbes.com/sites/davidhambling/2022/03/10/russia-reportedly-blocks-ukrainian-evacuation-route-with-air-dropped-butterfly-mines/?sh=165e514a1a32.

Robinson, C. Paul. *A White Paper: Pursuing a New Nuclear Weapons Policy for the 21st Century*. Sandia National Laboratories White Paper, March 22, 2001. https://www.sandia.gov/media/whitepaper/2001-04-Robinson.htm

ICRC. *Anti-Personnel Landmines: Friend or Foe? A Study of the Military Use and Effectiveness of Anti-Personnel Mines*. Geneva: ICRC, 1996. https://www.icrc.org/en/publication/0654-anti-personnel-landmines-friend-or-foe-study-military-use-and-effectiveness-anti

———. "Protocol for the Prohibition of the Use of Asphyxiating, Poisonous or Other Gases, and of Bacteriological Methods of Warfare. Geneva, 17 June 1925." Accessed April 24, 2022. https://ihl-databases.icrc.org/applic/ihl/ihl.nsf/States.xsp?xp_viewStates=XPages_NORMStatesParties&xp_treatySelected=280.

———. *Weapons That May Cause Unnecessary Suffering or Have Indiscriminate Effects: Report on the Work of Experts*. Geneva: ICRC, 1973. https://www.loc.gov/item/2011525354/.

Inai, Kouki. *Atlas of Mustard Gas Injuries: Building Bridges Between Iran and Japan Through the Relief of Victims Exposed to Mustard Gas*. Hiroshima: MOCT, 2012.

Inai, Kouki, and Yukio Takeshima. "Pathology of Respiratory Tract in Former Workers in Mustard Gas Factory: A Review." *Journal of Toxicologic Pathology* 8, no. 4 (1995): 343–353. https://doi.org/10.1293/tox.8.343.

International Campaign to Ban Landmines. "What is a Landmine?" Accessed April 29, 2022. http://www.icbl.org/en-gb/problem/what-is-a-landmine.aspx.

Jackson, Heather. "Severe Ocular Trauma due to Landmines and Other Weapons in Cambodia." *Community Eye Health Journal* 10, no. 23 (1997): 37–39. https://www.cehjournal.org/article/severe-ocular-trauma-due-to-landmines-and-other-weapons-in-cambodia/.

Jones, Edgar. "Terror Weapons: The British Experience of Gas and Its Treatment in the First World War." *War in History* 21, no. 3 (2014): 355–375. https://doi.org/10.1177/0968344513510248

Krasny, Jaroslav and Noriyuki Kawano, "Weapons of Mass Destruction and the Principle of Unnecessary Suffering: The Use of Nuclear Weapons in an Armed Conflict" *Hiroshima Peace Science* 36, (2014): 101–116. https://doi.org/10.15027/38055.

Kristensen, Hans M., and Matt Korda."United States Nuclear Forces, 2020." *Bulletin of the Atomic Scientists* 76, no. 1 (2020): 46–60. https://doi.org/10.1080/00963402.2019.1701286.

Laur, Timothy M., and Steven L. Llanso. *Encyclopedia of Modern U.S. Military Weapons.* New York: The Army Times Publishing Company, 1995.

Lederberg, Joshua, ed. *Biological Weapons: Limiting the Threat.* Cambridge, MA: MIT Press, 1999.

Los Alamos Scientific Laboratory and Norris E. Bradbury. *The Effects of Atomic Weapons.* Whitefish, MT: Literary Licensing, 2013.

Maresca, Louis, and Stuart Maslen. *The Banning of Anti-Personnel Landmines: The Legal Contribution of the International Committee of the Red Cross.* Cambridge: Cambridge University Press, 2000.

Mathur, Ritu. *Red Cross Interventions in Weapons Control.* London: Lexington Books, 2017.

Meuse, Alison. "U.S. – Led Coalition Has Used White Phosphorus In Fight For Mosul, General Says." *NPR*, August 1, 2022, https://www.npr.org/sections/parallels/2017/06/13/532809626/u-s-led-coalition-has-used-white-phosphorous-in-fight-for-mosul-general-says#:~:text=Press-,White%20Phosphorus%20Used%20Against%20Islamic%20State%20In%20Mosul%2C%20Coalition%20General,to%20get%20civilians%20out%20safely.%22.

Neer, Robert M. *Napalm: An American Biography.* Cambridge: Belknap Press of Harvard University Press, 2013.

NHS. "Carbon Monoxide Poisoning." Last reviewed April 10, 2019. https://www.nhs.uk/conditions/carbon-monoxide-poisoning/#:~:text=Prolonged%20exposure%20to%20carbon%20monoxide%20can%20cause%20memory%20problems%20and,tremors%2C%20stiffness%20and%20slow%20movement.

Nishimoto, Y., M. Yamakido, T. Shigenobu, K. Onari, and M. Yukutake. "Long-term observation of poison gas workers with special reference to respiratory cancers." *Journal of UOEH* 5 Suppl, (1983): 89–94.

Owen, Alan. "Global Health Survey 2020." LABRATS International Health Survey 2020. https://www.labrats.international/healthsurvey.

Patton, James. "Gas in the Great War." Medicine in the First World War. Accessed April 14, 2022. https://www.kumc.edu/school-of-medicine/academics/departments/history-and-philosophy-of-medicine/archives/wwi/essays/medicine/gas-in-the-great-war.html#:~:text=The%20minimal%20immediate%20effects%20are,%2C%20diphosgene%20(trichloromethane%20chloroformate).

Price, Richard M. *The Chemical Weapons Taboo.* New York: Cornell University Press, 1997.

Phillips, Charles, and Alan Axelrod, eds. *Encyclopedia of Wars.* New York: Zenda, Inc, 2005.

Razoux, Pierre. *The Iran-Iraq War.* Translated by Nicholas Elliott. Cambridge, MA: Belknap Press of Harvard University Press, 2015.

RERF. "About RERF." Accessed April 14, 2022a. https://www.rerf.or.jp/en/about/establish_e/.

———. *A Brief Description.* Hiroshima: RERF, 2016.

———. "Historical Materials." Accessed April 14, 2022b. https://www.rerf.or.jp/en/about/history_e/.

———. "Children of Atomic Bomb Survivors (F1) Study." Accessed April 14, 2022c. https://www.rerf.or.jp/en/programs/research_activities_e/outline_e/progfl-en/.

Rhodes, Richard. *Dark Sun: The Making of the Hydrogen Bomb.* New York: Simon & Schuster, 2005.

Saotome, Katsumoto. *Toukyo Daikuushuu: Zusetu* [Great Tokyo Air Raid: Illustrated]. Tokyo: Kawade Shobo Shinsha, 2015a.

Saotome, Katsumoto. *Tokyo Daikuushuu: Showa Nijyuunen Sangatsu Tooka no Kiroku [The Great Tokyo Air Raid: A Memory of March 10, 1945].* Tokyo: Iwanami-Shinsho, 2015b.

Sassoli, Marco. *International Humanitarian Law: Rules, Controversies, and Solutions to Problems Arising in Warfare.* Cheltenham: Edward Elgar, 2019.

Sassoli, Marco, Antoine Bouvier, Anne Quintin, and Julia Grignon. "Afghanistan/US, 'Mother of All Bombs.'" *How Does Law Protect in War?* Geneva: ICRC, 2014. Accessed April 14, 2022. https://casebook.icrc.org/case-study/afghanistanus-mother-all-bombs.

Saul, Ben, and Akande, Dapo, eds. *The Oxford Guide to International Humanitarian Law.* Oxford: Oxford University Press, 2020.

Schull, William J. *Effects of Atomic Radiation: A Half-Century of Studies from Hiroshima and Nagasaki.* New York: Wiley-Liss, 1995.

Shimizu, Y., H. Kato, and William J. Schull. "Studies of the Mortality of A-bomb Survivors. 9. Mortality, 1950–1985: Part 2. Cancer Mortality Based on the Recently Revised Doses (DS86)." *Radiation Research* 121, no. 2 (1990): 120–141.

Shigematsu, Itsuzo, Mitoshi Akiyama, Hideo Sasaki, Chikato Ito, and Nanao Kamada, eds. *Genbaku hoshasen no jintai eikyo* [Effects of A-bomb radiation on the human body]. Tokyo: Bunkodo, 1995.

Stanford Libraries. "Stanford Oral History Collections." Accessed April 24, 2022. https://exhibits.stanford.edu/oral-history.

Stockholm International Peace Research Institute. *Delayed Toxic Effects of Chemical Warfare Agents: A SIPRI Monograph*, Stockholm: Almqvist & Wiksell, 1975a.

———. *A Monograph: Incendiary Weapons.* Cambridge, MA: MIT Press, 1975b.

———. *The Problem of Chemical and Biological Warfare: The Rise of CB Weapons.* Stockholm: SIPRI, 1971.

Swopes, Bryan R. "9–10 March 1945: Operation Meetinghouse." This Day in Aviation, March 9, 2022. https://www.thisdayinaviation.com/tag/an-m69-incendiary-bomblet/.

The Effects of the Atomic Bombs at Hiroshima and Nagasaki: Report of the British Mission to Japan. London: His Majesty's Stationery Office, 1946.

UK Ministry of Defence. *The Manual of the Law of Armed Conflict.* Oxford: Oxford University Press, 2004.

UN Institute for Disarmament Research. *European Action on Small Arms and Light Weapons and Explosive Remnants of War: Final Report.* Geneva: UNIDIR, 2006. https://unidir.org/publication/european-action-small-arms-and-light-weapons-and-explosive-remnants-war-final-report.

US Department of Defense., Missile Defense Agency. "The Ballistic Missile Defense System (BMDS)." Accessed April 14, 2022. https://www.mda.mil/system/system.html.

US Department of Health and Human Services. *Toxicological Profile for White Phosphorus.* Atlanta, GA: Agency for Toxic Substances and Disease Registry, 1997.

US Air Force. *Doctrine for Joint Theater Nuclear Operations.* February 9, 1996. https://www.nukestrat.com/us/jcs/JCS_JP3-12-1_96.pdf.

UQAM, Faculte des sciences humaines. "Napalm." La Guerre d'Indochine, 1945–1956. Accessed April 14, 2022. https://indochine.uqam.ca/fr/le-dictionnaire/940-napalm.html.

Wood, Chris. "Nuclear Test Veterans: 'My Dad Was Treated Like a Guinea Pig.'" BBC, May 30, 2021. https://www.bbc.com/news/uk-wales-57157476.

Yanagisawa, N., H. Morita, and T. Nakajima. "Sarin Experiences in Japan: Acute Toxicity and Long-term Effects." *Journal of the Neurological Sciences* 249, no. 1 (2006): 76–85. https://doi.org/10.1016/j.jns.2006.06.007.

Young, Robert W., and Geroge D. Kerr. *Reassessment of the Atomic Bomb Radiation Dosimetry for Hiroshima and Nagasaki. Dosimetry System 2002. DS02. Volume 1.* Hiroshima: RERF, 2005.

CHAPTER 5

Contemporary Legal Framework and Unnecessary Suffering

5.1 Introduction

Following the order of the preceding chapter, Chap. 5 begins with a brief discussion regarding the Biological Weapons Convention and then proceeds on to the Convention on Certain Conventional Weapons (CCW)[1] as a law of armed conflict treaty containing specific protocols concerned with designated weapons. CCW shall not be understood as a disarmament treaty since its ultimate purpose is not disarmament but regulation of the use of particular weapons during hostilities.[2] It stems from two LOAC principles: distinction and prohibition of unnecessary suffering.[3] CCW includes five protocols, each for a particular weapon. A State doesn't need to become a party to every protocol; however, at least two are required to become bound by the agreement.[4]

In this chapter, I focus mainly on Protocol III, restricting incendiary weapons, and Protocol IV, prohibiting blinding lasers, since health effects

[1] Convention on Prohibitions or Restrictions on the Use of Certain Conventional Weapons which may be Deemed to be Excessively Injurious or to have Indiscriminate Effects (adopted 10 October 1980, entered into force 2 December 1983) 1342 UNTS 137.

[2] Andrew Clapham and Paola Gaeta, eds., *The Oxford Handbook of International Law in Armed Conflict* (Oxford: Oxford University Press, 2014), 63–64.

[3] William H. Boothby, *Weapons and the Law of Armed Conflict* (New York: Oxford University Press, 2016), 94.

[4] Boothby, *Weapons*, 97.

J. Krasny, *War Injuries*,
https://doi.org/10.1007/978-3-032-00737-7_5

played specific roles in these negotiations. Other protocols mention superfluous injury or unnecessary suffering (SIrUS) to prevent unwarranted modifications, such as adding glass to explosives, but focus predominantly on restricting their use, for example, not placing booby traps in children's toys.[5] The discussion then proceeds to the success story of the Chemical Weapons Convention (CWC),[6] concentrating on the negotiation process and its leading operative articles since the CWC is one of the most extensive and complex disarmament agreements. The Ottawa Treaty[7] follows as an example of novel humanitarian initiatives instigated by the extensive lobbying of nongovernmental organizations (NGOs) and civil society rather than States themselves, resulting in a legal document to eliminate another entire category of weapons, antipersonnel landmines. The Humanitarian Initiative and a campaign to ban landmines was one of the first partially successful attempts focusing on health effects and connecting them with the SIrUS principle. Activists and humanitarians tried to repeat this partial success later during the campaign to ban cluster munition, resulting in the Oslo Convention.[8] The author avoids extensive discussion of the Oslo Convention because the effects of unexploded cluster munition or duds are virtually the same as those of the antipersonnel landmines. Such health and humanitarian-centered initiatives then culminated in the Treaty on the Prohibition of Nuclear Weapons[9] as the latest newcomer in global disarmament treaties with a specific reference to unnecessary suffering.

In light of the long-term health effects the author has introduced in the previous chapter, particularly of chemical, nuclear, and incendiary

[5] Convention on Prohibitions or Restrictions on the Use of Certain Conventional Weapons which may be Deemed to be Excessively Injurious or to have Indiscriminate Effects: Protocol II: Protocol on Prohibitions or Restrictions on the Use of Mines, Booby-Traps and Other Devices (adopted 10 October 1980, entered into force 2 December 1983) 1342 UNTS 168.¶ Art.7(e).

[6] Convention on the Prohibition of the Development, Production, Stockpiling and Use of Chemical Weapons and on their Destruction (opened for signature 13 January 1993, entered into force 29 April 1997) 1974 UNTS 45.

[7] Convention on the Prohibition of the Use, Stockpiling, Production and Transfer of Anti-Personnel Mines and on their Destruction (concluded 18 September 1997, entered into force 1 March 1999) 2056 UNTS 211 (Ottawa Convention).

[8] Convention on Cluster Munitions (adopted 30 May 2008, entered into force 1 August 2010) (2009) 48 ILM 357.

[9] Treaty on the Prohibition of Nuclear Weapons (concluded 7 July, 2017, entered into force 22 January 2021) CN.475.2017.

weapons such as napalm, it is prudent to explore how the negotiations, the agreements themselves, and the movements to lobby for the conclusion of these treaties understood and interpreted the principle prohibiting unnecessary suffering and whether these agreements and negotiations contain any direct reference to the principle in their operational articles.

5.2 The Biological Weapons Convention

The use of biological weapons in modern international armed conflict on the battlefield is almost non-existent, or at least not well documented, besides allegations before 1945. There are indeed documented accusations of the use of biological warfare before the outbreak of WWII by the Empire of Japan.[10] However, none of these are documented enough to provide an array of evidence to scrutinize such deployments from the perspective of the LOAC norm against unnecessary suffering. The use of biological weapons in a contemporary international armed conflict is highly unlikely, although not impossible. Since this book is looking at the application and interpretation of SIrUS *lex lata* as a LOAC norm applicable to combatants in IAC, the discussion excludes any deliberations on possible terrorist attacks on soft targets.

While the 1925 Geneva Gas Protocol outlawed bacteriological weapons, these were still rather hypothetical, and even then, such use could still be possible as a reprisal. It was only with the 1975 Biological Weapons Convention that the weapons were banned as a whole category. The prohibition of biological weapons is also a customary norm.[11] Although the BWC does not ban the use of biological weapons in its operative paragraphs, such a ban is included in the preamble referring to the 1925 Geneva Gas Protocol and, as stated above, by customary law. Moreover, at the 2011 BWC Meeting of State Parties, the Member States reaffirmed the understanding that the Convention also bans the use.[12]

[10] Mark Wheelis, Lajos Rózsa, and Malcolm Dando, eds., *Deadly Cultures: Biological Weapons since 1945* (Cambridge, MA: Harvard University Press, 2006), 4.

[11] Jean-Marie Henckaerts and Louise Doswald-Beck, eds. *Customary International Humanitarian Law*. Vol.1, *Rules* (Cambridge: Cambridge University Press, 2005), 256.

[12] See Seventh Review Conference of the States Parties to the Convention on the Prohibition of the Development, Production and Stockpiling of Bacteriological (Biological) and Toxin Weapons and on Their Destruction Final Document of the Seventh Review Conference, Geneva, 5–22 December 2011, BWC/CONF.VII/7, available at: https://documents.un.org/doc/undoc/gen/g12/600/60/pdf/g1260060.pdf, last access October 22, 2024.

The global pandemic of Covid-19 and widespread misinformation regarding the origins of the disease calls for the necessity to reiterate the definition of biological weapons. This is codified in Article 1:

> 1. Microbial or other biological agents, or toxins whatever their origin or method of production, of types and in quantities that have no justification for prophylactic, protective or other peaceful purposes;
> 2. weapons, equipment or means of delivery designed to use such agents or toxins for hostile purposes or in armed conflict.

Pursuant to Article IV, to take any necessary measures to prevent the development of biological weapons, many States have developed their domestic legislation and adopted regulations to implement the prohibitions in the BWC and to strengthen their biosafety and biosecurity measures further.[13] Nevertheless, the BWC definition is based on intent. States can engage in research for peaceful or defensive purposes, and they often do. Such research is regularly conducted in specialized laboratories with a biosafety level (BSL) designation from one to four. BSL-4 is a laboratory containing the most dangerous viruses. This is nothing secret.[14] Such laboratories and research are crucial and necessary for medical research. The question then is, where is the line between peaceful and weapon research. This is, however, not a question of the weapons law. It often entails political connotations, as seen through the unfounded Russian accusations of biological weapons research by the US in Ukraine.[15]

Notwithstanding, the use of biological weapons would entail a disease outbreak. Combatants are regularly vaccinated. This was also the case in the Second Gulf War to prevent any adverse effects of possible exposure, in this case, weaponized anthrax. While terrorists, fanatics, rebel groups, or rogue governments might find BWs somewhat intriguing, it is unlikely that militarily significant States would rely on these weapons or even

[13] See UNIDIR-VERTIC, BWC National Implementation Measures Database, available at: https://bwcimplementation.org/, last access on October 31, 2024.

[14] See Global Labs, available at: https://www.globalbiolabs.org/map, last access on October 31, 2024.

[15] Ryan S. Houser, Gregory D. Koblentz, and Filippa Lentzos, "Understanding Biosafety and Biosecurity in Ukraine." *Health Security* 21 (1): 70–80, 2023, https://doi.org/10.1089/hs.2022.0095.

attempt to deploy them. This would be due to their unpredictability, global treaty and customary ban, and accompanying stigma they carry, inviting a harsh international response. As we can observe in the Ukraine-Russia conflict and conflicts in the Middle East, metal still plays a crucial role and wins the wars, meaning tanks, artillery, and explosives in general. Similar to ionizing radiation, the military advantage of such biological attack is limited, where the military would not wait to incapacitate the enemy after the incubation period. However, research into possible legitimate uses of biotechnology for the military is ongoing, as indicated in Chap. 7.

5.3 Convention on Certain Conventional Weapons

After a somewhat prolonged status quo, with most discussions revolving around nuclear weapons and testing, the Vietnam War can undoubtedly be regarded as a milestone. This conflict sparked an accelerated change in perception and rejuvenated the interest in understanding *the nature of* [emphasis added] unnecessary suffering. The extensive use of incendiaries and defoliants accompanied by horrific pictures in the media revitalized public interest in the issue of weaponry. The image of Ms. Kim Phuc running from the infernal fire of napalm in the background is an iconic photograph that triggered a public outcry against the use of napalm. This public demand or *public conscience* formed enough pressure on governments to act and, ultimately, to negotiate the CCW, which falls under the category of a law of war treaty specifically prohibiting unnecessary suffering as one of its *raisons d'être*. This is already apparent from its preamble:

> Basing themselves on the principle of international law that the right of the parties to an armed conflict to choose methods or means of warfare is not unlimited, and on the principle that prohibits the employment in armed conflicts of weapons, projectiles and material and methods of warfare of a nature to cause superfluous injury or unnecessary suffering,

The treaty's interpretation through the context of the preamble shall indeed be included, as stipulated in Art. 32(2)(a) of the Vienna Convention on the Law of Treaties. In the wake of the intensified use of incendiaries by the United States in North Vietnam, the Preamble of Resolution XXIII of the Tehran Conference on International Human Rights in 1968 singled out napalm as one of the most abhorrent weapons.[16] The Vietnam War, therefore, presented a dark "stimulus" that brought health effects regarding specific weapons back to the forefront.[17] A consulting group of experts supported by the UN, the World Health Organization (WHO), and the ICRC examined the nature, history, and use of incendiaries. On September 22, 1972, the UNGA met for the Conference of the Committee on Disarmament, where napalm was one of the main topics.[18] Later, "Napalm and Other Incendiary Weapons and All Aspects of Their Possible Use: Report of the Secretary-General" was issued, discussing extensively the health effects of the weapon.[19] The opinion was clear: incendiaries were powerful, "cruel," and indiscriminate.[20]

Consequently, in November 1972, the UNGA adopted Resolution 2932, declaring napalm unacceptable and in violation of laws prohibiting unnecessary suffering.[21] Interestingly enough, in Resolution 2932, Sweden referred to the Stockholm International Peace Research Institute (SIPRI) study of 1971 discussed in the previous chapter and points out that burns and shock are common to other conventional weapons, while not denying horrible injuries caused by napalm, and refers to the preamble of the St. Petersburg Declaration of 1868 that napalm "uselessly aggravates the suffering of combatants."[22] The United Kingdom then insisted such unnecessary suffering is concerning the use of incendiaries against personnel but not against vehicles or installations.[23] The chief user of napalm, the United States, did not participate in the conference nor offer any comment. Such fundamental disagreement in whether napalm violates

[16] Dietrich Schindler and Jiri Toman, eds., *The Laws of Armed Conflict: A Collection of Conventions, Resolutions and Other Documents* (Leiden: Martinus Nijhoff Publishers, 2004), 347.

[17] Robert M. Neer, *Napalm: An American Biography* (Cambridge: Belknap Press of Harvard University Press, 2013), 175.

[18] Marine Guillaume, "Napalm in US Bombing Doctrine and Practice, 1942–1975" *The Asia-Pacific Journal* 14, no. 23–25 (2016): Article 4893. https://apjjf.org/2016/23/Guillaume.html.

[19] UNGA Doc. A/9207: Napalm and other incendiary weapons and all aspects of their possible use. Report of the Secretary-General A_9207-EN.pdf, accessed April 15, 2022, https://digitallibrary.un.org/record/852668?ln=en.

[20] General and Complete Disarmament [1972] UNGA 32; A/RES/2932 (XXVII) (29 November 1972)

[21] See declarations of Australia, Czechoslovakia, Netherlands, Iran UNGA Doc. A/9207.

[22] See declaration of Sweden, A/9207, 19–21.

[23] A/9207, 24.

the norm against unnecessary suffering then resulted in Protocol III restricting napalm in densely populated areas rather than outright prohibition.

The XXII ICRC international conference, which sought to expand the organization's mandate from humanitarian law to the law of war, that is, Hague law, attempted to keep the spotlight on napalm and its prohibition based on extensive and unacceptable injuries, but its efforts were unsuccessful.[24] Napalm was not banned. During the 1977 plenary meeting of the Diplomatic Conference on the Reaffirmation and Development of International Humanitarian Law Applicable in Armed Conflicts, the United Nations discussed extensively unnecessary suffering concerning incendiary weapons.[25] In other words, the CCW is a by-product of the conference that codified the SIrUS in the Additional Protocol I (AP I) and a result of extensive work by the Ad Hoc Committee on Conventional Weapons as discussed in Chap. 3. During the proceedings and deliberations, the notion of unnecessary suffering was discussed regarding particular health effects of incendiaries, and the nature of burn injuries, carcinogenic effects, or asphyxiation came to dominate the discourse of discussion, as reflected in the United Nations General Assembly (UNGA) Resolution 3255 (XXIX).[26]

Therefore, the ICRC's expertise, medical analysis, and data played a significant role. While the ICRC's interventions in arms control have been somewhat controversial, the experience it gained through fieldwork lent a heavy weight to its opinion. By combining testimonialization, medicalization, and an effects-based approach, as Mathur (2017) categorized, the ICRC could offer well-informed input and subsequently affect or form a public opinion or "public conscience." Both public opinion and the humanitarian approach to arms control by the ICRC, while not sources of international law, undeniably played an essential role in forming or helping to shape domestic politics on the issue of weapons. Still, such an effort was

[24] Neer, 180.

[25] Schindler and Toman, 699–710.

[26] A/RES/3255(XXIX)[A] Napalm and other incendiary weapons and all aspects of their possible use Resolutions adopted by the General Assembly during its 29th session. Volume 1, 17 September-18 December 1974. - A/9631. - 1975. - p. 18–19. - (GAOR, 29th sess., Suppl. no. 31).

supported mainly by the UNGA Resolution 3255 in 1975 condemning the use of napalm.[27]

The Diplomatic Conference on the Reaffirmation and Development of International Humanitarian Law Applicable in Armed Conflicts, that is, the conference that adopted both 1977 Additional Protocols to Geneva Conventions, had, thus, set the stage for the diplomatic conference resulting in the adoption of the CCW and restriction of napalm under Protocol III.[28] It is worth noting, however, that none of the UNGA resolutions expressly mentioned SIrUS as codified in the Hague Conventions of 1899/1907 concerning napalm. Instead, the language used is "excessive injury," and the appeal is made regarding a strain placed on medical treatment. Such language is understandable. Should the UNGA declare a weapon violating the principle of unnecessary suffering as codified in the Hague Convention of 1907 or later in the 1977 AP I, it would *de jure* declare such a weapon unlawful under international law and, therefore, face stern opposition from affected States.

The CCW consists of a core treaty with protocols allowing States to reach separate agreements regarding specific weapons; however, formal negotiating sessions of the CCW proved medical debates to be inconclusive.[29] The conference met in two sessions, September 10–28, 1979, and September 15–October 10, 1980. As Swedish delegate H. Blix described, the cornerstone was laid in the negotiations leading up to the adoption of two additional protocols, especially the two ICRC conferences.[30] The problems of booby traps, fragments that are undetectable with X-ray, and landmines were not particularly contentious, and the diplomats reached an agreement on these points without persistent difficulties.[31] The contentious issue was, of course, napalm and incendiaries when the United States

[27] Napalm and other incendiary weapons and all aspects of their possible use. A/RES/3255(XXIX)A-B (1975)

[28] Convention on Prohibitions or Restrictions on the Use of Certain Conventional Weapons which may be Deemed to be Excessively Injurious or to have Indiscriminate Effects: Protocol III: Protocol on Prohibitions or Restrictions on the Use of Incendiary Weapons (adopted 10 October 1980, entered into force 2 December 1983) 1342 UNTS 171.

[29] Neer, 189.

[30] United Nations Conference on Prohibitions or Restrictions of use of certain conventional weapons which may be deemed to be excessively injurious or to have indiscriminate effects. Summary record of the 2nd meeting, September 11, 1979. A/CONF.95/SR.2.

[31] A/CONF.95/SR.2.

refused to ban incendiaries and their use against combatants.[32] The delegates did not single out napalm, and the discussion included fuel-air bombs as well, which are, as I have previously discussed, rather challenging to argue for violating the SIrUS norm. The US did not consider their effects as particularly excessive. As a compromise, excluding outright prohibition, incendiaries such as napalm were then restricted under Protocol III, and their use against civilians and concentrations of civilians was prohibited.[33]

Furthermore, the restrictions applied to incendiaries designed as anti-personnel weapons, illuminants, or other-purpose incendiaries, thus, would not fall under the restricted category, for example, white phosphorus. Therefore, the question of incendiaries ultimately became a question of discrimination between combatants and non-combatants rather than a question of unnecessary suffering. Given the fact that other weapons also include secondary incendiary effects, it is indeed rather challenging to argue that fuel-air bombs or flamethrowers are particularly barbaric when used against fortified targets instead of bunker-buster-type munitions. As is pointed out, "their use against combatants is not prohibited, and the international community has not concluded that they inflict unnecessary suffering or superfluous injury of combatants. Also, notwithstanding the restraint in the use of incendiary weapons, burn injuries are common to war, and there is extensive medical data on them."[34] Notwithstanding, pursuant to UNGA Resolution 2932 and the expertise offered by the ICRC,[35] I concur there is something intrinsically barbaric and against human nature in deliberately burning the enemy alive. Any State that dares to deploy napalm or flamethrowers extensively would face "public conscience." As Neer (2013) points out: "Ferocious denials [of napalm

[32] United Nations Conference on Prohibitions or Restrictions of use of certain conventional weapons which may be deemed to be excessively injurious or to have indiscriminate effects. Summary record of the 5th meeting, September 13, 1979. A/CONF.95/SR.5.para 19.

[33] Convention on Prohibitions or Restrictions on the Use of Certain Conventional Weapons which may be Deemed to be Excessively Injurious or to have Indiscriminate Effects: Protocol III: Protocol on Prohibitions or Restrictions on the Use of Incendiary Weapons (adopted 10 October 1980, entered into force 2 December 1983) 1342 UNTS 171. Art.(2) ¶ 1.

[34] Marie Donna Verchio, "Just Say No! The SIrUS Project: Well-Intentioned, But Unnecessary and Superfluous" *Air Force Law Review* 51, (2001): 183–228, 202.

[35] Napalm and other incendiary weapons and all aspects of their possible use, UNGA A/9207, 11 October 1973.

deployment] underlined the potency of the charge and echoed vituperative reactions of governments elsewhere accused of napalm deployments."[36]

Yet another case in point regarding the definition of unnecessary suffering as a long-term health effect is the prohibition of blinding lasers, designed as such and defined under Protocol IV of the CCW.[37] Numerous States had funded research into the potential military utility of blinding lasers since these were perceived as not notably worse than burning people alive or tearing them apart.[38] While prohibitions of lasers designed to blind are part of customary law codified in Art. 1 of the Protocol IV of the CCW,[39] the issue again is permanent damage resulting in subsequent psychological problems and extreme difficulties in social reintegration. Dinstein (2004) noted that these effects constitute superfluous injury, as they represent a severe and permanent injury.[40] This is a somewhat contradictory statement by Dinstein, who represented the traditionalist approach and had refused the medicalization of unnecessary suffering.[41] Therefore, untreatable, long-term health effects do play a significant role in defining the substance of SIrUS regardless of any military advantage possibly stemming from the use of such weapons. Blinding lasers are an outstanding example. Permanent blindness exceeds the temporal scope of application of the LOAC and persists for the rest of the life of the combatant. However, it is imperative to state that only lasers specifically designed to blind are prohibited, not lasers that cause blindness by improper use, such as navigational ones.[42] Losing a vision is exceptionally psychologically traumatizing. Losing eyesight is, therefore, linked to suffering in a psychosomatic sense and with extreme difficulties in returning to everyday life. As other

[36] Neer, *Napalm*, 207.

[37] Convention on Prohibitions or Restrictions on the Use of Certain Conventional Weapons which may be Deemed to be Excessively Injurious or to have Indiscriminate Effects: Protocol IV: Protocol on Blinding Laser Weapons (adopted 13 October 1995, entered into force 30 July 1998) 1380 UNTS 370.

[38] Dan Drollette Jr., "Blinding Them With Science: Is Development of a Banned Laser Weapon Continuing?" *Bulletin of the Atomic Scientists,* September 14, 2014. https://thebulletin.org/2014/09/blinding-them-with-science-is-development-of-a-banned-laser-weapon-continuing/.

[39] See Rule 86, Henckaerts and Doswald-Beck.

[40] Yoram Dinstein, *The Conduct of Hostilities Under the Law of International Armed Conflict* (Cambridge: Cambridge University Press, 2004), 73.

[41] Dinstein, *Conduct,* 59.

[42] Stuart Casey-Maslen, *Jus ad Bellum: The Law on Inter-State Use of Force,* (New York: Hart, 2020), 219.

weapons may cause blindness as well, it is clear that lasers that cause blindness deliberately are prohibited. In the case of blinding lasers, therefore, the medicalization meets the design-purpose interpretation.

Whether SIrUS was explicitly defined and applied during the deliberations on CCW or refuted for a particular weapon is irrelevant. What is important is that medical terms and discussions of health effects dominated the diplomatic conference, and such health-based discussions did, in fact, refer to unnecessary suffering. That is, not only military necessity but specific health aspects were dominant points of the debates, pointing to the fact that such health effects increasingly play a role and should not be disregarded or ignored on behalf of military necessity.

5.4 Chemical Weapons Convention

Before the Paris Conference of 1989, which led to the comprehensive prohibition of chemical weapons in 1993 in the Chemical Weapons Convention or CWC, several developments in the field of disarmament required consideration. Agent Orange (dioxin)[43] symbolized another controversial issue, noteworthy from the perspective of design purpose versus unnecessary suffering. The intended use of chemicals in the course of the Vietnam War was to defoliate the jungle, not target people, which would fall under a treaty prohibition such as the Hague Convention IV prohibiting the use of poison. Nevertheless, after public outcry, the UNSG submitted a report to the General Assembly in 1969 on "Chemical and Biological Weapons and the Effects of Their Possible Use."[44] Public pressure and condemnation of the use of defoliants were among the contributing factors that prompted the United States to ratify the Biological Weapons Convention (BWC)[45] in March 1975, which included obligations for negotiations regarding the effective prohibition of chemical weapons under Art. IX of the BWC. While the motive was political rather than pragmatic, the U.S. government sped up the ratification in response to public outcry regarding the use of Agent Orange in Vietnam. Hence,

[43] See Agent Orange Record, "What is Dioxin?" accessed April 25, 2022. https://agentorangerecord.com/what-is-dioxin-2/.

[44] UNSG "Report on Chemical and Bacteriological (Biological) Weapons and the Effects of their Possible Use" (August 1 1969) UN Doc. A/7575/Rev.1.

[45] Convention on the Prohibition of the Development, Production and Stockpiling of Bacteriological (Biological) and Toxic Weapons and on their Destruction (opened for signature on 10 April 1972, entered into force on 26 March 1975) 1015 UNTS 163.

while States are the lawmakers, public conscience—represented by civil society, international organizations, NGOs, and special-interest groups, such as victims' associations—helped form opinions and guide legislators in the appropriate direction. The testimonialization thus correlates and strongly affects the medicalization of the principle.

In March 1984, amid continuous allegations of deployment of chemical weapons on the battlefields of the Iran-Iraq War, U.S. President Ronald Reagan dispatched Vice President George H.W. Bush to the Conference on Disarmament to negotiate further progress on the CWC.[46] As stated earlier, legal obligations requiring negotiations regarding the effective prohibition of chemical weapons were already stipulated under Art. IX of the BWC, which the United States ratified on March 26, 1975. An effective path to such a universal disarmament instrument is, of course, complex in itself. For instance, an agreement on the most challenging issue, the on-site verification of the destruction of chemical weapons (CW) production facilities, first materialized only between 1986 and 1987, with the most controversial topic being the challenge inspections.[47] Every State seeks to protect its industrial secrets from espionage, and challenge inspections are often seen as unwelcome intrusions and threats to industrial secrets and know-how. Civil society, including the SIPRI and international Pugwash movements, actively supported negotiations that led to the adoption of the convention.[48] Of particular importance was the International Government-Industry Conference against Chemical Weapons in Canberra, which, most importantly, underlined the full support of the chemical industry for a global ban. At the same time, the chemical industry itself provided technical training for future inspectors of the Organisation for the Prohibition of Chemical Weapons (OPCW).[49] In the 1980s, meetings were held frequently between industrial and government representatives on a primarily national level.[50] National chemical industries were proactive and crucial in discussing verification, ratification,

[46] Jonathan B. Tucker, *U.S. Ratification of the Chemical Weapons Convention* (Washington, DC: National Defense University Press, 2011), 2.

[47] Walter Krutzsch, Eric Myjer, and Ralf Trapp, eds, *The Chemical Weapons Convention: A Commentary*. Oxford: Oxford University Press, 2014.

[48] Daniel Feakes, "Global Civil Society and Biological and Chemical Weapons" in *Global Civil Society Yearbook* edited by Kaldor, Mary, Helmut Anheier, and Marlies Glasius (Oxford: Oxford University Press, 2003), 98.

[49] Krutzsch, Myjer, and Trapp, 13–14.

[50] Krutzsch, Myjer, and Trapp, 38.

and inspections. With chemicals being the ultimate dual-use technology, the concern was about protecting trade and industrial secrets. Still, the industry realized it could benefit from partnering with the OPCW through the above-mentioned trainings, offering expertise and participation.

At the Paris Conference of January 1989 on chemical weapons, which was convened to prohibit CWs in a comprehensive agreement, numerous Arab nations requested the establishment of links between nuclear and chemical weapons to demand parallel disarmament.[51] The call for this pairing was against the backdrop of the revelation of the Israeli Nuclear Weapons Program by Mordechai Vanunu in 1986.[52] The link with nuclear weapons had already been expressed by the UN Commission for Conventional Armaments in 1948, which adopted the definition of weapons of mass destruction as "atomic explosive weapons, radioactive material weapons, lethal chemical and biological weapons, and any weapons developed in the future which have characteristics comparable in destructive effect to those of the atomic bomb or other weapons mentioned above with comparative effects."[53]

During the Gulf War (1990–1991), Tariq Aziz, the then-foreign minister of Iraq, stated that the Iraqi regime would not use CWs unless the United States used nuclear weapons first. This was later confirmed by the report of the United Nations Monitoring, Verification, and Inspection Commission (UNMOVIC) "that authority to launch biological and chemical warheads was pre-delegated if nuclear weapons hit Baghdad during the Gulf War."[54] This pairing of chemical weapons with nuclear weapons only further strengthened the perception of CWs as weapons of mass destruction, even though it is debatable that this is true. Therefore, the link of CWs to nuclear weapons to delegitimize them as weapons of mass destruction is a novel development that has served to prevent their use, together with their association with poison and historic abhorrence. This

[51] Richard M. Price, *The Chemical Weapons Taboo* (New York: Cornell University Press, 1997), 145.

[52] See Tony Long, "Oct.5, 1986: Israel's Secret Nuke Arsenal Exposed" *Wired*, October 5, 2011. https://www.wired.com/2011/10/1005israel-secret-nuclear-arsenal-exposed/.

[53] Resolutions Adopted by the Commission at its Thirteenth Meeting, 12 August 1948 and a Second Progress Report of the Commission UN Doc. S/C.3/32/Rev.1, para. 1.

[54] UNMOVIC Working Document, Unresolved Disarmament Issues Iraq's Proscribed Weapons Programmes, (6 March 2003), 159.

has effectively helped to remove CWs from standard and acceptable weapon arsenals.[55]

On September 3, 1992, the Conference on Disarmament (CD) in Geneva submitted the proposed Convention on the Prohibition of Chemical Weapons to the UN General Assembly, and the UNGA endorsed the document in November 1992.[56] The CWC was subsequently opened for signature in Paris in January 1993. However, the delegates at the CD could not resolve all of the complex issues during deliberations; thus, the UNGA created a Preparatory Commission, or PrepCom,[57] tasked with carrying out the essential preparations for the effective implementation of the Chemical Weapons Convention and organizing the first session of the State Parties.[58] Under Art. XXI, the CWC would enter into force 180 days after depositing the 65th ratification instrument with the UNSG but no earlier than two years after opening for signature. This was to secure time for the PrepCom to make all the necessary preparations. The First Session of the PrepCom was convened at the commission's seat at The Hague on February 8–12, 1993.[59] Since there was no experience with such intrusive verification regimes, the commission built on experiences of the International Atomic Energy Agency (IAEA), the United Nations Special Commission, and national investigations.[60] The PrepCom consisted of the Provisional Technical Secretariat (now the OPCW Technical Secretariat) and all signatory States.

The initial absence of the US and Russian Federation as signatories slowed down the ratification process, as many States observed whether these two superpowers had any intentions to join the agreement. On October 31, 1996, Hungary became the 65th nation to deposit its instruments of ratification, with the UN Secretary-General completing the necessary quorum. Then, the CWC entered into force on April 29, 1997. The participation of the United States was crucial to the success of the Convention because the United States had one of the largest stockpiles of

[55] Price, 162.

[56] UNGA Res. A/RES/47/39. Convention on the Prohibition of the Development, Production, Stockpiling and Use of Chemical Weapons and on Their Destruction.

[57] The PrepCom would become the Organization for the Prohibition of Chemical Weapons (OPCW) after the treaty's entry into force.

[58] Krutzsch, Myjer, and Trapp.

[59] OPCW, Preparatory Commission Documents, accessed 22 December 2020, https://www.opcw.org/resources/documents/preparatory-commission.

[60] Krutzsch, Myjer, and Trapp, 18.

chemical weapons. Participation of possessor States makes any agreement concerning weapons ban genuinely effective.[61] However, it took the United States four years to ratify the CWC since it did not initially stand out on the priority list of President Clinton, who assumed office shortly after the Paris Conference of 1993.[62] The year was busy for President Clinton, notably marked by the infamous Black Hawk Down incident during Operation Gothic Serpent in October 1993.

In 1984, the U.S. Congress had already ordered its Department of Defense (DoD) to begin destroying stockpiles of CWs, which were aging and posing significant health and environmental hazards.[63] Following the 1990 bilateral agreement with the USSR, chemical agents were to be retained only for training and defensive purposes.[64] For the United States, one of the contentious issues involved the use of riot control agents (RCAs) in armed conflict, ultimately leading to a reaffirmation of the right to deploy RCAs in special combat operations.[65] Should the United States fail to ratify the CWC, it would not be granted a seat on the 41-member OPCW Executive Council, and, therefore, U.S. citizens would be barred from serving in the Technical Secretariat.[66] Additionally, without ratification, the U.S. chemical companies would face trade restrictions on non-parties to the convention. Finally, the United States deposited its instrument of ratification on April 25, 1997, merely four days before the convention entered into force.[67] The PrepCom became the OPCW, and the primary principal organs are the Conference of State Parties, the Executive Council, and the Technical Secretariat (formerly the Provisional Technical Secretariat).[68] The CWC became legally binding, with 87 States

[61] Stuart Casey-Maslen, and Tobias Vestner, *A Guide to Disarmament Law* (New York: Routledge, 2019).

[62] See Ann Devroy and Ruth Marcus "Clinton Takes Oath as 42nd President Asking Sacrifice, Promising Renewal" *Washington Post*, January 21, 1993. https://www.washingtonpost.com/wp-srv/national/longterm/inaug/history/stories/clint92.htm.

[63] Tucker, 3.

[64] Agreement between the United States of America and the Union of Soviet Socialist Republics on Destruction and Non-Production of Chemical Weapons and on Measures to Facilitate the Multilateral Convention on Banning Chemical Weapons (1 June 1990) (1990) 29 ILM 934.

[65] Office of the Federal Register, "Executive Order 11850."

[66] Chemical Weapons Convention, at Art. VIII (23) and (44).

[67] Tucker, 23.

[68] Chemical Weapons Convention, at Art. VIII (4).

already having deposited their instruments of ratification.[69] State Parties began submitting their initial declarations in May, and in early June, the OPCW conducted its first inspections.

The Convention contains only 24 operative articles, yet it is one of history's most complex disarmament agreements. This complexity arises mainly from the requirements for stockpile destruction and verification detailed in its annexes, bringing the total agreement to nearly 160 pages. General obligations are set out in Art. I. The controversial issue of RCAs is mentioned in Art. II (9)(c) prohibits their use as a "method of warfare"; therefore, not applicable to their use for law enforcement purposes. Indeed, this issue can become quite complex in law enforcement operations, such as crowd control or POW control. The US maintains that such uses may be permissible for law enforcement purposes. This, however, is met with opposition from Russia and China, who point out that such a distinction between law enforcement and warfare can be blurred in armed conflict. Paradoxically, it is the Russian Federation that is now facing allegations of using chloropicrin and RCAs against Ukraine, which raises questions about their commitment to the convention.[70] Under Art. II (1), chemical weapons are defined as:

a. Toxic chemicals and their precursors, except where intended for purposes not prohibited under this Convention, as long as the types and quantities are consistent with such purposes;
b. Munitions and devices, specifically designed to cause death or other harm through the toxic properties of those toxic chemicals specified in subparagraph (a), which would be released as a result of the employment of such munitions and devices;
c. Any equipment specifically designed for use directly in connection with the employment of munitions and devices specified in subparagraph (b).[71]

[69] See Organisation for the Prohibition of Chemical Weapons, "OPCW by the Numbers," accessed December 11, 2020. https://www.opcw.org/media-centre/opcw-numbers.

[70] "The Alleged Use of Chemical Weapons in Ukraine: How the International Community Can Investigate," accessed 04 September 2024, available at: https://europeanleadershipnetwork.org/commentary/the-alleged-use-of-chemical-weapons-in-ukraine-how-the-international-community-can-investigate/.

[71] Convention on the Prohibition of the Development, Production, Stockpiling and Use of Chemical Weapons and on their Destruction (opened for signature 13 January 1993, entered into force 29 April 1997) 1974 UNTS 45.¶Art.II(1).

Art. II (2) further narrows the meaning of a "toxic chemical" as:

> Any chemical which through its chemical action on life processes can cause death, temporary incapacitation or permanent harm to humans or animals. This includes all such chemicals, regardless of their method of production, and regardless of whether they are produced in facilities, in munitions or elsewhere.

The next critical step for the CWC was to achieve universality by promoting the convention and actively engaging with non-member States to expand its membership. On December 5, 1997, the Conference of State Parties adopted a decision on tangible steps in a "Recommendation on Ensuring the Universality of the Convention"[72] and then on May 16, 2000, reviewed a report on the implementation of the recommendations,[73] which ultimately contributed to the adoption of the Action Plan on Universality in 2003 by the Executive Council.[74] In addition, during the Third Review Conference (RevCon) in 2013, civil societies were allowed to make statements for the first time. Civil societies play a vital role in the success of the CWC, which depends on the relationship between States, industry, and civil society in monitoring compliance with the convention. A case in point is the Chemical Weapons Convention Monitoring Coalition.[75]

The convention revolves more around design-purpose criterion rather than unnecessary suffering. Under the definition of purposes not prohibited by the convention, that is, Article II (9), any chemical can be used for military purposes, including as a weapon, provided that the primary effect is not toxicity toward humans or animals. As a result, even though some chemicals possess toxic properties, such as certain incendiaries like napalm

[72] Decision: Recommendation on Ensuring the Universality of the Convention, OPCW Doc. C-II/DEC.11. (5 December 1997).

[73] Report on the Implementation of the Recommendation of the Conference of the States Parties at its Fourth Session on Ensuring the Universality of the Chemical Weapons, OPCW Doc. C- V/DG.12 (16 May 2000).

[74] Technical Secretariat Background Paper on Universal Adherence to the Chemical Weapons Convention, TS Doc. RC-1/S/5, 2003 (25 April 2003).

[75] See OPCW, "Our Partners" accessed December 20, 2020, https://www.opcw.org/about/our-partners#:~:text=The%20CWC%20Coalition%20is%20a,for%20the%20Prohibition%20of%20Chemical.

and white phosphorous (used to generate smoke) and explosives, they do not fall under the scope of the CWC.

While humanitarian and civil society groups frequently discuss the concept of 'unnecessary suffering,' States tend to avoid addressing this issue directly. The reason is pragmatic: declaring or even suggesting a weapon at odds with the norm would render it unlawful under the well-established customary norm, as outlined in previous chapters. The CWC's success lies largely in the fact that nations with the largest chemical stockpiles were actively involved in negotiating the treaty. This momentum was also sustained by the extensive use of chemical weapons during the Iran-Iraq war, which further galvanized efforts to ban these weapons. However, the dynamic shifted with the growing involvement of non-governmental organizations and humanitarian initiatives that began influencing disarmament negotiations.

5.5 The Ottawa Treaty

The Ottawa Process arose from dissatisfaction with the negotiations of the Convention on Certain Conventional Weapons (CCW) Protocol II,[76] which was restricted in scope, with few ratifying States and a relatively meager overall reaction and support of the international community.[77] As explained earlier, the CCW is not a disarmament agreement but a LOAC treaty regulating the use of specific weapons under its protocols, including landmines. The CCW Protocol II concerning mines covered the specific technical and deployment aspects of allowed devices, such as detectability, thereby prohibiting the use of nondetectable landmines that could explode near mine detectors.[78] While the second protocol in Art. 3(3) prohibits unnecessary suffering, the wording slightly differs from Art. 35(2) of AP I. Therefore, Article 3(3) CCW Protocol II stipulates that: "It is prohibited in all circumstances to use any mine, booby trap, or other device which is designed or of a nature to cause superfluous injury or unnecessary."

[76] Convention on Prohibitions or Restrictions on the Use of Certain Conventional Weapons which may be Deemed to be Excessively Injurious or to have Indiscriminate Effects: Protocol II: Protocol on Prohibitions or Restrictions on the Use of Mines, Booby-Traps and Other Devices (adopted 10 October 1980, entered into force 2 December 1983) 1342 UNTS 168.

[77] Daniel Rietiker, *Humanization of Arms Control: Paving the Way for a World Free of Nuclear Weapons.* (New York: Routledge, 2018), 20–24.

[78] Art.3(5), Art.4.

The difference thus stems from the inclusion of the word "designed," denoting purpose and intent to cause excessive injuries. As such, a conceivable design to cause excessive injury could be the inclusion of glass fragments into a mine to obscure surgery or to use a material of a nature to cause such suffering without particular necessity, poisonous fragments, depleted uranium, or biological agents prohibited by the Biological Weapons Convention (BWC).

ICRC Medical Advisory Robin Coupland (1997b), a former field surgeon, strongly argued that landmines always cause unnecessary suffering by inflicting greater harm than necessary to incapacitate an enemy.[79] At the Second CCW Review Conference in 1996, the inadequate response to victims' needs led to the Ottawa Process, a series of diplomatic conferences that began later that year.[80] The following year, at the final conference on anti-personnel landmines, participating States signed the Ottawa Treaty, which entered into force on March 1, 1999.[81] The Ottawa Process saw extensive civil society involvement, particularly from NGOs like the International Campaign to Ban Landmines,[82] with prominent figures and organizations such as Princess Diana,[83] and of course, the ICRC yet again employing medicalization and testimonialization to achieve this ban. This contrasted with the Chemical Weapons Convention, where the key drivers were States, resulting in limited discussion of unnecessary suffering in the negotiations. This remarkable development marks what can now be called the humanitarian movement for the disarmament of particular weapons considered in violation of the principle of unnecessary suffering.

The first draft of the Ottawa Treaty submitted by Austria included a statement that "it is prohibited to use antipersonnel mines as they are

[79] Robin M. Coupland, "Abhorrent Weapons and 'Superfluous Injury or Unnecessary Suffering': From Field Surgery to Law" *BMJ: British Medical Journal* 315, no. 7120 (1997a): 1450–1452 http://www.jstor.org/stable/25176382.

[80] Rietiker, 22.

[81] Convention on the Prohibition of the Use, Stockpiling, Production and Transfer of Anti-Personnel Mines and on their Destruction (concluded 18 September 1997, entered into force 1 March 1999) 2056 UNTS 211 (Ottawa Convention).

[82] See International Campaign to Ban Landmines, "A Global Network Working for a World Free of Landmines," accessed April 25, 2022. http://www.icbl.org/en-gb/home.aspx.

[83] See Suyin Haynes, "Prince Harry Is Honoring His Mother's Work in Angola. Here's What to Know About Princess Diana's Landmines Walk" *Time*, September 27, 2019 https://time.com/5682006/princess-diana-landmines/.

deemed excessively injurious or have indiscriminate effects."[84] The SIrUS principle is hidden behind the word "excessively." Furthermore, the draft indirectly confirmed SIrUS as a customary principle by stating, "It is prohibited [by custom]." However, whether antipersonnel landmines do cause unnecessary suffering to combatants is contentious, as discussed in Chap. 4. This direct association of landmines and unnecessary suffering in the draft dismayed numerous States, particularly those not yet a party to the convention and not planning to become a party.[85] If the customary rule of unnecessary suffering prohibited antipersonnel landmines, their use would violate international law even for these non-parties. However, following the protests of such States, which would have jeopardized the entire convention and its conclusion, the text of the draft was subsequently changed to the all-encompassing sentence in disarmament treaties: "never under any circumstances" to use antipersonnel mines.[86] Of particular interest is the ICRC's reference to the SIrUS Project; during the deliberations, the ICRC referred to the project in defining objective criteria to determine whether the health effects violate SIrUS.[87] As for the effects of antipersonnel landmines in regards to the norm prohibiting unnecessary suffering, a statement by ICRC President Cornelio Sommaruga at the Ottawa Process on October 4, 1996, deserves to be quoted directly:

> If a person steps on a buried antipersonnel mine, his or her foot or leg is blown off. The force of the blast drives earth, grass, the vaporized mine case, and portions of the victim's shoe and foot upwards into the tissues of the other leg, buttocks, genitals, arms, and sometimes eyes. … If the person gets to a hospital, he or she will require several operations, stay in hospital for weeks and will require a safe blood transfusion. Awaiting the survivor is permanent and severe disability with all the social, psychological, and economic implications of being an amputee. Would not most people, including soldiers, describe the effects of mines just mentioned as superfluous and excessive to the military need?[88]

[84] Louis Maresca and Stuart Maslen. *The Banning of Anti-Personnel Landmines: The Legal Contribution of the International Committee of the Red Cross* (Cambridge: Cambridge University Press, 2000), 613.

[85] See Anti-Personnel Mine Ban Convention, "Membership," including declarations of non-member States at Anti-Personnel Mine Ban Convention, "Membership" accessed June 24, 2022 https://new.apminebanconvention.org/en/membership/.

[86] Maresca and Maslen, 613.

[87] Maresca and Maslen, 621.

[88] Maresca and Maslen, 478.

Thus, during the 1996 deliberations, the ICRC SIrUS Project was very much alive and helpful. It was only in 2005 that the organization had withdrawn the proposal. However, as is apparent, the ICRC has not changed its position on landmines as causing unnecessary suffering to combatants.[89] Therefore, it is a distinct illustration of attempts to define SIrUS in medical terms to achieve a practical result—a ban on a particular weapon category. What is different about the entire Ottawa Process compared to other attempts at disarmament—in addition to the ICRC's involvement in offering its medical expertise gained through field experience—is the massive participation of civil society with frequent references to the principle of unnecessary suffering concerning sustained injuries and the long-term untreatable health effects of these weapons.[90]

While the expertise of the ICRC is widely recognized, some members of civil society have at times reinterpreted or misinterpreted the application of the principle by conflating the Law of Armed Conflict (LOAC) with human rights law. There remains ongoing debate as to whether the non-use of landmines constitutes customary international law (lex lata), though current State practice suggests that the norm against anti-personnel landmines is not yet fully established as customary law and is, at best, still developing (lex ferenda).[91] Speaking from a perspective of realist theory, the interpretation of whether a particular weapon causes unnecessary suffering often hinges on whether a State perceives utility in that weapon. This demonstrates that the determination of unnecessary suffering is not solely a legal or humanitarian question but also reflects the practical considerations of States regarding the utility of certain weapons. As mentioned earlier, stating that a particular weapon, by its nature, causes SIrUS as codified in AP I Art.35(2) and as reaffirmed by the ICJ to be a customary norm of the LOAC would make the weapon ultimately unlawful for every State, regardless of it being a party to a particular treaty or not. This is important when discussing the dichotomy in interpreting the SIrUS principle. In many respects, the Oslo Convention adopted in 2008 mirrors

[89] See Peter Maurer, "20 Years After the Historic Treaty on Landmines, We Cannot Afford to Lose Momentum: ICRC President Peter Maurer's Address to the Sixtieth Meeting of the States Parties, Anti-Personnel Mine Ban Convention 18 December 2017, Vienna." accessed April 29, 2022. https://www.icrc.org/en/document/statement-20-years-after-historic-treaty-landmines-we-cannot-afford-lose-momentum.

[90] Maresca and Maslen, 621.

[91] Stuart Casey-Maslen, *The Treaty on the Prohibition of Nuclear Weapons: A Commentary.* (Oxford: Oxford University Press, 2019), 21.

the Ottawa Process, as do the arguments raised during deliberations. This is because the effects of cluster munitions closely resemble the issues behind antipersonnel landmines.[92]

While the ICRC's expertise on issues like unnecessary suffering is widely respected, the interpretation of such principles can vary significantly, particularly when civil society or other actors conflate LOAC with human rights law. The ongoing debate around the non-use of landmines and whether it constitutes customary law illustrates the evolving nature of norms in this area. Ultimately, whether a weapon is deemed to cause unnecessary suffering is often linked to the perceived utility of that weapon by States. This highlights that the SIrUS principle-whether a weapon inherently causes unnecessary suffering-cannot be viewed solely through a humanitarian lens but must also account for the practical and strategic considerations of States. This tension between legal norms and State practice plays a critical role in shaping how the principle of unnecessary suffering is applied in international law, particularly in the context of weapon legality.

5.6 Treaty on the Prohibition of Nuclear Weapons

While chemical weapons became progressively stigmatized and gradually acquired the degrading nickname of a "poor man's bomb," nuclear weapons were the opposite. Nuclear deterrence is considered by nuclear-weapon States (NWS) as crucial for security and is often used as an instrument of power and status.[93] That is why NWS sternly oppose attempts to link the weapons with unnecessary suffering. Civil society and anti-nuclear activists are thus repeating the process of stigmatization, taking the example of chemical weapons, emphasizing, inter alia, the long-term effects of nuclear explosions (i.e., the effects-based approach to SIrUS). The international community had already recognized the need for nuclear disarmament at the 17th plenary meeting of the newly established United Nations on January 24, 1946, which, in its very first resolution,

[92] For details see Oslo Process, accessed May 11, 2022, https://www.clusterconvention.org/oslo-process/.

[93] Scott D. Sagan, "Why Do States Build Nuclear Weapons? Three Models in Search of a Bomb" *International Security* 21, no. 3 (1996/1997): 54–86, https://doi.org/10.2307/2539273.

called for "the elimination from national armaments of atomic weapons and of all other major weapons adaptable to mass destruction."[94]

On November 24, 1961, at its 16th plenary session, the UNGA adopted a declaration calling for the prohibition of nuclear weapons in the Resolution of 1653.[95] The resolution further called for organizing a diplomatic conference to outlaw these weapons and to bring about complete disarmament.[96] The resolution, in its third preambular paragraph, explicitly declared nuclear weapons to be contrary to the principles of international law already codified in declarations and binding agreements, such as the St. Petersburg Declaration of 1868 and the Hague Declaration and Regulations of 1899/1907 mentioned earlier.[97] Unnecessary suffering was indirectly referenced as part of the recognized principles of international law, particularly through explicit mention of the St. Petersburg Declaration. This aligns with the broader international disarmament efforts, which have seen varying levels of success. For instance, the UNGA held three special sessions on nuclear disarmament in 1978, 1982, and 1988, but only the first resulted in consensus and a final document in 1978.[98] These efforts are intrinsically linked to the momentum generated by U.S. President Dwight Eisenhower's 'Atoms for Peace' speech, which led to the establishment of the IAEA in 1957. Building on this, on November 13, 1959, Ireland submitted a proposal for a new legally binding agreement aimed at curbing nuclear proliferation and promoting gradual disarmament.[99] Consequently, the UNGA adopted a resolution suggesting the ten-nation disarmament committee consider the feasibility of such an agreement.[100] The Irish proposal and the UN resolution laid the cornerstone of nuclear disarmament efforts. International tensions

[94] UNGA Resolution A/RES/1(I), Establishment of a Commission to Deal with the Problems Raised by the Discovery of Atomic Energy, at para 5(c). (24 January 1946).

[95] UNGA Resolution 1653 (XVI) 'Declaration on the Prohibition of the Use of Nuclear and Thermonuclear Weapons' (24 November 1961).

[96] UNGA Resolution 1653 (XVI), para 2.

[97] UNGA Resolution 1653 (XVI), para 3.

[98] Final Document of the Tenth Special Session of the General Assembly, UN Doc. A/S-10/4. (23 May–30 June 1978).

[99] Evgeny M. Chossudovsky, "The Origins of the Treaty on the Non-Proliferation of Nuclear Weapons: Ireland's Initiative in the United Nations (1958–1961)" *Irish Studies in International Affairs* 3, no. 2 (1990): 111–135 http://www.jstor.org/stable/30001773.111, 35.

[100] UNGA Res. 1340 (XIV). Prevention of the Wider Dissemination of Nuclear Weapons (21 November 1959).

during the Cuban missile crisis three years later helped to speed up the materialization of these efforts in the form of the Treaty on the Non-Proliferation of Nuclear Weapons,[101] or the Non-Proliferation Treaty (NPT), adopted on July 1, 1968, which is still the cornerstone of the non-proliferation regime and disarmament efforts under its Art. VI.

As the International Court of Justice (ICJ) advisory opinion (AO) on nuclear weapons unanimously decided, clearly referring to Art. VI of the NPT, "... there exists an obligation to pursue in good faith and conclude [the] negotiations leading to nuclear disarmament in all its aspects under strict and effective international control."[102] Several regional arrangements have already restricted the deployment and use of nuclear weapons in various regions of the world. These agreements have established "nuclear weapons free zones" or NWFZs in specific regions or even in outer space.[103] Creating these zones is endorsed by UNGA Resolution 3472 concerning the comprehensive study of the question of nuclear-weapon-free zones, in all of their aspects, stating that "Recognizing that the establishment of nuclear weapon-free zones can contribute to the security of members of such zones, to the prevention of the proliferation of nuclear weapons and to the goals of general and complete disarmament."[104]

[101] Treaty on the Non-Proliferation of Nuclear Weapons (adopted 1 July 1968, entered into force 5 March 1970) 729 UNTS 161.

[102] International Court of Justice, Legality of the Threat or Use of Nuclear Weapons, Advisory Opinion, July 8, 1996, I.C.J. Reports 1996, 226, para. 105(2)(F).

[103] These are the Antarctic Treaty (signed 1 December 1959, entered into force 23 June 1961) 402 UNTS 71. Treaty on Principles governing the Activities of States in the Exploration and Use of Outer Space, Including the Moon and Other Celestial Bodies (signed 27 January 1967, entered into force 10 October 1967) 610 UNTS 205. Treaty on the Prohibition of the Emplacement of Nuclear Weapons and Other Weapons of Mass Destruction on the Sea-Bed and the Ocean Floor and in the Subsoil Thereof (concluded 11 February 1971, entered into force 18 May 1972) 955 UNTS 115. Agreement governing the Activities of States on the Moon and Other Celestial Bodies (adopted 5 December 1979, entered into force 11 July 1984) 1363 UNTS 3. Treaty for the Prohibition of Nuclear Weapons in Latin America (done 14 February 1967, entered into force 22 April 1968) 634 UNTS 326 (Treaty of Tlatelolco). South Pacific Nuclear Free Zone Treaty (concluded 6 August 1985, entered into force 11 December 1988) 1445 UNTS 177 (Rarotonga Treaty). Treaty on the Southeast Asia Nuclear Weapon-Free Zone (signed 15 December 1995, entered into force 27 March 1997) (1996) 35 ILM 639. African Nuclear-Weapon-Free-Zone Treaty (signed 11 April 1996, entered into force 15 July 2009) (1996)35 ILM 698. Treaty on a Nuclear-Weapon-Free Zone in Central Asia (signed 8 September 2006, entered into force 21 March 2009). <http://cns.miis.edu/> (26 January 2012) (Treaty of Semipalatinsk).

[104] UNGA Resolution A/RES/3472 (XXX)A, Comprehensive study of the question of nuclear-weapon-free zones in all its aspects, at para. 5. (11 December 1975).

While member States of nuclear-weapon-free zones unilaterally renounce nuclear weapons, it is left to the discretion of nuclear weapons States or NWS whether to accede to additional protocols that pledge non-use of nuclear weapons against States within these zones. Such protocols are integral to strengthening the security assurances provided to non-nuclear weapon States (NNWS). A significant step in this regard came on April 11, 1995, when the United Nations Security Council or UNSC adopted Resolution 984.[105] Through this resolution, NWS provided formal security assurances against the use or threat of use of nuclear weapons against NNWS that are parties to the NPT. These assurances, although seen as positive, were still subject to reservations and conditions laid out by individual NWS, reflecting the geopolitical complexities at play. Resolution 984 marked a significant milestone but left ambiguity, particularly regarding its binding nature and enforcement in scenarios working with regional conflicts and their escalation. Over the years, these assurances have been revisited in international fora, as NNWS continues to seek legally binding guarantees, while NWS often emphasizes the strategic flexibility required by their nuclear deterrence policies.

This ongoing dialogue shifted in emphasis, particularly after the 2010 NPT Review Conference, when growing attention was directed toward the humanitarian consequences of the use of nuclear weapons, as reflected in statements made through multiple UN forums. These concerns led to three conferences on the humanitarian impact of nuclear weapons: Oslo (2013), Nayarit (February 2014), and Vienna (December 2014). As the head of the ICRC, Peter Maurer, stated in a speech in Vienna in 2014:

> There has been a fundamental change in the debate about nuclear weapons. After decades of focusing on nuclear weapons primarily in technical-military terms and as symbols of power, States have finally engaged in a long overdue discussion of what they would mean for people and the environment, indeed for humanity.[106]

This statement and praise by the ICRC are not surprising, given the previous effects-based approach on other weapons, such as napalm, landmines, or chemical weapons. We also cannot overlook the vital role of the

[105] UNSC Res 984 (1995) 'Security Assurances against Use of Nuclear Weapons to Non-Nuclear-Weapon States' (11 April 1995).

[106] Vienna Conference on the Humanitarian Impact of Nuclear Weapons (8–9 December 2014), Federal Ministry for Europe, Integration and Foreign Affairs, Republic of Austria.

survivors of Hiroshima and Nagasaki, including groups such as *Nihon Hidankyo*.[107] Survivors of the Hiroshima and Nagasaki bombings brought a profound sense of realism to the conferences and negotiations. Nuclear weapons were no longer seen as distant or abstract; their devastating human impact became undeniably real. Their health effects, including psychological impact, were present and visible, whether through the attendance of the WWII bombing survivors or those affected by nuclear testing in Semipalatinsk or the Marshall Islands.[108] Nihon Hidankyo was awarded the Nobel Peace Prize in October 2024 for their work in bringing this sense of realism into nuclear disarmament.[109] This recognition further reinforces the power of testimonialization, playing an essential part when arguing about the illegality of weapons.

On December 11, 2015, the UN adopted Resolution 70/33[110] in response to the failure of the 2015 NPT RevCon to produce a final document.[111] This resolution led to an open-ended working group, which, in its final report, recommended that the UNGA convene a 2017 conference. This conference, open to all States and including the participation of international organizations and civil society, was tasked with negotiating a legally binding instrument to prohibit nuclear weapons.[112] Consequently, through adopting Resolution 71/258, the General Assembly convened a diplomatic conference,[113] which successfully concluded with adopting the Treaty on the Prohibition of Nuclear Weapons (TPNW) on July 7, 2017.

Testimonies provided during the conference highlighted the long-term effects of a nuclear explosion, particularly ionizing radiation, linking unnecessary suffering through the prolonged torment of the survivors at

[107] See Nihon Hindankyo, available at: https://www.ne.jp/asahi/hidankyo/nihon/english/. Last access on October 28, 2024.

[108] See "Setsuko Thurlow Gives Final Remarks at Ban Treaty Adoption," Hibakusha Stories, July 7, 2017, accessed August 4, 2022, https://hibakushastories.org/setsuko-thurlow-gives-final-remarks-at-ban-treaty-adoption/.

[109] See The Nobel Peace Prize, Press Release, available at: https://www.nobelprize.org/prizes/peace/2024/press-release/, last access on 30 October 2024.

[110] Taking forward multilateral nuclear disarmament negotiations, UN Doc. A/RES/70/33 (11 December 2015).

[111] See 2015 NPT Review Conference, accessed May 11, 2022, https://www.un.org/en/conf/npt/2015/.

[112] Taking forward multilateral nuclear disarmament negotiations, UN Doc. A/71/371, at para. 67 (1 September 2016).

[113] Taking forward multilateral nuclear disarmament negotiations, UN Doc. A/RES/71/258 (11 January 2017).

side events of the diplomatic conference.[114] As expected, four NWSs voted against adopting Resolution 71/258, with China and 34 other States abstaining and 113 nations in favor.[115] Subsequently, the NWS and the States under the so-called nuclear umbrella boycotted the diplomatic conferences to negotiate the TPNW, apart from the Netherlands, which ultimately voted against the final adoption. The widespread boycott by NWS and nuclear umbrella States during the TPNW negotiations was likely influenced by the strategic and security concerns of these States. The International Campaign to Abolish Nuclear Weapons (ICAN) played a key role in advocating for the treaty, with an approach that sought to stigmatize the possession of nuclear weapons by emphasizing their humanitarian impact, including breach of the norm against unnecessary suffering. This approach may have contributed to the distancing of certain States from the negotiations, particularly those under nuclear deterrence arrangements, who did not want to be targets of criticism. However, given the deeply entrenched security interests tied to nuclear weapons, it is debatable whether a softer or more diplomatic approach from ICAN would have significantly altered the participation of NWS or umbrella States. As discussed in previous chapters, States often avoid engaging in discussions about unnecessary suffering due to its normative implications. This avoidance is even more pronounced when it comes to nuclear weapons, given their strategic importance, or better say, perceived strategic importance. Therefore, it is understandable that States would be particularly hesitant to address this issue in the context of nuclear disarmament.

ICAN effectively highlighted the humanitarian consequences of nuclear weapons, often linking their effects to the principle of unnecessary suffering. However, it is unclear whether ICAN's understanding of this principle was rooted in its historical applications and evolution, or if it reflected their own reinterpretation. The organization seldom elaborates on the principle, its interpretation, or its application using medical data with relevant analysis of legal instruments in the context of the TPNW.[116]

[114] See "Calendar of Side Events for Nuclear Weapon Ban Treaty Negotiations," Reaching Critical Will, last updated July 3, 2017, accessed August 4, 2022, https://www.reachingcriticalwill.org/disarmament-fora/nuclear-weapon-ban/negotiation/calendar.

[115] International Campaign to Abolish Nuclear Weapons (ICAN), "Voting on UN Resolution for Nuclear Ban Treaty," December 23, 2016, https://www.icanw.org/voting_on_un_resolution_for_nuclear_ban_treaty.

[116] ICAN, *The Nuclear Weapon Ban Treaty*. November 2017, accessed May 11, 2022. https://d3n8a8pro7vhmx.cloudfront.net/tectodevms/pages/2389/attachments/origi-

Notwithstanding, SIrUS is one of the principles of LOAC the TPNW is based on. In this book, I focus particularly on the statements made by the ICRC during negotiations as an international organization with a deep and established understanding of international humanitarian law (LOAC). While I prioritize their perspective over that of activists, the contribution of civil society to the eventual adoption of the TPNW cannot be overlooked. I acknowledge the significant role they played in mobilizing support for the treaty.

At a preparatory meeting on February 16, 2017, H.E. Elayne Whyte Gómez of Costa Rica, ambassador to the UN, was elected president of the UN Diplomatic Conference.[117] On March 27, 2017, at its first session, Mr. Kim Won-soo, who was then the under-secretary-general and UN high representative for disarmament affairs,[118] pledged the UN's full support of the Diplomatic Conference to President Whyte-Gómez, noting that the conference took place against the backdrop of rising tensions and that the risk of using nuclear weapons was as high as it had been for more than 60 years.[119] Mr. Kim Won-soo's warning about rising tensions against the backdrop of North Korea's nuclear ambitions eerily foreshadowed the nuclear threats we face today with conflicts in Ukraine and the Middle East.

At the first session of the Diplomatic Conference from March 27–31, 2017, States presented their views, which formed the basis for the president to draft the first version of the Treaty on the Prohibition of Nuclear Weapons. The second session held from June 15 to July 7, 2017, focused on reviewing the first draft, and on June 27, 2017, the second revised draft was presented,[120] followed by a third draft on July 3, where the most notable change was the initial exclusion of 'user or tester responsibility' for States that conducted atmospheric testing of nuclear weapons. This issue was corrected in the final draft of July 6, which reintroduced 'user or tester responsibility,' ultimately leading to the treaty's adoption by the UNGA on July 7, 2017. Notably, the Netherlands, a NATO member,

nal/1571070092/ican-2017-Oslo-final.pdf?1571070092.

[117] United Nations Office for Disarmament Affairs, *The United Nations Disarmament Yearbook*. Vol. 42 (Part II) (New York: United Nations Publications, 2017) 22.

[118] Succeeded by Ms. Izumi Nakamitsu on May 01, 2017. See UNODA, "Under-Secretary-General and High Representative for Disarmament Affairs" accessed February 12, 2022. https://www.un.org/disarmament/high-representative/.

[119] Casey-Maslen, *Treaty on Prohibition*, 48.

[120] Draft Treaty on the Prohibition of Nuclear Weapons, UN Doc.A/CONF.229/2017/CRP.1/Rev.1. (27 June 2017).

was the only participating State to vote against the treaty, citing its incompatibility with NATO obligation, concerns about undermining the NPT, and inadequate verification mechanisms.[121] Throughout the drafting process, there was no explicit reference to the concept of unnecessary suffering or its direct application to nuclear weapons. However, the implications of this principle were present indirectly through its emphasis on humanitarian consequences.

On the day of its adoption, the United States, the UK, and France responded by issuing a joint statement, declaring that they do not intend to ratify, accede to, or sign the TPNW and that the agreement does not represent customary international law as it stands (i.e., *lex lata*) or contribute in any way to the development of customary norms (i.e., *lex ferenda*).[122] These NATO States held a position that the agreement had the potential to further divide the international community, which could become a major obstacle at the upcoming NPT Review Conference, scheduled for 2022, at which the TPNW could paralyze negotiations such that the proceedings could end up, yet again, without a final document of the State parties. Indeed, the 2022 NPT RevCon ended up without adopting a final document. However, not because of the TPNW but because of issues surrounding Russian military activities in Ukraine, particularly concerning the Zaporizhzhia Nuclear Power Plant.[123]

In Art. 12 of the TPNW, State parties are obligated to promote the agreement, which could diverge focus from issues under the NPT (i.e., issues of progressive disarmament). Notably, several State parties to regional disarmament treaties did not ratify or even sign the TPNW.[124]

[121] See ICAN, *Netherlands*, available at: https://www.icanw.org/netherlands#:~:text=In%20explaining%20its%20vote%2C%20it,commitments%20as%20a%20NATO%20state%E2%80%9D, last access on 14 September 2024.

[122] US Mission to the United Nations, "Joint Press Statement from the Permanent Representative to the United Nations of the United States, United Kingdom, and France Following the Adoption" July 7, 2017. https://usun.usmission.gov/joint-press-statement-from-the-permanent-representatives-to-the-united-nations-of-the-united-states-united-kingdom-and-france-following-the-adoption/.

[123] See United Nations Meetings Coverage and Press Releases, Nonproliferation Treaty Review Conference Ends Without Adopting Substantive Outcome Document Due to Opposition by One Member State, August 26, 2022, available at: https://press.un.org/en/2022/dc3850.doc.htm, last access on January 14, 2023.

[124] For instance, Argentina, Uzbekistan, Kyrgyzstan and Tajikistan. UN Office for Disarmament Affairs, "Treaty on the Prohibition of Nuclear Weapons" accessed January 11, 2021. https://treaties.unoda.org/t/tpnw.

The preambular paragraphs of the TPNW, as is also the case with the CWC, reflect Arts. 1 and 2 of the UN Charter, representing a source of guidance on the treaty's object, principles, and purposes.[125] In the case of the TPNW, the preamble reflects the humanitarian approach, centering around the effects and consequences of *any* [emphasis added] use of nuclear weapons while drawing from the language of the humanitarian initiative. It already connects SIrUS with weapons and all of its effects in Preamble (9):

> *Basing themselves* on the principles and rules of international humanitarian law, in particular the principle that the right of parties to an armed conflict to choose methods or means of warfare is not unlimited, the rule of distinction, the prohibition against indiscriminate attacks, the rules on proportionality and precautions in attack, the prohibition on the use of weapons of a nature to cause superfluous injury or unnecessary suffering, and the rules for the protection of the natural environment.

Unfortunately, this remains the only reference to the SIrUS principle in the TPNW. While the treaty lists the fundamental rules of the law of armed conflict, it does so without any detailed explanation or elaboration. As a result, without a more precise application of these principles, each of them could be challenged by NWS, which could justify their positions through flexible deterrence strategies supported by relevant legal precedents and customary international law. Moreover, the SIrUS deserves a separate paragraph explicitly mentioning specific long-term health effects of ionizing radiation, including significantly increased risks of leukemia and solid cancers and effects on the second generation, as I have described in the previous chapter. In its current form, the link is vague, and indeed, NWS can refuse such a link, relying on traditional interpretation by maintaining that nuclear weapons offer great military advantage and thus do not violate SIrUS. Such ambiguous phrases merely hinting at fundamental principles of LOAC are present throughout the TPNW.

The catastrophic consequence of nuclear weapons that are mentioned in Preamble (4) would be more suited when formulated as in the UNGA Resolution 71/258,[126] which discusses nuclear *war*, since the use of

[125] Richard Gardiner, *Treaty Interpretation*, 2nd ed, (Oxford: Oxford University Press, 2017).

[126] UNGA Res. 71/258. *Taking Forward Multilateral Nuclear Disarmament Negotiations*, at para. 8.

nuclear *weapons* can be arguably limited.[127] Nuclear war would be exceedingly destructive, but nuclear weapons in themselves have different yields ranging from half a kiloton to megatons, as discussed in preceding chapters. Furthermore, the statement under Preamble (4) is not shared among the NWS, which argued at the ICJ that the use of nuclear weapons could be proportionate.[128] Certainly, nuclear weapons are not weapons of a single category or yield. While this can seem like a valid legal argument, neither are prohibited chemical weapons all lethal, and the ban applies to all uses on the battlefield, even irritants such as tear gas, as I have pointed out.

The *ethical* imperatives in the Preamble (5) apparently suggest the tremendous costs of nuclear weapons.[129] Arguing about the ethics of weapons is complex and problematic. Labeling nuclear weapons as 'unethical' implies that other weapons, like conventional explosives or incendiaries such as napalm, might be considered 'ethical' by comparison. Such activist-driven language can harm the perception of the treaty among NWS, whose participation is critical for its success. By focusing on ethics rather than strategic, legal, and humanitarian concerns, we risk alienating these key players, which could undermine the broader goal of disarmament.

In contrast to the Chemical Weapons Convention or CWC, which pragmatically grounds itself in previous legal agreements and UN resolutions, the TPNW often relies on vague moral and philosophical terms related to humanity, seemingly neglecting the traditional application of the law of armed conflict. While this critique may seem harsh, the TPNW nonetheless makes an important achievement: it bravely acknowledges the devastating health effects of nuclear weapons as unacceptable, regardless of any perceived military advantage.

Nonetheless, the Preamble (6) specifically includes the word hibakusha,[130] as a person suffering from nuclear weapons. However, the

[127] See Jeffrey A. Larsen, and Kerry M. Katchner, *On Limited Nuclear War in the 21st Century*, (Stanford: Stanford University Press, 2014).

[128] Laurence Boisson de Chazournes, and Philippe Sands, eds, *International Law, the International Court of Justice and Nuclear Weapons* (Cambridge: Cambridge University Press, 1999), 298.

[129] Casey-Maslen, *Treaty on Prohibition*, 80.

[130] The term *hibakusha* is mentioned, although not defined, in Preamble (6) TPNW. By its generic meaning, the term refers to a person affected by a nuclear explosion. This is a general definition offered by the Matsumura Japanese Language Dictionary, Vol. 3, at 2315. However, the Shinmura Japanese language dictionary, vol.7, at 2480, defines *hibakusha*

definition remains unclear and is, in reality, more complex than it might seem. The Japanese Ministry of Health, Labour, and Welfare divides *hibakusha* into four categories:

> **Category 1**, or direct hibakusha, who were present at the time of bombing in specified areas of Hiroshima and Nagasaki;
> **Category 2**, or early entrants to the cities, in other words, those who entered any of the cities within two weeks of the bombings (for Hiroshima before August 20, 1945, and for Nagasaki before August 23, 1945) and who entered the area within 2 km of the hypocenter.
> **Category 3**, or rescuers or people involved with disposals of dead bodies (immediately after the explosion of the atomic bomb or those who were due to activities or circumstances affected by ionizing radiation, such as emergency rescue operations or disposals of dead bodies).
> **Category 4**, or those born before June 3, 1946, in Nagasaki or those born before May 31, 1946, to a person falling under one or more of the above-specified categories. Based on acceptance into one of these four categories, survivors of atomic bombings are entitled to free medical care.[131]

However, even in Japan, there was a prolonged dispute concerning who would be entitled to the State benefits under a claim that fell within one of the above-mentioned categories, particularly those survivors affected by the so-called 'black rain'.[132] Preamble (6) further includes victims who were affected by testing. Research in areas such as Kazakhstan, which was heavily affected by nuclear testing, confirmed an increase in malignant tumors, leukemia, and genetic defects.[133] The risk and effects, as explained in Chap. 4, varies greatly, and in cases where the dose value cannot be measured under 1Gy, it is rather difficult to argue for a particular disease or tumor resulting from any exposure. This creates an inherent

more narrowly as a person affected by ionizing radiation (translated from the Japanese language by the author).

[131] See Ministry of Health, Labor and Welfare, Japan, "Who is Hibakusha?" accessed December 11, 2020. https://www.mhlw.go.jp/stf/newpage_13405.html.

[132] See Eric Johnston, "Japan to Fight Ruling Recognizing Hiroshima 'Black Rain' Victims" *The Japan Times,* August 12, 2020, https://www.japantimes.co.jp/news/2020/08/12/national/crime-legal/japan-fights-hiroshima-black-rain-ruling/#.XzXu3hMzZhF.

[133] Noriyuki Kawano, Yasuyuki Taooka, Takashi Hiraoka, Masaharu Hoshi, and Z. Z. Shaimardanovich. *Report on the Actual Conditions of the Radiation Exposed Residents Near the Former Semipalatinsk Nuclear Test Site* (Hiroshima: Hiroshima University Research Institute for Radiation Biology and Medicine and Hiroshima Peace Science Consortium, 2004), 26.

difficulty in proving a casual relationship, weakening the potential for legal claims based on these criteria. The SIrUS principle, when left undefined or inadequately measured, adds little practical value. To give these norms substance, concrete data must support the link between exposure and specific health outcomes.

In connection to the preceding paragraph of the preamble of the TPNW, Preamble (10) states that any use of nuclear weapons violates international law, particularly international humanitarian law. As Casey-Maslen (2019) points out, this statement was heavily criticized by Sweden and the Netherlands for going beyond the ICJ Advisory Opinion of 1996 on nuclear weapons.[134] Preamble (11) places weight on the customary principle of humanity under the LOAC. The principle is further codified under Art. 1(2) of the 1977 AP I to the Geneva Conventions (GCs) of 1949, as well as in the preamble of AP II. The ICJ further stressed the principle's applicability in its AO of 1996: "In cases not covered by this Protocol or by other international agreements, civilians and combatants remain under the protection and authority of the principles of international law derived from established custom, from the principles of humanity and from the dictates of public conscience."[135] As explained in Chap. 2, humanity under LOAC is principally understood in narrow terms as humane treatment of combatants *hors de combat* or POWs or as a secondary norm. This is because public conscience is a rather broad concept.[136] Surveys have found that the public favor disarmament but also support nuclear deterrence.[137] The results of such polls are often dubious, influenced by the fluctuating international security environment and the framing of survey questions. As a result, they may not provide a fully reliable measure of public opinion or 'conscience' on nuclear weapons, despite being frequently emphasized by activist groups.[138] Instead of relying on the subjective indicators, a more concrete understanding of the TPNW can be gained by examining its operative provisions.

[134] Casey-Maslen, *Treaty on Prohibition*, 101.

[135] *Legality of the Threat or Use of Nuclear Weapons (Advisory Opinion)* [1996] ICJ Rep 226.¶ 78.

[136] For a generic definition of conscience, see Waite, 147.

[137] See ICAN, "77% of Belgians Support Joining the TPNW – Poll" accessed December 11, 2020. https://www.icanw.org/77_of_belgians_support_joining_the_tpnw_poll.

[138] Clifton B. Parker, "Public opinion unlikely to curb a U.S. president's use of nuclear weapons in war. Stanford scholar finds" *Stanford News,* August 8, 2017 https://news.stanford.edu/2017/08/08/americans-weigh-nuclear-war/.

Article 1 of the TPNW clearly defines the scope of prohibitions, establishing a legal framework that directly addresses the possession, use, and transfer of nuclear weapons:

a. Develop, test, produce, manufacture, otherwise acquire, possess or stockpile nuclear weapons or other nuclear explosive devices;
b. Transfer to any recipient whatsoever nuclear weapons or other nuclear explosive devices or control over such weapons or explosive devices directly or indirectly;
c. Receive the transfer of or control over nuclear weapons or other nuclear explosive devices directly or indirectly;
d. Use or threaten to use nuclear weapons or other nuclear explosive devices;
e. Assist, encourage or induce, in any way, anyone to engage in any activity prohibited to a State Party under this Treaty;
f. Seek or receive any assistance, in any way, from anyone to engage in any activity prohibited to a State Party under this Treaty;
g. Allow any stationing, installation or deployment of any nuclear weapons or other nuclear explosive devices in its territory or at any place under its jurisdiction or control.

"Never under any circumstances" from Art. 1 includes both the use as a belligerent reprisal and the use in peacetime due to its all-encompassing and definite nature.[139] "Other nuclear explosive devices," as expressed in Art. 1(a) is not explicitly defined, and there is no established definition of what such a device would be like.[140] Casey-Maslen (2019) suggests the definition includes those devices that have not been "weaponized."[141]

Together with use, the prohibition on the threat of use of nuclear weapons is explicitly stated in Art. 1(d). Conditions necessary for such a threat to be in violation of Art. 1(d) are not defined. Therefore, it would

[139] As an example of peaceful detonations, in 1966, the Soviet Union exploded a nuclear device to extinguish burning gas. See Shabad, "Soviet Union."

[140] The TPNW does not include the definition of a nuclear weapon. The P5 Glossary of Nuclear Terms definition is a weapon assembly capable of producing an explosion and massive damage and destruction by the sudden release of energy that is instantaneously released from self-sustaining nuclear fission and/or fusion. See P5 Working Group on the Glossary of Key Nuclear Terms, *P5 Glossary of Key Nuclear Terms* (Beijing: China Atomic Energy Press, 2015), 1.3.5.

[141] Casey-Maslen, *Treaty on Prohibition,* 137.

depend on the nature and context of the armed conflict. Whether such a threat would have to be direct or indirect is also unclear. In the case of CWC, in addition to the use of chemical weapons, Art. I (c) prohibits State parties from "engaging in any military preparations to use chemical weapons." This formulation would coincide with the language of TPNW since "to threaten" is quite a broad concept.[142] Casey-Maslen (2019) argues that the notion of "threaten to use" would cover any act, whether physical or verbal, that would create the perception that nuclear weapons are going to be used.[143] These perceptions can, however, be subjective and often depend on circumstances, particular leaders' and their character.

Art. 2 concerning declarations does not require annual reporting for States that have joined the treaty; however, it emphasizes transparency whereby States must declare whether they have nuclear weapons or devices or disposed of such weapons or devices before joining the agreement. In comparison, the CWC, in its annex on implementation and verification, Part IV (A) (36), requires annual reports on the destruction process. Art. 4 of the TPNW is, without a doubt, one of the most frequently discussed provisions from the legal standpoint. It calls for the cooperation of a "competent international authority" for the purpose of verifying the irreversible destruction of nuclear weapons, should NWS decide to join in and then destroy their arsenals. Given the formulation of the article, the IAEA is the obvious candidate. However, the views differ among the Board of Governors member States of the IAEA regarding the practicality of the TPNW. Therefore, reaching a consensus would be extremely difficult. According to Art. 34 of the Vienna Convention on Treaties: "A treaty does not create either obligations or rights for a third state without its consent."[144] Accordingly, under Section 4 of the Vienna Convention regarding States and international organizations: "A treaty does not create either obligations or rights for a third State or a third organization without the consent of that State or that organization."[145] This is a generally

[142] For a generic definition, see Waite, Maurice, ed., *Paperback Oxford English Dictionary* (Oxford: Oxford University Press, 2012), 761.

[143] Casey-Maslen, *Treaty on Prohibition,* 155.

[144] Vienna Convention on the Law of Treaties (concluded 23 May 1969, entered into force 27 January 1980) 1155 UNTS 331, at Art. 34.

[145] Vienna Convention on the Law of Treaties between States and International Organizations or between International Organizations (adopted 20 March 1986, not yet entered into force) (1986) 25 ILM 543, at Section 4.

recognized customary rule of international law. Notwithstanding, under Art.4(2) of the TPNW, States shall:

> negotiate a legally binding, time-bound plan for the verified and irreversible elimination of their nuclear-weapon programme, including the elimination or irreversible conversion of all the nuclear weapon-related facilities. The State Party, no later than 60 days after their entry into force of this Treaty, shall submit this plan to the States Parties, or to a competent international authority designated by the States Parties. The plan shall then be negotiated with the competent international authority, which shall submit it to the subsequent meeting of States Parties or the review conference, whichever comes first, for approval in accordance with its rules of procedure.

The rising issue concerns what or who such a "competent international authority" is. The only international organization having efficient resources and further possessing international legal personality for such activity is the IAEA; however, as stated above, the treaty cannot bind an organization that is not a party to it, and it is unlikely that the IAEA will become a party in the foreseeable future. Nevertheless, Art. 4(2) calls for the agreement to be merely "negotiated" and not concluded, but how this would look in practice remains unclear. Moreover, it is worth noting that dismantlement of nuclear weapons would produce special fissionable material[146] exceeding any conceivable demand for civilian purposes for any subsequent megatons-to-megawatts-like program.[147]

Article 6 of the TPNW addresses victim assistance and reflects the humanitarian foundation of the treaty's negotiation, implicitly connecting it to the SIrUS principle. This provision is significant in the context of unnecessary suffering, as the effects of ionizing radiation on hibakusha and combatants would be identical from the biological perspective. However, the article is vague in certain respects. First, as noted earlier in the discussion on the classification of hibakusha, defining a 'victim or person affected by a nuclear explosion' is not straightforward. The article

[146] "Special fissionable material" means the following: plutonium-239; uranium-233; uranium enriched in the isotopes 235 or 233; any material containing one or more of the foregoing; and such other fissionable material as the Board of Governors shall from time to time determine; but the term 'special fissionable material' does not include source material. Statute of the International Atomic Energy Agency (done 26 October 1956, entered into force 29 July 1957) 276 UNTS 4, at Art. XX (1).

[147] Casey-Maslen, *Treaty on Prohibition*, 198.

does not specify the scientific basis for establishing criteria to determine who qualifies as a victim, raising concerns about the clarity and enforceability of this provision. As apparent from the "black rain" case in Hiroshima, continuous research into the dose-effect relationship by RERF, or exposure of the so-called "atomic bomb veterans," it is rather challenging to apply a set of criteria to objectively define a "victim of a nuclear explosion." NWS often skillfully employ legal counter-arguments based on vague definitions, particularly regarding the definition of a "victim of nuclear explosion." Without a doubt, such a definition is possible mainly based on medical data proving a link between exposures to various physical health issues. However, would psychological suffering, often resulting in crippling anxiety among the victims of the exposure, be covered by this provision?[148]

Any further discussion on the form of assistance and its extent requires a definition. In comparison to Art. X of the CWC on assistance and protection against chemical weapons, the TPNW is dim in scope and clarity. Discussions regarding amendments of provisions that relate to victim assistance and elaboration on who is a victim and how nuclear weapons affect survivors would offer a more sensible first meeting of the State parties. The Meeting of State Parties in 2022 and adopting the Vienna Declaration and Vienna Action Plan didn't bring much clarity. While the States Parties reiterated their commitments to abolishing nuclear weapons, no further elucidation was provided on the norm against unnecessary suffering, particularly its interpretation regarding the effects of nuclear explosion.[149]

In the early stages, the TPNW negotiations had a strong foundation. Discussions were grounded in the health effects and humanitarian impacts of nuclear weapons, and these were explicitly connected to the principle of unnecessary suffering bolstered by the ICRC's medical expertise. However, as the negotiations progressed and ICAN took over much of the advocacy, the dialogue began to lose its focus. The tone shifted toward moral condemnation and vague terminology, alienating NWS. The principles of

[148] A condition vividly described by a psychiatrist in Lifton, *Death in Life*. See Robert J. Lifton, *Death in Life: Survivors of Hiroshima* (Chapel Hill: University of North Carolina Press, 1991).

[149] See Annex I, Declaration of the first Meeting of States Parties to the Treaty on the Prohibition of Nuclear Weapons Our commitment to a world free of nuclear weapons, TPNW/MSP/2022/6, available at https://documents.un.org/doc/undoc/gen/n22/434/57/pdf/n2243457.pdf?OpenElement, last access on October 22, 2024.

LAOC were referenced but often without sufficient legal elaboration. While the TPNW embodies a humanitarian heart and soul, it ultimately lacks the legal rigor and political 'mind' necessary to engage all key stakeholders and ensure long-term success.

5.7 Conclusion

Effective and comprehensive disarmament treaties, and especially law of armed conflict treaties regulating or banning certain weapons, are rare. Once a weapon becomes part of a State's military arsenal, there is little urgency to eliminate it, especially if the weapon provides strategic or tactical advantages. States often invoke military necessity and argue that the benefits of such weapons outweigh concerns about unnecessary suffering. These States also resist evaluating the effects of weapons in purely medical terms, a position often taken by the ICRC and civil society. While the ICRC has the necessary expertise to interpret unnecessary suffering through a medical lens, activist groups sometimes apply the SIrUS principle too broadly or without sufficient rigor. This can dilute the principle's legitimacy. The LOAC is not utopian; it must remain grounded in pragmatism and realism. Activists risk weakening the effectiveness of SIrUS when it is invoked without careful consideration of military necessity or when used indiscriminately to promote a particular ban.

Despite these challenges, there have been notable successes in State-led disarmament initiatives, such the Chemical Weapons Convention (CWC), the Biological Weapons Convention (BWC), and the Convention on Conventional Weapons (CCW). In case of chemical weapons, the historical association with poison and the experiences of the Iran-Iraq War hastened the prohibition process. These initiatives benefited from State leadership, and the most effective humanitarian treaties, such as the Ottawa and Oslo treaties, depend on the participation of States that are in possession of such weapons and militarily significant.

During negotiations for the 1977 Additional Protocols to the Geneva Conventions of 1949, States frequently discussed the health effects of weapons, often referring to the work of the ICRC. This link between health and the impact of specific weapons was later formalized in the CCW. Therefore, when grounded in substantive discussion supported by data, the SIrUS principle can be powerful. Unfortunately, the TPNW, though a commendable initiative, still lacks this depth. Its success will likely depend on whether NWS eventually join, and even if they do, the treaty's operative paragraphs will need substantial amendments.

In the following chapter of this book, I look at the ICRC archives and explore the activities of the Committee in weapons control, then proceed to discuss specific cases brought before judicial and quasi-judicial bodies. Since LOAC lacks a dedicated implementation mechanism, enforcement is difficult. Enforcement is often left to the sole discretion of States. The International Humanitarian Fact-Finding Commission or IHFFC[150] exists but has seen limited action, with the exception of its work in Luhansk, Eastern Ukraine, in 2017.[151] As previously mentioned, LOAC remains left mainly to States, reluctant to discuss hostilities or weapons at an international court. In the next chapter, the author examines how judicial bodies interpreted and applied the norm against SIrUS, and how they interpreted the balance between military necessity and health effects.

References

Agent Orange Record. "What is Dioxin?" Accessed April 25, 2022. https://agentorangerecord.com/what-is-dioxin-2/.

Anti-Personnel Mine Ban Convention. "Membership." Accessed June 24, 2022. https://new.apminebanconvention.org/en/membership/.

Boisson de Chazournes, Laurence, and Philippe Sands, eds. *International Law, the International Court of Justice and Nuclear Weapons.* Cambridge: Cambridge University Press, 1999.

Boothby, William H. *Weapons and the Law of Armed Conflict.* New York: Oxford University Press, 2016.

Reaching Critical Will, Calendar of Side Events for Nuclear Weapon Ban Treaty Negotiations, last updated July 3, 2017, accessed August 4, 2022, https://www.reachingcriticalwill.org/disarmament-fora/nuclear-weapon-ban/negotiation/calendar.

Casey-Maslen, Stuart. *Jus ad Bellum: The Law on Inter-State Use of Force.* New York: Hart, 2020.

———. *The Treaty on the Prohibition of Nuclear Weapons: A Commentary.* Oxford: Oxford University Press, 2019.

Casey-Maslen, Stuart, and Tobias Vestner. *A Guide to Disarmament Law.* New York: Routledge, 2019.

[150] See International Humanitarian Fact Finding Commission, accessed August 4, 2022, https://www.ihffc.org/index.asp?Language=EN&page=home.

[151] Saul and Akande, 379.

Chossudovsky, Evgeny M. "The Origins of the Treaty on the Non-Proliferation of Nuclear Weapons: Ireland's Initiative in the United Nations (1958–1961)." *Irish Studies in International Affairs* 3, no. 2 (1990): 111–135. http://www.jstor.org/stable/30001773.

Clapham, Andrew, and Paola Gaeta, eds. *The Oxford Handbook of International Law in Armed Conflict*. Oxford: Oxford University Press, 2014.

Coupland, Robin M. "Abhorrent Weapons and 'Superfluous Injury or Unnecessary Suffering': From Field Surgery to Law." *BMJ: British Medical Journal* 315, no. 7120 (1997a): 1450–1452. http://www.jstor.org/stable/25176382.

———, ed. *The SIrUS Project: Towards a Determination of Which Weapons Cause "Superfluous Injury or Unnecessary Suffering."* Geneva: ICRC, 1997b. https://www.loc.gov/collections/military-legal-resources/?q=RC_SIrUS-project.html.

Devroy, Ann, and Ruth Marcus. "Clinton Takes Oath as 42nd President Asking Sacrifice, Promising Renewal." *Washington Post*, January 21, 1993. https://www.washingtonpost.com/wp-srv/national/longterm/inaug/history/stories/clint92.htm.

Dinstein, Yoram. *The Conduct of Hostilities Under the Law of International Armed Conflict*. Cambridge: Cambridge University Press, 2004.

Drollette Jr, Dan. "Blinding Them With Science: Is Development of a Banned Laser Weapon Continuing?" *Bulletin of the Atomic Scientists*, September 14, 2014. https://thebulletin.org/2014/09/blinding-them-with-science-is-development-of-a-banned-laser-weapon-continuing/.

Feakes, Daniel. "Global Civil Society and Biological and Chemical Weapons" in *Global Civil Society Yearbook* edited by Kaldor, Mary, Helmut Anheier, and Marlies Glasius. Oxford: Oxford University Press, 2003.

Gardiner, Richard. *Treaty Interpretation*. 2nd ed. Oxford: Oxford University Press, 2017.

Guillaume, Marine. "Napalm in US Bombing Doctrine and Practice, 1942–1975." *The Asia-Pacific Journal* 14, no. 23–25 (2016): Article 4893. https://apjjf.org/2016/23/Guillaume.html.

Haynes, Suyin. "Prince Harry Is Honoring His Mother's Work in Angola. Here's What to Know About Princess Diana's Landmines Walk." *Time*, September 27, 2019. https://time.com/5682006/princess-diana-landmines/.

Henckaerts, Jean-Marie, and Louise Doswald-Beck, eds. *Customary International Humanitarian Law*. Vol.1, *Rules*. Cambridge: Cambridge University Press, 2005.

Hibakusha Stories. "Setsuko Thurlow Gives Final Remarks at Ban Treaty Adoption," July 7, 2017, accessed August 4, 2022, https://hibakushastories.org/setsuko-thurlow-gives-final-remarks-at-ban-treaty-adoption/.

Houser, Ryan S., Gregory D. Koblentz, and Filippa Lentzos. 2023. "Understanding Biosafety and Biosecurity in Ukraine." *Health Security* 21 (1): 70–80. https://doi.org/10.1089/hs.2022.0095.

International Campaign to Ban Landmines. "A Global Network Working for a World Free of Landmines." Accessed April 25, 2022. http://www.icbl.org/en-gb/home.aspx.

International Campaign to Abolish Nuclear Weapons. "77% of Belgians Support Joining the TPNW – Poll." Accessed December 11, 2020. https://www.icanw.org/77_of_belgians_support_joining_the_tpnw_poll.

———. *The Nuclear Weapon Ban Treaty.* November 2017. Accessed May 11, 2022. https://d3n8a8pro7vhmx.cloudfront.net/tectodevms/pages/2389/attachments/original/1571070092/ican-2017-Oslo-final.pdf?1571070092.

International Campaign to Abolish Nuclear Weapons (ICAN), "Voting on UN Resolution for Nuclear Ban Treaty," December 23, 2016, https://www.icanw.org/voting_on_un_resolution_for_nuclear_ban_treaty.

Johnston, Eric. "Japan to Fight Ruling Recognizing Hiroshima 'Black Rain' Victims." *The Japan Times,* August 12, 2020. https://www.japantimes.co.jp/news/2020/08/12/national/crime-legal/japan-fights-hiroshima-black-rain-ruling/#.XzXu3hMzZhF.

Kawano, Noriyuki, Yasuyuki Taooka, Takashi Hiraoka, Masaharu Hoshi, and Z. Z. Shaimardanovich. *Report on the Actual Conditions of the Radiation Exposed Residents Near the Former Semipalatinsk Nuclear Test Site.* Hiroshima: Hiroshima University Research Institute for Radiation Biology and Medicine and Hiroshima Peace Science Consortium, 2004.

Krutzsch, Walter, Eric Myjer, and Ralf Trapp, eds. *The Chemical Weapons Convention: A Commentary.* Oxford: Oxford University Press, 2014.

Larsen, Jeffrey A., and Kerry M. Katchner. *On Limited Nuclear War in the 21st Century.* Stanford: Stanford University Press, 2014.

Lifton, Robert Jay. *Death in Life: Survivors of Hiroshima.* Chapel Hill: University of North Carolina Press, 1991.

Long, Tony. "Oct.5, 1986: Israel's Secret Nuke Arsenal Exposed." *Wired,* October 5, 2011. https://www.wired.com/2011/10/1005israel-secret-nuclear-arsenal-exposed/.

Maresca, Louis, and Stuart Maslen. *The Banning of Anti-Personnel Landmines: The Legal Contribution of the International Committee of the Red Cross.* Cambridge: Cambridge University Press, 2000.

Mathur, Ritu. *Red Cross Interventions in Weapons Control.* London: Lexington Books, 2017.

Matsumura, Akira. *Japanese Language Dictionary, Vol. 3.* 4th ed. Tokyo: Sanseido, 2019.

Maurer, Peter. "20 Years After the Historic Treaty on Landmines, We Cannot Afford to Lose Momentum: ICRC President Peter Maurer's Address to the Sixteeth Meeting of the States Parties, Anti-Personnel Mine Ban Convention 18 December 2017, Vienna." Accessed April 29, 2022. https://www.icrc.org/en/document/statement-20-years-after-historic-treaty-landmines-we-cannot-afford-lose-momentum.

Ministry of Health, Labor and Welfare, Japan. "Who is Hibakusha?" Accessed December 11, 2020. https://www.mhlw.go.jp/stf/newpage_13405.html

Neer, Robert M. *Napalm: An American Biography*. Cambridge: Belknap Press of Harvard University Press, 2013.

P5 Working Group on the Glossary of Key Nuclear Terms. *P5 Glossary of Key Nuclear Terms*. Beijing: China Atomic Energy Press, 2015.

Parker, Clifton B. "Public opinion unlikely to curb a U.S. president's use of nuclear weapons in war. Stanford scholar finds." *Stanford News*, August 8, 2017. https://news.stanford.edu/2017/08/08/americans-weigh-nuclear-war/.

Price, Richard M. *The Chemical Weapons Taboo*. New York: Cornell University Press, 1997.

Rietiker, Daniel. *Humanization of Arms Control: Paving the Way for a World Free of Nuclear Weapons*. New York: Routledge, 2018.

Sagan, Scott D. "Why Do States Build Nuclear Weapons?: Three Models in Search of a Bomb." *International Security* 21, no. 3 (1996/1997): 54–86. https://doi.org/10.2307/2539273.

Saul, Ben, and Akande, Dapo, eds. *The Oxford Guide to International Humanitarian Law*. Oxford: Oxford University Press, 2020.

Schindler, Dietrich, and Jiri Toman, eds. *The Laws of Armed Conflict: A Collection of Conventions, Resolutions and Other Documents*. Leiden: Martinus Nijhoff Publishers, 2004.

Shabad, Theodore. "Soviet Union Exploded a Nuclear Device to Extinguish Burning Gas." *New York Times*, December 2, 1971. Accessed April 21, 2022. https://www.nytimes.com/1971/12/02/archives/soviet-discloses-nuclear-blast-that-put-out-fire-in-gas-field.html.

Shinmura, Izuru. *Kojien* [Japanese language dictionary]. Vol. 7. Tokyo: Iwanami, 2018.

Summary record of the 2nd meeting, September 11, 1979. A/CONF.95/SR.2.

United Nations Conference on Prohibitions or Restrictions of use of certain conventional weapons which may be deemed to be excessively injurious or to have indiscriminate effects. Summary record of the 5th meeting, September 13, 1979. A/CONF.95/SR.5.para 19.

Tucker, Jonathan B. *U.S. Ratification of the Chemical Weapons Convention*. Washington, DC: National Defense University Press, 2011.

UNGA Doc. A/9207: Napalm and other incendiary weapons and all aspects of their possible use. Report of the Secretary-General A_9207-EN.pdf, accessed April 15, 2022, https://digitallibrary.un.org/record/852668?ln=en.

UN Office for Disarmament Affairs. "Treaty on the Prohibition of Nuclear Weapons." Accessed January 11, 2021. https://treaties.unoda.org/t/tpnw.

———. *The United Nations Disarmament Yearbook*. Vol. 42 (Part II). New York: United Nations Publications, 2017.

———. "Under-Secretary-General and High Representative for Disarmament Affairs." Accessed February 12, 2022. https://www.un.org/disarmament/high-representative/.

Organisation for the Prohibition of Chemical Weapons. "OPCW by the Numbers." Accessed December 11, 2020a. https://www.opcw.org/media-centre/opcw-numbers.

———. "Our Partners." Accessed December 20, 2020b. https://www.opcw.org/about/our-partners#:~:text=The%20CWC%20Coalition%20is%20a,for%20the%20Prohibition%20of%20Chemical.

US Mission to the United Nations. "Joint Press Statement from the Permanent Representative to the United Nations of the United States, United Kingdom, and France Following the Adoption." July 7, 2017. https://usun.usmission.gov/joint-press-statement-from-the-permanent-representatives-to-the-united-nations-of-the-united-states-united-kingdom-and-france-following-the-adoption/.

United Nations Conference on Prohibitions or Restrictions of use of certain conventional weapons which may be deemed to be excessively injurious or to have indiscriminate effects.

Verchio, Donna Marie. "Just Say No! The SIrUS Project: Well-Intentioned, But Unnecessary and Superfluous." *Air Force Law Review* 51, (2001): 183–228.

Waite, Maurice, ed. *Paperback Oxford English Dictionary*. Oxford: Oxford University Press, 2012.

Wheelis, Mark, Lajos Rózsa, and Malcolm Dando, eds. *Deadly Cultures: Biological Weapons since 1945*. Cambridge, MA: Harvard University Press, 2006.

CHAPTER 6

The Law in Practice: Judicial Interpretations and Insights

6.1 Introduction

This chapter builds on the previous discussions by examining legal precedents related to the health impacts of various weapons and how these have been interpreted through different legal frameworks. While terms like 'suffering' frequently appear in rulings from international courts and ad-hoc bodies, they are often used in a general sense rather than in the precise context of the law of armed conflict. The specific application of unnecessary suffering, a recognized LOAC principle, remains rare in judicial proceedings. Most relevant case law arises in national jurisdictions, where States often interpret the SIrUS principle through the traditional lens of balancing military necessity with the potential harm caused by a weapon without focusing specifically on health impacts or long-term health effects.

States seldom bring their armed forces before courts to litigate the use of weapons, particularly under the LOAC framework. Discussions on weapon use are often kept within military or governmental channels due to their sensitive nature, that is, national security. When cases do reach judicial or quasi-judicial bodies, it is typically through the lens of IHRL, which lacks the necessary legal instruments to assess SIrUS in its LOAC context directly. The concept of unnecessary suffering does not exist as a clearly defined norm in IHRL. Instead, IHRL bodies substitute it with broader principles, such as the right to life, as outlined in international conventions like the ECHR and ICCPR.

J. Krasny, *War Injuries*,
https://doi.org/10.1007/978-3-032-00737-7_6

This substitution, however, creates a significant gap. IHRL bodies, such as the European Court of Human Rights or ECtHR, are limited in their capacity to evaluate military actions through a purely law of armed conflict lens. These courts are bound by their mandate to interpret specific articles of human rights conventions, which do not provide for the enforcement of LOAC provisions. Additionally, the expertise required to properly balance military necessity against humanitarian principles, such as unnecessary suffering may be lacking in IHRL courts. As a result, there is often a disconnect between the intended humanitarian protections under LOAC and their application in IHRL cases, weakening the practical enforcement of the SIrUS principle.[1]

That said, IHRL undeniably plays an indispensable role in areas like non-international armed conflict or NIAC, belligerent occupation, and the protection of noncombatants. However, weapons law and the targeting of combatants are primarily the domain of LOAC, as confirmed by the ICJ.[2] Friction can occasionally arise between IHRL and LOAC, particularly due to differing interpretations of key concepts like proportionality and necessity as discussed in Chap. 3. Although IHRL plays a critical role, its influence on weapons law remains limited. However, exploring and strengthening the interaction between LOAC and IHRL is essential to maximize protection for those affected by hostilities.

In this chapter, the author explores how different legal mechanisms have interpreted and applied the norm against unnecessary suffering in relation to specific weapons. First, the focus will be on the use of nuclear weapons against Japan and the subsequent stance of the ICRC, which first began connecting SIrUS with long-term health effects. This analysis will draw on documents from the ICRC archives in Geneva, focusing on the vast material related to nuclear weapons. Included are the observations of Dr. Marcel Junod and his work in Hiroshima, as well as communications between the ICRC headquarters in Geneva and Junod.

After analyzing the ICRC's argument, the chapter will move on to explore judicial and semi-judicial decisions in cases involving unnecessary suffering, particularly in relation to nuclear and chemical weapons. These

[1] See Roberta Arnold and Noelle N. R. Quenivet, eds., *International Humanitarian Law and Human Rights: Towards a New Merger in International Law* (Leiden: Martinus Nijhoff Publishers, 2008), 292–293.

[2] Legality of the Threat or Use of Nuclear Weapons (Advisory Opinion) [1996] ICJ Rep 226.¶25.

include the Marshall Islands v. the UK, Victims of Agent Orange v. Dow Chemical, the Al-Anfal case, and the ICJ Advisory Opinion on the threat or use of nuclear weapons. I will also explore relevant national law, particularly Shimoda v. the State, concerning nuclear weapons, specifically the atomic bombings of Hiroshima and Nagasaki.

Given that LOAC lacks an international court specifically for enforcement, it is often the case that LOAC/IHL norms are interpreted through an IHRL lens. This trend is increasing and often provides the only remedy for victims of armed conflict. Whether this approach is positive or negative is beyond the scope of this chapter. What is clear, however, is that unnecessary suffering as a rule of LOAC has occasionally been brought before human rights courts. As IHRL does not include unnecessary suffering as a principle, this chapter will explore how courts have handled such cases, if at all. Although IHRL increasingly protects combatants, this protection does not extend to the hostilities phase.[3] The focus of this chapter, however, is not to analyze the interplay between LOAC, IHRL, and international criminal law but rather to assess how these mechanisms have specifically addressed SIrUS, whether they deliberated on medical effects and testimonies from victims, and the legal outcomes of their interpretations.

Similarly, friction can occasionally arise between IHRL and LOAC, particularly due to differing interpretations of key concepts like proportionality and necessity, as discussed in Chap. 3. Nonetheless, exploring and strengthening the interaction between LOAC and IHRL is crucial for maximizing the protection of those affected by hostilities. This requires a closer examination of how different legal mechanisms have interpreted and applied the SIrUS principle in relation to the use of specific weapons. Likewise, in this chapter, the author examines documents pertaining to the use of nuclear weapons against Japan and the stance and expertise of the International Committee of the Red Cross (ICRC) since it was the ICRC that first began to connect SIrUS with specific health effects.

The main objective of this chapter is to explore how the organization in the field connects unnecessary suffering with delayed and long-term health effects and how this connection is described in original documents. After exploring the ICRCs argument, in the next section, I explore judicial and semi-judicial decisions related to cases containing unnecessary suffering

[3] Stuart Casey-Maslen, ed., *Weapons Under International Human Rights Law* (Cambridge: Cambridge University Press, 2014), 220.

and associated with the weapons discussed in this book. These include the position of the ICJ, the case of *Marshall Islands v. the UK* and, of course, the advisory opinion on the threat or use of nuclear weapons. Especially noteworthy is the case of *La Tablada*, in which a group of combatants invoked SIrUS in front of the Inter-American Commission on Human Rights. Then, the author looks at national case law regarding nuclear and chemical weapons and their link to SIrUS.

As becomes apparent, since LOAC lacks proper judicial mechanisms for its enforcement, it is occasionally the case that particular rules are interpreted through IHRL lenses; in fact, this is increasing and often offers the only remedy for the victims. Whether such interpretation is positive or negative is outside the scope of this book. The fact is, however, that unnecessary suffering as a rule of the LOAC was brought before human rights courts on several occasions. Since IHRL does not include the principle of unnecessary suffering, it is worth exploring how these mechanisms dealt with such cases, if ever. Increasingly, combatants are protected by IHRL, but not during the active hostilities phase.[4] However, to reiterate, the purpose of this chapter is not to discuss the interplay between the LOAC (IHL) and IHRL or international criminal law. Rather, it is to explore how and whether these mechanisms specifically addressed SIrUS in their proceedings, whether they deliberated on medical effects and testimonies of the victims and what the legal outcome of their interpretation was.

6.2 ICRC Archives and the Legacy of Atomic Bombings of Japan

The ICRC archives in Geneva contain a wealth of material related to the atomic bombing of Hiroshima in 1945, including crucial documents and communications from Dr. Marcel Junod,[5] who played a pivotal role in the aftermath of the bombing. His firsthand observations and reports form the backbone of the ICRC's early understanding of the devastating effects of nuclear weapons. Junod's accounts, sent back to the ICRC headquarters, reflect a deep concern with the suffering caused by the

[4] Casey-Maslen, *Weapons*, 220.

[5] See Marcel Junod, accessed May 3, 2022, https://blogs.icrc.org/cross-files/marcel-junod/.

bomb-both its immediate impact and the delayed, long-term health effects suffered by survivors.[6]

A particular emphasis in this section is placed on how Junod's findings connected the concept of unnecessary suffering to the various phases of radiation exposure: immediate, delayed, or long-term. His insights laid the groundwork for the ICRCs humanitarian stance on nuclear weapons, a position that would later shape the organization's contributions to the Treaty on the Prohibition of Nuclear Weapons (TPNW). The ICRC's involvement in TPNW was grounded in its long history of documenting the excessive effects of nuclear weapons, beginning with Junod's pioneering work in Hiroshima, where he was amongst the first to organize medical aid for survivors.

ICRC field staff are often on the ground during or immediately following the use of controversial weapons, including incendiaries, white phosphorus, landmines, and, historically, nuclear weapons. For the ICRC, involvement in such cases is a delicate matter, as the organization must avoid being perceived as interfering in the legal assessment of weapons, which is considered the domain of States and often intertwined with national security concerns. Too much involvement in arms control or disarmament issues could undermine the trust that States place in the ICRC, jeopardizing its reputation for impartiality and potentially limiting its access to conflict zones where humanitarian assistance is critical. This would, in turn, prevent ICRC from its important work in the field, for example, accessing the POW camps or delivering medical help to the battlefields.

Nonetheless, Dr. Junod, before his arrival in Hiroshima, left Geneva in June 1945 and traveled through Paris, Cairo, Tehran, Moscow, and Siberia, arriving in Manchuria in July 1945. There, he worked with POWs and continued to Japan on August 6, 1945, the day of the bombing, to meet with Professor Suzuki of the Imperial University of Tokyo.[7] In his radiogram dated September 22, 1945, Dr. Junod recounts his four days in Hiroshima, describing the destruction of the city. His own overall estimates of civilian casualties—fatalities and the wounded—are in the hundreds of thousands. This shows the tremendous impression of the destruction caused by the bomb on Junod. However, Junod's estimates of fatalities immediately following the explosion were rather low, at 32,959

[6] See Marcel Junod, *Warrior Without Weapons* (London: Jonathan Cape, 1951).
[7] Junod, 293.

casualties, 23,963 seriously injured, and 43,517 slightly injured. Total military casualties were estimated to be equal to or higher than the civilian toll, and Junod mentions "numerous cases suffering later effects of irradiation, leukopenia, gingivitis, internal haemorrhage, acute anaemia. All hospitals destroyed with hundreds of medical staff fatalities"[8] This message was then sent by a subsequent note on January 3, 1946, to the chief delegate of the Japan delegation of the ICRC.[9]

There are two critical aspects in the statement. First, the estimate that military casualties were higher than the civilian toll focuses on military necessity. Indeed, higher numbers of military casualties do not immediately make the bombing proportionate under the LOAC. However, this statement reveals that the ICRC was aware of the military advantage created by the weapon. Second, even though the military aspect was apparent to Junod, he then linked suffering to the late effects of ionizing radiation without any distinction between combatants and civilians. Unlike the traditional view, that unnecessary suffering applies only to combatants, Junod interprets SIrUS without regard to this categorization. Undeniably, it is not particularly clear at first whether Junod talks of *suffering* in its generic term or refers to the norm prohibiting unnecessary suffering. However, this is clarified in the documents below.

In a document dated September 17, 1945, Junod discusses help for the POWs from the Hiroshima sector, specifying that the ICRC Hiroshima chapter was unable to offer assistance for POW transport due to the bombing and destruction of its medical and logistical capabilities.[10] Subsequently, in his letters of November 11, 1945, in addition to his efforts to help to transfer the POWs, Junod mentions a disease using the word *hiroshimitis* when he visited the city on September 9 for four days and after speaking with the local staff that described him the delayed effects of ionizing radiation.[11] The major comment of Junod, however, was centered around the distinction that the weapon, by its nature, is not capable of distinction between combatants and noncombatants. The scale of destruction and injuries was so severe that Junod refers to the suffering of civilians and *disabled combatants* [emphasis added] as well as the lack of

[8] ICRC Archives, Doc. No.: tok/t 22/9/45, G3/51.

[9] ICRC Archives, Doc. No.: Tokio 469 176/171 21/9 1650, G3/51.

[10] Junod, 286–300.

[11] Term used also by Lifton describing at that time unknown symptoms of ionizing radiation in Robert J. Lifton, *Death in Life: Survivors of Hiroshima* (Chapel Hill: University of North Carolina Press, 1991) 103–168.

health care. This is yet another essential testimonial: The fact that Junod refers to the suffering of disabled combatants—that is, those who are *hors de combat*—is a clear, albeit implicit reference to the violation of the principle of unnecessary suffering due to delayed and long-term health effects of the weapon. Since 1945, the ICRC has considered delayed and long-term health effects to cause unnecessary suffering unlike the effects of burns and blast.

At its XVII international conference, the ICRC recommended the prohibition of atomic weapons based on Junod's radiograms and reports. At the State Parties 17th Conference of August 1948, the president of the ICRC, Paul Ruegger, referred to LOAC principles and the health effects caused by nuclear weapons based on Junod's testimony in Hiroshima, portraying long-term health effects as unnecessary suffering to combatants who are already out of combat.[12] Junod's observations were later reaffirmed in an ICRC document appealing to the State Parties to the Geneva Conventions, which included the following quote (translated from the original by the author):

> *De plus, la bombe atomique cause à ses victimes des souffrances sans proportion avec les nécessites tactiques puisque beaucoup de ses victimes périssent des suites de leurs brulures après des semaines d'agonie, ou restent frappées, pour la vie, de douloureuses infirmités.*[13]
>
> [transl.: In addition, the atomic bomb causes its victims **suffering out of proportion to the tactical necessities** since many of its victims perish from their burns after weeks of agony, or remain **stricken for life** with painful illnesses.] [emphasis added]

Junod's observations regarding unnecessary suffering in relation to the use of atomic bombs present two key points. First, the initial effects of atomic bombs, such as intense heat and shockwaves, quickly render combatants incapable of continuing to fight. However, the ionizing radiation that follows adds further suffering to these incapacitated combatants, extending the harm far beyond the immediate battlefield. In this way, even by traditional interpretations of the SIrUS principle, which weighs military necessity against inflicted harm, these combatants, already incapacitated,

[12] Final report of the XVIIth ICRC conference, accessed May 11, 2022, https://tile.loc.gov/storage-services/service/ll/llmlp/RC_XVIIth-RC-Conference/RC_XVIIth-RC-Conference.pdf.

[13] Document titled *Armes Atomique et Armes aveugles* dated April 5, 1950.

continue to suffer unnecessarily from the prolonged effects of radiation. The long-term consequences, such as radiation sickness, exceed the immediate parameters of the LOAC, as they inflict continuous harm beyond the temporal boundaries of the conflict.

Second, even in the absence of detailed studies or assessments of the likelihood of diseases like leukemia or solid cancers at the time, Dr. Junod already acknowledged the long-term health effects of ionizing radiation as excessive and unnecessary. The connection between unnecessary suffering and ionizing radiation, which is best illustrated in the case of nuclear weapons, can extend to all weapons. LAOC does not distinguish between conventional and unconventional weapons when applying the SIrUS principle. As such, SIrUS, being a fundamental customary norm of the law of armed conflict, applies universally to all forms of weaponry.

6.3 Judicial Perspectives on SIrUS: Global, Regional, and National Mechanisms

When speaking of the sources of international law, it is a common practice among legal scholars to refer to Art. 38 of the ICJ Statute. The article serves as a basic orientation in legal sources. In this spirit, the author looked at international agreements and customs described in previous chapters. Next, it is pertinent to explore the SIrUS interpretation by international, regional, and national bodies. The purpose is to determine whether, in light of the preceding developments in codification and custom regarding unnecessary suffering, these mechanisms addressed the interpretation and application of SIrUR, and, if so, how and to what result. Therefore, Art. 38 of the ICJ Statute defines sources of law as the following:

a. international conventions, whether general or particular, establishing rules expressly recognized by the contesting states;
b. international custom, as evidence of a general practice accepted as law;
c. the general principles of law recognized by civilized nations;
d. subject to the provisions of Art. 59, judicial decisions and the teachings of the most highly qualified publicists of the various nations, as subsidiary means for the determination of rules of law.[14]

[14] Statute of the International Court of Justice (adopted 26 June 1945, entered into force 24 October 1945) 145 BSP 832¶38(1).

It is, however, vital to keep in mind that such judicial decisions or opinions as stipulated in Art. 38(d) have rather determinative functions and are not a source of law in themselves.[15] Therefore, these judicial findings serve as clarifications. States are the lawmakers. Moreover, regarding the rule of conventional nature, determination by doctrine and judicial decisions means interpretation. In contrast, for the rule of customary nature, determination has a broader scope, including establishing whether a custom exists or not.[16] This is often expressed by the Latin axiom *jura novit curia*, or "the court knows the law."[17] Hence, not "makes" the law. Such judicial decisions, therefore, represent an important reference in legal methodology. As States are sovereign entities, national or so-called municipal law may affect international law, particularly in providing evidence of a custom or State practice.[18]

One of the particular challenges of the law of armed conflict is the lack of a dedicated international mechanism for adjudicating LOAC violations. While there are international bodies like the International Criminal Court (ICC) and International Court of Justice (ICJ) that may deal with LOAC-related cases, these are not exclusively dedicated to LOAC enforcement. The implementation primarily relies on domestic legislation and practical measures taken by States prior to armed conflict.[19] Under Common Article 1 of the Geneva Conventions, States are obligated to respect and ensure respect for LOAC norms "in all circumstances." This obligation extends beyond merely adhering to the rules; it also includes taking steps to ensure that other States comply with LOAC norms. Many of these norms are considered *erga omnes*[20] obligations—legal duties that States owe to the international community as a whole. In other words, every State has an interest in ensuring that these rules are respected globally, and any State may call upon another to address violations of these obligations. Thus, while enforcement of LOAC is largely dependent on national systems, all States share a collective responsibility for upholding these international norms and can hold violators accountable through various legal avenues.

[15] Giovanni Distefano, *Fundamentals of Public International Law: A Sketch of the International Legal Order* (Leiden: Brill Nijhoff, 2019), 270–271.

[16] Distefano, 271.

[17] Malcolm Shaw, *International Law* (Cambridge: Cambridge University Press, 2017), 829.

[18] Shaw, 83.

[19] Marco Sassoli, *International Humanitarian Law: Rules, Controversies, and Solutions to Problems Arising in Warfare* (Cheltenham: Edward Elgar, 2019), 124.

[20] Sassoli, 90–91.

6.3.1 *International Criminal Tribunal for Former Yugoslavia (ICTY)*

It must be reiterated that the International Criminal Tribunal for Former Yugoslavia (ICTY) generally deals with another branch of public international law, that is, international criminal law (ICL), and must be distinguished from the law of armed conflict, which forms a separate branch of public international law (PIL). The purpose here is not to assess ICL with respect to unnecessary suffering or even the interplay between ICL and the LOAC. Rather, I examine the ICTY cases to determine if and how the tribunal dealt with the application of the principle and its interpretation not only *de iure* but *de facto*. As discussed earlier, to denote intent for criminal prosecution, the ICTY statute does not include weapons of a *nature* to cause unnecessary suffering but weapons *calculated* to cause unnecessary suffering.[21] However, there are no cases addressing the nature of weapons, or even those calculated to cause SIrUS at the ICTY.[22]

Indeed, the cases at the ICTY were not concerned with the means of warfare.[23] The Office of the President decided not to prosecute such crimes;[24] In addition, further investigations into the use of cluster bombs or depleted uranium were closed by the Office of the President.[25] The argument indeed was that there is still no consensus as to the excessive effects of depleted uranium, and the studies are ongoing, and "while it might be conceivable in the future that depleted uranium will, in fact, be banned, no such conclusion can be made today."[26] The legal issues behind cluster munitions are virtually the same as those regarding depleted uranium and further include the lack of definition of such munitions and the absence of conventional or customary prohibitions. Undeniably, since the ICTY was concerned with criminal prosecution and clarification of the law, such debates on the legality of weapons were irrelevant for the purposes of the tribunal. The International Criminal Court (ICC) works

[21] UNSC *Statute of the International Criminal Tribunal for the Former Yugoslavia* UNSC Res 827 (1993) (25 May 1993) SCOR 48th Year 29.¶Art.3(a).

[22] Stuart Casey-Maslen and Steven Haines, *Hague Law Interpreted: The Conduct of Hostilities under the Law of Armed Conflict* (New York: Hart, 2020), 223.

[23] In this regard, see Gideon Boas and William A. Schabas, eds., *International Criminal Law Developments in the Case Law of the ICTY* (Leiden: Martinus Nijhoff Publishers, 2003).

[24] ICTY, "Final Report to the Prosecutor."

[25] ICTY, para. 26–27.

[26] ICTY, para. 26.

based on the competency stemming from the Rome Statute.[27] The statute itself includes unnecessary suffering in Art. 8(2)(b)(xx) as a prosecutable crime, however, with the condition that such weapons are specifically included in the annex.[28] No weapon so far has been included, thereby indicating the reluctance of states to question the legitimacy of their arsenals.

6.3.2 International Court of Justice

In 1996, the ICJ delivered its Advisory Opinion (AO) on the legality of the threat or use of nuclear weapons. The ICJ had been tasked by the UNGA Resolution 49/75K to deliver an AO on the question: "Is the threat or use of nuclear weapons in any circumstance permitted under international law?"[29] Much has already been written about the substance of this opinion, and elaboration on it has been extensive.[30] Thus, looking at the AO and how it dealt with the norm against unnecessary suffering is essential. The court reaffirmed that SIrUS is one of the cardinal principles of the LOAC, applicable to combatants, not civilians.[31] In its interpretation of the principle, the court resorted to traditional understanding as "a harm greater than unavoidable to achieve legitimate military objectives."[32] The ICJ further states that "In view of the unique characteristics of nuclear weapons, the use of such weapons seems scarcely reconcilable with respect for such requirements [of IHL norms],"[33] which is a somewhat logically flawed statement, in a similar fashion as saying 'he is slightly dead'. A weapon is either reconcilable with the law or not.

[27] Rome Statute of the International Criminal Court (adopted 17 July 1998, entered into force 1 July 2002) 2187 UNTS 90.

[28] William Schabas, *An Introduction to the International Criminal Court,* 4th ed., (Cambridge: Cambridge University Press, 2011), 138.

[29] UNGA, General and Complete Disarmament A/Res/49/75, 9 January, 1995.

[30] See Laurence Boisson de Chazournes and Philippe Sands, eds., *International Law, the International Court of Justice and Nuclear Weapons* (Cambridge: Cambridge University Press, 1999).

[31] *Legality of the Threat or Use of Nuclear Weapons (Advisory Opinion)* [1996] ICJ Rep 226.¶ 78.

[32] *Legality of the Threat or Use of Nuclear Weapons (Advisory Opinion)* [1996] ICJ Rep 226.¶ 78.

[33] *Legality of the Threat or Use of Nuclear Weapons (Advisory Opinion)* [1996] ICJ Rep226. ¶ 95.

Anyway, to address the ICJ's statement regarding these unique characteristics, ionizing radiation is the unique characteristic since blast and heat are also produced by other weapons, albeit on a much lower scale. The wording "scarcely" suggests the court is leaving the door open for possible limited uses, for example, against military installations. However, since the SIrUS principle applies to combatants, as confirmed by the court itself, it is somewhat perplexing that the ICJ left this possibility as lawful, even though *scarcely*. Does this mean the court considers use against buildings, installations, or platforms lawful? Possibly, however, to assess the legality of any weapon, we have to consider its general and most common use, which, in the case of nuclear weapons, is against live force. No one would be there to argue for less lethal uses of chemical weapons on the battlefield. As explained in the preceding chapters, LOAC does not generally allow for derogations if it is not explicit. The 1996 Advisory Opinion was criticized in relation to IHL as an "empty exercise to stress the humanitarian rules and then basically to deprive them of any operation where they are most needed."[34] This paradox can be seen in the dissenting opinion of Judge Higgins:

> If the suffering is of the sort traditionally associated with the use of nuclear weapons—blast, radiation, shock, together with the risk of escalation, risk of spread through space and time— then only the most extreme circumstances (defence against untold suffering or the obliteration of a State or peoples) could conceivably "balance" the equation between necessity and humanity.[35]

The court balances military necessity with humanity, which, as explained in earlier chapters, is more of a secondary norm. Although, humanity is necessarily intertwined with the prohibition of unnecessary suffering. However, as such, even through traditional interpretation, the statement does not bring any further clarity into the matter and lacks substance, that is, naming precisely what the issue is. Moreover, such a formulation suggests the fundamental principles of the LOAC could be violated if the circumstances are "severe" enough. Contrary to Higgins' traditional interpretation, Judge Shahabuddeen even disputes its applicability only to combatants:

[34] Boisson de Chazournes and Sands, 292.

[35] *Legality of the Threat or Use of Nuclear Weapons* (Advisory Opinion), (Dissenting Opinion of Judge Higgins), p. 587.

> It may be said that the substance of the principle of unnecessary suffering operates for the benefit of civilians through the medium of other principles, such as that which prohibits indiscriminate attacks, but that the principle itself does not operate in relation to them. What, however, is the position where it is contended that an apparently indiscriminate attack on civilians is validated by recourse to the collateral damage argument?[36]

Speaking purely from the perspective of the LOAC and excluding other bodies of PIL such as IHRL, what Judge Shahabuddeen points out is that in case of an attack that has not indiscriminate character—in other words, an attack intended to be discriminate and lawful under the rule of distinction, but results in incidental harm and damage under the LOAC rule of proportionality even after all necessary precautions—noncombatant victims would enjoy less protection under the LOAC than combatants who are protected against unnecessary suffering.

Using a hypothetical example, if a low-yield tactical nuclear weapon is deployed, the radiation affects combatants as well as noncombatants. However, under the LOAC, combatants could claim violation of the norm against unnecessary suffering, while noncombatants could not, as they could be deemed part of collateral damage. In addition, do we need to accept that survivors of nuclear explosions are incidental or collateral damage and shall count as "fatalities" if they succumb to leukemia or radiation sickness? Of course, this is absurd, as would be the lesser protection of noncombatants under LOAC/IHL.

Essentially, though, Judge Weeramantry links suffering with radiation and further states "...that nuclear weapons are indeed deployed in part with a view to utilizing the destructive effects of radiation and fall-out."[37] Thus, Weeramantry rejects the argument of nuclear weapon states (NWS) that ionizing radiation is a secondary effect but rather one of the main effects of the weapon. This statement is further supported by scientific data on energy distribution and the resulting proportion of fatalities, as revealed by the first case study in Chap. 4 regarding the bombings of Japan.

In further support of the argument putting particular weight on ionizing radiation and medical effects, the dissenting opinion of Judge Koroma refers to the testimonies of inhabitants of the Marshall Islands

[36] *Legality of the Threat or Use of Nuclear Weapons (Advisory Opinion) (Dissenting Opinion of Judge Shuhabudeen)* [1996] ICJ Rep.375, p. 404.

[37] *Legality of the Threat or Use of Nuclear Weapons* (Advisory Opinion), (Dissenting Opinion of Judge Weeramantry), 1996, pp. 458–461.

regarding specific long-term health effects of exposure to high doses of radiation, including malignant tumors or cancer.[38] What such dissenting opinions reveal concerning the substance of unnecessary suffering is that long-term health effects experienced by the victims, whether combatant or non-combatant, were regarded by several judges as contrary to SIrUS prohibition. These dissenting opinions viewed the temporal aspect of such effects and interpreted the principle in medical terms rather than resorting to deliberating on military necessity.

In 2016, the ICJ delivered a judgment in four cases brought by the Marshall Islands against three NWS: India, Pakistan, and the United Kingdom.[39] While the cases concerned NWS obligations for nuclear disarmament under Art. VI of the NPT and the nonfulfillment of this obligation by NWS, the court elaborated on the principle of unnecessary suffering in several paragraphs. Judge Trinidad, in his dissenting opinion, opined that the fundamental principle of the prohibition of unnecessary suffering is not only customary or *cardinal,* as stated in the AO of 1996, but also *jus cogens.*[40] Judge Trindade reminded the ICJ of its rather vague and abstract AO of 1996, referring to the AO as an enigmatic form of *non liquet*, that is, a situation where the law is not clear.[41] Trindade points out that unnecessary suffering could be substantively determined through the experiences of the Marshallese people. Furthermore, Judge Trindade refers to the statement of the ICRC that nuclear weapons cause unnecessary suffering to the population.[42] That is, the data that were obtained by Junod were implicitly referred to by the ICJ judge in reference to the norm prohibiting unnecessary suffering to give it a substance.

From the perspective of the ICJ and statements of particular judges in the AO and the case of the Marshall Islands, it can be observed that while the court acknowledges massive destruction caused by heat and blast, this would fall under the rule of distinction as understood by the

[38] *Legality of the Threat or Use of Nuclear Weapons* (Advisory Opinion), (Dissenting Opinion of Judge Koroma) 1996, pp. 569–570.

[39] *Obligations concerning Negotiations relating to Cessation of the Nuclear Arms Race and to Nuclear Disarmament* (Marshall Islands v. United Kingdom), Preliminary Objections, Judgment, I.C.J. Reports 2016, p. 833.

[40] *Obligations concerning Negotiations relating to Cessation of the Nuclear Arms Race and to Nuclear Disarmament* (Marshall Islands v. United Kingdom), (Dissenting Opinion of Judge Trindad), 2016, para. 186.

[41] Ibid., para 166.

[42] Ibid., para. 278.

LOAC. Individual judges refer particularly to ionizing radiation with regard to unnecessary suffering. Indeed, such is not the conclusion of the AO of 1996 or the Marshall Islands case but, rather, individual dissenting opinions. Nevertheless, judicial experts apparently interpret specific long-term health effects as violating the norm against unnecessary suffering. They further interpret SIrUS in medical terms rather than simply as a balance to military necessity.

Finally, as a supportive example of such medicalization of unnecessary suffering, it is worth mentioning that the former Yugoslavia brought a case against several NATO countries—France, Belgium, Spain, the Netherlands, and the United States—to the ICJ as demonstrated in *Serbia and Montenegro v. United States.* The case included violations of laws and customs of war, particularly the use of cluster munitions and depleted uranium by NATO forces. In his dissenting opinion, Judge Kreca highlights the long-term health effects of depleted uranium, including an increased risk of leukemia and lung cancer.[43] Judge Kreca argues that "the arsenal used in the attacks on Yugoslavia contains also weapons whose effects have no limitations either in space or in time. In the oral proceedings before the Court, the Agent of the United States explicitly stressed that depleted uranium is in standard use of the United States Army."[44]

What is important here is the judge's point regarding no limitation of effects in space or in time of depleted uranium; as in previous cases, the judge highlighted the temporal scope of the health effects of a particular weapon. Furthermore, these long-term health effects were implied to be concerning excessive injuries, thus violating the prohibition of unnecessary suffering. However, unlike in previous cases, Judge Kreca included medical description of what happens after inhalation of depleted uranium particles to determine long-term health effects caused by ionizing radiation emitted from depleted uranium.[45] Such an inclusion of specific medical data into an argument by an ICJ judge is particularly noteworthy and

[43] *Legality of the Use of Force* (Yugoslavia v. United States of America), ICJ. Rep. 959 (Dissenting Opinion of Judge Kreca).

[44] *Legality of the Use of Force* (Yugoslavia v. United States of America), ICJ. Rep. 959 (Dissenting Opinion of Judge Kreca), 951.

[45] *Legality of the Use of Force* (Yugoslavia v. United States of America), ICJ. Rep. 959 (Dissenting Opinion of Judge Kreca), 959. Kreca cites "The report by Marvin Resnikoff of Radioactive Waste Management Associates," which elaborates on carcinogenic effects of depleted uranium. See Marvin Resnikoff, accessed May 11, 2022, https://www.rwma.com/about-us.

further indicates that individual judges do, in fact, increasingly incorporate medical analysis when determining whether a weapon causes unnecessary suffering.

6.3.3 IACHR: La Tablada Case

The Inter-American Commission for Human Rights or IACHR provides for an intriguing perspective in the *La Tablada* case. While the Inter-American Court of Human Rights (IACtHR) admits it lacks the competence to assess IHL violations, it does reiterate that it is competent to observe that certain acts of omission that violate the American Convention on Human Rights also violate IHL treaties.[46] The IACHR thus established the court is eligible to deliberate on and consider the case. As cases involving unnecessary suffering are, for applicability reasons, rather limited or almost nonexistent at human rights courts, the *La Tablada* case stands out.[47] Albeit, the case in the end did not reach IACtHR.

On January 23, 1989, a group of approximately 40 armed persons launched an attack on the Mechanized Infantry Regiment of the Argentinian Army, allegedly to thwart a planned coup.[48] A two-day battle ensued in the area of the barracks of the regiment, with the military decisively regaining control the next day. However, the attackers claimed that they were subjected to torture, arbitrary execution, and inhumane treatment following their defeat. The perpetrators also insisted that, during the battle at the barracks, the Argentinian military deployed incendiary weapons or white phosphorus and thereby breached the LOAC principle prohibiting weapons of a nature to cause unnecessary suffering.[49]

As explained earlier, since the law of armed conflict doesn't apply in all cases of internal disturbances, the crucial part is that the IACHR ruled that this attack triggered the Common Art. 3 of the GC of 1949 and,

[46] Sassoli, 113.

[47] *Juan Carlos Abella v. Argentina*, Case 11.137, Report N° 55/97, Inter-Am.C.H.R., OEA/Ser.L/V/II.95 Doc. 7 rev. at 271 (1997).

[48] See also details of the case *Juan Carlos Abella v Argentina* at Inter-American Commission on Human Rights, accessed December 12, 2021, https://www.cidh.oas.org/annualrep/97eng/argentina11137.htm.

[49] *Juan Carlos Abella v. Argentina*, Case 11.137, Report N° 55/97, Inter-Am.C.H.R., OEA/Ser.L/V/II.95 Doc. 7 rev. at 271 (1997)¶10(e).

therefore, IHL and LOAC norms were indeed applicable.[50] Hence, there is no dispute whether LOAC norms apply. In regards to admissibility, the court refers to Art. 25 of the American Convention on Human Rights or ACHR[51] to provide "legal remedy to violations by state agents of rights recognized by the constitution or laws of the state concerned."[52] Because every member of the Organization of American States has ratified one or more humanitarian law instruments, the court assumes jurisdiction.[53] Consequently, under Art. 44 of the ACHR, any person or group of persons may file complaints about violations.[54]

More importantly, though, as the applicability of LOAC norms was established, both belligerents, including the attacking party, were granted the status of combatants, and thus, the applicability of the SIrUS principle was without a contest. Leaving aside human rights and complementarity issues with other norms considered in this case, the important question is how the Commission approached the applicability of SIrUS. Regarding means and methods of warfare, the petitioners claimed the Argentinian military violated two fundamental LOAC norms: prohibition of a denial of quarter and use of weapons of a nature to cause SIrUS.[55]

Leaving aside the first claim, as a part of the burden of proof, the Commission received video evidence of the alleged assault by incendiaries on the barracks where the assaulting group was positioned. This attack was also reported extensively on public television in Argentina.[56] By invoking the above rules of the LOAC, the attackers (the petitioners) appealed the ad hoc committees and expert opinions of the ICRC, leading to the adoption of the 1977 Additional Protocol I (AP I), discussed in Chap. 3, which

[50] *Juan Carlos Abella v. Argentina*, Case 11.137, Report N° 55/97, Inter-Am.C.H.R., OEA/Ser.L/V/II.95 Doc. 7 rev. at 271 (1997)¶156.

[51] American Convention on Human Rights (signed 22 November 1969, entered into force 18 July 1978) 1144 UNTS 123 (Pact of San José).

[52] *Juan Carlos Abella v. Argentina*, Case 11.137, Report N° 55/97, Inter-Am.C.H.R., OEA/Ser.L/V/II.95 Doc. 7 rev. at 271 (1997)¶163.

[53] *Juan Carlos Abella v. Argentina*, Case 11.137, Report N° 55/97, Inter-Am.C.H.R., OEA/Ser.L/V/II.95 Doc. 7 rev. at 271 (1997)¶162.

[54] Alison Bisset, *Blackstone's International Human Rights Documents*, 11th ed., (Oxford: Oxford University Press, 2018), 383.

[55] *Juan Carlos Abella v. Argentina*, Case 11.137, Report N° 55/97, Inter-Am.C.H.R., OEA/Ser.L/V/II.95 Doc. 7 rev. at 271 (1997). ¶180(a)(b).

[56] See DiFilm, *La Tablada 1989*.

codified the prohibition of SIrUS[57] and also led to the 1980 Convention on Certain Conventional Weapons (CCW), particularly protocol III regarding incendiary weapons.[58] The petitioners claimed the use of force was excessive to military necessity and, as such, violated customary LOAC and even breached the CCW by the use of incendiary weapons.[59]

The IACHR first reviewed the submitted video evidence of the alleged attack by incendiaries. It held that it was unable to determine the precise nature of the weapon used since the effects, such as fire and smoke, may be produced by other means that are "not specifically designed to cause burn injury to persons, such as piercing munition."[60] Second, the Commission stated that even if incendiaries were used, such munitions are not prohibited by any conventional or customary law, and although Argentina did not become a party to the CCW until 1995, the CCW itself does not prohibit incendiaries.[61] In the following paragraph, the Commission concluded that the killings that occurred "were legitimately combat-related and did not constitute violations of the American Convention or applicable humanitarian law rules."[62]

Indeed, from the perspective of examining the interpretation of the SIrUS principle, this ruling might appear to be inconclusive or even admissive of incendiaries as not violating the principle prohibiting unnecessary suffering, but the court highlighted a few important factors. First, in its argumentation, the IACHR uses the term "specifically designed to cause."[63] Such wording denotes intent and is closer to the Hague Convention of 1907 as "weapons calculated to cause" than to the 1977 AP I, which codifies the principle as weapons "of a nature to cause," which is also the wording in its customary form. Indeed, such wording was related to the Commission's attempt to classify the weapon as incendiary and not whether it violates SIrUS, in other words, whether the weapon was *designed to* cause burns or not.

[57] The constant reference throughout the case to the ICRC by the petitioners as well as by the Court itself further confirms exceptional position and weight of the Red Cross Committee and its opinions and analysis even though not a source of law in itself.

[58] *Juan Carlos Abella v. Argentina*, Case 11.137, Report N° 55/97, Inter-Am.C.H.R., OEA/Ser.L/V/II.95 Doc. 7 rev. at 271 (1997) ¶17.

[59] *Juan Carlos Abella v. Argentina*, ¶137(h).

[60] *Juan Carlos Abella v. Argentina*, ¶186.

[61] *Juan Carlos Abella v. Argentina*, ¶187.

[62] *Juan Carlos Abella v. Argentina*, ¶188.

[63] *Juan Carlos Abella v. Argentina*, ¶186.

Ultimately, the IACHR resorted to the design purpose criteria of weapons advocated by the traditional interpretation of SIrUS. It might have been different and more legally curious if the petitioners invoked specific health effects to support their argument for unnecessary suffering, giving it a substance, including toxic effects or particular burns. It seems, however, that the plaintiffs and the court worked with the traditional interpretation of military necessity balanced against injury, which is not specified in medical terms. Indeed, the IACHR could have elaborated further on the notion of military necessity concerning the use of the particular weapon during the assault on the barracks where the attackers were concentrated. This would, in turn, indirectly examine SIrUS concerning the use of weapons and their effects as balanced against a military necessity.

Still, the IACHR did not shy away from including the SIrUS rule and was ready to elaborate should there be more substantial evidence. This could mean that human rights mechanisms in the future might not refrain from interpreting and applying the rule, and even combatants may seek such a remedy. However, supporting arguments against violating the norm against SIrUS with medical data would equip plaintiffs with stronger arguments.

6.3.4 ECtHR: *Isayeva v. Russia*

The notorious case of *Isayeva v. Russia* is noteworthy for an indirect reference to SIrUS and its application.[64] Since the LOAC or IHL lacks international judicial implementing bodies and relies mainly on the self-help of States—and partially on universal jurisdiction for the prosecution of grave breaches, as stated in Chap. 3—IHRL mechanisms, as illustrated in the *La Tablada* case, sometimes serve, albeit controversially, as a way of implementing the LOAC. As discussed in previous chapters, IHRL does not consider unnecessary suffering to be a legal norm, nor does it differentiate legal standing between combatants and noncombatants. Therefore, the principle must be "turned" to an IHRL norm, such as the right to life and its arbitrary deprivation. However, in 2005, the European Court of Human Rights (ECtHR) delivered a judgment in a case involving the use of heavy combat weapons in the Chechen village of Katyr-Yurt, where armed Chechen rebels were taking refuge and were hiding among

[64] *Isayeva v. Russia*, 57950/00, Council of Europe: European Court of Human Rights, 24 February 2005.

noncombatants.[65] To engage these rebels, Russian armed forces deployed the high-performing explosives FAB-250 and FAB-500.[66] As a result of this bombardment, "the applicant's two children and three relatives were killed, her nephew was disabled, and the applicant herself was wounded."[67]

Relying on Art. 2 of the European Convention of Human Rights (right to life), the applicant claimed her right to life and that of her relatives were violated. The Russian government did not dispute the death of the noncombatants. Still, Russia claimed that the attack was legitimate under Art. 2 para 2(a) as "force absolutely necessary in the circumstances for the protection of persons from unlawful violence."[68] The mingling of combatants with noncombatants makes the case quite complex because of the concurrent applicability of LOAC and IHRL norms and principles, which have the same name but different meanings, such as necessity and proportionality. While the case is not a LOAC case per se, the court, in its judgment, indirectly referred to SIrUS and its application in non-international armed conflict (NIAC) and to the means employed as a "balance" with the pursued military aim.[69] While such a statement refers to the necessity under LOAC, the reference to the weapons (FAB-250 and FAB-500) indicates that the court is taking note of the nature of the means. However, in the following sentence, the court states it "will now consider whether the actions in the present case were no more than absolutely necessary for achieving the declared purpose."[70] Unlike the previous statement, the wording here is closer to the restrictive interpretation under IHRL than the LAOC. To reiterate, "necessity" under the LOAC means all lawful means necessary to accomplish a military objective. In contrast, "necessity" under IHRL means using force as an absolute last resort after exhausting any available nonlethal option. It appears that the court confuses these two separate terms. This is apparent in the statement that, when force is used even in the course of military operation, armed forces

[65] See European Human Rights Advocacy Center, "*Isayeva v Russia*."

[66] See *Isayeva v Russia*, case summary at Weapons Law Encyclopedia.

[67] See *Isayeva v. Russia*, accessed November 11, 2021, https://hudoc.echr.coe.int/fre#{%22itemid%22:[%22002-3996%22]}.

[68] See Sassoli et al., "ECHR, *Isayeva v Russia*."

[69] *Isayeva v. Russia*, 57950/00, Council of Europe: European Court of Human Rights, 24 February 2005¶181.

[70] *Isayeva v. Russia*, 57950/00, Council of Europe: European Court of Human Rights, 24 February 2005¶182.

are allowed to apply only "the least amount of foreseeable physical and mental suffering."[71]

This is not so in the law of armed conflict, where necessity refers to the necessity of means to accomplish a lawful military objective without mentioning "the least" amount of suffering. Thus, LOAC focuses on means capable of accomplishing such objectives given the circumstances and not "increasing" the suffering. This is an essential difference in interpretation and why legal scholars focusing on IHRL occasionally misread traditional principles of the law of armed conflict. Another important aspect the court highlights is the mix of noncombatants and combatants in the case. If one accepts that SIrUS applies to combatants, the noncombatants in such a scenario are left with less protection under the LOAC (although more protection under IHRL). Then again, as *La Tablada* confirmed, particularly in NIAC, the body of law offering the most protection shall be applied.[72]

The only explicit reference to the norms as understood by LOAC is regarding proportionality, stating that the attack shall be calculated to reduce the probability of harm to noncombatants.[73] Proportionality, as understood by LOAC, indeed aims to avoid, if not minimize, collateral damage and does not require force to be proportionate to the threat. Particularly noteworthy is the statement that the norms of NIAC shall be construed in conformity with IHRL governing the right to life and humane treatment. The court then referred to its ruling in *Gulec v. Turkey*[74] where it ruled that the State should make nonlethal weapons available to its armed forces for use against mixed targets.[75] The court refers to a three-part test that the attack in NIAC on a mixed group was lawful only

> as a last resort, that means, and methods employed could cause only the least amount of physical and mental suffering, and that armed forces should

[71] *Isayeva v. Russia*, 57950/00, Council of Europe: European Court of Human Rights, 24 February 2005¶166.

[72] *Juan Carlos Abella v. Argentina*, Case 11.137, Report N° 55/97, Inter-Am.C.H.R., OEA/Ser.L/V/II.95 Doc. 7 rev. at 271 (1997). ¶166.

[73] *Isayeva v. Russia*, 57950/00, Council of Europe: European Court of Human Rights, 24 February 2005¶165.

[74] *Güleç v. Turkey*, 54/1997/838/1044, Council of Europe: European Court of Human Rights, 27 July 1998, accessed August 4, 2022, https://www.refworld.org/cases,ECHR,3ae6b6a918.html.

[75] *Isayeva v. Russia*, 57950/00, Council of Europe: European Court of Human Rights, 24 February 2005¶166.

be used for the neutralization or deterrence of hostile forces by surrender, arrest, withdrawal, or isolation of enemy combatants, not solely by killing and wounding.[76]

Furthermore, the court repeats that such a rule requires States to make available nonlethal weapons technologies.[77] While such requirements make sense for cases of NIAC, the military usually aims at developing weapons that can accomplish military objectives and go through enemy defenses. Indeed, these statements reveal the inevitable friction between the LOAC regarding the regulation of means and methods of warfare dating back to the Hague Regulations of 1899/1907 and the modern human rights approach. Such interpretations of LOAC principles, including SIrUS, are heavily influenced by the underlying ideas of human rights law rather than the traditional LOAC. The suffering mentioned by the court that methods must result in only the least amount of suffering is an interpretation of SIrUS through restrictive human rights concepts of necessity and proportionality.

Therefore, what is important is that while the court refers to suffering, this is not the SIrUS as understood by the traditional LOAC. The traditional view does not refer to the least suffering but to the weapons necessary to achieve an objective compared to alternate, less injurious weapons. There is no lower threshold in the LOAC regarding the least suffering, but there is a higher threshold, meaning the prohibition of *excessive* suffering. While the interplay between the LOAC and IHRL is outside the scope of this book, these two cases brought before human rights mechanisms reveal that human rights bodies are willing to apply LOAC norms, albeit sometimes controversially and with a level of confusion. The basic principles of IHRL and the LOAC are simply different and, as such, are interpreted differently. The case further indicates an inevitable friction amongst the norms applicable to the conduct of hostilities under the LOAC and specific rules of IHRL when combatants mingled with noncombatants. This causes a legal paradox in the applicability of SIrUS only to combatants in a modern, urban battlefield where combatants are mingled with noncombatants and where noncombatants would, as a result, enjoy less protection under LOAC.

[76] Güleç v. Turkey, App. No. 21593/93, Judgment of 27 July 1998, § 70–73 (Eur. Ct. H.R.). This is the author's paraphrase of the Court's reasoning under Article 2 ECHR; see also McCann and Others v. United Kingdom, Judgment of 27 September 1995, § 149.

[77] *Isayeva v. Russia*, 57950/00, Council of Europe: European Court of Human Rights, 24 February 2005¶167.

As a rather bizarre case brought before the Human Rights Committee (HRCtee) in 1990 involving unnecessary suffering as a LOAC norm, the *J.P.K. v. the Netherlands* is worth a brief discussion.[78] In this case, a Dutch citizen known by the initials J.P.K., brought a complaint to the HRC regarding his refusal to attend the Netherlands' compulsory military service in 1987. J.P.K. argued that the Dutch military would force him to contribute to the training and preparation for the use of nuclear weapons.[79] He further claimed that to be credible, nuclear strategies of flexible response or deterrence and forward defense must be based on actual intent to resort to nuclear weapons.[80] J.P.K. invoked multiple legal instruments, including the 1977 Geneva Protocol, the 1949 Geneva Convention, UNGA Resolution 95(I), the UN Charter, and even the Martens-Clause referring to humanity. He further noted the principle that violence liable to cause unnecessary suffering must be avoided.[81] J.P.K.'s claim is chaotic, confusing, and without any normative substance. Accordingly, the Committee dismissed the case, stipulating, inter alia, that compulsory military service is not precluded by the International Covenant on Civil and Political Rights (ICCPR).[82] It would have been interesting if the court had chosen to elaborate on the claims made by J.P.K., but since these were unsubstituted from the beginning, there was no point. However, this case reveals that virtually anyone can lodge a claim with human rights bodies without understanding the LOAC, twisting and misinterpreting the norm, and then relying on these human rights bodies to correct this. Whether they are adequately equipped to make such corrections is debatable. Should they decide to do so, the question is whether such interpretation through IHRL bodies and mechanisms adds to confusion and reinterpretation of this fundamental LOAC principle to align it with the human rights perspective.

[78] *J.P.K. v. The Netherlands*, CCPR/C/43/D/401/1990, UN Human Rights Committee (HRC), 18 November 1991, accessed August 4, 2022, https://www.refworld.org/cases,HRC,3ae6b6f88.html.

[79] *J.P.K. v. The Netherlands*, CCPR/C/43/D/401/1990, UN Human Rights Committee (HRC), 18 November 1991, para 3.2.

[80] *J.P.K. v. The Netherlands*, CCPR/C/43/D/401/1990, UN Human Rights Committee (HRC), 18 November 1991, para 3.2.

[81] *J.P.K. v. The Netherlands*, CCPR/C/43/D/401/1990, UN Human Rights Committee (HRC), 18 November 1991, para 3.1.

[82] *J.P.K. v. The Netherlands*, CCPR/C/43/D/401/1990, UN Human Rights Committee (HRC), 18 November 1991, para 6.5.

The Human Rights Council (HRC), at times, issues reports on particular situations of violence in which it focuses on the use of specific weapons such as white phosphorus or napalm. Since these weapons are not prohibited, the report often elaborates on necessity and proportionality as understood by IHRL.[83] Nevertheless, it is vital to point out one additional inquiry by the HRC, the Commission of Inquiry on the Syrian Arab Republic, where it did mention SIrUS in relation to particular weapons and their effects.[84] The commission, in its seventh report, concluded that the use of incendiary weapons—in this case, incendiary bombs—violated the rule prohibiting unnecessary suffering.[85] The report included health effects of a "napalm-like substance" on the victims, such as disfigurement, second and third-degree burns on up to 80 percent of the body surface, and extreme pain.[86] The Council states that: "By using incendiary bombs in the Urem Al-Koubra school incident, the Government violated rules of international humanitarian law prohibiting the use of weapons that cause superfluous injury, unnecessary suffering or that are indiscriminate by nature."[87] In light of all that has been said in this book, such a statement is obviously quite stretched. First and foremost, SIrUS does not apply to noncombatants as the Council suggests such bombs were used against schools. Second, the Council does not elaborate on why and how it came to the general conclusion that incendiaries violate SIrUS. Such is not the understanding of numerous States and even the Protocol III of the Convention on Certain Conventional Weapons.

Such misinterpretation and rather simplistic approach are thus one of the reasons why there is confusion in the interpretation of the principle. It would have been much more beneficial if the Council had taken the time to explore thoroughly the language of the instruments of international humanitarian law, including SIrUS as a norm, such as Additional Protocol I to the Geneva Conventions and Hague Regulations. The Council would then be better off thoroughly elaborating on the effects of such weapons and connecting them to unnecessary suffering and military objectives.

[83] UN Human Rights Council, *Report of Commission of Inquiry on Lebanon*, para. 80.

[84] See UN Human Rights Council, "Independent International Commission."

[85] 7th Report of the Commission of Inquiry on Syria, UN doc. A/HRC/25/65, 12 February 2014, §§130–131.

[86] 7th Report of the Commission of Inquiry on Syria, UN doc. A/HRC/25/65, 12 February 2014, §§130–131, para 130.

[87] 7th Report of the Commission of Inquiry on Syria, UN doc. A/HRC/25/65, 12 February 2014, §§130–131, para.131.

This would give the argument more substance helpful to the victims rather than empty phrases. The incident involving an attack on the school is thus, under humanitarian law, not a question of SIrUS but of distinction and proportionality.

Indeed, cases before international judicial or quasi-judicial bodies where SIrUS was invoked correctly and explored are almost nonexistent. Since this book is not concerned with the interplay between IHRL and IHL, the human rights mechanisms serve as illustrative examples.

However, several observations stem from the above cases brought before human rights bodies. Indeed, the rules of Hague law, that is, of conduct of hostilities, while predominantly created for an international armed conflict, do apply in NIAC, including the application of the SIrUS norm.[88] Accordingly, it may be invoked by nonstate armed groups (NSAGs) that enjoy combatant status. However, due to the ambiguity of the SIrUS rule and human rights instruments' quite different "conceptual" origin, invoking the right to life in NIAC stemming from human rights instruments makes much more sense and offers better protection. Combatants, meaning regular members of the armed forces, do not usually bring claims to human rights courts arguing about being subjected to weapons of a nature to cause unnecessary suffering in the course of international armed conflict.

Additionally, applying this principle to civilians is highly controversial. Civilians are protected under IHRL and LOAC by norms against arbitrary killing, and unnecessary suffering would not make much sense. As a norm, there is no necessary suffering that a civilian must endure under an IHRL or LOAC framework; indeed, such suffering would be contrary to the underlying idea of human rights. Since the book examines SIrUS as a law-of-war principle, I have excluded further deliberations on IHRL and its interpretation of unnecessary suffering. It is more relevant to look at how the traditional enforcers of the LOAC, in other words, States, interpret and apply the rule prohibiting weapons of a nature to cause unnecessary suffering.

[88] *Prosecutor v. Tadic* (Judgement) IT-94-1-A (15 July 1999) ¶23.

6.4 National Courts

From the perspective of interpreting and applying SIrUS, municipal or national law is indeed the most relevant when enforcing the norms of the LOAC, particularly those pertaining to international armed conflicts (IACs). While IHRL mechanisms can sometimes seem inefficient in applying LOAC norms, particularly those relating to the means and methods of warfare, national law often refers to national legislation and involves the armed forces themselves.

This section explores two particular judicial procedures related to the use of weapons with a specific focus on the application of *Hague law* and SIrUS. As national courts affect international law, municipal law may offer insights into understanding of the interpretation and substance of the principle. As Judge Shahabuddeen puts it in his dissenting opinion in the 1996 AO on nuclear weapons, "Though not of course binding, it [the Shimoda case] ranks as a judicial decision under Art. 38, paragraph 1(d), of the Statute of the Court; it qualifies for consideration."[89] The two cases—*Shimoda v. The State* and *Vietnam Association for Victims of Agent Orange v. Dow Chemical*—are significant in relating health effects to unnecessary suffering in light of previous chapters on nuclear and chemical weapons and their effects.

6.4.1 *Shimoda v. The State*

The bombings of Hiroshima, Nagasaki, and other cities, such as Tokyo, remain controversial to this day. It is not my intent to examine the legal background of the attack on Hiroshima from the perspective of the entire law of war.[90] Instead, the author wishes to point out deliberations that may further the understanding of weapons and their relationship with the SIrUS norm. The issue of the bombing of Hiroshima was raised already at the International Military Tribunal for the Far East, also known as the Tokyo War Crimes Trial. U.S. Army Maj. Ben Bruce Blakeney, an American lawyer best known for his work for the defense at the trial, was convinced

[89] Legality of the Threat or Use of Nuclear Weapons (Advisory Opinion) (Dissenting Opinion of Judge Weeramantry) [1996] ICJ Rep.375¶400.

[90] In this matter see McKinney, Katherine E, Scott D. Sagan, and Allen S. Weiner, "Why the Atomic Bombing of Hiroshima Would Be Illegal Today" *Bulletin of the Atomic Scientists* 76, no. 4 (2020): 157–165. https://www.tandfonline.com/doi/full/10.1080/00963402.2020.1778344.

that the bombing of the civilians in Hiroshima and Nagasaki was in clear violation of the Hague Convention IV (1907), and thus violating the prohibition of unnecessary suffering.[91]

Nonetheless, *the Shimoda case* was launched by Shoichi Okamoto, a defense attorney for General Okada at the Tokyo Trial.[92] Due to Art. 19(a) of the peace treaty stipulating that Japan will not bring any claims arising from the state of war against the Allies,[93] Okamoto decided to appeal to a local Japanese court, and five *hibakusha* from Hiroshima and Nagasaki were selected to become the plaintiffs.[94] Later, Okamoto eventually joined hands with Yasuhiro Matsui, a lawyer, a *hibakusha,* and the soon-to-be mayor of Hiroshima. In April 1955, the appeal was issued to the Tokyo district court. Ryuichi Shimoda was among the five selected *hibakusha* and became the icon of the case due to the suffering that he and his family endured as a result of the bomb. His children died, and he suffered hiroshimitis, an illness resulting from exposure to high doses of ionizing radiation, a term coined by Dr. Junod, as previously explained.[95]

The plaintiffs raised several arguments based on applicable international law and the LOAC, particularly norms against indiscriminate bombardment. In addition, the plaintiffs raised arguments regarding violations of laws and customs of war as codified in the Hague Convention of 1907, that is, Art. 23(a) and (e) prohibiting poison, poisoned weapons, and unnecessary suffering, respectively. Moreover, they invoked the 1925 Geneva Protocol banning asphyxiating gases and bacteriological warfare.[96] Therefore, the argument was "that the use of an atomic weapon was contrary to the fundamental principle of the laws of war that unnecessary pain

[91] Yuki Tanaka and Richard Falk, "The Atomic Bombing, the Tokyo War Crimes Tribunal and the Shimoda Case: Lessons for Anti-Nuclear Legal Movements" *The Asia-Pacific Journal* 7, no. 44–43 (2009): Article 3245. https://apjjf.org/-Yuki-Tanaka/3245/article.html.

[92] Tanaka and Falk, 3–4.

[93] Treaty of Peace with Japan (signed 8 September 1951, entered into force 28 April 1952) 136 UNTS 45.¶19(a). Full quotation: "*(a) Japan waives all claims of Japan and its nationals against the Allied Powers and their nationals arising out of the war or out of actions taken because of the existence of a state of war, and waives all claims arising from the presence, operations or actions of forces or authorities of any of the Allied Powers in Japanese territory prior to the coming into force of the present Treaty.*"

[94] Tanaka and Falk, 6.

[95] Tanaka and Falk, 6.

[96] Tanaka and Falk, 9.

must not be inflicted."[97] It seems that the plaintiffs, as well as the court, were unaware of the applicability of the principle only to combatants.

Besides, the plaintiffs argued unnecessary suffering without its traditional balancing principle of military necessity or advantage. In other words, the plaintiffs did not raise the traditional counterbalance either, simply because they did not know or considered Hiroshima not to be a military objective. It is necessary to point out a prevalent misunderstanding of the principle that is apparent in the article of Tanaka and Falk (2009) concerning the interpretation of the ruling in the *Shimoda* case. Against the argument of the defense that the belligerents may "choose the means of injuring the enemy in order to attain the special purpose of war, subject to certain conditions imposed by international customary law and treaties,"[98] Tanaka and Falk summarized, "In other words, the defense implied that any weapon could be utilized no matter how destructive, lethal and inhumane it would be, as long as there was no positive law or treaty to explicitly prohibit the use of such a weapon."[99] Such summarization, while not entirely correct, is indeed close to the underlying concepts of modern human rights law but not the LOAC. Undeniably, belligerents, as explained in Chap. 2, may choose any *lawful* weapon to accomplish their military objectives. In 1945, the understanding of customary rules of the LOAC was highly traditional, including the interpretation of SIrUS. States did not take medical effects into account. However, they were considered by the ICRC, as apparent from the Junod Report, but not by States themselves, who concentrated on the military advantage of a particular weapon as a balancing principle, as can be seen from the St. Petersburg Declaration and The Hague Conventions.

Tanaka and Falk (2009) simplify LOAC norms and arguments too excessively. Notwithstanding, Falk's (1965) is the first notable attempt to offer a legal analysis of this important decision.[100] Falk (1965) points out that the court is "obviously impressed by the added horror that stems from this atomic effect that spread the suffering through time and space for an unknown duration and scope with uncertain consequence."[101] Such

[97] Tanaka and Falk, 9.

[98] Tanaka and Falk, 10.

[99] Tanaka and Falk, 10.

[100] Richard A. Falk, "The Shimoda Case: A Legal Appraisal of the Atomic Attacks Upon Hiroshima and Nagasaki" *American Journal of International Law* 59, no. 4 (1965): 759–793. https://doi.org/10.2307/2197093.

[101] Falk, 769.

observation palpably comes from the court's description of the destructive impact of the blast, heat, and ionizing radiation. The case of Ryuichi Shimoda and four other plaintiffs from Hiroshima for compensation for the nuclear bombing, which they saw as illegal, represented the first time that a judicial body had addressed nuclear weapons.

Although the Tokyo district court ultimately dismissed the case because an individual does not possess a legal personality in international law,[102] nevertheless they discussed the LOAC and the application of its norms. While the court elaborated extensively on the notion of a defended and undefended city, it is germane to focus on its explanations of two particular norms of the LOAC—military necessity and, primarily, SIrUS—as these two rules are intertwined according to traditional interpretation. The court deliberated on the notion of total war in which the distinction between combatants and noncombatants is blurred or even nonexistent, stating that a broader context must be considered as the military objective, "that the outcome of the war is decided also by other factors, including the general population and the labour force."[103] Such construction of military necessity as closely related to the so-called ***kriegsraison*** discussed in Chap. 2 is clarified by Falk (1965) to concern only those contributing to the war effort, not the general population.[104] While contributing noncombatants may not be military objectives per se, the factory, ammunition depot, electricity station, or other installations contributing to the war effort can become such an objective, as discussed in Chap. 2 under the fundamental principles of the LOAC. Consequently, indirect participation is collateral damage.[105]

The court admits the atomic bombing "is believed to be contrary to the prohibition of means of injuring the enemy that cause unnecessary suffering or are inhumane."[106] Then, the district court refers to the traditional balancing of military necessity and effectiveness against humanitarian considerations, and as an example, it cites the St. Petersburg Declaration

[102] Traditionally, did not possess legal personality in international law, that is, right to participate, it was the State that chose whether to act on an individual's behalf. See Shaw, 156. The concept of whether and to what extent an individual possesses legal personality under international law is widely debated even today.

[103] *Shimoda et al. v. the State*, 633.

[104] Falk, 773–774.

[105] See Nils Melzer, *Interpretive Guidance on the Notion of Direct Participation in Hostilities Under International Humanitarian Law* (Geneva: ICRC, 2009).

[106] *Shimoda et al. v. the State*, 634.

prohibiting exploding bullets. However, as mentioned in Chap. 2, the *raison de être* for the St. Petersburg declaration was not entirely humanitarian as such bullets were prohibited only amongst "civilized" nations. The court further compares the use of atomic bombing to Art. 23(a) of The Hague Conventions, Declaration IV on asphyxiating gases, and the 1925 Geneva Protocol, arguing that there is no legal agreement between international lawyers on the differences between poison, poisonous gas, and bacteria. The reasoning is based on considering these gases as further increasing the suffering of combatants *hors de combat*. In the following paragraph 11(e), the court states that "it can safely be concluded that besides poisons, poisonous gases and bacteria, the use of means of injuring the enemy which cause injury at least as great as or greater than these prohibited materials is prohibited by international law."[107] In its most relevant passage, the court states that while it is doubtful whether the use of the bomb was necessary, it is a fact that many citizens live with long-term effects of ionizing radiation and continuous suffering. Therefore, it concludes, concerning SIrUS, that the suffering attributed to the atomic bomb is greater than that caused by poisons and poisonous gases. The proceedings took place in the 1960s, in other words, before the Vietnam War and the Iran-Iraq War. Therefore, rather than a moral comparison of health effects, the statement should be interpreted as a comment regarding the prohibition of poison under The Hague Conventions and not CWs as understood under the Chemical Weapons Convention (CWC).

However, it is important to note that the Shimoda case proceedings did refer to unnecessary suffering as it relates to long-term health effects. They did disregard military advantage, and they did include consideration of medical aspects. The court took eight years to consider the matter, concluding its work in 1963. The decision was published the next year in English in The Japanese Annual of International Law, vol. 8, 1964, p. 231. Even though the decision was available to the international legal community, it did not stir much attention, and besides Judge Shahabuddeen's dissenting opinion cited above, it was not even referred to in the ICJ AO of 1996. Indeed, the final AO does not include any reference to *Shimoda*; however, the ICJ did comment on the case in the form of the dissenting opinions of Judge Weeramantry and Judge Shahabuddeen. Judge Weeramantry acknowledges *Shimoda* as the first deliberation of the legality of nuclear weapons but does not draw any precedence or cite passages

[107] *Shimoda et al. v. the State*, 634.

from the ruling.[108] On the contrary, Judge Shahabuddeen pointed out that the court, "assisted by professors of international law, as well as a full team of advocates, seemed unaware that the SIrUS principle applies to combatants and not to civilians."[109]

It is paradoxical that the court, in its central argument, admitted that the bomb causes unnecessary suffering to civilians. This is probably due to the court's initial disregard for the differentiation of military objectives and civilian objects in the doctrine of total war. Indeed, a combatant's body is no different from a civilian's, and the effects are the same. However, it should be stated that civilians, as a rule, cannot invoke and raise the principle of unnecessary suffering. It does not apply to them. It is important to emphasize, however, that the *Shimoda* case is not concerned with the legality of nuclear weapons as such but about the specific historical incidence of their use.[110]

6.4.2 *Vietnam Association for Victims of Agent Orange v. Dow Chemical*

In the course of the Vietnam War, the United States sprayed toxic herbicides in South Vietnam in an attempt to reveal hidden combatants.[111] The intended purpose, therefore, was not antipersonnel but as a defoliant. Nevertheless, the herbicides have affected those near this spraying with delayed and long-term health effects, even stretching to the second generation. The victims complained of long-term health injuries due to these toxic chemicals that include multiple forms of cancer, such as lung, prostate, and breast, as well as birth defects. Since the Vietnamese plaintiffs were not citizens of the United States, they brought the case to the U.S. national court under the Alien Tort Statute,[112] which states, "The district courts shall have original jurisdiction of any civil action by an alien for a tort only, committed in violation of the law of nations or a treaty of

[108] *Legality of the Threat or Use of Nuclear Weapons (Advisory Opinion) (Dissenting Opinion of Judge Weeramantry)* [1996] ICJ Rep 429. ¶439.

[109] *Legality of the Threat or Use of Nuclear Weapons (Advisory Opinion) (Dissenting Opinion of Judge Weeramantry)* [1996] ICJ Rep 429 ¶404.

[110] Falk, 784.

[111] See International Crimes Database, *Vietnam Association for Victims of Agent Orange v Dow Chemical*, case summary, accessed June 5, 2022, https://www.internationalcrimesdatabase.org/Case/196/Vietnam-Association-for-Victims-of-Agent-Orange-v-Dow/.

[112] 28 U.S. Code § 1350 - *Alien's action for tort.*

the United States."[113] In other words, under specified conditions, a non--U.S. citizen may bring claims of violations of conventional or customary law committed by the United States to the U.S. district courts.

On September 10, 2004, the Vietnam Association for Victims of Agent Orange and several individuals filed suit against various chemical companies producing the agent, particularly Dow Chemical, which also supplied napalm.[114] In addition to reliance on the Geneva Convention (GC) of 1949, the plaintiffs invoked the 1907 Hague Conventions Art. 23(a), the Annex to the 1907 Hague Convention (IV) regarding asphyxiating gases, and the 1925 Geneva Gas Protocol.[115] Leaving aside the question of admissibility—which in itself is quite problematic because the plaintiffs brought the case against private companies that could not be a party to the above-mentioned international agreements—the case deserves examination of how the court addressed the invoked principle of unnecessary suffering that comprised one of the main arguments of the plaintiffs.[116]

However, the United States was not a party to the Geneva Gas Protocol until 1975, and by then, the Vietnam War was over.[117] Primarily, though, the plaintiffs claimed that "the use of Agent Orange was disproportionate to military necessity because it caused unnecessary human suffering…."[118] That is, the plaintiffs interpreted the norm in its traditional sense by weighing military necessity with SIrUS, which, without supporting medical data, is, as I have explained before, problematic to maintain against a State.

Furthermore, since the plaintiffs referred to the Hague Convention of 1907 and AP I was not applicable, the unnecessary suffering rule under Art. 23(e) required intent, that is, "weapons calculated to" as referred to

[113] 28 U.S. Code § 1350, Ch. 646, 62 Stat. 934.

[114] *Vietnam Association For Victims Of Agent Orange/Dioxin and ors v Dow Chemical Company and ors*, First Instance, 373 F.Supp.2d 7 (E.D.N.Y. 2005), ILDC 123 (US 2005), 10th March 2005, United States; New York; District Court for the Eastern District of New York [EDNY].

[115] *Vietnam Association For Victims Of Agent Orange/Dioxin and ors v Dow Chemical Company and ors*, First Instance, 23.

[116] *Vietnam Association For Victims Of Agent Orange/Dioxin and ors v Dow Chemical Company and ors*, First Instance, 18.

[117] *Vietnam Association For Victims Of Agent Orange/Dioxin and ors v Dow Chemical Company and ors*, First Instance, 24.

[118] *Vietnam Association For Victims Of Agent Orange/Dioxin and ors v Dow Chemical Company and ors*, First Instance, 26.

by the court.[119] The court argues that "It does not apply to lethal weapons that collaterally cause injury or suffering to achieve an appropriate (in war) military objective of incapacitating enemy troops, let alone to herbicides that may cause harm to human beings as the side-effect of an application intended to destroy plants."[120] The court maintained that such a prohibition on SIrUS applies to weapons that cause unnecessary or superfluous injury to "an already-incapacitated combatant," in other words, *hors de combat*—those who are wounded, sick, or no longer engaging in hostilities. Using the example of bullets containing a poisonous agent, the court further pointed out that such is not necessary to add for the legitimate military objective of disabling enemy combatants.[121]

As evident in the *Shimoda* case, there was no broad agreement about what constitutes poison or poisoned gases. The 1899 Hague Convention was not enough to prevent WWI, and the French believed it prohibited only the most toxic substances, as explained in Chap. 4. However, as the court points out, poison applied to weapons increases suffering above the necessary objective of the bullet or bayonet. Such discussion is now irrelevant with the CWC and its customary prohibition on CWs. Since the Agent Orange case was filed in 2004, the medicalization of the principle and the intertwining of IHL with IHRL caused certain confusion. However, the court ruled using the applicable LOAC in place in 1975.

In other words, defoliants were not categorized as CWs at that time, and the 1925 Geneva Gas Protocol did not prohibit their use. The understanding at that time pertains to the design-purpose idea of weapons law that the primary effects shall be considered rather than every possible effect that is not intended. Such an interpretation is similar to that of the United States regarding ionizing radiation from nuclear weapons. It is apparent here that the plaintiffs confused several notions of the LOAC with the restrictive interpretation of human rights. Three essential principles are mentioned in the case: military necessity, proportionality, and unnecessary suffering. As explained in Chap. 3, it is crucial to differentiate the interpretation of these principles of the LAOC from IHRL; they are not the same principles and norms. The principle of proportionality under

[119] *Vietnam Association For Victims Of Agent Orange/Dioxin and ors v Dow Chemical Company and ors*, First Instance, 31.

[120] *Vietnam Association For Victims Of Agent Orange/Dioxin and ors v Dow Chemical Company and ors*, First Instance, 185.

[121] *Vietnam Association For Victims Of Agent Orange/Dioxin and ors v Dow Chemical Company and ors*, First Instance, 183.

the LOAC refers to incidental damage with regard to the value of a military objective, not as a proportionality to a particular threat. Such confusion is apparent from the above-quoted statement that the use violated proportionality and thus caused unnecessary suffering.

The proceedings concluded that "the plaintiffs did not demonstrate a violation of international law" and that the United States used the defoliant against foliage to reveal hidden troops, not as an antipersonnel means of warfare.[122] The plaintiffs appealed to the appellate court on February 22, 2008. The District Court confirmed the 2005 reasons for dismissal and found no new developments in the appeal. In its reasoning, the appellate court argued:

> In this respect, it is significant that Plaintiffs nowhere allege that the government *intended to* harm human beings through its use of Agent Orange. In their Amended Complaint, Plaintiffs recognize that "[t]he stated *purpose of the [herbicide]* spraying was twofold: (a) to defoliate forests and mangroves to destroy the vegetative cover used by the [Democratic Republic of Vietnam] and [National Liberation Front] troops for concealment, and (b) to destroy crops to deprive them of food." In addition, Plaintiffs acknowledge that the herbicide defoliation campaign "heavily targeted," among other things, vegetative cover adjacent to U.S. military bases and surrounding areas, making it all the more implausible that the government intended to use the herbicide as a poisonous weapon during war.[123] [emphasis added]

The appellate court's decision in the 2008 case involving Vietnamese Agent Orange victims emphasized the intended purpose of the chemical weapon in question, not its misuse. As discussed in Chap. 4, chemical weapons (CWs) have toxic effects on humans or animals as their primary purpose, distinguishing them from other weapons that may cause toxic effects as a secondary result. Defoliants like Agent Orange were used primarily for their plan-destroying properties, although their toxic effects on humans have become well-documented.

The court acknowledged that while the US was not a party to the 1925 Geneva Gas Protocol at the time of the Vietnam War, it was bound by the

[122] *Vietnam Association For Victims Of Agent Orange/Dioxin and ors v Dow Chemical Company and ors*, First Instance, 208.

[123] *Vietnam Association for Victims of Agent Orange/Dioxin v. Dow Chemical Co.*, 05-1953-cv, United States Court of Appeals for the Second Circuit, 22 February 2008, accessed August 5, 2022, https://www.refworld.org/cases,USA_CA_2,47d7981e2.html, 27.

1907 Hague Convention. Article 23(a) of this convention prohibits the use of poisons, and the Nuremberg International Military Tribunal (IMT) confirmed that such prohibitions had become customary international law. Therefore, the plaintiffs argued that the use of Agent Orange could be considered in violation of international law under the Hague IV provisions, which prohibit the use of poisons and deleterious gases. The Court also recognized the severe health effects of Agent Orange, including an increased risk of lung cancer and genetic deformities in descendants, issues which were supported by risk assessments of pesticides and herbicides. The deliberations included medical evidence that linked these toxic substances to unnecessary suffering, a concept applicable to combatants under international law.

However, despite these arguments, the court ultimately ruled that the use of Agent Orange did not violate international law as it was not classified as a poison or chemical weapon under the conventions applicable at the time. While the court acknowledged the significant harm caused to human health,[124] it concluded that the defoliant's primary purpose was not to cause harm to humans, thus falling outside the legal definition of prohibited weapons under the Hague Convention.

6.4.3 *Iraqi High Tribunal: Al-Anfal*

In connection with the preceding chapters focusing on chemical weapons, it is worth mentioning the second Iraqi High Tribunal case decision on July 24, 2007, the so-called Al-Anfal case.[125] The case refers to the chemical attacks against Kurdish villages in northern Iraq, particularly Halabja, as discussed in Chap. 4 during the operation Al-Anfal (1988). In other words, the case did not deal with Iraq's use of chemicals against Iran and combatants in an IAC, but against its own population, the Kurds. As such, it could not argue for reservation under the Geneva Protocol on gas that it acted in retaliation. The court relied on its domestic code from 1968 to

[124] *Vietnam Association for Victims of Agent Orange/Dioxin v. Dow Chemical Co.*, 05-1953-cv, United States Court of Appeals for the Second Circuit, 22 February 2008, accessed August 5, 2022, https://www.refworld.org/cases,USA_CA_2,47d7981e2.html, 13–14. First instance *Vietnam Association For Victims Of Agent Orange/Dioxin and ors v Dow Chemical Company and ors*, First Instance, 373 F.Supp.2d 7 (E.D.N.Y. 2005), ILDC 123 (US 2005), 10th March 2005, United States; New York; District Court for the Eastern District of New York [EDNY], 71–73.

[125] See *Al Anfal* at the International Crimes Database.

2003 that included *erga omnes* crimes such as genocide, war crimes, and crimes against humanity.[126] The Court referred to wanton destruction in violation of military necessity.[127] Several defendants were brought to the court, including Ali Hassan al-Majid, infamously known as "Chemical Ali."[128] Al-Majid ordered "special strikes" against the Kurdish population in northern Iraq, including the massacre in Halabja, Iraq.[129] The Court of Appeals confirmed the death sentence for al-Majid for multiple war crimes and crimes against humanity and stated, "When some of the plaintiffs stood before it, the court acknowledged the chemical gases' poisonous effects, as most of them suffer from problems in their respiratory systems, scars over the body, and psychological damages caused by these horrible prisons."[130]

The important aspect here is the judicial recognition of long-term health effects going beyond the temporal scope of the conflict. The court did not particularly elaborate on unnecessary suffering as a LOAC norm caused by chemical weapons; it was unnecessary because of the prevailing rule of distinction. The Al-Anfal campaign was led against noncombatants, and while the weapons were used in the course of the Iran-Iraq War against Iranian combatants, the Iraqis argued that the attack was a reprisal allowed by its reservation in the 1925 Geneva Protocol on gas, as discussed in Chap. 4.

6.5 Conclusion

This chapter examined primary sources through documentary analysis of letters and radiograms sent by Dr. Junod from Hiroshima to the ICRC headquarters in Geneva. His testimony was particularly important during the 17th Conference of State parties to GCs in 1948, at which the president of the ICRC called for the prohibition of nuclear weapons based on the effects of ionizing radiation and unnecessary suffering, among other relevant principles and rules.

Further evidence linking long-term health effects to unnecessary suffering was offered in a ruling of a domestic court in Japan when the Tokyo

[126] *Al Anfal,* Case No. l/CSecond/2006, 24.

[127] *Al Anfal,* Case No. l/CSecond/2006, 19.

[128] John Kevin Heller, "Convictions in the Anfal Trial" *OpinioJuris.* June 24, 2007, http://opiniojuris.org/2007/06/24/convictions-in-the-anfal-trial/.

[129] *Al Anfal,* Case No. l/CSecond/2006, 12.

[130] *Al Anfal,* Case No. l/CSecond/2006, 5.

district court ruled that radiation indeed inflicts unnecessary suffering upon its victims. In a similar case related to Dow Chemical and the use of Agent Orange in Vietnam, the issue was the purpose of the chemical. As a defoliant, Agent Orange was not designed to be deployed against human targets, so it was not treated as a weapon. Indeed, it would be much more relevant if the Vietnam War victims had included napalm and its effects in their complaint about Agent Orange and argued, putting predominant weight on medical data and SIrUS from a medical perspective, including references to the work of the ICRC.

In the international arena, particular judges of the ICJ have reaffirmed several times that the long-term effects of ionizing radiation are contrary to military necessity and, therefore, are in violation of the SIrUS principle. Here, it can be confidently said that the estimated relative risk due to the possibility of developing cancer or leukemia would be included as unnecessary suffering. Since LOAC does not differentiate between conventional and unconventional weapons, such a case and ruling may be used in other proceedings, for instance, regarding controversial incendiaries such as white phosphorus or napalm.

La Tablada and *Isayeva v. Russia* demonstrated the use of regional mechanisms in applying the rules of IHL. While outside their treaty scope, these judicial mechanisms may be the only effective remedy in case of grievances. As a result of the growing intertwining of IHL/LOAC and IHRL, the predominance of NIACs, and the blurring of boundaries between military and law enforcement operations, such cases will only increase. The progress of codification of the principle prohibiting SIrUS from its initial black-letter codification in the late nineteenth century has revealed specific changes in interpretation during the mid-twentieth century. These changes were particularly affected by the dominance of NIACs and the use of new weapons since the end of WWII. With IHRL entering the scene with the particular support of citizen groups, the responsibility for weapons and their effects was no longer left entirely to the States. Positive law theory became natural law, and human rights advocates gained momentum. Not only were particular weapons restricted or banned because they caused unnecessary suffering, but human rights mechanisms gradually incorporated IHL and referred to it in their opinions, judgments, or decisions.

The cases indeed confirmed that unnecessary suffering relates to a combatant, already incapacitated. As long-term effects on health persist, such combatants are still under the "attack" of such weapons even if they are no longer fighting. While poison was discussed to incur such injuries, it is apparent that continuous long-term effects are becoming unacceptable and, as such, part of SIrUS interpretation precisely because they affect a combatant *hors de combat*. More often than not, the judicial and quasi-judicial bodies did not shy away from employing the ICRC studies or other medical data to examine whether the effects of a particular weapon are excessive to the military necessity. While the bodies retained the purpose-design interpretation, they often included medical elaboration when touching upon the norm prohibiting unnecessary suffering.

References

Arnold, Roberta, and Noelle N. R. Quenivet, eds. *International Humanitarian Law and Human Rights: Towards a New Merger in International Law*. Leiden: Martinus Nijhoff Publishers, 2008.

Bisset, Alison. *Blackstone's International Human Rights Documents*. 11th ed. Oxford: Oxford University Press, 2018.

Boas, Gideon, and William A. Schabas, eds. *International Criminal Law Developments in the Case Law of the ICTY*. Leiden: Martinus Nijhoff Publishers, 2003.

Boisson de Chazournes, Laurence, and Philippe Sands, eds. *International Law, the International Court of Justice and Nuclear Weapons*. Cambridge: Cambridge University Press, 1999.

Casey-Maslen, Stuart, ed. *Weapons Under International Human Rights Law*. Cambridge: Cambridge University Press, 2014.

Casey-Maslen, Stuart, and Steven Haines. *Hague Law Interpreted: The Conduct of Hostilities under the Law of Armed Conflict*. New York: Hart, 2020.

DiFilm. "Copamiento Regimiento 3 de Infanteria Mecanizada de La Tablada 1989." YouTube video, 00:01:18. April 16, 2014. https://www.youtube.com/watch?v=EsNFTlfsMf0.

Distefano, Giovanni. *Fundamentals of Public International Law: A Sketch of the International Legal Order*. Leiden: Brill Nijhoff, 2019.

Falk, Richard A. "The Shimoda Case: A Legal Appraisal of the Atomic Attacks Upon Hiroshima and Nagasaki." *American Journal of International Law* 59, no. 4 (1965): 759–793. https://doi.org/10.2307/2197093.

Heller, Kevin Jon. "Convictions in the Anfal Trial." *OpinioJuris*. June 24, 2007. http://opiniojuris.org/2007/06/24/convictions-in-the-anfal-trial/.

Junod, Marcel. *Warrior Without Weapons*. London: Jonathan Cape, 1951.

Lifton, Robert Jay. *Death in Life: Survivors of Hiroshima*. Chapel Hill: University of North Carolina Press, 1991.

McKinney, Katherine E, Scott D. Sagan, and Allen S. Weiner. "Why the Atomic Bombing of Hiroshima Would Be Illegal Today." *Bulletin of the Atomic Scientists* 76, no. 4 (2020): 157–165. https://www.tandfonline.com/doi/full/10.1080/00963402.2020.1778344.

Melzer, Nils. *Interpretive Guidance on the Notion of Direct Participation in Hostilities Under International Humanitarian Law*. Geneva: ICRC, 2009.

Sassoli, Marco. *International Humanitarian Law: Rules, Controversies, and Solutions to Problems Arising in Warfare*. Cheltenham: Edward Elgar, 2019a.

Sassoli, Marco. *International Humanitarian Law: Rules, Controversies, and Solutions to Problems Arising in Warfare*. Cheltenham: Edward Elgar, 2019b.

Schabas, William. *An Introduction to the International Criminal Court*. 4th ed. Cambridge: Cambridge University Press, 2011.

Shaw, Malcolm. *International Law*. Cambridge: Cambridge University Press, 2017.

Tanaka, Yuki, and Richard Falk. "The Atomic Bombing, the Tokyo War Crimes Tribunal and the Shimoda Case: Lessons for Anti-Nuclear Legal Movements." *The Asia-Pacific Journal* 7, no. 44–43 (2009): Article 3245. https://apjjf.org/-Yuki-Tanaka/3245/article.html.

CHAPTER 7

Challenges and Future Technology

7.1 Introduction

Practical implementation and general interpretation of the norm against unnecessary suffering present considerable challenges. Previous judicial case studies illustrate that applying the norm without substantial medical data often renders the principle prohibiting superfluous injury and unnecessary suffering ambiguous and without substance, open to contests in interpretations. Such ambiguities are then often employed to circumvent the norm regarding particular weapons, such as nuclear weapons or incendiaries.

Moreover, novel domains of combat present additional challenges to the norm. In naval warfare, where vessels are the primary targets, the norm against SIrUS frequently faces opposition for its application that relates to the definition of military objectives. The rapid development of novel military technologies has added further complications. Emerging fields, such as cyber and space warfare and artificial intelligence, present novel domains for the application of LOAC. Likewise, the advancement of directed energy weapons, CRISPR/Cas9 gene-editing technology, the use of robotics and exoskeletons, nanotechnology, and space-based weapons further challenge the application of the norm against unnecessary suffering in contemporary and future armed conflicts.

Notwithstanding, to ensure new weapons comply with the principles of the law of armed conflict, particularly the most fundamental ones, States

J. Krasny, *War Injuries*,
https://doi.org/10.1007/978-3-032-00737-7_7

must evaluate, during the study, development, acquisition, or adoption of new weapons, means, and methods of warfare, whether their use would be prohibited by international law in all or certain circumstances. As the Additional Protocol I to the Geneva Conventions of 1949 stipulates:

> In the study, development, acquisition or adoption of a new weapon, means or method of warfare, a High Contracting Party is under an obligation to determine whether its employment would, in some or all circumstances, be prohibited by this Protocol or by any other rule of international law applicable to the High Contracting Party.[1]

In "some or all circumstances" would mean that there could be just specific restrictions placed on deployment. Such as the case of the CCW Protocol and the restriction on napalm and its use.[2] Given that few States have adopted this obligation in their weapons review processes, it is unlikely this obligation is customary and thus universally applicable, irrespective of a State's status as a contracting party to Additional Protocol I of the Geneva Conventions.[3] In reality, not all States conduct such weapons reviews, even those that are Parties to the Additional Protocol I. Boothby (2016) argues that many States do not have such a system in place.[4] Indeed, the implementation of Article 36 of API differs across different nations and regions. For instance, the United Kingdom has implemented a thorough framework to guarantee that any new weapon adheres to the principles of the law of armed conflict. The UK Ministry of Defence conducts this review process through qualified legal staff considering not only *lex lata*, or law as it stands, but also *lex ferenda*, that is, likely future developments in LOAC.[5] Likewise, the United States, despite not being a Party to API, upheld the norm and were, in fact, conducting these reviews before the codification of the obligation in API.[6] Furthermore, in order to

[1] See AP I, Art. 36.

[2] See CCW, Protocol III, Art. 2.

[3] Geoffrey S. Corn, Victor Hansen, Richard Jackson, M. Christopher Jenks, Eric Talbot Jensen, and James A. Schoettler. *The Law of Armed Conflict: An Operational Approach.* (New York: Wolters Kluwer, 2012), 203.

[4] William H. Boothby, *Weapons and the Law of Armed Conflict* (New York: Oxford University Press, 2016), 343.

[5] UK Ministry of Defence, *The Manual of the Law of Armed Conflict* (Oxford: Oxford University Press, 2004), 119.

[6] US Department of Defense, *Law of War Manual* (Washington, DC: General Counsel of the Department of Defense, 2016), 1038.

help States implement Article 36, the ICRC has developed a guide for weapons review.[7] This helps States Parties to ensure it is unlikely their new weapons before their production would violate the fundamental norms of LOAC by virtue of their "nature." Nevertheless, weapons development is an expensive endeavor, and it would be against the interests of the State to develop a weapon that is, in the end, in violation of the basic principles of LAOC. Thus, States, in their own interests, must thoroughly assess new technologies to ensure adherence to basic LOAC principles, particularly fundamental customary norms such as distinction, proportionality, necessity, precautions, prohibition of unnecessary suffering, and humanity, prior to the development of any new weapons in conflict. This fulfills legal obligations and upholds international humanitarian law, minimizing collateral damage and preventing the breach of the norm against unnecessary suffering.

In this chapter, the author looks at several challenging and emerging scenarios relevant to the norm against unnecessary suffering. However, since these are all future scenarios, the author refrains from overtly hypothesizing on what could or should be, that is, *lex ferenda*. Instead, the author applies the norm against SIrUS according to *lex lata*. Initially, the author examines maritime warfare because the principal military objective frequently involves the destruction of a vessel rather than direct incapacitation of soldiers. The chapter thereafter moves to the realms of cyber and space warfare. Cyber warfare is progressively incorporated into contemporary conflicts, frequently in a hybrid form that may sometimes complicate the application of the law of armed conflict due to the distinctive characteristics of the virtual battlefield. Considering these complications, the author further examines the applicability of the norm against excessive suffering in outer space. While this chapter and discussion are predominantly hypothetical, it strives to deliberate on practical challenges when interpreting the norm against unnecessary suffering in these new areas. Finally, the author discusses emerging weapon technologies, pinpointing particular difficulties that could hinder their compliance with the prohibition of unnecessary suffering.

[7] "A Guide to the Legal Review of New Weapons, Means and Methods of Warfare." 2021. International Committee of the Red Cross. December 20, 2021. https://www.icrc.org/en/publication/0902-guide-legal-review-new-weapons-means-and-methods-warfare-measures-implement-article.

7.2 Naval Warfare and Unnecessary Suffering

As Casey-Maslen and Haines (2020) point out, the principles and rules of LOAC apply to all weapons deployed against or by naval platforms.[8] Although, applying the norm against SIrUS in naval combat presents specific difficulties. In such a combat environment, the principal military objective or target is usually a platform, such as a vessel or submarine rather than an attempt to incapacitate naval combatants directly or individually. Consequently, the San Remo Manual doesn't provide any additional clarification regarding the application of the principle in naval warfare.[9] This emphasis on platform destruction imparts distinct attributes to naval warfare. First, we may generally disregard non-combatants from consideration, as these platforms, which are legitimate military objectives, are predominantly manned by naval personnel. Any adjacent civilian vessel would be an issue of distinction or proportionality.

Since the rule against unnecessary suffering pertains specifically to combatants, injuries sustained in naval warfare are typically indirect. The most common of these injuries would be burns, penetrating wounds, and asphyxiation.[10] However, in situations involving the deployment of nuclear weapons in maritime warfare, sailors will encounter ionizing radiation, resulting in significant long-term health effects previously outlined in earlier chapters. Exposure to such radiation presents an additional layer, subjecting naval personnel to unnecessary and potentially excessive harm beyond the immediate impacts of conventional weaponry. Such an attack may be led by direct deployment of nuclear weapons against a fleet or use of nuclear mines.[11] Thus, arguing against the application of the norm against SIrUS in naval warfare is absurd, as it exposes contradictions when comparing the effects of ionizing radiation on land combatants versus those on naval ships. Naval personnel who survive the initial explosion will experience comparable long-term health effects due to radiation exposure.

[8] Stuart Casey-Maslen, and Steven Haines, *Hague Law Interpreted: The Conduct of Hostilities under the Law of Armed Conflict* (New York: Hart, 2020), 289.

[9] Louise Doswald-Beck, ed., *San Remo Manual on International Law Applicable to Armed Conflicts at Sea* (Cambridge: Cambridge University Press, 1995).

[10] Derek A. Benham, Matthew C. Vasquez, Jakob Kerns, Kyle D. Checchi, Ross Mullinax, Theodore D. Edson, and Matthew D. Tadlock. 2023, "Injury trends aboard US Navy vessels: A 50-year analysis of mishaps at sea" *Journal of Trauma and Acute Care Surgery* 95 (2S): S41–49. https://doi.org/10.1097/ta.0000000000004047.

[11] Boothby, *Weapons*, 290

Furthermore, individuals may encounter specific hazards inherent to the maritime context, including drowning, being stranded at sea, or becoming stuck in a sinking ship or submarine. Each situation presents significant challenges for surviving personnel, exacerbating their suffering and introducing complex ethical considerations regarding the norm against unnecessary suffering. These, however, are inevitable outcomes of warfare. The objective for SIrUS and LOAC/IHL, in general, is not to humanize warfare but to alleviate the unnecessary suffering of combatants by outlawing the cruelest, unnecessary conduct and weapons. Injuries resulting from blasts, burns, and drowning are intrinsic to lawful means and methods of warfare within the maritime domain. Conventional weapons, including torpedoes, mines, and missiles, can inflict immediate casualties and fulfill military objectives, such as sinking or incapacitating a vessel, without subjecting survivors to extended radiological suffering, ending in leukemia or various forms of cancer.

Thus, maintaining the position that the norm against unnecessary suffering does not apply in naval warfare could set a dangerous precedent. Such a stance would justify the use of any controversial weapon that causes long-term health injuries by claiming that their primary target is merely a platform, that is, a vehicle or a piece of equipment. It is, therefore, essential to prevent obfuscating and relativizing LOAC norms and to uphold these standards diligently in order to give LOAC full effect and further substance to the norm against SIrUS. This can only be accomplished by an effects-based approach, presenting evidence of health effects on combatants that are out of proportion to any military objective.

7.3 Cyber and Space Warfare

The question of what constitutes a breach of the norm against unnecessary suffering in cyber warfare is open to debate. In this sense, Boothby (2016) argues that since a cyber-attack is defined as a cyber operation that causes injury, death, damage, or destruction, any tool or software causing such effects would be considered a cyber weapon.[12] The Tallinn Manual argues that manipulating a combatant's pacemakers-stopping and starting it intermittently-could cause significant suffering and thus violate the

[12] Boothby, *Weapons*, 238.

norm.[13] Likewise, targeting a life support system on a military base or in a bunker could produce similar effects. If the intention is to cause suffering, such as disabling thermal regulation or cutting off oxygen, such actions would likely breach the principle. Additionally, interfering with pain management devices could result in unnecessary suffering for combatants. Devices such as transcutaneous electrical nerve stimulation (TENS) units, advanced smart patches, or neurostimulation headbands, if app-controlled or connected to Wi-Fi, might be vulnerable to such attacks. The impact would depend on whether these devices are linked to other electronic systems, making them susceptible to cyber manipulation. The question therefore would be whether any program is developed for the purposes of causing such prolonged suffering or always produces such accompanying effects that cause unnecessary injuries or suffering well above what is necessary to put combatants out of combat. Such real-life cases are, however, still rare.

Cyber warfare frequently targets critical infrastructure, such as power grids, hospitals, and transportation systems. While these attacks often impact civilian populations, adherence to the principles of proportionality and necessity can help minimize their effects on civilians. By carefully assessing the anticipated military advantage against potential civilian harm, it is possible to conduct these operations in a way that reduces unnecessary suffering. One often cited case is the Stuxnet malware, a cyber weapon developed to disrupt Iran's nuclear enrichment efforts by targeting the uranium enrichment facility in Natanz, Iran. What is significant is that this was an unprecedented cyber-attack that caused physical damage. It is exactly physical damage that experts consider a prerequisite to categorize a cyber weapon as a weapon. The Stuxnet malware used overpressure and rotor speed alteration attacks. As such the centrifuges moved above and below safe operating ranges, which caused frequent malfunctions and overall slowed down the whole enrichment process.[14] Leaving aside question of jus ad bellum, that is, legitimacy of the use of force and whether such action could or could not be considered an armed attack, from the perspective of unnecessary suffering, the effects are important. Indeed, if

[13] International Groups of Experts at the Invitation of the NATO Cooperative Cyber Defence Centre of Excellence, *Tallinn Manual 2.0 on the International Law Applicable to Cyber Operations* (Cambridge: Cambridge University Press, 2017), 455.

[14] Ralph Langner, *To Kill a Centrifuge: A Technical Analysis of What Stuxnet's Creators Tried to Achieve*. Arlington, Hamburg, and Munich: The Langner Group, November 2013.

we accept such an attack triggered the application of LOAC. Whether it, in fact, did or did not is not important for our purposes. If we assume it did, and imagine that there would be injuries of combatants, then the requirements for the application of the norm against SIrUS would be fulfilled. However, again, assuming such centrifuges operated for military purposes, the injuries would most probably involve common instantaneous patterns, that is, injuries from blast, fragments, or burns. It would thus be quite difficult to argue that the norm against SIrUS was breached. Rather, other principles come to mind, such as necessity, distinction, proportionality, and precautions. This would also be the case of recent attacks on Hezbollah members in Lebanon. On September 17, 2024, hundreds of pagers of Hezbollah members exploded, killing at least 12, including two children and wounding thousands since the Hezbollah members were caught wherever they were at the moment, grocery stores, cars, shops. It is also suggested that an explosive was installed in the pagers and exploded remotely using radio signal.[15] While this is not a cyber-attack per se, we can imagine that such attacks may occur also using cyber weapons, as illustrated by the Stuxnet malware. Again, if we disregard particular circumstances, assume the law of war applies, it is rather challenging to argue how in such instances the norm against unnecessary suffering may be violated. Similar arguments apply to the case of exploding the cellphone of Yahya Ayyash aka "the Engineer," a Hamas member killed when his phone containing explosive detonated.[16] These cases would not invoke the norm against unnecessary suffering but depending on circumstances could cause issues concerning distinction, proportionality, and necessity, as well as precautions. This is apparent with the Lebanon case where the detonation was not really controlled and affected a large portion of non-combatants. The question is what precautions did the attacker take to avoid civilian casualties and were such casualties proportionate?

While such attacks would not invoke unnecessary suffering, targeting exoskeletons and mobility aids could lead to unnecessary injuries for combatants by manipulating these devices to function in harmful manner. Such interference could not only incapacitate the combatants but also

[15] Grantham-Philips, Wyatte, Michael Biesecker, Sarah El Deeb, and Sarah Parvini. 2024. "Lebanon Pager and Walkie-talkie Explosions: What We Know so Far | AP News." AP News. September 19, 2024. https://apnews.com/article/lebanon-israel-hezbollah-pager-explosion-e9493409a0648b846fdcadffdb02d71e#.

[16] Byman, Daniel. "Do Targeted Killings Work?" *Foreign Affairs* 85, no. 2 (2006): 95–111. https://doi.org/10.2307/20031914.

cause physical injuries, such as through twisting limbs, delivering electrical shocks, or forcing unwanted movement, for example, into hazardous areas where they may be exposed to radiation, burns, drowning, or other excessive dangers. These effects would result in avoidable suffering, violating the norm against SIrUS.

The international legal framework regarding cyber operations is still underdeveloped and is lacking profoundly behind the fast-paced technological development in AI and cyber tools. It is apparent that to apply the SIrUS prohibition to a cyber-attack, this will require physical consequences, that is, injury or harm to a combatant. In such a sense, these effects are not notably different from kinetic weapons. The effects thus would matter; blowing up centrifuges could release radiation and affect nearby combatants; as such, the scenario vis-à-vis the application of the norm against SIrUS is the same as with a nuclear attack.

Cyber warfare is already an integral part of armed conflict. However, States are gradually developing their legislation to be transparent and set legal boundaries when it comes to the use of cyber weapons.[17] Nevertheless, the norm against SIrUS would indeed be violated if such weapons are designed and of a nature to cause such effects, that is, if they are specifically designed to manipulate pacemakers or other devices such as exoskeletons to neutralize combatants through prolonged and unnecessary suffering.

As Pobjie and Ortega (2024) point out, while it is prohibited to place nuclear weapons in orbit, international law does not regulate non-nuclear weapons.[18] Space-based kinetic attacks, such as the destruction of satellites, generate space debris that can harm other satellites, impacting both military and civilian infrastructure. The debris can continue to orbit Earth for years, potentially damaging other assets in space, indirectly affecting civilian services on the ground, such as communication, weather forecasting, and navigation systems. Space debris presents a severe danger to astronauts, spacecrafts, and the space station. In 2007, China conducted an anti-satellite missile test that created thousands of pieces of debris.[19]

[17] See UNIDIR, "Cyber Policy Portal." n.d. https://cyberpolicyportal.org/.

[18] Erin Pobjie & Almudena Azcárate Ortega. "Space Security Legal Primer 1 – Outer Space & Use of Force", UNIDIR, Geneva, 2024. https://doi.org/10.37559/WMD/24/Space/02, 11.

[19] Weeden, Brian. "2007 Chinese Anti-Satellite Test" (2010), available at: https://swfound.org/media/9550/chinese_asat_fact_sheet_updated_2012.pdf, last access October 22, 2024.

This debris continues to threaten other space assets, illustrating how even limited space engagements can cause enduring, indiscriminate harm to global services and danger to astronauts and the International Space Station (ISS). In this sense, space warfare's unique characteristics call for SIrUS to consider indirect, cumulative suffering. The potential deployment of nuclear or radiological weapons in space raises significant humanitarian concerns.[20] An explosion in orbit could expose future space missions to harmful radiation or compromise the safety of those on space stations. These long-term effects affecting both military personnel and civilians indirectly (such as astronauts on international missions). While the Outer Space Treaty prohibits nuclear weapons in space, it does not cover non-nuclear radiological threats or space-based directed energy weapons. Expanding the SIrUS principle to include protection against radiological or nuclear exposure in space could provide a framework for limiting these weapons. Therefore, yet again, it comes to long-term health effects as being rather incompatible with the norm prohibiting unnecessary suffering.

In addition, many satellites serve both civilian and military purposes, such as GPS systems used for both civilian navigation and military targeting. An attack on these assets could lead to indirect effects for civilians who rely on GPS for transportation, emergency services, and economic activities. GPS and similar systems (e.g., Russia's GLONASS or Europe's Galileo) illustrate how military and civilian infrastructures are intertwined in space. A deliberate attack on GPS satellites, which guide everything from civilian flights to disaster response, could indirectly lead to civilian casualties. However, it is challenging in such cases to see how the principle of unnecessary suffering would apply.

Directed energy weapons (DEWs), such as space-based lasers, could disable or destroy targets without creating debris. However, if misused or miscalibrated, they might still affect dual-use satellites, disrupting civilian services. A DEW attack, if not precisely calibrated, could still cause collateral damage. As apparent, cyber and especially space warfare doesn't traditionally fit within the physical injury model of unnecessary suffering. Moreover, there are no combatants in space, at least yet. However, it is

[20] See NTI, "Russian Biological Facility Build-Up Underscores Need for Enhanced Transparency" (October 28, 2024), available at: https://www.nti.org/atomic-pulse/russian-biological-facility-build-up-underscores-need-for-enhanced-transparency/, last access October 29, 2024.

theoretically possible an astronaut can turn into a civilian directly participating in hostilities. Such hypothesizing is, however, too much in the realm of sci-fi for the purposes of this book. Since even application to traditional kinetic weapons is challenging, any expanding of SIrUS to recognize non-physical suffering would be quite dangerous, obfuscating current application and unnecessarily complicating the interpretation of the norm. While not much is available on the application of the norm against SIrUS in space for the above reasons, there are several resources on use of force in space. However, these are not legal sources. States increasingly develop their legislation to clarify their stance when it comes to the use of force in space.[21] Thankfully, conduct of hostilities amongst combatants in outer space is still, at least for the time being, highly theoretical.

7.4 New Weapons Technology

In general, any new weapon needs to undergo revision under Article 36 of Additional Protocol I. States continuously modernize and develop yet effective weaponry to maintain their security. Among these new developments are the above-mentioned cyber weapons, directed energy weapons, CRISPR-Cas9 gene technologies, nanotechnologies, autonomous weapon systems, hypersonic missiles and many other new weapons remaining secret. In addition, AI could significantly help with the creation of more powerful and accessible weapons, even chemical or biological weapons as illustrated by the MegaSyn Experiment.[22] In fact, it doesn't really matter what kind of technology is used. What matters is the injurious effects on combatants. While traditionalists would disagree and stress military necessity and advantage vis-à-vis effects, the ICRC, as explained in previous chapters, increasingly adopts the effects-based approach. As such, the ICRC helps to give much-needed substance to the principle. Therefore, when looking at any of the new weapons, it is important to consider the effects on combatants and whether any other less-injurious weapon is available that could accomplish the same objective.

[21] "Space Security Portal." n.d. https://spacesecurityportal.org/.

[22] An experiment conducted by the researchers at Collaborations Pharmaceuticals in the US in 2022. The experiment was aimed at exploring if drug development specialized AI could be misused to potentially develop or help with development of new chemical weapons. Drexel, Bill, and Caleb Withers. "AI Safety and Biosecurity." *AI and the Evolution of Biological National Security Risks: Capabilities, Thresholds, and Interventions.* Center for a New American Security, 2024. http://www.jstor.org/stable/resrep62401.6.

Directed energy weapons such as lasers, microwaves, or high-power electromagnetic devices cause damage through energy transfer. This may cause unique injuries. Such injuries can include burns or even radiation exposure. Moreover, burns may be internal, making it difficult to spot such injuries. Secondary injuries for eyes would be difficult to argue for as violating the norm against SIrUS given the intent-based Protocol IV of the CCW.[23] The answer could be regulations of the levels necessary to achieve military objectives or focusing such weapons on equipment.

The rapid advancements in recent years in neuroscience and technology present another set of new challenges for LOAC and the norm against unnecessary suffering in particular. Neuroweapons could affect the structure and function of the combatant's nervous system for warfare purposes.[24] Examples would be using neuropharmacological agents such as tranquilizers and neurotoxins or neurological devices such as transcranial neuromodulatory systems and brain-machine interfaces.[25] Further, the use of neurodata could target individuals based on genetic vulnerabilities or behavior patterns.[26] Gene-editing technologies such as CRISPR/Cas9[27] could be used to create biological agents targeting specific populations including, of course, combatants.

As an illustrative example of such research for military purposes, the People's Liberation Army (PLA) is allegedly interested in exploring such gene editing technologies for human enhancement.[28] Allegedly, the PLA research is not for weaponization but rather enhancement and development of less injurious techniques to incapacitate combatants. Any use of biological agents for warfare purposes would be covered by the BWC. A similar issue is nanotechnology and miniaturizing of weapons. These when inhaled could cause unnecessary injuries to combatants. When inhaled,

[23] See Art. 1, Protocol IV, CCW.

[24] Joseph DeFranco, Diane DiEuliis, and James Giordano. "Redefining Neuroweapons: Emerging Capabilities in Neuroscience and Neurotechnology." *PRISM* 8, no. 3 (2019): 48–63. https://www.jstor.org/stable/26864276.

[25] DeFranco et al., "Redefining Neuroweapons".

[26] DeFranco et al., "Redefining Neuroweapons".

[27] Clustered Regularly Interspaced Short Palindromic Repeat/Cas9 is a technology that allows modifications of virus genomes. See Dance, Amber. "Core Concept: CRISPR Gene Editing." *Proceedings of the National Academy of Sciences of the United States of America* 112, no. 20 (2015): 6245–6246. https://www.jstor.org/stable/26462797.

[28] Kania, Elsa B. "Minds at War: China's Pursuit of Military Advantage through Cognitive Science and Biotechnology." *PRISM* 8, no. 3 (2019): 82–101. https://www.jstor.org/stable/26864278.

they could cause damage to respiratory systems that is untreatable, causing prolonged health damage beyond military objective.

Autonomous Weapons Systems (AWS), that is, fully autonomous weapons systems are still in the future. Meaning, the terminator is not happening, yet. There is a wide discussion on what autonomy actually means and this discussion is not so straightforward.[29] However, technology is making giant leaps forward. Drones, robots and other AI-driven platforms designed to select targets and engage with them will increasingly appear on the battlefield. For now, a human is still needed in the loop, at least to switch on the machine. While the question for AWS is mostly in the area of distinction and criminal responsibility in cases such systems commit war crimes, attributing responsibility would be relevant should AWS cause unnecessary injuries to combatants. Therefore, what would matter is how and with what AWS did cause such injuries. As Scharre (2019) puts it, since the norm against unnecessary suffering deals with the mechanism of injury rather than the decision to target, its particular effect on AWS as such is limited.[30]

7.5 Conclusion

The swift evolution of military technology poses considerable difficulties for the implementation and enforcement of the norm prohibiting unnecessary suffering. Emerging technologies, including directed energy weapons, gene-editing tools, cyber warfare, and space-based weapons, present novel forms of harm and ethical challenges, thereby challenging the limits of international humanitarian law. The assessment of harm and suffering in traditional weapons and combat domains is more straightforward; however, the indirect, cumulative, and frequently non-physical effects of modern warfare technologies necessitate a reevaluation of current legal frameworks.

To uphold the SIrUS principle, States must engage in systematic examination of these new technologies, ensuring their deployment adheres to the core principles of the law of armed conflict, including distinction, proportionality, necessity, precautions, and the norm against

[29] Bhuta, Nehal, Susanne Beck, and Hin-Yan Liu. 2016. Autonomous Weapons Systems: Law, Ethics, Policy. Cambridge University Press, 352–354.

[30] Paul Scharre, *Army of None: Autonomous Weapons and the Future of* War (New York: WW Norton, 2019), 258.

SIrUS. Furthermore, as cyber and space warfare increasingly converge with civilian infrastructure, the establishment of more effective accountability mechanisms is crucial. These should specifically address possible patterns of injuries as well as psychological suffering, which are frequently neglected by conventional interpretations of international law. Future international agreements must define explicit thresholds for unnecessary suffering in contemporary conflict scenarios. Addressing these gaps enables the international community to reduce human suffering in warfare, ensuring that technological advancement aligns with ethical considerations and the principle of humanity. A commitment to maintaining humanitarian principles amidst advancing military capabilities is essential for the protection of both combatants and civilians in future conflicts.

It is, however, apparent that the issues for new technologies are the same and that the effects-based approach is the only way to give the norm against SIrUS at least some substance. Increasingly though, with the new technologies, there is a danger of increasing attempts to obfuscate and marginalize the principle on behalf of military necessity. After all, military necessity shall not trump the prohibition of unnecessary suffering and the principle of humanity, even in warfare. If that happens, history shows us, where it leads.

References

Benham, Derek A., Matthew C. Vasquez, Jakob Kerns, Kyle D. Checchi, Ross Mullinax, Theodore D. Edson, and Matthew D. Tadlock. 2023. "Injury trends aboard US Navy vessels: A 50-year analysis of mishaps at sea." *Journal of Trauma and Acute Care Surgery* 95 (2S): S41–49. https://doi.org/10.1097/ta.0000000000004047.

Boothby, William H. *Weapons and the Law of Armed Conflict*. New York: Oxford University Press, 2016.

Bhuta, Nehal, Susanne Beck, and Hin-Yan Liu. 2016. Autonomous Weapons Systems: Law, Ethics, Policy. Cambridge University Press.

Byman, Daniel. "Do Targeted Killings Work?" *Foreign Affairs* 85, no. 2 (2006): 95–111. https://doi.org/10.2307/20031914.

Casey-Maslen, Stuart, and Steven Haines. *Hague Law Interpreted: The Conduct of Hostilities under the Law of Armed Conflict*. New York: Hart, 2020.

Corn, Geoffrey S., Victor Hansen, Richard Jackson, M. Christopher Jenks, Eric Talbot Jensen, and James A. Schoettler. *The Law of Armed Conflict: An Operational Approach*. New York: Wolters Kluwer, 2012.

Dance, Amber. "Core Concept: CRISPR Gene Editing." *Proceedings of the National Academy of Sciences of the United States of America* 112, no. 20 (2015): 6245–6246. https://www.jstor.org/stable/26462797.

DeFranco, Joseph, Diane DiEuliis, and James Giordano. "Redefining Neuroweapons: Emerging Capabilities in Neuroscience and Neurotechnology." *PRISM* 8, no. 3 (2019): 48–63. https://www.jstor.org/stable/26864276.

Doswald-Beck, Louise, ed. *San Remo Manual on International Law Applicable to Armed Conflicts at Sea.* Cambridge: Cambridge University Press, 1995.

Drexel, Bill, and Caleb Withers. "AI Safety and Biosecurity." *AI and the Evolution of Biological National Security Risks: Capabilities, Thresholds, and Interventions.* Center for a New American Security, 2024. http://www.jstor.org/stable/resrep62401.6.

Erin Pobjie & Almudena Azcárate Ortega. "Space Security Legal Primer 1 – Outer Space & Use of Force", UNIDIR, Geneva, 2024. https://doi.org/10.37559/WMD/24/Space/02, 11.

Grantham-Philips, Wyatte, Michael Biesecker, Sarah El Deeb, and Sarah Parvini. 2024. "Lebanon Pager and Walkie-talkie Explosions: What We Know so Far | AP News." AP News. September 19, 2024. https://apnews.com/article/lebanon-israel-hezbollah-pager-explosion-e9493409a0648b846fdcadffdb02d71e#.

International Groups of Experts at the Invitation of the NATO Cooperative Cyber Defence Centre of Excellence. *Tallinn Manual 2.0 on the International Law Applicable to Cyber Operations.* Cambridge: Cambridge University Press, 2017.

Kania, Elsa B. "Minds at War: China's Pursuit of Military Advantage through Cognitive Science and Biotechnology." *PRISM* 8, no. 3 (2019): 82–101. https://www.jstor.org/stable/26864278.

Langner, Ralph. *To Kill a Centrifuge: A Technical Analysis of What Stuxnet's Creators Tried to Achieve.* Arlington, Hamburg, and Munich: The Langner Group, November 2013.

Scharre, Paul. *Army of None: Autonomous Weapons and the Future of* War. New York: WW Norton, 2019.

NTI, "Russian Biological Facility Build-Up Underscores Need for Enhanced Transparency (October 28, 2024), available at: https://www.nti.org/atomic-pulse/russian-biological-facility-build-up-underscores-need-for-enhanced-transparency/, last access October 29, 2024.

UK Ministry of Defence. *The Manual of the Law of Armed Conflict.* Oxford: Oxford University Press, 2004.

US Department of Defense. *Law of War Manual.* Washington, DC: General Counsel of the Department of Defense, 2016.

Weeden, Brian. "2007 Chinese Anti-Satellite Test" (2010), available at: https://swfound.org/media/9550/chinese_asat_fact_sheet_updated_2012.pdf, last access October 22, 2024.

Final Reflections: The Legal Norm Against Unnecessary Suffering

This book examined the formation and interpretation of the fundamental principle of the law of armed conflict, which prohibits the employment of weapons and methods of warfare that cause superfluous injury or unnecessary suffering (SIrUS). Article 35(2) of the 1977 Additional Protocol I to the 1945 Geneva Conventions codifies the concept of needless suffering, but its origins go back much further in time. The book adhered to this chronological structure. The author has explored the traditional concept of SIrUS under the classic law of armed conflict and the process of the first codification of the principle beginning with the St. Petersburg Declaration. Such examination has revealed that SIrUS is traditionally understood and interpreted as a balance between the value of the military objective, that is, an advantage stemming from reaching such an objective, and poised against harm caused by a particular weapon deployed to reach such objective. Accordingly, SIrUS is connected to military necessity, as understood by LOAC, that is, all lawful and necessary means to accomplish military objectives.[1] Hence, the link between military necessity and unnecessary suffering is apparent from the wording of military "necessity" and "unnecessary" injury. In other words, means that exceed the force necessary to accomplish such objectives are deemed excessive. The traditional narrative

[1] Yoram Dinstein, *The Conduct of Hostilities Under the Law of International Armed Conflict* (Cambridge: Cambridge University Press, 2004), 57–61.

J. Krasny, *War Injuries*,
https://doi.org/10.1007/978-3-032-00737-7

thus did not delve into deliberations on particular health effects of weapons on combatants.

Following the traditional narrative, the author explored the emergence of what can be called a humanitarian approach to the conduct of hostilities. At its inception, the ICRC was predominantly engaged in humanitarian activities to alleviate the suffering of wounded personnel.[2] Following WWI, the organization started calling attention to the effects of gas extensively used on the battlefields of Europe.[3] Not only did the organization advocate for a ban, but it also utilized the experience of its staff in the field to point out specific injuries and health effects of chemical gas. Such advocacy marked the first "clash" between traditional Hague law and the emerging health effects approach. This novel development initiated by the ICRC was further intensified at the end of WWII when Dr. Junod arrived in Hiroshima. Junod pointed out the long-term effects of ionizing radiation on combatants who no longer pose any threat.[4] As in the case of gas, the ICRC once again pointed out the health effects of a particular weapon (the atomic bomb) and argued for its ban. While in the nineteenth century, Hague law played the dominant role, after WWII, it turned to a predominant focus on Geneva law, i.e., the humanitarian approach. The ICRC continuously witnesses the use of weapons on the battlefield through its medical experts. One of such weapons drew attention in the 1960s and 1970s—napalm. The ICRC once again delved into weapon issues, offering its expertise in assessing the health effects of incendiaries and further of anti-personnel landmines and fragmentation weapons. This expertise culminated in an arms regulation effort that eventually adopted the Convention on Certain Conventional Weapons. The process of medicalization can thus be divided into three chronological stages: the first stage following the use of chemical weapons in WWI, the second stage following the use of atomic bombs in WWII, and the third stage following the use of incendiaries in the course of the Vietnam War. While instantaneous kinetic injuries are not particularly difficult to assess, continuous long-term injuries pose a challenge. The first codification of SIrUS happened in the late nineteenth century, when weapons were not particularly complex or sophisticated. Thus, pointing out excessively

[2] David P. Forsythe, *The Humanitarians* (Cambridge: Cambridge University Press, 2005), 15–20.

[3] Forsythe, *The Humanitarians,* 248.

[4] Marcel Junod, *Warrior Without Weapons* (London: Jonathan Cape, 1951), 286–300.

injurious arms was not difficult, e.g., dum-dum bullets. The development of more effective projectiles follows the progress in body armor, so increasing the effectivity of bullets is understandable. Instantaneous injuries are thus an inevitable effect of war. Given that no unnecessary modifications are done to the ammunition or weapon itself, these immediate injuries represent unavoidable combat wounds.

Regulation of weapons causing instant kinetic injuries and, for that matter, also burns have to be therefore made upon the availability of other means capable of accomplishing the same objective. Delayed and particularly lifelong health effects pose a challenge. Often, there is no available remedy to redress these effects. Moreover, such effects are frequently not understood well enough by the medical professionals to offer proper treatment. While instantaneous and, to a certain extent, delayed effects occur under the applicable temporal scope of the law of armed conflict during the hostilities, long-term effects exceed such temporal applicability. This temporal surpassing is vividly evident in the case of chemical and nuclear weapons. The toxic effects of gas and ionizing radiation, respectively, keep affecting a combatant long after the conflict ends and the law of armed conflict ceases to apply. A combatant's health is in such case affected by a weapon used during armed conflict, and these effects continue even after he or she ceases to be a combatant and returns to civilian life. Furthermore, as explained in Chap. 4, the occurrence of deadly diseases such as leukemia in those surviving and affected by a nuclear explosion is increased almost five-fold than those unexposed. A combatant who survives an attack with nuclear weapons has a significantly high chance of dying long after an armed conflict is over. There is no cure, no remedy, and the health effects are not one-time; they keep changing and worsening throughout the life of such combatant. It is as if the combatant was still being attacked by such a weapon, even though he is no longer a combatant. While humanitarian initiatives stressed the health effects of weapons, whether landmines or nuclear weapons, offering testimonies of victims supported by medical data, they ignored the traditional balancing concept of military necessity. These initiatives showed a growing focus of governmental, non-governmental organizations, and civil societies exclusively on health effects by employing the field data gathered by the ICRC. However, civil societies and NGOs are not obligated to protect a nation; States are, so the reluctance to give up a particular weapon they deem effective is understandable.[5] The balancing principle of military necessity thus cannot be completely disregarded. Necessity of a weapon has to go hand in hand with medical assessment of injuries it causes. Incorporating the utility of a particular weapon and juxtaposing it against injuries makes the discussion pragmatic rather than constant reiterations of inhumanity and morality, which are somewhat vague concepts, as there is no humane or moral weapon. Ex-combatants and medical practitioners thus offer the most reliable source when discussing unnecessary suffering vis-à-vis particular weapons rather than activists. This combination of testimony and medicalization gives the principle demonstrable evidences.

These tangible features through medicalization were apparent in the judicial deliberations, revealing that an increased focus on health since the nineteenth century is being reflected and recognized by judicial bodies, including increased application of medical data and analysis. This is further confirmed by the fact that the ICRC and its medical data and field experience are often quoted and included in the proceedings, i.e., the ICRC data offer tangible substance to the principle. Therefore, clinging to the traditional interpretation of unnecessary suffering only balanced against military necessity is dangerous, allowing for a broad interpretation and legitimization of the use of even the most horrific weapons. Including specific medical data gives the principle a substance. As such, while military necessity is still an essential balancing principle, further medical data offer another tool for assessment to be used, not in general, but concerning specific means of warfare.

The origin of the disparity in interpretation of the norm against SIrUS lies in the active involvement of the ICRC in traditional State-dominated field of LOAC, i.e., weapons law. To give the principle of unnecessary suffering a normative substance and increase its applicability to protect combatants, the ICRC strived to include health effects (with supporting field data) as a balancing principle against military necessity. The medicalization of the principle by the ICRC occurred in three phases following the use of particular weapons. Namely, after the use of gas in WWI, atomic bomb in WWII, and incendiaries during the Vietnam War.

Arms control activities of the ICRC through medicalization then stand in contrast with States which weigh particular weapons not against injuries

[5] Roberts, Brad. "Ban the Bomb? Or Bomb the Ban? Next Steps on the Ban Treaty." Global Security Policy Brief, March 22, 2018. European Leadership Network. https://www.europeanleadershipnetwork.org/policy-brief/ban-the-bomb-or-bomb-the-ban/.

it causes but against the military advantage it offers and availability of alternatives. Unlike the ICRC, which tries to give normative substance to the general principle applicable to all weapons, States are willing to discuss unnecessary suffering only concerning specific weapons. This was apparent since the St. Petersburg Declaration concerning exploding bullets, the Hague Regulations prohibiting expanding bullets, CCW Protocol IV prohibiting blinding lasers, and anti-personnel use of chemical weapons as a means of warfare. Civil society and NGOs then usually further pick up the narrative of the ICRC in their campaigns strengthening the predominant focus on health effects as opposed to military utility.

In sum, the disparity in interpretation is caused by the ICRC emphasizing specific health effects and employing medical means when discussing weapons at diplomatic conferences. Because of the general respect for the work of the ICRC and its expertise, its testimony following the use of new weapons in major conflicts, and supplemented by advocacy for the experiences of survivors offering their own testimonies to support the ICRC's medicalization efforts, such activities are shifting the balance of the principle away from military necessity and toward specific health effects explained in proper medical terms and supported by field data.

While states prefer traditional interpretation and their initiatives have yielded tangible results, the motivation was rarely humanitarian and rarely concerned with combatants and their suffering. Exploding bullets were prohibited only between signatories of the St. Petersburg Declaration and "civilized" nations. Under the Hague Convention, expanding bullets are also prohibited. Despite this prohibition, the British used expanding bullets extensively in India.[6] Under CCW Protocol IV, blinding lasers are prohibited, but lasers that can accidentally blind, such as navigational lasers, are not. Only regulations apply to incendiaries. Chemical weapons are prohibited as a form of warfare, but riot control agents and incapacitants that can be lethal are not as evidenced by the Moscow Theater Siege case. Landmines, cluster munitions, white phosphorus, and depleted uranium all cause unnecessary suffering in the traditional sense, i.e., these weapons can be replaced with less gruesome weapons that achieve the same goal. Nonetheless, states are hesitant to replace them, citing the military advantages they provide and the precautions they take. It is therefore not surprising that the ICRC offers its expertise to assess the health effects

[6] Alex Ogston, "The Peace Conference And The Dum-Dum Bullet," *The British Medical Journal* 2, no.2013 (1899): 278–281. http://www.jstor.org/stable/20261388.

of weapons, regardless of their military advantage. Ultimately, arguments for military advantage cannot lead to violations of humanitarian standards.

Therefore, the fundamental principle of the law of armed conflict prohibiting means and methods of warfare designed to cause unnecessary suffering must be interpreted in light of military necessity and must include medical data and supporting medical evaluations of the effects of weapons. Including medical analysis and data provides argumentative support and gives the principle material substance. Without it, the norm against SIrUS can be ignored and its ambiguity misinterpreted to justify violations of the law of war. Long-term health effects, as understood from the testimonies of survivors, continue to affect and injure ex-combatants for the rest of their lives in the forms described in this book and, as such, exceed the scope of application of the law of armed conflict. Furthermore, these long-term health effects are not yet fully comprehended by the community of medical experts. Without an accurate comprehension of the health impact, treatment is impossible. This distinguishes such effects from instantaneous injuries.

While instantaneous effects are no less traumatic, they are immediate and have limited degree of injury. Continuous long-term effects besides not being fully known have unending consequences. Consequently, the most original aspect of my book is that it provides specific medical evidence to support the argument that long-term continuous effects exceed the temporal scope of application of the law of armed conflict, thereby causing unnecessary suffering because there is no longer a corresponding military objective after a combatant has ceased to be a combatant. Further, since such lifelong effects are not yet fully comprehended an effective remedy is in fact non-existent.

It is essential to continue focusing on and following the application and interpretation of SIrUS as a LOAC norm. As such, it is bound to progress, and the focus on health will be dominant. Novel interpretations will emerge particularly due to the IHRL and LOAC/IHL interplay. However, human rights law is inadequate in the realm of conduct of hostilities. The law of armed conflict is the *lex specialis* for regulating the conduct of hostilities and the use of weapons, particularly during international armed conflict. As such, researchers focusing on weapons and targeting in armed conflict in military operations shall not confuse this with the human rights approach. The underlying *raison d' etre* is simply different. Unnecessary suffering is the least of the least of law of war norms that strive to protect the lives and well-being of combatants engaging in combat.

Its application during a conflict on high seas, cyber or outer space is largely unexplored. With new weapons such as cyber weapons or weapons in outer space, their definition, interpretation, and application of SIrUS will become increasingly relevant. With the ongoing trend in the development of non-lethal means of warfare, the threshold for unnecessary suffering is set relatively high. Dazzling lasers to temporarily blind the enemy are undoubtedly welcome developments, although their misuse is just another side of the same coin as any weapon.[7] The same goes for microwave or long-range acoustic weapons. Here it is essential to follow the design purpose of such weapons. As in the case of cyberweapons, a possible attack on the pacemaker of an enemy soldier with the intent to stop its function, then revive, then stop again[8] involves *mens rea* or an intent to cause suffering. Application of the traditional rules of LOAC will need to be interpreted and maybe even re-interpreted in light of these changes and developments in weaponry and methods of warfare.

The work on this book is being completed during the ongoing international armed conflict between Ukraine and the Russian Federation. The conflict began on February 24, 2022, and is the largest armed confrontation on the European continent since the dissolution of former Yugoslavia. As such, it includes a wide spectrum of modern, modernized, and powerful means of warfare. Among reports of serious violation of rules and customs of war emerge particular grave breaches of all four Geneva Conventions, including norms of the 1977 Additional Protocol I. The rules pertaining to the conduct of hostilities are being violated by a lack of consideration for precautions, distinction, proportionality, and necessity as understood by the law of war. This includes deployments of weapons without any consideration of proportionality and distinction under LOAC. The suffering caused by violations of the conduct of hostilities only results in reprisals and further violations.

The law of armed conflict is not a utopian fantasy or an unrealistic set of vague norms. It is pragmatic. It is explicit. As such, following its rules not only limits suffering but ensures the effectivity of military operations.

[7] Dan Drollette Jr, "Blinding Them With Science: Is Development of a Banned Laser Weapon Continuing?" *Bulletin of the Atomic Scientists*, September 14, 2014. https://thebulletin.org/2014/09/blinding-them-with-science-is-development-of-a-banned-laser-weapon-continuing/.

[8] International Groups of Experts at the Invitation of the NATO Cooperative Cyber Defence Centre of Excellence, *Tallinn Manual 2.0 on the International Law Applicable to Cyber Operations* (Cambridge: Cambridge University Press, 2017), 455.

Disproportional attacks, targeting of non-combatants, use of restricted and prohibited weapons offer no advantage to the belligerents whatsoever. Weapons law in this sense strives to delegitimize the cruelest weapons whatever their "alleged" advantage might be without taking away legitimate means of defense. The law of armed conflict together with human rights law shall overcome its areas of friction, become truly complementary and offer the maximum possible protection and remedy to the victims of armed violence and related unlawful acts.

References

Dinstein, Yoram. *The Conduct of Hostilities Under the Law of International Armed Conflict.* Cambridge: Cambridge University Press, 2004.

Drollette Jr, Dan. "Blinding Them With Science: Is Development of a Banned Laser Weapon Continuing?" *Bulletin of the Atomic Scientists,* September 14, 2014. https://thebulletin.org/2014/09/blinding-them-with-science-is-development-of-a-banned-laser-weapon-continuing/.

Forsythe, David P. *The Humanitarians.* Cambridge: Cambridge University Press, 2005.

International Groups of Experts at the Invitation of the NATO Cooperative Cyber Defence Centre of Excellence. *Tallinn Manual 2.0 on the International Law Applicable to Cyber Operations.* Cambridge: Cambridge University Press, 2017.

Junod, Marcel. *Warrior Without Weapons.* London: Jonathan Cape, 1951.

Ogston, Alex. "The Peace Conference And The Dum-Dum Bullet." *The British Medical Journal* 2, no. 2013 (1899): 278–281. http://www.jstor.org/stable/20261388.

Roberts, Brad. "Ban the Bomb? Or Bomb the Ban? Next Steps on the Ban Treaty." Global Security Policy Brief, March 22, 2018. European Leadership Network. https://www.europeanleadershipnetwork.org/policy-brief/ban-the-bomb-or-bomb-the-ban/.

Bibliography

Agent Orange Record. "What is Dioxin?" Accessed April 25, 2022. https://agentorangerecord.com/what-is-dioxin-2/.

Al-Dawoody, Ahmed. *The Islamic Law of War: Justifications and Regulations*. New York: Palgrave Macmillan, 2011.

ANHA Hawar News Agency. "Halabja...Massacre Whose Effects Still Linger Today." March 16, 2020. http://www.hawarnews.com/en/haber/halabjamassacre-whose-effects-still-linger-today-h15286.html.

Anti-Personnel Mine Ban Convention. "Membership." Accessed June 24, 2022. https://new.apminebanconvention.org/en/membership/.

Aoki, Fukiko. *731: Ishii Shiro to Saikinsen Butai no Yami wo Abaku* [731: Exposing the darkness of Ishii Shiro and the bacteriological unit]. Tokyo: Shinchosha, 2005.

Arkin, William M., and Hans M. Kristensen. "US Deploys New Low-Yield Nuclear Submarine Warhead." Federation of American Scientists, January 29, 2020. https://fas.org/blogs/security/2020/01/w76-2deployed/.

Arms Control Association. "Biological Weapons Convention Signatories and States-Parties." Last reviewed March 2022. https://www.armscontrol.org/factsheets/bwcsig#:~:text=The%20Biological%20Weapons%20Convention%20(BWC,South%20Sudan%2C%20and%20Tuvalu).

Arnold, Roberta, and Noelle N. R. Quenivet, eds. *International Humanitarian Law and Human Rights: Towards a New Merger in International Law*. Leiden: Martinus Nijhoff Publishers, 2008.

J. Krasny, *War Injuries*,
https://doi.org/10.1007/978-3-032-00737-7

Asbarez Staff. "Use of White Phosphorus Bombs by Azerbaijan Confirmed." *Asbarez,* October 30, 2020. https://asbarez.com/use-of-white-phosphorous-bombs-by-azerbaijan-confirmed/.

Aust, Anthony. *Modern Treaty Law and Practice.* Cambridge: Cambridge University Press, 2013.

Baetens, Freya. "Hague Conferences (1899, 1907)." Oxford Bibliographies. Last modified November 21, 2012. https://www.oxfordbibliographies.com/view/document/obo-9780199743292/obo-9780199743292-0115.xml#obo-9780199743292-0115-bibItem-0012.

Bantekas, Ilias, and Lutz Oette. *International Human Rights: Law and Practice.* 3rd ed. Cambridge: Cambridge University Press, 2020.

BBC. "Agent Orange appeal in US Court." Last updated June 19, 2007. http://news.bbc.co.uk/2/hi/asia-pacific/6766139.stm.

Bennett, Angela. *The Geneva Convention: The Hidden Origins of the Red Cross.* Cheltenham: The History Press, 2006.

Benham, Derek A., Matthew C. Vasquez, Jakob Kerns, Kyle D. Checchi, Ross Mullinax, Theodore D. Edson, and Matthew D. Tadlock. 2023. "Injury trends aboard US Navy vessels: A 50-year analysis of mishaps at sea." *Journal of Trauma and Acute Care Surgery* 95 (2S): S41–S49. https://doi.org/10.1097/ta.0000000000004047.

Berlin, Michael J. "U.N. Team Says Chemical Agents Used in Gulf War." *Washington Post,* March 27, 1984. https://www.washingtonpost.com/archive/politics/1984/03/27/un-team-says-chemical-agents-used-in-gulf-war/a515ae16-5d8b-4d2c-ae0f-7d33eb45d07f/.

Bhuta, Nehal, Susanne Beck, and Hin-Yan Liu. 2016. Autonomous Weapons Systems: Law, Ethics, Policy. Cambridge University Press.

Bisset, Alison. *Blackstone's International Human Rights Documents.* 11th ed. Oxford: Oxford University Press, 2018.

Boas, Gideon, and William A. Schabas, eds. *International Criminal Law Developments in the Case Law of the ICTY.* Leiden: Martinus Nijhoff Publishers, 2003.

Boeke, Sergei. *Transitioning from Military Interventions to Long-Term Counter Terrorism Policy: The Case of Mali (2013-2016).* Leiden: Leiden University – Institute of Security and Global Affairs, 2016.

Boisson de Chazournes, Laurence, and Philippe Sands, eds. *International Law, the International Court of Justice and Nuclear Weapons.* Cambridge: Cambridge University Press, 1999.

Bolus, Norman E. "Basic Review of Radiation Biology and Terminology." *Journal of Nuclear Medicine Technology* 45, no. 4 (2017): 259–264. https://doi.org/10.2967/jnmt.117.195230.

Boniface, Susie. "Nuclear Heroes Betrayed by Ministry of Defence Pen-Pushers Over Medals." *Mirror,* December 10, 2020. https://www.mirror.co.uk/news/

uk-news/nuclear-heroes-betrayed-pen-pushers-23149346?fbclid=IwAR2bVUGg_Et6Rh9qRWtrj2Z36awq1Vbpzvf4nZ7PFEdGLZYM8UYwIsDdx8g.
Boothby, William H. *The Law of Targeting*. Oxford: Oxford University Press, 2012.
———. *Conflict Law: The Influence of New Weapons Technology, Human Rights and Emerging Actors*. The Hague: T.M.C. Asser Press, 2014.
———. *Weapons and the Law of Armed Conflict*. New York: Oxford University Press, 2016.
Bowen, Thomas E., ed. *Emergency War Surgery*. Collingdale, PA: Diane Publishing Co., 2005.
Bowyer, Richard. *Dictionary of Military Terms*. 3rd ed. London: A&C Black, 2007.
British Medical Association. *Illustrated Medical Dictionary*. 1st ed. London: Dorling Kindersley, 2002.
Bryant, Michael S. *A World History of War Crimes: From Antiquity to the Present*. 2nd ed. New York: Bloomsbury Academic, 2021.
Buhler, George. *The Laws of Manu*. Pinnacle Press, 2017.
Bunn, George. "Banning Poison Gas and Germ Warfare: Should the United States Agree?" *Wisconsin Law Review*, no. 2 (1969): 375–420.
Byman, Daniel. "Do Targeted Killings Work?" *Foreign Affairs* 85, no. 2 (2006): 95–111. https://doi.org/10.2307/20031914.
Cambodian Mine Action and Victim Assistance Authority. "Monthly Report of February 2022." Accessed May 2, 2022. https://www.cmaa.gov.kh/detail/content/rzlUAsxfrSDhHmGktDHP.
Cambodian Self-Help Demining. "About CSHD." Accessed April 14, 2022. https://www.cambodianselfhelpdemining.org/about/
Casey-Maslen, Stuart. *Jus ad Bellum: The Law on Inter-State Use of Force*. New York: Hart, 2020.
———. *The Treaty on the Prohibition of Nuclear Weapons: A Commentary*. Oxford: Oxford University Press, 2019.
———, ed. *Weapons Under International Human Rights Law*. Cambridge: Cambridge University Press, 2014.
Casey-Maslen, Stuart, and Steven Haines. *Hague Law Interpreted: The Conduct of Hostilities under the Law of Armed Conflict*. New York: Hart, 2020.
Casey-Maslen, Stuart, and Tobias Vestner. *A Guide to Disarmament Law*. New York: Routledge, 2019.
Center For Arms Control and Non-Proliferation. "Fact Sheet: Russia's Use of Thermobaric Weapons in Ukraine." March 1, 2022. https://armscontrolcenter.org/fact-sheet-russias-use-of-thermobaric-weapons-in-ukraine/.
Chemical and Biological Weapons Nonproliferation Program. "The Moscow Theater Hostage Crisis: Incapacitants and Chemical Warfare." James Martin Center for Nonproliferation Studies, November 4, 2002. https://nonproliferation.org/the-moscow-theater-hostage-crisis-incapacitants-and-chemical-warfare/.

Chetail, Vincent. "The Fundamental Principles of Humanitarian Law Through the Case Law of the International Court of Justice." *Refugee Survey Quarterly* 21, no. 3 (2002): 199–211. https://ssrn.com/abstract=1645121.

Choate, Joseph H. *The Two Hague Conferences*. Princeton: Princeton University Press, 1913.

Chossudovsky, Evgeny M. "The Origins of the Treaty on the Non-Proliferation of Nuclear Weapons: Ireland's Initiative in the United Nations (1958-61)." *Irish Studies in International Affairs* 3, no. 2 (1990): 111–135. http://www.jstor.org/stable/30001773.

Clapham, Andrew, and Paola Gaeta, eds. *The Oxford Handbook of International Law in Armed Conflict*. Oxford: Oxford University Press, 2014.

Clark, Roger S. "Methods of Warfare That Cause Unnecessary Suffering or Are Inherently Indiscriminate: A Memorial Tribute to Howard Berman," *California Western International Law Journal* 28, no. 2 (1997): Article 4. https://scholarlycommons.law.cwsl.edu/cwilj/vol28/iss2/4.

Clausewitz, Carl von. *On War*. Translated by Michael Howard and Peter Paret. Oxford: Oxford University Press, 1976.

Columbia Law Review, *Harvard Law Review* Association, *University of Pennsylvania Law Review*, and *Yale Law Journal*, eds. *The Bluebook: A Uniform System of Citation*. 21st ed. Cambridge, MA: Harvard Law Review Association, 2020.

Committee for the Compilation of Materials on Damage Caused by the Atomic Bombs in Hiroshima and Nagasaki. *Hiroshima and Nagasaki: The Physical, Medical and Social Effects of the Atomic Bombings*. Tokyo: Iwanami Shoten, 1981.

Corn, Geoffrey S., Victor Hansen, Richard Jackson, M. Christopher Jenks, Eric Talbot Jensen, and James A. Schoettler. *The Law of Armed Conflict: An Operational Approach*. New York: Wolters Kluwer, 2012.

Coupland, Robin M. "Abhorrent Weapons and 'Superfluous Injury or Unnecessary Suffering': From Field Surgery to Law." *BMJ: British Medical Journal* 315, no. 7120 (1997a): 1450–1452. http://www.jstor.org/stable/25176382.

———. *The Red Cross Wound Classification*. Geneva: ICRC, 2020. https://www.icrc.org/en/publication/0498-red-cross-wound-classification.

———, ed. *The SIrUS Project: Towards a Determination of Which Weapons Cause "Superfluous Injury or Unnecessary Suffering."* Geneva: ICRC, 1997b. https://www.loc.gov/collections/military-legal-resources/?q=RC_SIrUS-project.html.

Coupland, Robin M., and Adriaan Korver. "Injuries From Antipersonnel Mines: The Experience of the International Committee of the Red Cross." *British Medical Journal* 303, no. 6816 (1991): 1509–1512. https://doi.org/10.1136/bmj.303.6816.1509.

Crawford, Neta. *Accountability for Killing: Moral Responsibility for Collateral Damage in America's Post-9/11 Wars*. Oxford: Oxford University Press, 2013.

Dance, Amber. "Core Concept: CRISPR Gene Editing." *Proceedings of the National Academy of Sciences of the United States of America* 112, no. 20 (2015): 6245–6246. https://www.jstor.org/stable/26462797.

DeFranco, Joseph, Diane DiEuliis, and James Giordano. "Redefining Neuroweapons: Emerging Capabilities in Neuroscience and Neurotechnology." *PRISM* 8, no. 3 (2019): 48–63. https://www.jstor.org/stable/26864276.

Doswald-Beck, Louise, ed. *San Remo Manual on International Law Applicable to Armed Conflicts at Sea.* Cambridge: Cambridge University Press, 1995a.

Drexel, Bill, and Caleb Withers. "AI Safety and Biosecurity." *AI and the Evolution of Biological National Security Risks: Capabilities, Thresholds, and Interventions.* Center for a New American Security, 2024. http://www.jstor.org/stable/resrep62401.6.

Darnton, Geoffrey. *Nuclear Weapons and International Law: From the London Nuclear Warfare Tribunal Via the International Court of Justice Advisory Opinion to Contemporary Developments.* 2nd ed. Bournemouth: Requirements Analytics, for Peace Analytics, 2015.

Deplano, Rossana, and Nicholas Tsagourias, eds. *Research Methods in International Law: A Handbook.* Cheltenham: Edward Elgar Publishing Limited, 2021.

Devroy, Ann, and Ruth Marcus. "Clinton Takes Oath as 42nd President Asking Sacrifice, Promising Renewal." *Washington Post*, January 21, 1993. https://www.washingtonpost.com/wp-srv/national/longterm/inaug/history/stories/clint92.htm.

DiFilm. "Copamiento Regimiento 3 de Infanteria Mecanizada de La Tablada 1989." YouTube video, 00:01:18. April 16, 2014. https://www.youtube.com/watch?v=EsNFTlfsMf0.

Dinstein, Yoram. *The Conduct of Hostilities Under the Law of International Armed Conflict.* Cambridge: Cambridge University Press, 2004.

———. *War, Aggression and Self-Defence.* 6th ed. Cambridge: Cambridge University Press, 2017.

Distefano, Giovanni. *Fundamentals of Public International Law: A Sketch of the International Legal Order.* Leiden: Brill Nijhoff, 2019.

Doswald-Beck, Louise, ed. *San Remo Manual on International Law Applicable to Armed Conflicts at Sea.* Cambridge: Cambridge University Press, 1995b.

Douhet, Giulio. *The Command of the Air.* Translated by Dino Ferrari. Maxwell Air Force Base, Alabama: Air University Press, 2019.

Drollette Jr, Dan. "Blinding Them With Science: Is Development of a Banned Laser Weapon Continuing?" *Bulletin of the Atomic Scientists,* September 14, 2014. https://thebulletin.org/2014/09/blinding-them-with-science-is-development-of-a-banned-laser-weapon-continuing/.

Dunant, Henry. *A Memory of Solferino.* Geneva: International Committee of the Red Cross, 1959.

The Effects of the Atomic Bombs at Hiroshima and Nagasaki: *Report of the British Mission to Japan*. London: His Majesty's Stationery Office, 1946.

Erin Pobjie & Almudena Azcárate Ortega. "Space Security Legal Primer 1 – Outer Space & Use of Force", UNIDIR, Geneva, 2024. https://doi.org/10.37559/WMD/24/Space/02

European Human Rights Advocacy Centre. "*Isayeva v Russia*." February 24, 2005. https://ehrac.org.uk/en_gb/resources/isayeva-v-russia/.

Falk, Richard A. "The Shimoda Case: A Legal Appraisal of the Atomic Attacks Upon Hiroshima and Nagasaki." *American Journal of International Law* 59, no. 4 (1965): 759–793. https://doi.org/10.2307/2197093.

Feakes, Daniel. "Global Civil Society and Biological and Chemical Weapons" in *Global Civil Society Yearbook* edited by Kaldor, Mary, Helmut Anheier, and Marlies Glasius. Oxford: Oxford University Press, 2003.

Fellmeth, Aaron X., and Maurice Horwitz. *Guide to Latin in International Law*. New York, Oxford University Press, 2009.

Fetter, Steve. "Ballistic Missiles and Weapons of Mass Destruction: What is the Threat? What Should be Done?" *International Security* 16, no. 1 (1991): 5–42. https://doi.org/10.2307/2539050.

Fleck, Dieter. *The Handbook of International Humanitarian Law*. New York: Oxford University Press, 2008.

Forsythe, David P. *The Humanitarians*. Cambridge: Cambridge University Press, 2005.

France 24. "France in Mali: A Year of Hunting Jihadists in West Africa." January 11, 2014. https://www.france24.com/en/20140111-france-mali-military-intervention-operation-serval-anniversary-timeline.

Frankland, Noble, and Charles Webster. *The Strategic Air Offensive Against Germany: 1939 – 1945*. Vol. 4. Uckfield: Naval & Military Press, 2006.

Gallagher, Gary W., Stephen D. Engle, Robert K. Krick, and Joseph T. Glatthaar. *The American Civil War: This Mighty Scourge of War*. Oxford: Osprey Publishing, 2003.

Gardiner, Richard. *Treaty Interpretation*. 2nd ed. Oxford: Oxford University Press, 2017.

Garrett, Benjamin C., and John Hart. *The A to Z of Nuclear, Biological and Chemical Warfare*. Lanham, MD: Scarecrow Press, 2009.

Geneva Academy of International Humanitarian and Human Rights Law. "RULAC: Rule of Law in Armed Conflicts." Accessed April 21, 2022. https://www.rulac.org/.

Gesley, Jenny. "The 'Lieber Code' – the First Modern Codification of the Laws of War." Library of Congress blog. April 24, 2018. https://blogs.loc.gov/law/2018/04/the-lieber-code-the-first-modern-codification-of-the-laws-of-war/.

Gillis, Melissa. *Disarmament: A Basic Guide*. 3rd ed. New York: United Nations, 2012. http://www.un.org/disarmament/HomePage/ODAPublications/AdhocPublications/PDF/Basic_Guide-2011-web-Rev1.pdf.

Gordon, Michael R. "Paris Conference Condemns the Use of Chemical Arms." *New York Times*, January 12, 1989. https://www.nytimes.com/1989/01/12/world/paris-conference-condemns-the-use-of-chemical-arms.html.

Grantham-Philips, Wyatte, Michael Biesecker, Sarah El Deeb, and Sarah Parvini. 2024. "Lebanon Pager and Walkie-talkie Explosions: What We Know so Far | AP News." AP News. September 19, 2024. https://apnews.com/article/lebanon-israel-hezbollah-pager-explosion-e9493409a0648b846fdcadffdb02d71e#.

Grotius, Hugo. *The Rights of War and Peace*. (Vol. I–III). Edited by Richard Tuck. Indianapolis: Liberty Fund, 2005.

Grunden, Walter E. "No Retaliation in Kind: Japanese Chemical Warfare Policy in World War II. In Friedrich, Bretislav, Dieter Hoffmann, Jürgen Renn, Florian Schmaltz, and Martin Wolf. *One Hundred Years of Chemical Warfare: Research, Deployment, Consequences*. Springer, 2018.

Guillaume, Marine. "Napalm in US Bombing Doctrine and Practice, 1942–1975." *The Asia-Pacific Journal* 14, no. 23–25 (2016): Article 4893. https://apjjf.org/2016/23/Guillaume.html.

Guldner, Gregory T., and Curtis Knight. *Napalm Toxicity*. Treasure Island, FL: StatPearls Publishing, 2021. https://www.ncbi.nlm.nih.gov/books/NBK537127/#:~:text=Napalm%20burns%20result%20in%20severe,to%20napalm%20may%20be%20severe.

Gupta, Ramesh C., ed. *Handbook of Toxicology of Chemical Warfare Agents*. 2nd ed. Oxford: Academic Press, 2015.

Hambling, David. "Russia Accused of Using Air-Dropped Butterfly Mines to Block Ukrainian Evacuation Route." *Forbes*, March 10, 2022. https://www.forbes.com/sites/davidhambling/2022/03/10/russia-reportedly-blocks-ukrainian-evacuation-route-with-air-dropped-butterfly-mines/?sh=165e514a1a32.

Hayashi, Nobuo. "Using Force by Means of Nuclear Weapons and Requirements of Necessity and Proportionality *Ad Bellum*." In *Nuclear Weapons Under International Law*, edited by Gro Nystuen, Stuart Casey-Maslen, and Annie G. Bersagel, 15–30. Cambridge: Cambridge University Press, 2014.

Haynes, Suyin. "Prince Harry Is Honoring His Mother's Work in Angola. Here's What to Know About Princess Diana's Landmines Walk." *Time*, September 27, 2019. https://time.com/5682006/princess-diana-landmines/.

Heller, Kevin Jon. "Convictions in the Anfal Trial." *OpinioJuris*. June 24, 2007. http://opiniojuris.org/2007/06/24/convictions-in-the-anfal-trial/.

Henckaerts, Jean-Marie. "Study on customary international humanitarian law: A contribution to the understanding and respect for the rule of law in armed conflict." *International Review of the Red Cross* 87, no. 857 (2005): 175–212.

Henckaerts, Jean-Marie, and Louise Doswald-Beck, eds. *Customary International Humanitarian Law*. Vol. 1, *Rules*. Cambridge: Cambridge University Press, 2005.

Hippler, Thomas. *Bombing the People: Gulio Douhet and the Foundations of Air-Power Strategy, 1884–1939*. Cambridge: Cambridge University Press, 2013.

Holquist, Peter. "The Laws of War: From the Lieber Code to the Brussels Conference." Accessed April 12, 2022. https://www.americanacademy.de/the-laws-of-war/.

Houser, Ryan S., Gregory D. Koblentz, and Filippa Lentzos. 2023. "Understanding Biosafety and Biosecurity in Ukraine." *Health Security* 21 (1): 70–80. https://doi.org/10.1089/hs.2022.0095.

Hull, William I. *The Two Hague Conferences and Their Contributions to International Law*. Boston: For International School of Peace, Ginn, 1908.

ICRC. *Anti-Personnel Landmines: Friend or Foe? A Study of the Military Use and Effectiveness of Anti-Personnel Mines*. Geneva: ICRC, 1996. https://www.icrc.org/en/publication/0654-anti-personnel-landmines-friend-or-foe-study-military-use-and-effectiveness-anti

———. "Atomic Weapons and Non-Directed Missiles: ICRC Statement, 1950. 05-04-1950 Article, International Review of the Red Cross, - Supplement, Vol. III, No. 4." Accessed April 13, 2022a. https://www.icrc.org/en/doc/resources/documents/article/other/5kylur.htm.

———. "Conference of Government Experts On Weapons Which May Cause Unnecessary Suffering or Have Indiscriminate Effects." *International Review of the Red Cross*. Accessed April 22, 2022b. https://international-review.icrc.org/sites/default/files/S002086040001 6041a.pdf.

———."Expert Meeting on Legal Reviews of Weapons and the SIrUS Project. 30-06-2001 Article, International Review of the Red Cross, No. 842." Accessed April 13, 2022c. https://www.icrc.org/en/doc/resources/documents/article/other/57jr5z.htm.

———. *Weapons That May Cause Unnecessary Suffering or Have Indiscriminate Effects: Report on the Work of Experts*. Geneva: ICRC, 1973. https://www.loc.gov/item/2011525354/.

———. "World War I: The ICRC's Appeal Against the Use of Poisonous Gases. 8 February 1918." Accessed April 13, 2022d. https://www.icrc.org/en/doc/resources/documents/statement/57jnqh.htm.

ICRC. IHL Database: Customary IHL. "Military Manuals." Accessed April 19, 2022e. https://ihl-databases.icrc.org/customary-ihl/eng/docs/src_iimima.

———. "Practice Relating to Rule 70. Weapons of a Nature to Cause Superfluous Injury or Unnecessary Suffering." Accessed April 12, 2022f. https://ihl-databases.icrc.org/customary-ihl/eng/docindex/v2_rul_rule70.

———. "Rule 70. Weapons of a Nature to Cause Superfluous Injury or Unnecessary Suffering." Accessed April 12, 2022g. https://ihl-databases.icrc.org/customary-ihl/eng/docindex/v1_rul_rule70.

———. "Rule 74. Chemical Weapons." Accessed April 13, 2022h. https://ihl-databases.icrc.org/customary-ihl/eng/docs/v1_rul_rule74#:~:text=The%20use%20of%20chemical%20weapons%20is%20prohibited.&text=Volume%20II%2C%20Chapter%2024%2C%20Section,and%20non%2Dinternational%20armed%20conflicts.

ICRC. Treaties, States Parties and Commentaries. "Additional Articles relating to the Condition of the Wounded in War. Geneva, 20 October 1868." Accessed April 13, 2022i. https://ihl-databases.icrc.org/applic/ihl/ihl.nsf/Treaty.xsp?documentId=ECB39EA050F80A5DC12563CD002D6624&action=openDocument.

———. "Convention for the Amelioration of the Condition of the Wounded and Sick in Armies in the Field. Geneva, 6 July 1906." Accessed April 13, 2022j. https://ihl-databases.icrc.org/applic/ihl/ihl.nsf/Treaty.xsp?documentId=C64C3E521F5CC28FC12563CD002D6737&action=openDocument.

———. "Convention Relative to the Treatment of Prisoners of War. Geneva, 27 July 1929." Accessed April 13, 2022k. https://ihl-databases.icrc.org/applic/ihl/ihl.nsf/INTRO/305?OpenDocument.

———. "Commentary of 2016. Article 3: Conflicts Not of an International Character." Accessed April 13, 2022l. https://ihl-databases.icrc.org/ihl/full/GCI-commentaryArt3.

———. "Final Act of the Diplomatic Conferences of Geneva 1974 – 1977." Accessed May 2, 2022m. https://ihl-databases.icrc.org/ihl/INTRO/465.

———. "Protocol Additional to the Geneva Conventions of 12 August 1949, and Relating to the Protection of Victims of International Armed Conflicts (Protocol I), 8 June 1977." Accessed April 13, 2022n. https://ihl-databases.icrc.org/ihl/INTRO/470.

———. "Protocol for the Prohibition of the Use of Asphyxiating, Poisonous or Other Gases, and of Bacteriological Methods of Warfare. Geneva, 17 June 1925." Accessed April 24, 2022o. https://ihl-databases.icrc.org/applic/ihl/ihl.nsf/States.xsp?xp_viewStates=XPages_NORMStatesParties&xp_treatySelected=280.

International Groups of Experts at the Invitation of the NATO Cooperative Cyber Defence Centre of Excellence. *Tallinn Manual 2.0 on the International Law Applicable to Cyber Operations.* Cambridge: Cambridge University Press, 2017.

IHL in Action. "About the Project." Accessed April 20, 2022a. https://ihl-in-action.icrc.org/about.

———. "Iraq, Computer Modelling in Collateral Damage Estimates and Choice of Weapons." Accessed April 20, 2022b. https://ihl-in-action.icrc.org/case-study/iraq-computer-modelling-collateral-damage-estimates-and-choice-weapons.

———. "Libya, Canada's Operation Mobile and the Principles of Proportionality and Precautions in Attack." Accessed April 20, 2022c. https://ihl-in-action.icrc.org/case-study/libya-canadas-operation-mobile-and-principles-proportionality-and-precautions-attack.

———. "Mali, France's Operation Serval, Minimising Civilian Casualties." Accessed April 20, 2022d. https://ihl-in-action.icrc.org/case-study/mali-frances-operation-serval-minimising-civilian-casualties

Imanaka, Tetsuji. "Casualties and Radiation Dosimetry of the Atomic Bombings on Hiroshima and Nagasaki". In *Radiation Risk Estimates in Normal and Emergency Situations*, edited by Arrigo A. Cigna and Marco Durante, 149–156. Dordrech: Springer, 2006. https://doi.org/10.1007/1-4020-4956-0_15.

Inai, Kouki. *Atlas of Mustard Gas Injuries: Building Bridges Between Iran and Japan Through the Relief of Victims Exposed to Mustard Gas.* Hiroshima: MOCT, 2012.

Inai, Kouki, and Yukio Takeshima. "Pathology of Respiratory Tract in Former Workers in Mustard Gas Factory: A Review." *Journal of Toxicologic Pathology* 8, no. 4 (1995): 343–353. https://doi.org/10.1293/tox.8.343.

Inazo, Nitobe. *Bushido: The Soul of Japan.* New York: Kodansha, 2002.

International Campaign to Abolish Nuclear Weapons. "77% of Belgians Support Joining the TPNW – Poll." Accessed December 11, 2020. https://www.icanw.org/77_of_belgians_support_joining_the_tpnw_poll.

———. *The Nuclear Weapon Ban Treaty.* November 2017. Accessed May 11, 2022a. https://d3n8a8pro7vhmx.cloudfront.net/tectodevms/pages/2389/attachments/original/1571070092/ican-2017-Oslo-final.pdf?1571070092.

———. "Signature and Ratification Status." Accessed April 14, 2022b. https://www.icanw.org/signature_and_ratification_status.

International Campaign to Ban Landmines. "A Global Network Working for a World Free of Landmines." Accessed April 25, 2022a. http://www.icbl.org/en-gb/home.aspx.

———. "Voting on UN Resolution for Nuclear Ban Treaty" Accessed April 29, 2022b. https://www.icanw.org/voting_on_un_resolution_for_nuclear_ban_treaty

———. "What is a Landmine?" Accessed April 29, 2022c. http://www.icbl.org/en-gb/problem/what-is-a-landmine.aspx.

International Court of Justice. "Letter Dated 20 June 1995 From the Acting Legal Adviser to the Department of State, Together with Written Statement of the Government of the United States of America." 1995. https://www.icj-cij.org/public/files/case-related/95/8700.pdf.

International Crimes Database. *Al-Anfal.* July 24, 2007. https://www.internationalcrimesdatabase.org/Case/1233.

———. *Frans Cornelis Adrianus van Anraat v. The Netherlands.* July 6, 2010. https://www.internationalcrimesdatabase.org/Case/869.

———. *Shimoda et al. v. the State*. December 7, 1963. https://www.asser.nl/upload/documents/DomCLIC/Docs/NLP/Japan/Shimoda_TokyoDistrictCourt_7-12-1963.pdf.

———. *Vietnam Association for Victims of Agent Orange v. Dow Chemical Co.* March 28, 2005. https://www.internationalcrimesdatabase.org/Case/896.

———. *Ct. of Appeal of Vietnam Association for Victims of Agent Orange v. Dow Chemical Co.* February 22, 2008. https://www.internationalcrimesdatabase.org/Case/196.

International Law Commission. Annual Reports. *Report on the Work of the Seventy-First Session (2019)*. Last updated December 10, 2019. https://legal.un.org/ilc/reports/2019/.

Jackson, Heather. "Severe Ocular Trauma due to Landmines and Other Weapons in Cambodia." *Community Eye Health Journal* 10, no. 23 (1997): 37–39. https://www.cehjournal.org/article/severe-ocular-trauma-due-to-landmines-and-other-weapons-in-cambodia/.

Jeannesson, Stanislas (2020). "The International Hague Conferences of 1899 and 1907." *Encyclopedie d'histoire numerique de l'Europe*. June 22, 2020. https://ehne.fr/en/node/12230.

Jevglevskaja, Natalia. "St. Petersburg, 1868: First International Agreement Prohibiting the Use of Certain Weapons." *Online Atlas on the History of Humanitarianism and Human Rights*. Accessed April 9, 2022. https://hhr-atlas.ieg-mainz.de/articles/jevglevskaja-st_petersburg

Johnston, Eric. "Japan to Fight Ruling Recognizing Hiroshima 'Black Rain' Victims." *The Japan Times*, August 12, 2020. https://www.japantimes.co.jp/news/2020/08/12/national/crime-legal/japan-fights-hiroshima-black-rain-ruling/#.XzXu3hMzZhF.

Jones, Edgar. "Terror Weapons: The British Experience of Gas and Its Treatment in the First World War." *War in History* 21, no. 3 (2014): 355–375. https://doi.org/10.1177/0968344513510248

Junod, Marcel. *Warrior Without Weapons*. London: Jonathan Cape, 1951.

Kalshoven, Frits, and Liesbeth Zegveld. *Constraints on the Waging of War*. 4th ed. Cambridge: Cambridge University Press, 2011.

Kapossy, Bela, and Richard Whatmore, eds. *Emer de Vattel: The Law of Nations, Or, Principles of the Law of Nature, Applied to the Conduct and Affairs of Nations and Sovereigns, with Three Early Essays on the Origin and Nature of Natural Law and on Luxury*. Indianapolis: Liberty Fund, 2008.

Kawano, Noriyuki, Yasuyuki Taooka, Takashi Hiraoka, Masaharu Hoshi, and Z. Z. Shaimardanovich. *Report on the Actual Conditions of the Radiation Exposed Residents Near the Former Semipalatinsk Nuclear Test Site*. Hiroshima: Hiroshima University Research Institute for Radiation Biology and Medicine and Hiroshima Peace Science Consortium, 2004.

Keefer, Scott. "'Explosive Missals': International Law, Technology, and Security in Nineteenth-Century Disarmament Conferences." *War in History* 21, no. 4 (2014): 445–464. Accessed May 11, 2022. http://www.jstor.org/stable/26098618

Khateri, Shahriar, and Ahmad Jannati Muhib. *Iraq's Use of Chemical Weapons Against Iran: UN Documents 1984 – 1988.* Tehran: Foundation of Preservation of Works and Dissemination of the Values of Holy Defense, 2010.

Khorram-Manesh, Amir, Krzysztof Goniewicz, Fredereick M. Burkle, and Yohan Robinson. "Review of Military Casualties in Modern Conflicts – The Re-Emergence of Causalities From Armored Warfare." *Military Medicine* 187, no. 3–4 (2022): e313–e321. https://doi.org/10.1093/milmed/usab108.

Kneubuehl, Beat P., Robin M. Coupland, Markus A. Rothschild, and Michael J. Thali. *Wound Ballistics: Basics and Applications.* New York: Springer, 2008.

Kolb, Robert, and Richard Hyde. *An Introduction to the International Law of Armed Conflicts.* Portland: Hart Publishing, 2008.

Krasny, Jaroslav. "Do Tactical Nukes Break International Law?" *Bulletin of The Atomic Scientists,* December 31, 2020. https://thebulletin.org/2020/12/do-tactical-nukes-break-international-law/.

Krasny, Jaroslav, and Noriyuki Kawano. "Weapons of Mass Destruction and the Principle of Unnecessary Suffering: The Use of Nuclear Weapons in an Armed Conflict." *Hiroshima Peace Science* 36, (2014): 101–116. https://doi.org/10.15027/38055.

Krasny, Jaroslav. "Use of Nuclear Weapons in Armed Conflict." *Hiroshima Peace Science* 41, (2019): 73–84. https://doi.org/10.15027/49035.

Kristensen, Hans M., and Matt Korda. "United States Nuclear Forces, 2020." *Bulletin of the Atomic Scientists* 76, no. 1 (2020): 46–60. https://doi.org/10.1080/00963402.2019.1701286.

Krutzsch, Walter, Eric Myjer, and Ralf Trapp, eds. *The Chemical Weapons Convention: A Commentary.* Oxford: Oxford University Press, 2014.

Larsen, Jeffrey A., and Kerry M. Katchner. *On Limited Nuclear War in the 21st Century.* Stanford: Stanford University Press, 2014.

Laur, Timothy M., and Steven L. Llanso. *Encyclopedia of Modern U.S. Military Weapons.* New York: The Army Times Publishing Company, 1995.

Lazenby, John F. *The Peloponnesian War: A Military Study.* London: Routledge, 2004.

Lechner, R., G. Achatz, T. Hauer, H.G. Palm, A. Lieber, and C. Willy. Verletzungsmuster und-ursachen in modernen Kriegen [Patterns and causes of injuries in a contemporary combat environment]. *Unfallchirurg* 113, no. 2 (2010):106–113. https://doi.org/10.1007/s00113-009-1732-9

Lederberg, Joshua, ed. *Biological Weapons: Limiting the Threat.* Cambridge, MA: MIT Press, 1999.

Lesaffer, Randall. Grotius on the Use of Force. Perfect, Imperfect and Civil Wars: An Introduction. *Grotiana* 41, no. 2 (2020): 255–262. https://doi.org/10.1163/18760759-41020001.

Lifton, Robert Jay. *Death in Life: Survivors of Hiroshima*. Chapel Hill: University of North Carolina Press, 1991.

Long, Tony. "Oct.5, 1986: Israel's Secret Nuke Arsenal Exposed." *Wired,* October 5, 2011. https://www.wired.com/2011/10/1005israel-secret-nuclear-arsenal-exposed/.

Longuet, Samuel. "Permitted for Law Enforcement Purposes but Prohibited in the Conduct of Hostilities: The Case of Riot Control Agents and Expanding Bullets." *International Review of the Red Cross* 98, no. 901 (2016): 249–274. https://doi.org/10.1017/S1816383117000108.

Los Alamos Scientific Laboratory and Norris E. Bradbury. *The Effects of Atomic Weapons.* Whitefish, MT: Literary Licensing, 2013.

Maresca, Louis, and Stuart Maslen. *The Banning of Anti-Personnel Landmines: The Legal Contribution of the International Committee of the Red Cross.* Cambridge: Cambridge University Press, 2000.

Mathur, Ritu. *Red Cross Interventions in Weapons Control.* London: Lexington Books, 2017.

Matsumura, Akira. *Japanese Language Dictionary*, Vol. 3. 4th ed. Tokyo: Sanseido, 2019.

Maurer, Peter. "20 Years After the Historic Treaty on Landmines, We Cannot Afford to Lose Momentum: ICRC President Peter Maurer's Address to the Sixteenth Meeting of the States Parties, Anti-Personnel Mine Ban Convention 18 December 2017, Vienna." Accessed April 29, 2022. https://www.icrc.org/en/document/statement-20-years-after-historic-treaty-landmines-we-cannot-afford-lose-momentum.

McKinney, Katherine E, Scott D. Sagan, and Allen S. Weiner. "Why the Atomic Bombing of Hiroshima Would Be Illegal Today." *Bulletin of the Atomic Scientists* 76, no. 4 (2020): 157–165. https://www.tandfonline.com/doi/full/10.1080/00963402.2020.1778344.

NTI, "Russian Biological Facility Build-Up Underscores Need for Enhanced Transparency (October 28, 2024), available at: https://www.nti.org/atomic-pulse/russian-biological-facility-build-up-underscores-need-for-enhanced-transparency/, last access October 29, 2024.

Patton, James. "Gas in the Great War." Medicine in the First World War. Accessed April 14, 2022. https://www.kumc.edu/school-of-medicine/academics/departments/history-and-philosophy-of-medicine/archives/wwi/essays/medicine/gas-in-the-great-war.html#:~:text=The%20minimal%20immediate%20effects%20are,%2C%20diphosgene%20(trichloromethane%20chloroformate).

Melzer, Nils. *Interpretive Guidance on the Notion of Direct Participation in Hostilities Under International Humanitarian Law*. Geneva: ICRC, 2009.

Ministry of Health, Labor and Welfare, Japan. "Who is Hibakusha?" Accessed December 11, 2020. https://www.mhlw.go.jp/stf/newpage_13405.html

National Geographic. *National Geographic Visual History of the World*. Washington, DC: National Geographic Society, 2005.

NATO. "Arms Control, Disarmament and Non-Proliferation in NATO." Last updated June 23, 2022. https://www.nato.int/cps/en/natohq/topics_48895.htm

Neer, Robert M. *Napalm: An American Biography*. Cambridge: Belknap Press of Harvard University Press, 2013.

Newton, Michael A., ed. *The United States Department of Defense: Law of War Manual Commentary and Critique*. Cambridge: Cambridge University Press, 2018.

NHS. "Carbon Monoxide Poisoning." Last reviewed April 10, 2019. https://www.nhs.uk/conditions/carbon-monoxide-poisoning/#:~:text=Prolonged%20exposure%20to%20carbon%20monoxide%20can%20cause%20memory%20problems%20and,tremors%2C%20stiffness%20and%20slow%20movement.

Meuse, Alison. "U.S. – Led Coalition Has Used White Phosphorus In Fight For Mosul, General Says." *NPR*, August 1, 2022, https://www.npr.org/sections/parallels/2017/06/13/532809626/u-s-led-coalition-has-used-white-phosphorous-in-fight-for-mosul-general-says#:~:text=Press-,White%20Phosphorus%20Used%20Against%20Islamic%20State%20In%20Mosul%2C%20Coalition%20General,to%20get%20civilians%20out%20safely.%22.

Nishimoto, Y., M. Yamakido, T. Shigenobu, K. Onari, and M. Yukutake. "Long-term observation of poison gas workers with special reference to respiratory cancers." *Journal of UOEH* 5 Suppl, (1983): 89–94.

Nystuen, Gro, Stuart Casey-Maslen, and Annie G. Bersagel, eds. *Nuclear Weapons Under International Law*. Cambridge: Cambridge University Press, 2014.

O'Connor, Simon. "Nuclear Weapons and the Unnecessary Suffering Rule." In *Nuclear Weapons Under International Law*, edited by Gro Nystuen, Stuart Casey-Maslen, and Annie G. Bersagel, 128–147. Cambridge: Cambridge University Press, 2014.

Office of the Federal Register. "Executive Order 11850." National Archives. April 8, 1975. https://www.archives.gov/federal-register/codification/executive-order/11850.html.

Official Records of the Diplomatic Conference on the Reaffirmation and Development of International Humanitarian Law Applicable in Armed Conflicts, Geneva (1974-1977). Bern: Federal Political Department, 1978. https://www.loc.gov/item/2011525500/.

Ogston, Alex. "The Peace Conference And The Dum-Dum Bullet." *The British Medical Journal* 2, no. 2013 (1899): 278–281. http://www.jstor.org/stable/20261388.

Olsen, John Andreas, ed. *A History of Air Warfare*. Washington: Potomac Books, 2010.

———. *Strategic Air Power in Desert Storm*. New York, Routledge, 2006.

Organisation for the Prohibition of Chemical Weapons. "List of Participants of the Twenty-First Session of the Conference of the States Parties." Society for Chemical Weapons Victims Support. December 2, 2016. https://www.opcw.org/sites/default/files/documents/CSP/C-21/en/c21inf03r1_e_.pdf.

———. "OPCW by the Numbers." Accessed December 11, 2020a. https://www.opcw.org/media-centre/opcw-numbers.

———. "Our Partners." Accessed December 20, 2020b. https://www.opcw.org/about/our-partners#:~:text=The%20CWC%20Coalition%20is%20a,for%20the%20Prohibition%20of%20Chemical.

Owen, Alan. "Global Health Survey 2020." LABRATS International Health Survey 2020. https://www.labrats.international/healthsurvey.

P5 Working Group on the Glossary of Key Nuclear Terms. *P5 Glossary of Key Nuclear Terms*. Beijing: China Atomic Energy Press, 2015.

Parker, Clifton B. "Public opinion unlikely to curb a U.S. president's use of nuclear weapons in war. Stanford scholar finds." *Stanford News,* August 8, 2017. https://news.stanford.edu/2017/08/08/americans-weigh-nuclear-war/.

Phillips, Charles, and Alan Axelrod, eds. *Encyclopedia of Wars*. New York: Zenda, Inc, 2005.

Price, Richard M. *The Chemical Weapons Taboo*. New York: Cornell University Press, 1997.

PRIO. "Malvern Lumsden." Accessed April 14, 2022. https://www.prio.org/people/5054.

Program on Humanitarian Policy and Conflict Research at Harvard University. *HPCR Manual on International Law Applicable to Air and Missile Warfare*. Cambridge: Cambridge University Press, 2013.

Razoux, Pierre. *The Iran-Iraq War*. Translated by Nicholas Elliott. Cambridge, MA: Belknap Press of Harvard University Press, 2015.

RERF. "About RERF." Accessed April 14, 2022a. https://www.rerf.or.jp/en/about/establish_e/.

———. *A Brief Description*. Hiroshima: RERF, 2016.

———. "Historical Materials." Accessed April 14, 2022b. https://www.rerf.or.jp/en/about/history_e/.

———. "Children of Atomic Bomb Survivors (F1) Study." Accessed April 14, 2022c. https://www.rerf.or.jp/en/programs/research_activities_e/outline_e/progf1-en/.

Rhodes, Richard. *The Making of the Atomic Bomb.* London: Simon & Schuster, 2012.

———. *Dark Sun: The Making of the Hydrogen Bomb.* New York: Simon & Schuster, 2005.

Rietiker, Daniel. *Humanization of Arms Control: Paving the Way for a World Free of Nuclear Weapons.* New York: Routledge, 2018.

Roberts, Brad. "Ban the Bomb? Or Bomb the Ban? Next Steps on the Ban Treaty." Global Security Policy Brief, March 22, 2018. European Leadership Network. https://www.europeanleadershipnetwork.org/policy-brief/ban-the-bomb-or-bomb-the-ban/.

Robinson, C. Paul. *A White Paper: Pursuing a New Nuclear Weapons Policy for the 21st Century.* Sandia National Laboratories White Paper, March 22, 2001. https://www.sandia.gov/media/whitepaper/2001-04-Robinson.htm

Roser, Max, Joe Hasell, Bastian Herre, and Bobbie Macdonald. "War and Peace After 1945." Our World in Data. Accessed April 12, 2022. https://ourworldindata.org/war-and-peace.

Rousseau, Jean-Jacques. *The Social Contract and the First and Second Discourses.* Edited by Susan Dunn. New York: Yale University Press, 2020.

Sagan, Scott D. "Why Do States Build Nuclear Weapons?: Three Models in Search of a Bomb." *International Security* 21, no. 3 (1996/1997): 54–86. https://doi.org/10.2307/2539273.

Sandoz, Yves, Christophe Swinarski, and Bruno Zimmerman, eds. *Commentary on the Additional Protocols of 8 June 1977 to the Geneva Conventions of 12 August 1949.* Geneva: International Committee of the Red Cross, 1987.

Sanskriti. "Pashupatastra: Weapon of Lord Shiva." Accessed April 12, 2022. https://www.sanskritimagazine.com/indian-religions/hinduism/pashupatastra-weapon-of-lord-shiva/.

Saotome, Katsumoto. *Toukyo Daikuushuu: Zusetu* [Great Tokyo Air Raid: Illustrated]. Tokyo: Kawade Shobo Shinsha, 2015a.

Saotome, Katsumoto. *Tokyo Daikuushuu: Showa Nijyuunen Sangatsu Tooka no Kiroku* [The Great Tokyo Air Raid: A Memory of March 10, 1945]. Tokyo: Iwanami-Shinsho, 2015b.

———. *The Great Tokyo Air Raid: Illustrated Book,* [in Japanese]. Tokyo: Kawade Publishing, 2015c.

Sassoli, Marco. *International Humanitarian Law: Rules, Controversies, and Solutions to Problems Arising in Warfare.* Cheltenham: Edward Elgar, 2019.

Sassoli, Marco, Antoine Bouvier, Anne Quintin, and Julia Grignon. "Afghanistan/US, 'Mother of All Bombs.'" *How Does Law Protect in War?* Geneva: ICRC, 2014. Accessed April 14, 2022. https://casebook.icrc.org/case-study/afghanistanus-mother-all-bombs.

Sassoli, Marco. "Derogations." Accessed April 21, 2022a. https://casebook.icrc.org/glossary/derogations.

———. "Dum-dum Bullets." Accessed March 14, 2022b. https://casebook.icrc.org/glossary/dum-dum-bullets.
———. "ECHR, *Isayeva v. Russia*." Accessed October 23, 2021. https://casebook.icrc.org/case-study/echr-isayeva-v-russia.
———. "Hors de Combat." Accessed April 12, 2022c. https://casebook.icrc.org/glossary/hors-de-combat.
———. "Martens Clause." Accessed April 20, 2022d. https://casebook.icrc.org/glossary/martens-clause.
Saul, Ben, and Akande, Dapo, eds. *The Oxford Guide to International Humanitarian Law.* Oxford: Oxford University Press, 2020.
Schabas, William. *An Introduction to the International Criminal Court.* 4th ed. Cambridge: Cambridge University Press, 2011.
———. *The International Criminal Court: A Commentary on the Rome Statute.* 2nd ed. Oxford: Oxford University Press, 2016.
Schachter, Oscar. *International Law in Theory and Practice.* Springer, 1991.
Scharre, Paul. *Army of None: Autonomous Weapons and the Future of War.* New York: WW Norton, 2019.
Schindler, Dietrich, and Jiri Toman, eds. *The Laws of Armed Conflict: A Collection of Conventions, Resolutions and Other Documents.* Leiden: Martinus Nijhoff Publishers, 2004.
Schull, William J. *Effects of Atomic Radiation: A Half-Century of Studies from Hiroshima and Nagasaki.* New York: Wiley-Liss, 1995.
Schutter, Olivier de. *International Human Rights Law: Cases, Materials, Commentary.* Cambridge: Cambridge University Press, 2010.
Seventh Review Conference of the States Parties to the Convention on the Prohibition of the Development, Production and Stockpiling of Bacteriological (Biological) and Toxin Weapons and on Their Destruction Final Document of the Seventh Review Conference, Geneva, 5–22 December 2011, BWC/CONF.VII/7, available at: https://documents.un.org/doc/undoc/gen/g12/600/60/pdf/g1260060.pdf, last access October 22, 2024.
Sevitt, S. "Death After Burning." *Medicine, Science & Law* 6, no. 1 (1966): 36–44.
Shabad, Theodore. "Soviet Union Exploded a Nuclear Device to Extinguish Burning Gas." *New York Times,* December 2, 1971. Accessed April 21, 2022. https://www.nytimes.com/1971/12/02/archives/soviet-discloses-nuclear-blast-that-put-out-fire-in-gas-field.html.
Shaw, Malcolm. *International Law.* Cambridge: Cambridge University Press, 2017.
Shigematsu, Itsuzo, Mitoshi Akiyama, Hideo Sasaki, Chikato Ito, and Nanao Kamada, eds. *Genbaku hoshasen no jintai eikyo* [Effects of A-bomb radiation on the human body]. Tokyo: Bunkodo, 1995.
Shimizu, Y., H. Kato, and William J. Schull. "Studies of the Mortality of A-bomb Survivors. 9. Mortality, 1950-1985: Part 2. Cancer Mortality Based on the

Recently Revised Doses (DS86)." *Radiation Research* 121, no. 2 (1990): 120–141.

Shinmura, Izuru. *Kojien* [Japanese language dictionary]. Vol. 7. Tokyo: Iwanami, 2018.

Simcox, Kenneth. "Poetry Critique: Dulce Et Decorum Est." 2000. Accessed August 8, 2022. http://www.wilfredowen.org.uk/poetry/dulce-et-decorum-est.

Solis, Gary D. *The Law of Armed Conflict: International Humanitarian Law in War.* 2nd ed. Cambridge: Cambridge University Press, 2016.

Stanford Libraries. "Stanford Oral History Collections." Accessed April 24, 2022. https://exhibits.stanford.edu/oral-history.

Stockholm International Peace Research Institute. *Delayed Toxic Effects of Chemical Warfare Agents: A SIPRI Monograph,* Stockholm: Almqvist & Wiksell, 1975a.

———. *A Monograph: Incendiary Weapons.* Cambridge, MA: MIT Press, 1975b.

———. *The Problem of Chemical and Biological Warfare: The Rise of CB Weapons.* Stockholm: SIPRI, 1971.

Swopes, Bryan R. "9–10 March 1945: Operation Meetinghouse." This Day in Aviation, March 9, 2022. https://www.thisdayinaviation.com/tag/an-m69-incendiary-bomblet/.

Tanaka, Yuki, and Richard Falk. "The Atomic Bombing, the Tokyo War Crimes Tribunal and the Shimoda Case: Lessons for Anti-Nuclear Legal Movements." *The Asia-Pacific Journal* 7, no. 44-3 (2009): Article 3245. https://apjjf.org/-Yuki-Tanaka/3245/article.html.

Tokuoka, S., Y. Hayashi, K. Inai, H. Egawa, Y. Aoki, H. Akamizu, R. Eto et al. "Early Cancer and Related Lesions in the Bronchial Epithelium in Former Workers of Mustard Gas Factory." *Acta Pathologica Japonica* 36, no. 4 (1986): 533–542. https://doi.org/10.1111/j.1440-1827.1986.tb01042.x.

Trigt, Evan. "The Martens Clause: A New Research Guide." Peace Palace Library blog, August 31, 2017. https://peacepalacelibrary.nl/blog/2017/martens-clause-new-research-guide.

Tucker, Jonathan B. *U.S. Ratification of the Chemical Weapons Convention.* Washington, DC: National Defense University Press, 2011.

UK Ministry of Defence. *The Manual of the Law of Armed Conflict.* Oxford: Oxford University Press, 2004.

UN Digital Library. *Napalm and Other Incendiary Weapons and All Aspects of Their Possible Use. Report of the Secretary-General.* New York: UN, 1973. https://digitallibrary.un.org/record/852668?ln=en.

UN Human Rights Council. *Report of the Commission of Inquiry on Lebanon Pursuant to Human Rights Council Resolution S-2/1, A/HRC/3/2,* 23 November 2006. https://documents-dds-ny.un.org/doc/UNDOC/GEN/G06/150/97/PDF/G0615097.pdf?OpenElement

———. "Independent International Commission on Inquiry on the Syrian Arab Republic." Accessed April 26, 2022. https://www.ohchr.org/en/hr-bodies/hrc/iici-syria/documentation.

UN Institute for Disarmament Research. *European Action on Small Arms and Light Weapons and Explosive Remnants of War: Final Report*. Geneva: UNIDIR, 2006. https://unidir.org/publication/european-action-small-arms-and-light-weapons-and-explosive-remnants-war-final-report.

UN International Criminal Tribunal for the Former Yugoslavia. *Final Report to the Prosecutor by the Committee Established to Review the NATO Bombing Campaign Against the Federal Republic of Yugoslavia*. Accessed April 28, 2022. https://www.icty.org/en/press/final-report-prosecutor-committee-established-review-nato-bombing-campaign-against-federal#IVA2.

UN Office for Disarmament Affairs. "Treaty on the Prohibition of Nuclear Weapons." Accessed January 11, 2021. https://treaties.unoda.org/t/tpnw.

———. "Under-Secretary-General and High Representative for Disarmament Affairs." Accessed February 12, 2022. https://www.un.org/disarmament/high-representative/.

———. *The United Nations Disarmament Yearbook*. Vol. 42 (Part II). New York: United Nations Publications, 2017.

UN Office of Legal Affairs. *Yearbook of the International Law Commission* 1980, Vol. II/2. New York: UN, 1981. https://legal.un.org/ilc/publications/yearbooks/english/ilc_1980_v2_p2.pdf.

UN War Crimes Commission, *Law Reports of Trials of War Criminals*. 1949, Vol. VIII, London. UQAM, Faculte des sciences humaines. "Napalm." La Guerre d'Indochine, 1945–1956. Accessed April 14, 2022. https://indochine.uqam.ca/fr/le-dictionnaire/940-napalm.html.

US Air Force. *Doctrine for Joint Theater Nuclear Operations*. February 9, 1996. https://www.nukestrat.com/us/jcs/JCS_JP3-12-1_96.pdf.

US Department of Defense. *DOD Dictionary of Military and Associated Terms*. Washington DC: The Joint Staff, 2019.

———. *Law of War Manual*. Washington, DC: General Counsel of the Department of Defense, 2016.

———. *Nuclear Posture Review*. Accessed March 22, 2022a. https://dod.defense.gov/News/SpecialReports/2018NuclearPostureReview.aspx.

———, Missile Defense Agency. "The Ballistic Missile Defense System (BMDS)." Accessed April 14, 2022b. https://www.mda.mil/system/system.html.

US Department of Health and Human Services. *Toxicological Profile for White Phosphorus*. Atlanta, GA: Agency for Toxic Substances and Disease Registry, 1997.

US Mission to the United Nations. "Joint Press Statement from the Permanent Representative to the United Nations of the United States, United Kingdom, and France Following the Adoption." July 7, 2017. https://usun.usmission.

gov/joint-press-statement-from-the-permanent-representatives-to-the-united-nations-of-the-united-states-united-kingdom-and-france-following-the-adoption/.

US Nuclear Regulatory Commission. "Lethal Dose (LD)." Last updated March 9, 2021. https://www.nrc.gov/reading-rm/basic-ref/glossary/lethal-dose-ld.html.

Van Dijk, Boyd. *Preparing for War: The Making of the Geneva Conventions.* Oxford: Oxford University Press, 2022.

Verchio, Donna Marie. "Just Say No! The SIrUS Project: Well-Intentioned, But Unnecessary and Superfluous." *Air Force Law Review* 51, (2001): 183–228.

Waite, Maurice, ed. *Paperback Oxford English Dictionary.* Oxford: Oxford University Press, 2012.

Weapons Law Encyclopedia. "*Isayeva v. Russia* (ECtHR)." Accessed November 14, 2021. http://www.weaponslaw.org/cases/ecthr-isayeva-2005.

———. "White Phosphorus Petition (Israeli High Court of Justice)." Accessed April 24, 2022. http://www.weaponslaw.org/cases/israel-hcj-white-phosphorus-2013.

Weeden, Brian. "2007 Chinese Anti-Satellite Test" (2010), available at: https://swfound.org/media/9550/chinese_asat_fact_sheet_updated_2012.pdf, last access October 22, 2024.

Wheelis, Mark, Lajos Rózsa, and Malcolm Dando, eds. *Deadly Cultures: Biological Weapons since 1945.* Cambridge, MA: Harvard University Press, 2006, 4.

WHO. *Health Aspects of Chemical and Biological Weapons.* Geneva: WHO, 1970. http://whqlibdoc.who.int/publications/24039.pdf.

Wood, Chris. "Nuclear Test Veterans: 'My Dad Was Treated Like a Guinea Pig.'" BBC, May 30, 2021. https://www.bbc.com/news/uk-wales-57157476.

Woolf, Amy M. "Russia's Nuclear Weapons: Doctrine, Forces, and Modernization." Federation of American Scientists. Last updated April 21, 2022. https://fas.org/sgp/crs/nuke/R45861.pdf.

XXth International Conference of the Red Cross. Accessed May 10, 2022, https://international-review.icrc.org/sites/default/files/S002086040000 8901a.pdf.

XXIst International Conference of the Red Cross. Accessed May 10, 2022, https://international-review.icrc.org/sites/default/files/S0020860400063555a.pdf.

XXIInd International Conference of the Red Cross. Accessed May 10, 2022, https://international-review.icrc.org/sites/default/files/S0020860 400004605a.pdf.

Yanagisawa, N., H. Morita, and T. Nakajima. "Sarin Experiences in Japan: Acute Toxicity and Long- term Effects." *Journal of the Neurological Sciences* 249, no. 1 (2006): 76–85. https://doi.org/10.1016/j.jns.2006.06.007.

Young, Robert W., and Geroge D. Kerr. *Reassessment of the Atomic Bomb Radiation Dosimetry for Hiroshima and Nagasaki. Dosimetry System 2002. DS02. Volume 1.* Hiroshima: RERF, 2005.

Index[1]

[1] Note: Page numbers followed by 'n' refer to notes.

J. Krasny, *War Injuries*,
https://doi.org/10.1007/978-3-032-00737-7

I

FSC
www.fsc.org
MIX
Papier | Fördert gute Waldnutzung
FSC® C083411

Kolibri 360 GmbH
Ferdinand-Jühlke-Straße 7
99095 Erfurt, Deutschland
produktsicherheit@kolibri360.de